MW01198956

Street Diplomacy

Street Diplomacy

The Politics of Slavery and Freedom in Philadelphia, 1820–1850

ELLIOTT DRAGO

Johns Hopkins University Press
Baltimore

Johns Hopkins University Press
2715 North Charles Street
Baltimore, Maryland 21218-4363
www.press.jhu.edu

Library of Congress Cataloging-in-Publication Data

Names: Drago, Elliott, 1984– author.
Title: Street diplomacy : the politics of slavery and freedom in Philadelphia,
1820–1850 / Elliott Drago.
Description: Baltimore : Johns Hopkins University Press, [2022] |
Includes bibliographical references and index.
Identifiers: LCCN 2021056397 | ISBN 9781421444536 (hardcover) |
ISBN 9781421444543 (ebook)
Subjects: LCSH: Fugitive slaves—Pennsylvania—Philadelphia—History. |
Free African Americans—Pennsylvania—Philadelphia—Social
conditions—19th century. |
Kidnapping—Pennsylvania—Philadelphia—History—19th century. |
Abolitionists—Pennsylvania—Philadelphia—History—19th century. |
Antislavery movements—Pennsylvania—Philadelphia—History. |
Philadelphia (Pa.)—Race relations—History—19th century. |
Philadelphia (Pa.)—Politics and government—19th century.
Classification: LCC F158.9.N4 D75 2022 |
DDC 305.8009748/11—dc23/eng/20211206
LC record available at https://lccn.loc.gov/2021056397

A catalog record for this book is available from the British Library.

*Special discounts are available for bulk purchases of this book. For more information,
please contact Special Sales at specialsales@jh.edu.*

CONTENTS

Acknowledgments *vii*

Introduction: Terror in an Age of Slavery 1

1 A Precarious Freedom 17

2 Street Diplomacy 53

3 Fugitive Freedom in Philadelphia 85

4 Domestic Sanctuary 115

5 A Theatre of Scenes 148

6 Interlocking Opportunities 187

Epilogue: The Famous Grasshopper War 218

Notes *233*
Primary Sources *277*
Index *279*

ACKNOWLEDGMENTS

Simone Weil once wrote, "Attention is the rarest and purest form of generosity." I consider myself the recipient of so many blessings in the spirit of Weil's words that I could easily spend an entire bookshelf thanking these wonderful human beings. Alas, editors and readers have lives, too!

Thank you to my teachers, old and new. Mike Solon and Thomas Stewart always reminded me that critical thought required humor and vice versa. I would not be the historian I am today without the empathy and patience of the entire Saint Joseph's University history department, a department constantly badgered by a scruffy-haired college lad known as me. Thank you, Jeff Hyson, Richard Warren, Alison Lewin, Thomas Marzik, Jay Carter, and Ian Petrie for all of your encouragement.

I am so fortunate for the support of Katie Sibley and Randall Miller. Katie's energy and optimism pushed me to avoid the low-hanging fruit of perpetual cynicism. Randall Miller went beyond the call of duty in his efforts to encourage me to study history after undergrad. His counsel, passion, and friendship embody caritas, and I hope that I inspire my students as much as he inspires me.

I hit the jackpot with my first internship opportunity at the National Archives and Records Administration. Thank you to V. Chapman-Smith for forgiving me for missing my first day as well as her timeless words of advice, words for all of us: "Cynicism is not a survival instinct." Matt DiBiase, Patrick Connelly, Robin Morris, and Jefferson Moak's archival aptitudes presented me with plenty of dusty dreamscapes under the streets of Philadelphia and made summers at NARA true halcyon days.

I received first-rate encouragement from my professors at Villanova University and Temple University. Thank you to Maghan Keita, Paul Steege, Karen Kauffman, Paul Rosier, Marc Gallicchio, David Waldstreicher, Susan Klepp, Bryant Simon, Liz Varon, David Watt, Beth Bailey, Petra Goedde,

Arthur Schmidt, Andrew Isenberg, and Jessica Roney. Thank you to Judy Giesberg, who always made it a point to challenge me as a writer and thinker. Harvey Neptune also deserves a special thanks for his insights and humor as well as always insisting that I consider the irony of irony.

I would like to thank my extended scholarly community, especially Andrew Diemer, Chris Bouton, Kate Masur, Scott Hancock, Larry Tise, Stanley Harrold, Paul Finkelman, Robert Forbes, Milt Diggins, Richard Blackett, David Fiske, Hilary Green, Richard Bell, Kellie Carter-Jackson, Walter Johnson, Seth Rockman, Gary Nash, Julie Winch, Edward Turner, Bill Nelson, Matthew Pinsker, William Cooper, John Ashworth, Eric Foner, Richard Newman, Jean Soderlund, Sally E. Hadden, Nancy Isenberg, Chandra Manning, Joshua Rothman, Manisha Sinha, Thomas D. Morris, Carol Wilson, Elise Lemire, Aldo Schiavone, William Freehling, Whitney Howell, Josh Mattingly, Matt Nixon, Dylan Gottlieb, Carly Goodman, Tommy Richards, and Noam Chomsky.

Thank you to my friends, especially the Cummings, Johnson, Pearson, Quinn, and Weber families, Peter Canale, Matt McGuire, Bo Schambelan, Tom Potterfield, Mark Jacobs, Lisa Chen, and Sean Loomis. And who could forget the sublimity of the Fab Four, Ray Davies, and the comedic philosopher sage? Memento Mori.

I would also like to thank the staff at the Historical Society of Pennsylvania, especially Christina Larocco. Portions of chapter one originally appeared in "A Precarious Freedom: The 1820 Philadelphia Kidnapping Crisis," *Pennsylvania Magazine of History and Biography* 145, no. 2 (April 2021): 119–152. Thank you to the kind folks at the Philadelphia City Archives and the American Philosophical Society. A special thank you to archivist David Murray is in order, as he joined me in a number of meaningful research quests.

I am thankful to have worked with Laura Davulis and Ezra Rodriguez from Johns Hopkins University Press. While I do not recommend finishing a book during a pandemic, Laura's and Ezra's patience and accessibility provided stability in an otherwise interesting time. Thanks to Mike Baker for his keen eyes and astute suggestions.

Jon Wells's patience, levity, and empathy guided me through the wonders of graduate school. Knowing that I could rely on him for countless reasons enabled me to earn my degree and speak with confidence as a scholar and more importantly, as a human being. I am forever in his debt. Both his and Heather Ann Thompson's perfectly timed advice and thoughtful assurances continue to motivate me.

My ineffable love for my family matches my perpetual pride in my family.

I am nothing without my family—teachers all—and thus I dedicate this book to them. Thank you Dad, Mom, Brian, Keith, and Michael for enduring my eccentricities and giving me the time to become who I am today. Thank you to Betty, Bud, Jane, Len, Regina, Angela, and Alan as well as the Drago, Stirling, Lavers, Morales, and Rivera families for their continued love and support.

Vanessa, John, and Freida: you light my life from the morning until the end of the day. Thank you for all of the lessons you have taught me and continue to teach me. My love for you remains instant, always, and cosmic. Amor, amor, amor. Omnia vincit amor, ad maiora! Little children, love one another.

Street Diplomacy

Terror in an Age of Slavery

The notorious Philadelphia slave catcher George F. Alberti sat patiently while the abolitionist James Miller McKim asked him how many enslaved human beings he had caught in his lifetime. Reflecting on his infamous career then in 1859, Alberti answered, "I have been forty years in the business: *forty years. A hundred isn't so many when you think of the length of time I have been at it.*" Alberti then enumerated tale after hair-raising tale, painful anecdotes that involved tearing families apart, remanding men, women, and children to unscrupulous slaveholders, and rescinding the hopes of generations of African Americans who lived in Philadelphia.[1]

McKim, a close confidante of Underground Railroad doyen William Still, continued to pepper Alberti with queries in order to understand what motivated him to engage in slave catching. Alberti justified his practices with language not unfamiliar to Southerners: religion sanctioned slave catching and slavery as did the Constitution of the United States. Plus, Alberti added, a number of African Americans assisted his man-stealing efforts, including a local Black preacher. In fact, his most controversial trial occurred in 1851, when Alberti and an African American kidnapped a Black woman and her two-year-old child. For this crime Alberti and his accomplice, James Frisby Price, were sentenced to ten years in Eastern State Penitentiary. Within a year Pennsylvania governor William F. Bigler pardoned the pair as a way to prove his state's loyalty to the Slave South.[2]

Alberti, McKim, and Still shared vital connections to Philadelphia's African American community. Alberti's despicable yet at times legal act of hunting African Americans ran counter to the actions of his uncle, Thomas Shipley, a

white abolitionist who at the time of his death in 1836 served as the vice president of the Pennsylvania Abolition Society. These intimate relationships between slaveholders, slave catchers, fugitives from slavery, and Black and white
activists epitomized the dangerous reality of Black life in Pennsylvania. A
friend of Still and McKim, and protégé to Thomas Shipley, the Black activist
Robert Purvis realized this fact of life for Philadelphia's Black community,
remarking that at any moment he or any other African American "may fall a
victim to the hellish talons of a northern kidnapper, be thrown into the presence of a prejudiced judge, and, without an intercessor, doomed to hopeless,
hapless, interminable bondage."[3]

This book examines the conflicts over slavery and freedom experienced by
the African American community in Philadelphia from 1820 to 1850. Struggles that arose over removing fugitives from slavery and the kidnappings of
free African Americans forced Philadelphians to confront the politics of slavery that sought to protect slaveholders' right to property across the Union.
Although Pennsylvania was a free state officially and Philadelphia was a bastion of abolitionism, I argue that at the street level Pennsylvania was in many
ways akin to a slave state.

As the southernmost Northern city in a state that bordered three slave
states, Philadelphia maintained both a long tradition of abolitionism as well
as the activity of fugitives from slavery. Similar to other cities in the Early
Republic that experienced the shocks of the market, transportation, abolitionist, and proslavery revolutions, Philadelphia possessed several key geographical features that made it stand out to African Americans, slaveholders,
slave catchers, and kidnappers alike. The city's prime location near the slave
states of Delaware, Maryland, and Virginia provided a constant stream of African Americans into the city and state. Unlike the rural hinterlands where
African Americans were crucial to farm labor, Philadelphia offered a wider
variety of job opportunities and acted as a more attractive destination. So
while rural areas in Pennsylvania endured similar crises, Philadelphia's precarious borders facilitated greater numbers of human beings seeking refuge
and as a result a greater number of incidents in the history of slavery and
freedom in the state. Slaveholders, kidnappers, and their allies utilized a
number of means by which they could abduct African Americans and secret
them out of Philadelphia, Pennsylvania: by foot, by wagon, and by water, or a
combination thereof. Consequently, clashes between the forces of slavery
who traveled to Philadelphia and the forces of freedom within the city erupted
in multiple ways.[4]

Riots, rescues, street battles, and arbitrary arrest and removal were not un-common sights in Philadelphia. Whether these clashes arose through riots or "mundane" arrests, these experiences changed the lives of the participants: the arrest of an innocent African American forged links to their opponents and allies in the city, state, and nation. Many opponents and allies were well known and powerful figures in their time, but they alone did not drive history then or now. Put simply, I celebrate how ordinary people produce extraordi-nary historical change. These changes that linked the local to the national speak to a trend within the historiography to emphasize the complicity of Northerners in enslaving African Americans, and in doing so, betray any notion of safety for these same people of the urban north during the Early Republic and Antebellum Era.[5]

Whether emancipated during the liberating fervor of the Revolutionary Era or freeing themselves through direct action, the "steady traffic" of African Americans entering Pennsylvania from the South gave both the state of Penn-sylvania and the city of Philadelphia a central role in crafting what it meant to live as a free person in a slaveholding republic. African Americans came to Philadelphia to enjoy a freedom with the country's largest, most vibrant, most strident, and best-organized Black community in the North during the Early Republic. In the words of the historians Erica Armstrong Dunbar and Gary Nash, Philadelphia served as both "the epicenter of emancipation" and a "city of refuge" for many African Americans, replete with lived experiences that showcased caution and hope. Caution lay within the fact that at any time the forces of slavery could question Black freedom. The willingness of Black and white activists to strive together and adopt a variety of means of asserting and protecting themselves made Philadelphia special. From the 1688 German-town protest to the 1847 Pennsylvania liberty law and beyond, a mobile Afri-can American population combined with the city's abolitionist legacy re-sulted in the inevitable increase in conflicts over interstate comity, that is, the union of peaceful relationships and expectations of reciprocity between the states.[6]

While it may seem obvious, Philadelphia will always retain its unique sta-tus in the history of slavery and freedom precisely because it is the only city that can claim to have hosted both the signing of the Declaration of Indepen-dence and the Constitutional Convention. As Gary Nash has argued, Phila-delphians understood the historical importance of their city: they resided in or wished to reside in a colony, and then a state, declared a "Holy Experiment." Both the City of Brotherly Love and Sisterly Affection and this Holy Experi-

ment existed in a nation bound by the central paradox of slavery and freedom. Thus, Philadelphians, Black and white possessed a crucial role in meeting the perils and promises of the American republic. Nonetheless, my work
owes a tremendous debt to historians who study the urban North. Yet I would
rather be in Philadelphia, as street battles over slavery often ended in the same
space devoted to promoting human equality: the "old Statehouse" known to
us as Independence Hall, the site where the vast majority of cases involving
fugitives from slavery and kidnapping victims transpired. Philadelphia connects the local, the state, and the nation like no other place in America, and
in doing so, the city is essential to our understanding of where we came from,
who we are, and who we can become as human beings.[7]

It would be appropriate at this juncture to sketch the relationship between
the US federal government and the institution of slavery at the nation's founding. As the historian David Waldstreicher has argued, the Constitution acted
(and still acts) as a tool used by politicians to govern, and thus, the Founders
"sought to govern slavery" in a variety of ways through this living document.
The infamous Three-Fifths Clause gave slaveholders an outsized representation in Congress, a reality that over time meant that slaveholding politicians
would pressure Northern politicians to heed their clarion calls to protect
slavery; the protection of the international slave trade for twenty years after
ratification ensured at least another generation of enslaved people in the
United States; and of course, the "fugitive slave" clause (Article 4, Section 2,
Clause 3) stated, persons "held to service or labor" who escaped from one
state and into another "shall be delivered up" to the state from which the
person fled. As Waldstreicher explained, these concessions to Southern slavery were open-ended and thus primed to face resistance by nonslaveholders,
whether politicians or ordinary people living outside of the Slave South. Crises stemming from the "fugitive slave" clause faced resistance along the border between Pennsylvania and the slave states of Virginia and Maryland,
whose consequent failures to retrieve fugitives from slavery in Pennsylvania
excited slaveholders to lobby the federal government in 1793 to devise stronger safeguards to recapture their so-called property.[8]

The 1793 Fugitive Slave Act passed by Congress and signed into law by
President George Washington spoke to the reality of precarious borders. As a
legal mechanism to retrieve supposed fugitives from slavery, the legislation
buttressed the fugitive slave clause but went further and imposed fines and
jail time upon those who aided fugitives. However, the federal government at
this point in the Early Republic faced a personnel issue: there were not enough

federal officials to enforce this act in the country. Therefore, the question of how the act would be executed fell to states like Pennsylvania, a state that had already passed a gradual emancipation act in 1780 as well as a 1788 act devoted to protecting African Americans from kidnappers. A federal government with staffing concerns and a state with a budding legacy of emancipation to uphold left the enforcement of the 1793 act to ordinary people, Black or white, Northern or Southern, free or enslaved. Here we see the ease with which the issue of alleged fugitives from slavery and kidnapping victims became conflated.[9]

Writing a decade after the passage of the Fugitive Slave Act, in 1803, the Philadelphia abolitionist Thomas P. Cope, claimed that "not a day passes but free Blacks are stolen by force or decoyed by the most wicked artifices from the Northern and Middle States and sold for slaves in the Southern." What Cope described in essence was what the historian Ira Berlin called "the second middle passage," that period from the Early Republic to the outbreak of the Civil War in which over one million African Americans were sold and thus forced from the Upper South to the Deep South. The expansion of the domestic slave trade to the cotton states brought forth a number of deadly consequences for free African Americans "at risk" in states like Pennsylvania. The lure of the United States' ever-expanding slave country, replete with rising cotton prices and enshrining the chattel principle allowed slaveholders to enforce the 1793 act themselves, often with the help of sometimes Southern, sometimes Northern minions.[10]

Despite the presumption of living in a free city in a free state, Philadelphia's African American community faced innumerable threats to their safety and freedom throughout the nineteenth century. These threats linked their existential terror on the streets to state and national concerns. The expansion of the domestic slave trade encouraged slaveholders and kidnappers to prowl around Philadelphia, which increased anti-Black prejudices that culminated in brutal anti-Black riots. Such disorder on the streets mirrored the increasingly fractious contests at the state and national level. Pennsylvania state politicians and elite white Philadelphians grappled with the meaning of African American freedom and found themselves flummoxed when attempting to discern "fugitives" from kidnapping victims. Actions at the local level pushed Pennsylvania politicians to grapple with the meaning of African American freedom in their state, and in doing so inspired states' rights arguments that threatened comity. African Americans and their allies initiated and contested Pennsylvania's politics of slavery and freedom at the local, state, and national levels by exploiting precarious borders more imagined than real within Philadelphia.[11]

Ordinary African Americans living in Philadelphia bore the burden of comity through practicing what I call "street diplomacy." Street diplomacy functioned on multiple levels by collapsing space. The word "street" of course, refers to the local politics of slavery and freedom within Philadelphia. The city's streets served as the stages upon which ordinary people, in particular African Americans, negotiated and exercised freedom while yoked to a national politics of slavery. The word "street" also encourages the study of the day-to-day activities of abolitionists and their allies, what the historian Graham Russell Gao Hodges has termed "practical abolition." These daily strivings to protect and liberate African Americans in Philadelphia matter because they contain as much tension as popular culture's obsession with what Eric Foner has called the "dramatic escapes." Furthermore, the streets mattered because these confrontations between the struggles over slavery and freedom happened in public spaces. Slave catching, kidnappings, rescues, riots—all of these spectacles served as America's original "open secret" of enslavement extending across borders, rendering them illusory. Throughout this study I showcase how contests at the street level influenced politics and politicians at the state and national levels.[12]

The "diplomacy" of "street diplomacy" serves as an homage to the historian Stanley Harrold's term "interstate diplomacy." As Harrold argued, fugitives from slavery who escaped across borders brought together state governments who strove to define exactly whose rights they could protect within their borders. Thus, slave state "diplomats" traveled to Northern state legislatures to convince the latter to enforce the 1793 Fugitive Slave Act and even encourage the passage of state legislation to assist slaveholders with retrieval efforts. Northern state legislatures, Pennsylvania's in this case, would in turn debate these pleas from neighboring states while at the same time endeavoring to define their own sense of states' rights. While a useful way of understanding interactions between Americans, Northern and Southern, my issue with interstate diplomacy is that many, if not most, of these interstate diplomats were elite white males. Focusing too much on their efforts of course elides the roles that other Americans played in these debates, whether on the streets or in the legislature. Therefore, I expand upon exactly who filled the ranks of these diplomats by premising street diplomacy on interracial activism, those Black and white street diplomats who fostered local, state, and national political crises.[13]

Slaveholders, kidnappers, and street diplomats abided by and ignored borders when the borders suited their purposes. Political borders past and present represent in many ways how the dominant culture can arbitrarily divide physical geography and, in doing so, create "legal" and "illegal" spaces and human beings. As their work defines them as criminals both then and now, kidnappers eschew legal borders, break them at will, and even use them strategically to their own illegal benefit. Likewise, Black and white street diplomats viewed kidnappers and slaveholders as human beings who committed crimes against humanity. After all, how else would one describe ripping a human being from their life, family, and future? Kidnappers, slaveholders, fugitives from slavery, and street diplomats defied borders because they all knew that human beings would willingly break the law either to enslave others or liberate themselves.[14]

Street diplomacy consisted of the interactions at street level between human beings who could enslave and human beings who could liberate. Street diplomats viewed every attempt to arrest, "remove," and enslave African Americans as no different from kidnappings, and thus, labored to conflate illegal and legal acts to disrupt the "removal" process. Over time, street diplomacy convinced Pennsylvania lawmakers to adopt similar views in light of an exacerbated comity with the slaveholding states. In a larger sense, street diplomacy in Philadelphia magnified the stakes of comity by showing how identifying states by their condition of bondage remained impossible due to permeable geographic borders that fostered perpetual crises over kidnappings and fugitives from slavery. These up-close and personal struggles over freedom and slavery spawned local, state, and national ramifications that complicated the best efforts of proslavery forces to deny Black freedom. In sum, I view street diplomacy in terms of ordinary people's actions, in particular African Americans, whose potential enslavement or kidnapping in Philadelphia unconsciously bore the burden of keeping the Union together.

The work of proslavery forces, namely, slaveholders, their agents, white and Black kidnappers, and their local, state, and national political allies, undermined state laws designed to protect the freedom of Black Pennsylvanians. Commonly referred to as "liberty laws," these state laws exposed the inherent difficulty in determining the free or enslaved status of both fugitives from slavery and kidnapping victims. As mentioned, African Americans and their allies did not distinguish between kidnapping victims and fugitives from slavery: they viewed both examples as kidnappings, regardless of the law. The three liberty laws under consideration in this book were not without precedent, as the 1780 Gradual Emancipation Act in Pennsylvania represented the first post-nati emancipation law in the Americas. In the decades following the 1780 act, Pennsylvania's reputation for liberty resulted in Philadelphia hosting the largest number of free African Americans outside of the slave states as well as a burgeoning and mobile population of fugitives from slavery. Rather than overemphasizing the "luck" of an African American being born and living in Pennsylvania, I emphasize how the presence of free, freed, and "fugitive" African Americans prompted a grim consequence to Philadelphia being the center of Black life in the nation: slaveholders, kidnappers, and slave catchers infested the city.[15]

The Black community sought, and capitalized on having, white allies in Philadelphia. Analyzing the dynamic and convoluted relationships between African Americans and whites exposes fascinating moments of both interracial cooperation and conflict. Regarding interracial cooperation, I argue against historians' views of the conservative and at times elitist strategies of the Pennsylvania Abolition Society (PAS). Instead of focusing on the dictums of elite and cautious whites at the top of the PAS hierarchy, I analyze the on-the-ground activities of the PAS, which is part and parcel with an "any means necessary approach" to protecting and emancipating African Americans. As the historian Chris J. Bonner has acknowledged, while many African Americans participated in the larger direct actions to rescue or protect alleged fugitives, still many more African Americans (and of course, their allies) cautiously worked within the legal system to denounce "the injustices of slavery." I highlight the junior members of the PAS who worked alongside African Americans on a daily basis, people like McKim and Shipley, and who often did so at their own personal risk. I also examine the work of African American activists like James Forten and Robert Purvis, both of whom collaborated with whites for decades. Fleshing out these collaborations, as argued by the historian Eric Foner, means examining "interlocking" abolitionist networks within Philadelphia. The basis of these positive interracial networks derived from the strength of the core belief expressed and actualized by African Americans and their white allies: human beings were innately free, and any attempt to enslave or capture an African American was tantamount to kidnapping. To be sure, these abolitionist forces struggled for decades to convince Americans of this basic fact of human existence: what remains vital is that they struggled together.[16]

Regarding interracial conflict, the violence inherent in slavery and kidnapping as well as potential and actual riots permeated Philadelphia and consisted mainly, but never exclusively, of working-class whites who attacked

African Americans and destroyed their property. While riots may have occurred sporadically, the day-to-day brutality and terror exacted upon African
Americans in Philadelphia fostered racism and, if left unopposed, more violence. Yet focusing too much on interracial conflict often obscures the intra-
racial fault lines within the African American community, as one discovers
repeated examples of African Americans working for both slave catchers and
kidnappers. The fragmentary nature of this evidence, though extant, speaks
to the perpetual terror of being African American and projecting a safe and
free future in Philadelphia during the nineteenth century. I hope that this
book works to understand better how at times race functioned as a strategy
of convenience and a weapon of the marginalized within the history of slavery rather than an either/or proposition, especially when analyzed through
conflicts over street diplomacy.[17]

Conflict at the local level became inextricably fused to national politics as
white politicians' ability to classify enslaved African Americans as property
and as human beings represented a fundamental tension throughout the
United States. As with the work of Daina Ramey Berry, who examined prices
and the attendant experiences of enslaved people from birth to death, I position my study around the chattel principle as conceived by James Pennington.
Pushing the chattel principle past the realm of bodies, prices, and numbers
and toward ontology, conflicts over slavery and freedom in Philadelphia revealed how African Americans, flesh and blood human beings with potential
futures, embodied potential property regardless of their status of servitude or
location in the nation. I consider the ontological meaning of existing as a
potentially free, potentially enslaved unity-in-opposites within the lived experiences of African Americans. In other words, African Americans struggled to exist with their lives, freedoms, and futures intact despite constant
interruptions by nefarious forces that considered them ready-to-hand instruments; instruments denied engaging in the world with others; instruments
without lives, freedoms, or futures. The forces of slavery who enslaved or
kidnapped recognized and acted upon the principle that African Americans
were free and not-free at the same time, regardless of laws and borders but
always inclusive of violence and terror. African Americans living north of
slavery prior to the Civil War embodied both freedom and slavery, the unity-
in-opposites that made their ontological status, their way of being, subject to
perpetual suspicion.[18]

Those African Americans enslaved or kidnapped experienced both the
short asthmatic breath of freedom afforded them in Philadelphia and the

stultifying sickness of the long enslavement that awaited them if captured or kidnapped; the long lives lived under the lash of slavery destroyed the lives, futures, and families of the enslaved and the kidnapped. Each person in this book, many of whom disappear from the historical record altogether with the "conclusion" of their cases, remind us that we will never fully understand the depth of the account of a single African American life being ripped off the streets of Philadelphia by a slaveholder, slave catcher, or kidnapper: an historical unease. We grow closer to those lives and projections of an uncertain, hopeful future: we all know that feeling of one's own life being felt. By studying the specific fugitive or kidnapping cases that inspired Pennsylvania's three liberty laws, one finds that time and again African Americans and their allies forced politicians to grapple with the reality that Philadelphia was not a safe haven for African Americans.[19]

Studying these struggles within Philadelphia reveals how physical violence and legislative endeavors exist in a dialectical relationship. As the historian Christopher J. Bonner has cogently argued, while historians have little trouble viewing crafting laws as political acts, historians ought to pay even closer attention to those moments in which lawbreaking became "political." Desperate rescues of fugitives from slavery, bloody race riots, and normalized daily bloodletting directed toward Philadelphia's African American community produced civil wars in miniature, thus reflecting the negotiated and compromised realities of Black freedom in the city. Local contests over slavery and freedom mutually constituted the legislative processes at the state and national level and underscored the inability of white politicians to resolve what it meant for an African American to inhabit a free state within a slave society. Black Philadelphians' local encounters with proslavery zealots and politicians complicated both slaveholders' rights to retrieve their "property" under the 1793 Fugitive Slave Act and Pennsylvania state laws designed to protect free Black Pennsylvanians. As a result, African Americans and their allies forced Pennsylvania politicians to grapple with increasingly desperate compromises with slavery. In short, I explore how, through fits and starts and by no means a teleological road to freedom, slavery ended in Pennsylvania.[20]

Chapter 1 examines Pennsylvania's 1820 anti-kidnapping law, commonly referred to as the state's first personal liberty law. I study specific kidnappings and cases involving fugitives from slavery as a way to connect the local to the state and national and to show how ordinary African Americans forced white politicians to confront the terror of daily life in Philadelphia. Many of these politicians worked pro bono for the PAS and linked their local and state efforts to the national political issue related to the expansion of slavery westward. As slavery crept north under the guise of kidnappings and fugitives from slavery, Black Philadelphians and their allies pressured white politicians to take a stand against slavery at the state and national level. In addition, I discuss the politicking and debates over Black freedom in the Pennsylvania state legislature, where white politicians discussed the 1793 Federal Fugitive Slave Act in relation to the case studies under consideration within the chapter. Ultimately, the 1820 act limited state involvement in removing fugitives from slavery, increased fines and penalties for kidnapping, and allowed abolitionists to conflate removing fugitives from slavery with illegal kidnappings. This final consequence of the 1820 law spurred the rise of what I term "street diplomacy."

Chapter 2 analyzes how the 1820 anti-kidnapping law played out on the streets of Philadelphia, and how unintended consequences stemming from the execution of the law fostered hostilities between state officials from Pennsylvania and Maryland. Here I introduce the term "street diplomacy" as a way to connect ordinary African Americans and their allies living in Philadelphia to broader state national concerns over maintaining comity and the Union. Black Philadelphians and their allies resisted removal efforts and kidnappings through Pennsylvania's 1820 anti-kidnapping law, while slaveholders continued to uphold faith in the 1793 federal Fugitive Slave Act.

Chapter 3 highlights specific cases of kidnapping and fugitives from slavery and connects them to local, state, and national politics. Fed-up by a perceived lack of success in extraditing so-called fugitives from Pennsylvania, the state of Maryland sent representatives to the Pennsylvania state legislature in 1826 to demand protections for slaveholders' right to own, pursue, and remove human beings. African Americans and their allies brought their demands as street diplomats into the state legislature by attending the debates over the 1826 law and confronting Pennsylvania politicians face to face. The resulting 1826 liberty law both reaffirmed Pennsylvania's right to protect its residents and served to succor Southern slaveholders, leaving African American freedom an open question in the state.

Chapter 3 also analyzes how comity worked and did not work. The 1826 kidnappings of Black children from Philadelphia resulted in a successful display of comity between states and added insights into how kidnappers operated in and around the city. A subsequent kidnapping incident involving a man named Emory Sadler did not bode well for comity between Pennsylvania and Maryland, and it showed that at times rescue efforts depended more on the particular slave state's governor. Focusing on how street diplomats refused to be passive, the chapter also explores how they brought matters of comity to the street level. Black and white activists in Philadelphia collaborated in a variety of ways, from holding conventions, sharing information, and petitioning government officials to pursuing kidnappers and rescuing their victims. Crucial here is the fundamental understanding held by Black and white street diplomats: slavery was kidnapping, plain and simple.

When street diplomacy broke down, African Americans and their allies mobbed courtrooms and defended themselves from white rioters. Emphasizing again how the local influenced the state and national debates over freedom and slavery, this chapter analyzes the effects of Nat Turner's rebellion on Philadelphia. The political effects of Turner led both local organizers and state politicians to debate registering Blacks and preventing them from immigrating into Pennsylvania. These debates became tangled with the issues of fugitives from slavery and kidnappings, and as a result, spawned further anti-Black resentment from white Philadelphians.

Chapter 4 delves deeper into two major riots experienced by Philadelphians in 1834 and 1835. The source of both riots lay within white Philadelphians' growing fears of race mixing, a perceived "problem" facilitated by the strength of the Black community, the presence of fugitives from slavery, and the burgeoning interracial and immediate abolitionism within the city. The aggressive stances taken by some African Americans during these riots spoke to the success of street diplomacy, as Black and white abolitionists linked violence in Philadelphia to the terror of enslavement across the Union. Many whites, including influential politicians, clamored for Pennsylvanians to tamp down the new wave of interracial activism as a way to prevent the collapse of comity and the country itself. Yet civil disorder plagued Black life in Philadelphia, from the roles played by overzealous constables and ambivalent judges to well-attended meetings of whites who pledged to stand with the South in the face of a potential race war.

As these violent consequences gripped Philadelphians, abolitionists struggled to maintain comity and distanced themselves from any apparent catalysts of disorder. However, their work or at the very least knowledge of the "Great Postal Campaign" of 1835 acted as a catalyst for further disorder, as their aspirations for immediate abolition flew in the face of white Philadelphians who rioted against them and their Black allies multiple times within the previous year. In sum, this chapter shows how street diplomats' innate interracial strivings and ability to conflate kidnappings and fugitives from slavery left comity and loyalty to a Union with slavery an open question.

Chapter 5 analyzes how street diplomats confronted the "theatre of scenes" that embodied their work. The deaths of Thomas Shipley and James Forten gave rise to Robert Purvis, a mixed-race man who, along with other street diplomats, employed a variety of strategies, from print to physical action, to resist slaveholders and kidnappers. Again, street diplomacy continued to pivot upon interracial activism and the assumption that any attempt to arrest a supposed fugitive from justice equated to a kidnapping. The drastic increase in the state's Black population having been disproved by Philadelphia state senator Samuel Breck did little to thwart the Democracy from conflating "fugitive" and free African Americans living in Philadelphia. This association fueled the Democracy and succeeded in disenfranchising the state's Black population in 1838.

Street diplomats who made public pronouncements of fundamental human equality collaborated to construct a temple of liberty, Pennsylvania Hall, in Philadelphia for that very purpose. White rioters aligned with both the national Democracy and local constabulary destroyed Pennsylvania Hall within three days of its dedication. These public displays of anti-Black violence spoke to the continued depredations faced by African Americans in the city, not least of all when individuals faced kidnapping and permanent slavery. Once again, street diplomats, male and female, black and white, redoubled their efforts to form vigilant committees to protect the African American community. Ordinary people who sought their protection enacted their own street diplomatic strategies as well, from gathering information to writing politicians and drastically confronting packed courtrooms with the stakes of their possible enslavement.

Chapter 5 also analyzes *Prigg v. Pennsylvania,* a case whose outcome nullified one of the major successes of Philadelphia's street diplomats, the 1826 liberty law. Ironically, *Prigg* inspired new waves of fugitives from slavery to free themselves and flee to Pennsylvania. Specifically, these arrivals fled to the home of Robert Purvis and other members of the revitalized Vigilant Committee, replete with a female auxiliary. By 1842 the Vigilant Committee boasted 1,000 members, and in keeping with the bravery inherent in street diplomacy, helped organize a parade as a celebration of West Indian emancipation and more importantly, a show of force. Many whites did not take kindly to these displays of Black achievement and community strength, and they initiated a series of riots against African Americans living in Philadelphia, regardless of who they were or where they lived.

Chapter 6 explores the aftermath of *Prigg* by tracing the local, state, and national factors that contributed to Pennsylvania's 1847 liberty law. While the 1793 federal Fugitive Slave Act permitted slaveholders to remand their human property anywhere in the nation, Pennsylvanians' inability to handle fugitives from slavery in the state, which as the former chapters discuss, often became conflated with illegal kidnapping efforts. State politicians mulling over the role of Pennsylvania in the nation mirrored the inextricable nature of the local fights over slavery and freedom. Several cases involving fugitives from slavery in Pennsylvania from the 1840s again broached the question regarding to what extent free state Pennsylvanians might honor slaveholders' demands for comity. The *Prigg* ruling sustained this open question and gave space to slaveholders, politicians, and street diplomats to take legal and extralegal means to answer it. Street diplomats continued to implement covert and overt means to protect African Americans after *Prigg*. Their work created the foundation for the success of what became the nineteenth century's most important and successful American project: the Underground Railroad. Black and white "conductors" operated across Philadelphia and the houses of street diplomats like James Forten, Robert Purvis, and William Still became "stations" that welcomed a long stream of African Americans from the South.

Similar to previous chapters, chapter 6 discusses how slavery anywhere intertwined local and national politics everywhere. The debates over slavery's expansion, this time into Texas, once again raised the ire of Pennsylvanians, many of whom were not devout abolitionists but instead, zealous about Pennsylvania states' rights. While politicians debated Texas at the national level, Pennsylvania Democrats clamored for expansion as a way of promoting and maintaining the Union. Although not completely Whig partisans, many Philadelphia abolitionists shuddered at how the Democracy espoused the spread of slavery at the national level without apparent regard for the freedom of citizens within Pennsylvania. Here the discourse of "Union" became the watchword not of liberty but of slavery, with the fate of African Americans and the "Union" hanging in the balance.[21]

The fragile comity present within a national politics dependent on street diplomacy on the local level thrust the question of Pennsylvania's "free state" status toward the state legislature. An attempted slave catching that occurred on the streets of the state capital in Harrisburg in 1847 mere blocks away from the legislature meant that Pennsylvania politicians could not avoid the perpetual clash between slavery and freedom in the state. Through abolitionist conventions and an all-out petitioning effort, African Americans and their allies thrust the national issues over slavery, including the Mexican War, Wilmot Proviso, and the Walker Tariff of 1846 onto Pennsylvania state lawmakers, who in 1847 debated and passed legislation that made slave sales within the state illegal, rescinded state assistance to remand fugitives under the 1793 Fugitive Slave Act, and rendered punishments to any slaveholder who brought an enslaved person into the state. In essence, the interlocking local, state, and national forces came together in this 1847 legislation and presaged the passage of the 1850 Fugitive Slave Act.

The epilogue highlights the central question I analyzed throughout the book, namely, when slavery ended in Pennsylvania. Unlike traditional periodizations that place emancipation in the aftermath of the Civil War, I prefer to invoke how slavery in Pennsylvania (and in a larger sense, the nation) became transposed over time, as Americans confronted the looming specter of a national union with slavery in the 1850s and beyond. Furthermore, I consider how African Americans and their allies pushed white politicians to consider Pennsylvania's role in the national union with slaveholders, and how the process of street diplomacy placed the burden of the Union and comity on the backs of African Americans, free, freed, or fugitive.[22]

To conclude, I analyze a fascinating case of a fugitive from slavery that originated in Philadelphia. The cast of characters included not only the "fugitive" herself, Catherine Thompson, but her infant child Joel, the notorious slave catcher George Alberti, proslavery ideologues, abolitionists, and the governor of Pennsylvania, Democrat William Bigler. Within this case I plan to discuss the themes prevalent throughout my work: Catherine Thompson attempted to negotiate her freedom through street diplomacy; George Alberti justified his nefarious trade with the help of staunch proponents of slavery; interracial abolitionism galvanized its efforts to protect Black freedom in Pennsylvania; and the Pennsylvania politician Bigler, after the trial, pardoned Alberti to appease Southern slaveholders.

Few scholars have studied the Thompson case, though a wealth of material regarding the trial exists, including a pro- and anti-Alberti pamphlet, numerous newspaper accounts from across the country, and an interview with Alberti himself. The central figure in the case, Catherine Thompson, contested Alberti's claims despite the fact that she, like many other African Americans, received reassurances from an African American man who worked as a slave catcher with Alberti. In fact, given that many scholars have insisted on the importance of relatively obscure activists, African American or otherwise, what I hope to show is how people like Alberti, however supposedly obscure (more likely ignored by scholars), were known quantities within the minds of Black Philadelphians (and pushed further, many other African Americans living outside of Philadelphia), which in a similar way reveals the importance of such figures as well as the true stakes of freedom and slavery that lay within the nature of every interaction between slave catchers and African Americans in Philadelphia.

That African Americans in Pennsylvania, and in many ways the free states as a whole, failed to disentangle their fates from enslaved people living in the slave states underscored the wide range of tactics employed by Black Philadelphians to exercise street diplomacy and resist slave hunters and kidnappings: working with white allies, crafting abolitionist pamphlets and literature for the general public, petitioning white politicians, and resorting to violence if needed. As a major contention in the book, the failure of white politicians to completely separate legal and illegal removals of African Americans from Pennsylvania ensured the ebb and flow of Black freedom in the state through the passage of the state's liberty laws. These legal developments depended on the local efforts of Black Philadelphians and their white allies, and through the contests of street diplomacy, entwined local, state, and national politics and politicians in the debate over the abolition of slavery in Pennsylvania.

CHAPTER ONE

A Precarious Freedom

An African American freedman and Philadelphia resident named Perry Frisby knelt at his bedside to pray one autumn night in 1819. Suddenly he heard several loud bangs at his front door. A male voice urged him to come outside and console a dying woman. Frisby ran out of his house and came face to face with the Philadelphia constable George F. Alberti, Jr., who welcomed Frisby with a blow to the head. Alberti dragged Frisby down the street, ignoring pleas from bystanders to cease in his assault. Soon the pair arrived in Southwark on the southern outskirts of Philadelphia. There an unnamed Philadelphia alderman granted Alberti a certificate of removal for Frisby to Maryland, where Alberti sold him for $600. Frisby's travails did not end in Maryland: within days of arriving in that state he was sold even farther south to New Orleans. How he escaped that hellish reality of the Deep South we may never know, but what we do know is that Frisby, a "respectable man of colour," combined his efforts with abolitionist groups in New York and Pennsylvania and made it back to Philadelphia by October 19, 1819. With the help of the Pennsylvania Abolition Society (PAS) Acting Committee member Thomas Shipley, Frisby pressed assault and battery charges against Alberti in the Mayor's Court. Several witnesses, including Frisby's wife, Flora, offered testimony. On December 31, 1819, the court decided that Frisby lacked enough witnesses to prove Alberti's guilt, and thus discharged him.[1]

As Frisby's plight shows all too clearly, African Americans living in the North experienced a precarious freedom throughout the Early Republic. Mundane activities such as praying, walking down the street, or scrounging for work brought danger. Living in a free city within a slaveholding republic exposed Black Philadelphians to both slave catchers and kidnappers as the proximity to slave states made such dangers all the more immediate. Slave catchers throughout the Philadelphia region used legal means, namely, the 1793 Fugitive Slave Act, to capture suspected fugitives from slavery and "deliver" them to a slaveholder. Kidnappers, on the other hand, employed illegal means to steal free African Americans.

Philadelphians grappled with the ambiguous relationship between these two forms of removal. Perry Frisby established positive relationships with his neighbors, white and Black, living a free and respectable life in Philadelphia absent the yoke of his former enslavement. However, Frisby's prior enslavement followed him across space and time: his former owner's widow had her husband's will "set aside," in other words, ignored. A pattern emerged in Frisby's case as well as countless others: a slaveholder pursued a freed person regardless of their location, ripped them from their lives, and enslaved them. In the words of the historian Sarah L. H. Gronningsater, this process betrayed any notion of a "rosy, uncomplicated, or teleological view" of becoming or living while free in Philadelphia. The "imperfect" politics of slavery and freedom provided a dynamic context for every American, regardless of their position on slavery. We grapple with the allies that slaveholders found in Philadelphia, allies like law enforcement officials, allies like George Alberti, and in doing so, consider how ordinary African Americans like Frisby wielded their own alliances, from family members to neighbors to abolitionists and politicians. Both slaveholders and African Americans knew the stakes of their contest, the sacred Union which formed in Philadelphia barely a half-century before Frisby answered his door.[2]

Building off of the "chattel principle," a term devised and experienced by the "fugitive Blacksmith" James W. C. Pennington to explain how an enslaved person's identity was bound to a price, the terror of removing fugitives from slavery and kidnappings bound African Americans, even those who were ostensibly free, to slavery no matter their location in the Union. While historians have placed fugitives from slavery at the center of late-antebellum politics, few have examined how kidnappings worked in tandem with and thus complicated retrieving fugitives from slavery in earlier decades, in particular those cases that precipitated the 1820 personal liberty law debates in Pennsylvania. African Americans in Philadelphia produced political crises in Pennsylvania and forced both Black and white Pennsylvanians to ponder the extent to which the state should protect Blacks within the state's borders. The geography of Lower North states exacerbated legal and racial boundaries, thus confounding early Americans' role in engaging in the politics of slavery and freedom in Pennsylvania. Put simply, the African American community in Philadelphia was too close to slavery to completely enjoy freedom.[3]

This chapter analyzes the cases that precipitated the 1820 "Act to Prevent Kidnapping" in Pennsylvania. Illegal removals of African Americans from Philadelphia encouraged state politicians to pass this act, the nation's first "personal liberty law" and a states' rights measure designed to foil kidnappers and their "legal" counterparts, slaveholders and their agents. The catch, of course, was that Pennsylvania remained bound to a Federal Constitution that demanded respect for slaveholders' property rights in human beings. Similar to other struggles over such laws in the Early Republican North, antislavery principles in Pennsylvania emerged over the course of the debates surrounding these cases because ordinary African Americans and their allies believed that they had a right to live in freedom in Pennsylvania. These cases represented a broad spectrum of kidnapping plots, many of which the key players conflated with so-called legal removals. While the realities of other means of kidnapping, or "removing," existed, these five cases acted as potentialities in terms of how specific kidnappings happened and influenced the 1820 liberty law. Ultimately, the combined efforts of African Americans and their allies at the local level convinced Pennsylvania politicians to restrict the power of the Federal Constitution by devising stringent punishments for kidnapping and limiting the number of state officials allowed to assist in federally approved and legal removals.[4]

Pennsylvania Legislation, Federal Law, and Kidnapping, 1780–1817

Pennsylvania governor William Findlay addressed a variety of concerns in his 1819 address to the Pennsylvania state legislature. He proposed new laws to suppress "vice and immorality," highlighted the potential of interstate canal building, and suggested awarding medals to Pennsylvanians who served under Oliver Hazard Perry at Lake Erie in the late war against Britain. After speaking to these state and regional interests, Findlay made a crucial link between local, state, and national politics when he addressed instances that embodied this link: the kidnapping of free Blacks and the legal renditions of fugitives from slavery within Pennsylvania: "I cannot forbear to urge upon your attention the necessity of some provisions for the punishment of the crime of kidnapping, more adequate to the prevention of the offence, as well as more proportioned to other punishments for crimes of inferior grade. It is a melancholy fact, that our laws regard the stealing of a horse a more heinous offence than that of stealing a man."[5]

Findlay's public pronouncement buttressed the intimacies and ambiguities regarding African Americans shared by many whites of his time, politicians or otherwise. His family owned an African American named George, a man whom Findlay grew quite fond of and emancipated two years prior to this address. To commemorate this occasion Findlay stated that "the principles of slavery are repugnant to those of justice." The Philadelphia-based *Franklin's Gazette* noted that Findlay's actions were not "merely an unmeaning declaration [but one] accompanied by a sacrifice of interest." Findlay's interest, in this case, lay within what it meant to treat Blacks like human beings: one must sacrifice one's financial interest by emancipating people with prices, but one must also take care not to become too cozy with the notion of abolishing slavery, even if the institution itself was repugnant.[6]

Like many politicians in the North during the Early Republic, Findlay could not avoid the politics of slavery. Barely a month after his address to the state legislature, he affixed his signature to a resolution "preventing the introduction of Slavery into new States," a resolution directly opposed to the spread of "the crimes and cruelties of slavery, from the banks of the Mississippi to the shores of the Pacific." In a time believed by historians to represent a lapse in antislavery activity, Findlay agreed that Pennsylvania's duty was to provide civil freedom for its residents while respecting rights guaranteed to the slave states. The threat of the spread of slavery into new territories ran counter to Findlay's emancipation of George, and in doing so, thrust Findlay and the state of Pennsylvania into the center of debates over slavery and freedom. Most significantly, Findlay's 1819 address connected emancipation to the "natural concomitant": the kidnapping of free Blacks in Pennsylvania.[7]

The Pennsylvania legislature had long grappled with defining Pennsylvania as a "free" state in a slaveholding republic. While slavery declined across the state over the course of the eighteenth century, metropolitan Philadelphia boasted a population of approximately 12,000 African Americans in 1820, many of whom were recently emancipated during and after the American Revolution and even more who could claim enslaved ancestors. Sensing the porous borders engendered by the war, the Pennsylvania legislature passed the Gradual Abolition Act of 1780, which offered African Americans what the historians Gary Nash and Jean Soderlund have called "freedom by degrees":

children of enslaved people born after the passage of the act were to be freed at age 28, and visiting slaveholders were required to register the enslaved within six months of entering the state or risk their immediate emancipation. Furthermore, a "Supplementary Act" passed by the state legislature in 1788 dictated that slaveholders who intended to establish residency in Pennsylvania could not bring enslaved people with them and, crucially, established that any person who "sent or carried away" (i.e., kidnapped) a Black person would face a fine of 100 pounds and six months in prison.[8]

As Pennsylvania slaveholders began to emancipate the enslaved and African Americans who enjoyed the post-nati emancipation act, these strides obscured the strengthened relationship between the presence of slavery across the United States and the kidnapping of free Blacks. As early as 1802 the Quaker abolitionist Isaac Hopper reported that he worked with several African Americans to detain a Maryland slave catcher named David Lea. Describing Lea as "a very ill looking fellow, filthy in his person, and bore the appearance of being intemperate," Hopper questioned Lea's motives for visiting Philadelphia. Lea responded that he had no business in the city and that he had no money. Upon hearing this rationale Hopper declared Lea "dangerous" and convinced Philadelphia alderman John Hunter to confine him in prison. When Hopper and the jailer searched Lea's clothing, they found his pockets stuffed with advertisements for more than fifty fugitives from slavery. Hopper speculated that Lea went to Philadelphia to find fugitives, "inform their masters, and get a reward for apprehending them." Lea admitted to this plan and stated that slaveholders would pay him for his services. Lea's statements, while repugnant, did not violate the laws of Pennsylvania or the United States: he exercised his right to retrieve human beings, and if he stole the wrong person, he possessed enough advertisements in his pocket to find the "right" victim.[9]

Given how human beings always make time at the end of hostilities to sow the seeds of future conflict, Hopper, his African American allies, and those who fought with them battled against the plausible deniability and inhumanity exercised by Lea and his allies in a war that in many ways broke out at the end of the War of 1812. The historian Matthew Mason has argued that the end of this conflict "set in motion" the actions of the enslaved in the South, many of whom capitalized on wartime chaos to venture to Philadelphia, where they could blend in and forge a free future. The end of the war also increased the pace of Native American removal from the southeastern portion of the United States. The demand for enslaved labor in that region swelled in the minds of slaveholders and kidnappers alike, with both groups setting their sights on Philadelphia. Slaveholders and kidnappers traced African Americans to the city and thus emphasized the primacy of Philadelphia as a flashpoint for conflicts over slavery with local, state, and national consequences. African Americans could enjoy "a tenuous but meaningful freedom" regardless of their origin in Philadelphia, while Pennsylvania legislation on emancipation and kidnapping reflected its status as a "free" state within a slaveholding republic and meant that state officials and African Americans were subject to the federal Fugitive Slave Act of 1793.[10]

In practice, the 1793 act required state officials to intervene on behalf of the federal government, even where state laws protected African Americans. In 1820 the federal judiciary consisted of a skeleton crew, as most states possessed one district judge and circuit judges rode circuits but resided in only nine states. In short, federal support was lacking in local enforcement and slaveholders relied on state magistrates—city recorders, judges, and aldermen—to issue certificates of removal. Many slaveholders, aware of the physical risks associated with retrieving and then traveling with a "fugitive," enlisted local law enforcement, typically constables, to act as their agents in the state to which the fugitive from slavery fled.[11]

Constables and aldermen represented the everyday and familiar faces of law enforcement in Philadelphia. In 1820 Philadelphia possessed fourteen constables, one from each city ward. Locally elected since the colonial era, constables were empowered to "to arrest and apprehend all night-walkers, malefactors and duly-suspected persons, who shall be found wandering, and misbehaving themselves." In a way, these duties presaged powers given to federal officers under the 1850 Fugitive Slave Act. Constables were allowed to recruit bystanders—and if the bystanders refused (again, similar to the 1850 Fugitive Slave Act)—they would be fined. Aldermen, for their part, had the power to jail suspected fugitives. However, given the violent and rapid manner in which fugitives were apprehended and detained, questions remained as to the true condition of accused Blacks. Under the 1793 law, local magistrates, state or federal judges, or the city recorder decided the free or enslaved status of African Americans brought before them. Yet prior to their decision, the actions of constables and aldermen proved essential to successful legal retrievals under the 1793 act—and thus earned them an ignominious distinction in the eyes of Black and white abolitionists. Broad local powers limited to Philadelphia proper enabled local law enforcement to apply federal law to African Americans with impunity.[12]

STATE-HOUSE

The "Old State-House" to nineteenth-century Americans, "Independence Hall" to Americans living today. This building hosted not only the signing of the Declaration of Independence and the Constitutional Convention but also held dozens of trials featuring slaveholders, kidnapping victims, and so-called fugitives from slavery throughout the nineteenth century. Courtesy of the Library Company of Philadelphia

Living while Black in Philadelphia, 1787–1820

The heart of Black Philadelphia was situated in Cedar Ward. Located in the southern part of Philadelphia, the Black community straddled Philadelphia City and County and abutted the Delaware River. Philadelphia City hosted many of Black Philadelphians' white abolitionist supporters and in later decades would decidedly vote Whig in local, state, and national elections. Always the humbler of the two, Philadelphia County barely made a dent as an urban enclave, and in many ways resembled rural outskirts; here, then, many impoverished Philadelphians of all races and backgrounds lived due to cheap housing. Unlike Philadelphia City, the white residents of Philadelphia County, especially later arrivals from Ireland, would go on to vote overwhelmingly for the Democratic Party. The Delaware River also offered plenty of jobs for semi- or unskilled day laborers, from hauling goods from ship to wharf, to plying simple wares, or even working as sailors. African Americans perceived and sought out Philadelphia as a city of opportunity, one located in the "the only state in the union wherein the Black man is treated equally to the white," according to the wealthy African American sailmaker and Philadelphia native James Forten.[13]

More than inexpensive living arrangements or job opportunities, African Americans flocked to Cedar Ward to live near the comfort, security, and vicinity of Black cultural institutions. Founded in 1787 by African Americans Absalom Jones and Richard Allen, the Free African Society provided aid to freed people, many of whom arrived in the city nearly destitute once they left or fled from their enslavement. The society also interacted with Quaker abolitionists and wealthy whites as a way to strengthen both groups' goal of abolition. For example, by the 1790s the PAS found itself "inundated" with requests for legal aid for kidnapping victims, again an early nod toward the interracial abolitionism so crucial to understanding slavery and freedom in Philadelphia. Richard Allen's Mother Bethel AME Church, founded in 1794, advanced the moral leadership of Black Philadelphia by acting as the "Liberty Bell for Black folks": there congregants adhered to Allen's views of protecting the recently freed and free from discrimination or worse, kidnapping. No coincidence, then, that as the preeminent Black church, Mother Bethel would collect money for those kidnapped and still in bondage and by the 1830s become a vital station on the Underground Railroad.[14]

Black leaders reinforced the work of Black cultural institutions by committing to the "essential political act" of petitioning both the federal and state government. It will be remembered that Philadelphia reigned as the nation's capital until 1800, and so petitioning the federal government meant more than sending scrolls to a far-flung locale. A 1797 petition delivered to Congress by four freed people from North Carolina expressed disgust at the "men of cruel disposition" who not only enslaved them but liberated them in such a way that they would have to abandon North Carolina altogether. Thankfully, they arrived in Philadelphia, where they could live in freedom—but a precarious one at that, as it was "pathetically easy" to kidnap free people of color. Black Philadelphians echoed this complaint: Absalom Jones and seventy other Black men from the city drafted and submitted a petition to the House of Representatives in 1799 that went further and claimed that the constant harassment and kidnapping of free African Americans violated the federal compact, i.e., comity, the friendly relationships and expectation of reciprocity between states. The Fugitive Slave Act of 1793 produced "Man-stealers" who defied borders "under colour of this law, [and] cruelly treated, shot, or brought back in chains to those who have no just claim upon them." Commodifying human beings in one part of the country defined how people across the country who looked like them would be treated. The petitioners argued that extending the opposite notions of "justice and equity to all Classes" represented the true spirit of the Constitution and Declaration of Independence. Like the 1797 petition, this petition from 1799 stoked a heated debate in Congress. Unlike the 1797 petition, which received thirty votes of support for African Americans to petition Congress, the 1799 petition garnered a single supporter, the outspoken Representative George Thatcher of Massachusetts, who presented the 1797 position.[15]

It is hard to disagree with the historian Edward Raymond Turner that the entire history of Blacks in Pennsylvania after 1800 consisted of "race prejudice" and preventing African American emigration into Pennsylvania. Unfortunately, these dual realities blended well, for in 1813 Pennsylvania lawmakers attempted to ban Black emigration into the state and fine, imprison, or outright sell African Americans who lived in Pennsylvania and did not register themselves with the state. The bill's sponsors included representatives from Philadelphia City: Lewis Rush and his colleague Jacob Mitchell harangued legislators about the supposed "nuisances" of some 4,000 fugitives from slavery they alleged had crossed into Pennsylvania. The bill's detractors included the Pennsylvania Abolition Society, who through the vehicle of the antislavery stalwart and Philadelphia City representative Thomas Sergeant presented a memorial to protect Blacks from the "spirit of hostility" emanating from the Pennsylvania legislature, including resisting measures to prevent their sale upon being convicted of "certain" crimes. Interesting here is the fact that debates over banning Black immigration featured the remnants of slavery. After all, the proponents of the ban linked the mobility exercised by fugitives from slavery to free Black criminality, with the latter being a stand-in for people whom they believed deserved to be sold as enslaved human beings regardless of being free Pennsylvania residents.[16]

Black leader James Forten crafted a series of elegant responses to the manufactured fears of Black migration into Pennsylvania. "Where shall the poor African look for protection, should the people of Pennsylvania consent to oppress him?" Forten pondered. Once liberated, African Americans who reached Pennsylvania ought not to suffer being auctioned off and reenslaved. Forten and his allies recognized that slaveholders and many white Pennsylvanians used the migration issue as a smokescreen to obscure how Pennsylvania lawmakers tread dangerously close to legalizing the kidnappings of free people.

Thus Forten also criticized a law that would require African Americans to register with the state within a day of their arrival. Registration reified the handing-over of manumission papers to law enforcement, papers that every African American needed to carry with them to avert enslavement. Who were these "registers" who required proof of freedom? Forten knew: "Probably a cruel man" who would encourage constables to "seize and confine everyone who dare to walk the streets without a [slave] collar on his neck." Although the 1813 bill was defeated, Blacks traveling into or within Pennsylvania remained under constant scrutiny, as kidnappers and slave catchers often ignored or flat-out destroyed manumission papers. For example, in 1814 erstwhile Philadelphia constables Joseph Robinson and George Alberti tore up Richard Keen's freedom papers. The pair then confined Keen for seven weeks, waiting for Keen's "owner" or a prospective slave trader or kidnapper. Fortunately, Keen and the PAS took Alberti and Robinson to court, where Judge Joseph Hemphill fined them $250 for false imprisonment.[17]

Alleged waves of fugitives from slavery migrating into the state notwithstanding, the impunity that Black Philadelphians faced daily came about in large part to whites associating African Americans with slavery. Other than the quantitative realities that African Americans composed about 10 percent of the Philadelphia population, the best estimates for freed Blacks in the city varies from the vast majority of Blacks (approximately eleven of every twelve) in the city in 1790 to an 1838 census by the white abolitionist Benjamin Bacon and the Black minister Charles Gardner that revealed about one-quarter of Black households contained one family member who was born into slavery. That residential segregation did not typify Philadelphia throughout the Early Republic meant that African Americans were, indeed, a population that rubbed shoulders with whites daily and a population on the move.[18]

As a "versatile" labor force, many Black Philadelphians remained on the economic margins, leaving them susceptible to abuse by white Philadelphians. This position of relative economic independence neither protected them from the vicissitudes of economic life in the city nor slave catchers and kidnappers, to say nothing of the growing white resentment that fed into anti-Black racism and violence. Sources of resentment included not only the strength and security of Black leadership and cultural institutions, but the increase of Black home ownership in Philadelphia from 1800 to 1820, which represented community vitality, as did the rise of a small yet ambitious and confident Black middle class in the city primed to devote their time to "live an antislavery life." Put simply, African American mobility took many forms: in many

ways Blacks traveled freely from one geographic state to another as much as
they passed from one status of servitude to another, from one social class to
the next, and in doing so, drove whites to acts of senseless violence that contained the seeds of legislative debates.[19]

Philadelphia hosted violent street spectacles that forced African Americans to maneuver their way through a hopeful yet perilous freedom. Imagining an honest streetscape in 1820, ordinary Philadelphians who surveyed the
scene might not look twice when they saw constables or slaveholders dragging African Americans bloody-heeled down Market Street to the "old State-
house," Independence Hall. James Forten explained the terror evoked by such
incidents:

> The Constable, whose antipathy generally against the Black is very great, will
> take every opportunity of hurting his feelings! Perhaps, he sees him at a dis-
> tance and having a mind to raise the boys in hue and cry against him, exclaims,
> "Halloa! Stop the Negro?"—The boys, delighting in the sport immediately begin
> to hunt him, and immediately from a hundred tongues, is heard the cry—"Hoa,
> Negro, where is your Certificate!"—Can anything be conceived more degrad-
> ing to humanity!

Forten's remarks ought to give us pause. He identified the mask of Southern
slavery eagerly donned by many Philadelphians, especially those who relished the "sport" of assaulting and capturing supposed fugitives from slavery.
Richard Allen experienced a similar episode at the hands of a would-be slave
catcher. Being one of the most famous Black Philadelphians saved Allen from
enslavement. Many African Americans cornered by a slave catcher or constable, who in many instances were one and the same person, were not so lucky.
Complicating matters further, both slave catchers and constables found willing assistants in the "boys" who inundated the streets of Philadelphia. Often
just as impoverished as their Black neighbors, these rowdy gangs of youths
added to the general mise-en-scène of terror that pervaded Black life.[20]

Black cultural institutions were also targeted by whites precisely because
they were beacons of hope and safe havens for the Black community. As the
cases of Perry Frisby and Richard Allen showed, praying in one's house or
being the leader of a congregation did not prevent white harassment. In one
infamous incident in 1825, a group of young white men burst through the
doors of Mother Bethel demanding the right to smoke cigars during the service. When African Americans refused to allow them to do so, the white men
stormed off to the back of the church and threw handfuls of salt and cayenne

pepper onto the church's stove. The pandemonium that ensued from this affront included a massive pell-mell rush of 1,500 Black Americans to the exit, which precipitated a stampede that injured dozens and even resulted in the deaths of two congregants. Coughing, gasping, and no doubt vomiting from the potent spiced miasma, these innocent men and woman avoided each other's footsteps and dashed for fresh air and freedom. Those who bore witness to this street scene believed that had the windows and doors not been opened, "the whole congregation would have been strangled." Such perils in the midst of a church service reminded contemporaries that some white Philadelphians felt little discomfort in terrorizing the Black community at its most vulnerable moments.[21]

The PAS Acting Committee

The more slaveholders depended on state officials and local law enforcement to help them execute the 1793 act, the more Philadelphia's African American community and its allies thrust "complicated legal and human questions" related to kidnapping and removal into politics. Likewise, the more kidnappers and slave catchers traveled to Philadelphia, the more abolitionists took notice of the increase in "man-stealing." Philadelphia federal judge and PAS member Richard Peters, Jr. wrote to "The Abolition and Manumission Societies in the United States" in 1817 to encourage abolitionists to pressure their respective state legislatures into remedying the "unjustifiable and nefarious" practices of kidnapping. Peters echoed Forten's thoughts on the overzealous, often illegal role played by constables in Philadelphia and urged the friends of abolition to "be aroused to continual watchfulness" for wayward slaveholders and kidnappers.[22]

Philadelphia's African American community relied not just on the support of influential figures like Peters but also on the daily actions and countersurveillance measures best exemplified by the work of the enforcer group within the PAS: the Acting Committee. The PAS created the Acting Committee in 1787 and assigned it to meet and discuss problems plaguing Black life between the general meetings of the PAS. Acting Committee members were composed of a revolving set of young, entrepreneurial white men who interacted with members of the Black community. This white and Black alliance represented "first movement" abolitionists, as termed by the historian Paul J. Polgar, and brought together shared ideals of protecting and enforcing emancipation in states like Pennsylvania through street-level activism. In this way Philadelphia abolitionists of all phenotypes elided the epistemological isola-

tion that many historians decree when examining "Black" or "white" abolitionism. The Acting Committee remained fundamentally committed to integrating knowledge systems of ordinary people, mostly African American,
into their shared goals of investigation, protection, and emancipation. Most
importantly, the Acting Committee investigated kidnapping activities within
Philadelphia by corroborating evidence, pursuing leads, speaking with informants, and referring cases to the standing committee of exceptional lawyers
who worked pro bono for the PAS.[23]

While phenotypical realities and consequential discrimination may have
prevented the young white men of the Acting Committee from completely
embodying the Black experience in Philadelphia, they adopted much more
than just "Black hearts." These white men went into the most downtrodden
areas of Philadelphia, areas where the ghastly realities of living while poor,
not just Black, informed how they conceptualized strategies to protect those
who needed the most protection. Their work with African Americans and
devotion toward their mutual goals engendered successes. The PAS delegation reported to the 1817 American Convention of Abolition Societies, which
met in Philadelphia that year, that the Acting Committee had successfully
prevented thirty cases of kidnapping out of the fifty-four that received their
attention that year alone. "Notwithstanding the numerous and increasing demands on the attention of our acting committee," the PAS believed that the
committee, "had a tendency to thwart the designs of those avaricious and unprincipled marauders, who have extensively combined for the purpose of enslaving their fellow beings." In sum, the Acting Committee worked together
with Black Philadelphians to push state lawmakers to revise kidnapping legislation. When Pennsylvania lawmakers met in 1820 to debate what became
"An Act to Prevent Kidnapping," they referenced kidnapping cases recorded
by the Acting Committee.[24]

Exploring the Cases

The 1820 liberty law debates in the Pennsylvania state legislature reflected the
illusory borders between freedom and slavery in Pennsylvania. Like cases examined by other historians of slavery, these featured ordinary people whose actions
worked to heighten sectional tensions during a time period in which antislavery political activity appeared "neglected" or waning. These Philadelphia-based
cases featured influential white politicians precisely because some of these
same state legislators worked as abolitionists, too. Furthermore, these cases
demonstrated that the fears of fugitives from slavery intruding into Pennsyl-

vania tapped into larger concerns regarding the role the state would play in defining freedom within its borders.[25]

All of the cases cited by Pennsylvania lawmakers during the 1820 liberty law debates reinforced how local contests over slavery and freedom became dialectically linked to state and national politics. The burden of maintaining friendly relationships and reciprocity between states reflected this local-as-national connection: accusing a Black person on the streets of Philadelphia of being a fugitive from slavery summoned and potentially threatened the property rights enshrined by the Federal Constitution. The stakes of human freedom were (and will always be) that high, even when one reversed the process: debating the morality or legality of the 1793 Fugitive Slave Act hastened real, drastic, and often negative consequences in the lived experiences of individual African Americans, whose freedom was always subject to scrutiny. Pennsylvania state lawmakers balanced vicious and violent local realities with their competing commitments to residents of their own state, neighbors in slave states, and ultimately, the bonds of Union that preserved the country. And yet the burden of comity rested squarely on the backs of African Americans, who at any time could have their futures snuffed out by slaveholders or kidnappers. Local kidnapping events and cases of fugitives from slavery in Philadelphia conjured sympathy toward African Americans and as a result dictated state legislation.

The Case of Abraham Quomoney

The 1816 kidnapping of Abraham Quomoney in Philadelphia, mentioned in the 1820 debates, began as a local event that caught the attention of state politicians mired in the controversy over the spread of slavery into Missouri. The PAS Acting Committee recorded that John Adams, Samuel Talbot, and Samuel Neales, all of Milford, Delaware, informed them that a certain Captain John Milnor and William Miller of the sloop *Betsey* of Philadelphia hired a free Black boy named Abraham Quomoney, also of Philadelphia, under false pretenses in 1816. Milnor and Miller convinced Quomoney to join them aboard the sloop for a short voyage to Cohansey Creek, New Jersey, to pick up a load of wood. Quomoney's age and marginal economic position betrayed his vulnerability and susceptibility to being kidnapped. Instead, Miller and Milnor took Quomoney to Sussex County, Delaware, where they sold him to the notorious Cannon-Johnson kidnapping gang (see below). Chained and beaten by the gang for three days, somehow Quomoney managed to escape and met with Adams, Talbot, and Neales, who sent him back to Philadelphia. As a result, the Acting Committee convinced Philadelphia mayor Robert Wharton to issue an arrest warrant for Milnor and Miller. Philadelphia constable Anthony Elton apprehended both men in Delaware and brought them to Philadelphia, where they and Quomoney appeared in the Mayor's Court.[26]

Quomoney's kidnapping had local, state, and national implications. A lifelong friend of the PAS, Wharton prided himself in later years as never having returned a fugitive from slavery to a slaveholder, although often called upon to perform such an act. He admitted to the Philadelphia abolitionist Isaac T. Hopper that he "could not conscientiously do it" and would rather resign his office than breach the sacred principles enshrined in the Declaration of Independence; interestingly enough, this trial and all others pertaining to kidnappings and fugitives from slavery took place in the aforementioned "old statehouse": Independence Hall. In Wharton's court Milnor and Miller admitted that they took Quomoney aboard the sloop, but they testified that the boy jumped off the boat and refused to board again because he wished to go to work at Milford. Wharton weighed the evidence, ruled that Milnor and Miller be held on $2,000 bail, and pushed the case to the next session of the Mayor's Court. The trial came to court in November 1817, at which time Wharton found Miller guilty of kidnapping, fined him $100, and sentenced him to a year in prison. Disappointed by this mild punishment, the Acting Committee requested that the PAS General Committee send a memorandum to the state legislature urging the politicians to address "some of the evils to which the people of color are subjected."[27]

The PAS viewed its connections with influential national political figures as vital to revising state and national legislation on kidnapping and consequently fugitives from slavery, especially since these politicians offered their legal skills gratis on behalf of the PAS to aid African Americans. The PAS General Committee kept in close contact with sympathetic Pennsylvania legislators in Washington. In March 1817, the PAS received letters from Pennsylvanian politicians, US Senator Jonathan Roberts and US Representative Joseph Hopkinson, both of whom presented the PAS memoranda to their respective chambers in early February to little effect. Though expelled from the Society of Friends due to his support of President James Madison during the War of 1812, Roberts adopted the Quaker principles that worked to end the "iniquity" of slavery throughout his political career. During the debates over expanding slavery into Missouri, for instance, Roberts remarked that he would prefer to bring Maine into the Union and have Congress reconsider the admission of Missouri, but to link these states "was an extraordinary mode of proceeding which ought to be met at the threshold." Key here, then, was Roberts's caution toward tying the fortunes and futures of the free states to a runaway slave system. Given his long work in the service of Black freedom as a PAS lawyer, Hopkinson, too, was obviously troubled by the expansion of slavery into Missouri and made at least one stirring speech on the topic at a "large and highly respectable [Philadelphia] meeting" in 1819.[28]

Philadelphia abolitionists watched as slavery evolved into kidnappings that swept across borders into Pennsylvania. The PAS petitioned Pennsylvania congressmen in January 1818 to fend off a proposal made by Representative James Pindall of Virginia to revise the Fugitive Slave Act of 1793. The proposed amendments were, the PAS wrote, "a clear and complete statement of the proslavery viewpoint" since they forced Northern state magistrates to honor certificates of ownership issued in Southern states and remove alleged fugitives from slavery, thus circumventing habeas corpus and encouraging the kidnapping of free Blacks. Pennsylvania senator John Sergeant responded to Pindall by recommending instead to "change the nature of the bill by making judges of the State in which apprentices, slaves, etc., are seized, the tribunal to decide the fact of slavery, instead of the judges of the States whence the fugitives escaped." Sergeant's advice spoke to his contentious position as a white politician confronted by white slaveholders. On the one hand, he defended the right of Africans to move around Pennsylvania unmolested to ensure that African Americans received a trial in a Pennsylvania court. On the other hand, he respected the right to remove African Americans from Pennsylvania as a way to maintain interstate comity.[29]

Although Pindall's proposals never mustered enough votes to pass both houses of Congress, Quomoney's kidnapping and the PAS confirmed the difficulty of separating fugitives from slavery from kidnapping victims. This difficulty became propounded when lawmakers sought to preserve comity, which meant preserving the Union. Whether preserving African American freedom or maintaining the right to enslave, ordinary people created extraordinary episodes in which local, state, and national figures depended upon each other for success. African Americans depended on white support at the local level to encourage political support at the state and even national level. Again, the process of dependence worked in reverse, especially when antislavery stalwarts from Pennsylvania aligned themselves with the PAS and its local operatives, the Acting Committee and its most necessary allies, ordinary African Americans. In short, kidnappings and the removal of fugitives from slavery created spaces for Blacks and whites to work together and influence political decisions. Whether these interracial interactions promoted freedom or slavery was another matter.

The Case of William Young

An African American man named William Young exposed a hard truth for African Americans living in the North: some African Americans kidnapped other African Americans. Termed "counterfeit kin" by the historian Richard Bell, these men and women of the "reverse" or "other" Underground Railroad added yet another complicated and terrifying layer to Black life. Young work as a Black kidnapper, demonstrating how the "mercurial" nature of race exerted its power through its malleability. Pushing this notion a bit further, race did and did not matter when it came to kidnapping. Kidnappers, Black or white, viewed African Americans as people without futures, or futures that Black kidnappers in particular might one day suffer due to their own physical appearance. The malleability of race dispensed with the illusion that racial solidarity "happened" amongst a free, freed, and potentially "fugitive" population of African Americans living in Philadelphia. Kidnappers like Young could and did, in effect, hide in plain sight while at the same time pursuing people who looked just like them, people who could in no way avoid being seen as members of a particular race whose freedom was always subject to questioning.[30]

An African American abolition society brought Young's case to the PAS Acting Committee in December 1817. While this Philadelphia Black abolition society's name did not survive in the historical records, it clearly functioned as a covert anti-kidnapping vigilance group. Once again, the PAS relied almost exclusively on Black reconnaissance and knowledge to subdue Young. The Black activists accused Young of kidnapping two Black men and a Black girl. This unnamed society had already contacted the Philadelphia lawyer John Swift, who brought the case before Philadelphia City alderman Samuel Badger. Working at street level, African Americans relied not only upon word of mouth and constant vigilance to deter kidnappers but also upon appeals to white law enforcement officials, whose sympathy and legal imprimatur preserved an individual's future freedom. Badger's name appears frequently throughout the PAS records, and more often than not, he chose to err on the side of "further examination" when confronted with a fugitive case. In the case of a victim of an attempted kidnapping, or supposed fugitive from slavery, an alderman's responses bought the accused crucial time to gather allies and information that would prove their freedom. Alderman Badger committed

Young to the Court of Quarter Sessions. Having "progressed in the case as far as they [felt] competent," the Black abolition society chose to have the Acting Committee take the case under its care, perhaps suggesting the society's awareness of the optics of Black-on-Black kidnapping and the efficacy of partnering with whites.[31]

Young's case came before Judge Richard Rush in late September 1818. According to reports, a year earlier Young "seduced" three African American men, John Wood, John Dorden, and Benjamin Bennet, from the southern suburbs outside the city limits to sail to Delaware to cut wood; since then no one in the community had seen the men. However, many witnesses did see Young transformed upon his return to Philadelphia: he appeared "better clad, and had the command of more money." Much like a slaveholder who sold an enslaved person to purchase sartorial accoutrements, Young converted his victims into clothing, objects without a future. When one of Bennet's friends confronted Young about Bennet, Young told him that a constable put Bennet in the workhouse. Given how constables who surveilled the African American community routinely seized Black men for vagrancy, Young sought to frame Bennet as an idle body. Suggesting the evolving sense of race during the nineteenth century, it was revealing how Young appealed to racist stereotypes as an alibi. Nonetheless, Young explained that Wood and Dorden had left the shallop and returned to the city on another boat and that he was the "*only* person of Colour" onboard. An eyewitness who piloted another shallop alongside Young for two hours swore that Young was accompanied by "*two* coloured Men, and a *Black Man*." Judge Rush reasoned from Young's "lies and inconsistent tales" that he was a kidnapper and found him guilty. Authorities never recovered Wood, Dorden, or Bennet.[32]

Young's defense and Rush's ruling reflected how permeable borders supported interminable slavery. First, Rush remarked on the growing significance of the internal slave trade by commenting upon the ease with which kidnappers ignored borders: "Considering all the circumstances, it is to be feared, some inhuman monster in the State of Delaware, stood ready to receive the victims, and has hurried them, ere now, to the Banks of the Mississippi, to the utmost verge of Georgia, or even to some Island in the West Indies, where they may be at this moment suffering under the daily lash of a merciless Task-Master."[33] Rush did not exaggerate the scope and distances: kidnappings that began in Philadelphia as deals between individuals in neighboring slave states often extended across the entire United States. After all, the rise of the dreadful internal slave trade after 1809 made it common for kidnapping victims to find themselves thousands of miles (and thousands of memories) away from their homes and loved ones. Second, Rush emphasized the barbarity of kidnapping: if it were in his power to do so, he would make Young "experience a state of servitude *for life*, equally galling and severe, with that you have brought upon your Fellow Creatures." Rush's rationale for such a harsh punishment may have reflected his antislavery upbringing, being the son of Benjamin Rush, signer of the Declaration of Independence and former secretary of the PAS; but even the younger Rush reified slavery, condoning it to the extent that a criminal might face lifelong servitude as punishment for illegally enslaving another human being.[34]

Rush also commented on Young's racial identity, which white and Black abolitionists viewed as a "delicate" situation. What made Young's crime heinous was that he was a "Man of Colour" who kidnapped two "coloured" men and one "Black" one. Distinguishing between these terms meant identifying specific phenotypes that would be obvious to everyone in the courtroom: Young was mixed-race, "a yellow man" according to the *Hallowell Gazette*. Depending on his intentions, Young utilized the malleability of his race to present himself as either an employer or a kidnapper.[35]

Although correlation may not equate to causation, the fact that Pennsylvania legislators sought to revise kidnapping legislation shortly after the Quomoney and Young cases is significant. Rush bemoaned the incommensurate penalties for kidnapping in Pennsylvania: "While [the law] punishes a man, who steals a *Horse*, with hard labour for *seven* years, it imposes for stealing a *Man*, a fine of *one hundred* pounds, and hard labour not exceeding *one* year." Not coincidentally, Governor William Findlay used the exact same language when advocating for revised kidnapping legislation. That elite whites borrowed wholesale from each other's words to remain on point once again established how ordinary people, nefarious kidnappers like Young or otherwise, drove politics and history. With no other recourse but to punish Young, Rush reasoned that Young deserved the maximum sentence: a 300-pound fine and three years hard labor.[36]

While Rush lamented the fact that Pennsylvania law prevented him from exacting a harsher penalty on Young, African Americans and their PAS allies faced a graver threat to their anti-kidnapping efforts due to an 1819 decision by Pennsylvania Supreme Court judge William Tilghman. In *Wright v. Deacon*, Tilghman upheld the constitutionality of the 1793 Fugitive Slave Act and stated at that time that "whatever may be our private opinions on the subject of slavery, it is well known that our southern brethren would not have consented to become parties to a Constitution under which the *United States* have enjoyed so much prosperity, unless their property in slaves had been secured." Thus, to Tilghman, state courts could not, nor were they ever intended to, prevent removing fugitives from slavery or deny slaveholders their right to retrieve their property throughout the United States. This dangerous yet "necessary bargain" (Tilghman's words) forced Pennsylvanians to heed the 1793 federal Fugitive Slave Act at the expense of Black freedom in the state. This underlying tension between protecting a state's citizens and affirming a slaveholder's right to property continued to plague abolitionists, Black and white, in locales like Philadelphia.[37]

With Tilghman's ruling fresh in their minds, the PAS pressured Governor Findlay to address the kidnapping of Black Pennsylvanians in December 1819. As mentioned earlier, Findlay employed the same logic and language conveyed by Rush in his sentencing of Young. Kidnappers threatened Black freedom in Pennsylvania and, in doing so, flouted any respect for Pennsylvania borders and laws. Findlay recommended establishing harsher punishments to afford "security for life, liberty and property" for Pennsylvania residents. Findlay's comments proved auspicious and resonated with national politics in 1819: while Pennsylvanians debated kidnapping laws, Congress debated the spread of slavery into Missouri.[38]

The Missouri Debates: Slavery Local and National?

The Missouri debates of 1819–1822 forced Congress to address the issue of whether it had the power to restrict slavery as the United States expanded into new territories. As the historian Elizabeth R. Varon has noted, these debates spoke to the "prophetic" nature of disunion. Politicians grappled with the fate of the Union, especially in how slavery might affect and even drive expansion. While Southern slaveholding politicians cited the diffusion of slavery as a means to gradually emancipate enslaved African Americans, Northerners like the Pennsylvania politician John Sergeant decried the diffusion argument as a way to smuggle slavery and its symbiotic counterpart, kidnappings, across the North. The prophetic stakes of the debate hinted at a continued national discord over the presence of slavery in the United States. On the street level these moments of disunion occurred in the lives of ordinary African Americans in Pennsylvania, whose freedom was subject to questioning by slaveholders, kidnappers, and local law enforcement officials.[39]

Thus the Missouri Compromise debates began in 1819, when New York Republican congressman James Tallmadge proposed to amend a bill allowing for Missouri statehood. The "Tallmadge amendment" sought to prohibit slavery from the state and ensured a gradual emancipation scheme. The debates fomented a crisis when Northern Congress members met with a fierce proslavery defense concocted by their Southern slaveholding colleagues. However, Southerners could not dismiss the idea of restricting the spread of slavery as mere New England or Federalist-inspired sectionalism. The Missouri debates placed middle states like Pennsylvania in a disproportionately important position.[40]

Kidnappings in Philadelphia became magnified when Pennsylvania politicians linked local contests to national politics. As the historian Matthew Mason has explained, these links exposed the weakness of the Union. Elite whites who worked to promote abolition in the North collided with the reality of street-level dangers created and exacerbated by slaveholders and kidnappers. Senator John Sergeant of Pennsylvania played a key role during the Missouri debates. He delivered a speech to Congress in early February 1820 in which he argued that Pennsylvania could not both abolish slavery in its own territory and ignore the spread of slavery into new territories: "Can it be, that we sincerely believe it to be an evil, and yet will gravely insist that it is a right of every new state, to do what? I was going to say, enjoy this evil, but that would be a perversion of terms—afflict and injure herself, and her associates, too by admitting it within her limits?" Allowing slavery to spread over space, Sergeant explained, extended an evil not only to the enslaved but also to African Americans born afterward—free or otherwise—who bore the "unalterable physical mark" of slavery.[41]

In a similar prophetic vein, Sergeant linked the obvious dynamics of the growing interstate slave trade with an increase in kidnappings of free African Americans. Philadelphia's central role in attracting African Americans who freed themselves in a variety of ways embodied the perpetual risk that African Americans took in maintaining the Union. Sergeant noted that if Congress failed to restrict the further spread of slavery into Missouri then a "great inland domestic slave trade" would be established in the United States, complete with "the horrors of the middle passage" and the "most cruel accompaniments of that hateful traffic": kidnappers. As a Pennsylvanian and PAS supporter, Sergeant witnessed firsthand how the frayed borders of Southern slavery encouraged the kidnappings of free Blacks in Philadelphia. Slaveholders who sought to retrieve their so-called property from Northern locales intensified the pressures placed on Pennsylvania politicians. National considerations about property ran headfirst into states like Pennsylvania, which attempted to define freedom on their own terms. By the time these debates reached the streets of Philadelphia, local realities—interracial activism and resistance—conflated "legal" removals with kidnappings. African Americans and their allies considered both forms of removal one and the same and made Pennsylvania and Philadelphia hotspots for conflict that linked local and national concerns over slavery. The precariousness of Black freedom exhibited by the Quomoney and Young cases influenced how white politicians debated the interlocked notions of slavery spreading west and kidnapping spreading north.[42]

The Case of Henry Hudson

The third case mentioned by Pennsylvania state legislators in their debates over the revised kidnapping law explored the confusing process of establishing whether an African American man named Henry Hudson was an actual kidnapping victim. Hudson was born enslaved in Kent County, Delaware, in 1797. In 1805 Hudson was bound to Smith Forsett of Wilmington, who told him that he would free him upon his twenty-first birthday. However, when Forsett died in 1814 his will dictated that Hudson work for Nathaniel and Alice Luff, also of Wilmington. Hudson served the Luff family for four years until his twenty-first birthday on May 30, 1818, at which point the Luffs freed him. Alice Luff and Hudson then traveled to Philadelphia to write up his official certificates of freedom. Having the notarized certificates in hand, Hudson journeyed to Germantown in the northwest corner of Philadelphia, where he scrounged for and eventually found work on a farm owned by the Quaker Reuben Haines III.[43]

Haines lived his entire life in the Philadelphia area. Born in 1786 at his family's ancestral home of "Wyck" in Germantown, he worked briefly as a merchant in Philadelphia, where he maintained ties to Philadelphia's elite, including his cousin Roberts Vaux and friend William Rawle, both members of the PAS leadership. By 1820, Haines decided to remain with his family in Germantown year-round so that he could devote his attention both to them and "improvement" projects such as developing the agricultural potential of his home and the infrastructure of Germantown. Thus, when Hudson met Haines, both men were in a state of transition and self-definition. The former explored his freedom, while the latter fixated on improving his home and community.[44]

Hudson vanished in broad daylight while working at Wyck on April 30, 1819. Haines enlisted the help of his uncle and PAS member Abraham Garrigues of Philadelphia to investigate Hudson's apparent kidnapping. Garrigues interviewed nine Philadelphia justices of the peace from across the city, but none were of any help. Eyewitnesses from Germantown offered contradictory claims: John Snovel's wife saw a yellow carriage driven by two or more men turn past her house on the afternoon of the 30th; Christian Dillman's wife and daughter saw a yellow or orange hack driven by a Black man speed by their house. These clashing accounts produced great anxiety in Garrigues, who, after suffering "a sleepless night," theorized that Hudson "had fallen a Sacrifice to some remorseless Tyrant."[45]

Newspapers covered Hudson's disappearance because of the reality of kidnapping activity in Philadelphia as well as Haines's social standing. Typically friendly to the PAS, *Poulson's* newspaper warned that Philadelphia was "infested with men stealers" and that it behooved every good citizen to be vigilant. Haines contacted the Baltimore abolitionist Isaac Tyson and asked him to place a $100 reward advertisement in the *Baltimore Patriot*. The *Patriot* described Hudson as a "very civil, inoffensive man." Here Haines appealed to refinement and exculpated any fears regarding Hudson's temperament as a free Black man. The advertisement alluded to the dueling realities of African American and kidnapper mobility by requesting that "keepers of turnpike gates, toll bridges and taverns, are particularly requested to give such information as may by in their power." Expecting that other Southerners, Americans all, would abide by comity and assist in the search, Haines's friend James Canby brought the reward advertisement to Norfolk, Virginia, and placed it in several Southern newspapers. Despite disseminating Hudson's story across the country's newspapers, by mid-May, no one had heard from or seen Henry Hudson.[46]

Haines's advertisement displayed how interstate comity demanded respect and reciprocity. The reward advertisement reaped benefits and confirmed Haines's expectations that he would receive support from Southerners. On May 18 Haines received a letter from a man named Ephraim Carsons of Warwick, Maryland, who claimed he knew the kidnappers who captured Hudson. Carsons told Haines to disregard the reward because he wanted "nothing more than to have such wretches brought to the most condign punishment," a fitting sentiment in the interest of comity and honor between white men. Carsons urged Haines to hurry to Warwick because Hudson was to be sold to a trader in Georgia. Haines left for Maryland; not only did he expect Southerners to assist him but as a white man he passed over borders unmolested. Haines believed that legal categories were meaningful, and he brought Hudson's certificate of freedom and a deposition testifying to Hudson's emancipation with him as he traveled south.[47]

Compounding the unpredictability of recovering kidnapping victims, Haines also procured a letter from the "notorious" slave catcher Richard Lockwood of Middletown, Delaware, in the hope of securing his "prompt and efficient aid." Lockwood regularly implemented the 1793 federal Fugitive Slave Act yet seemed to respect Hudson's freedom, albeit through the efforts of Haines. While as beneficial as Lockwood's help may have been, he may have assisted Haines to avoid any implication in kidnapping Blacks or even to expect reciprocity when he himself ventured north to retrieve fugitives from slavery. Haines and Lockwood collapsed the border between freedom and slavery, north and south, precisely because they were powerful white men; in essence, Haines placed his faith and Hudson's fate in the hands of a "notorious" slave catcher.[48]

Haines left Wilmington on the 25th with the Delaware abolitionist Evan Lewis and met with Lockwood, who advised them to wait until morning to recover Hudson and "seize and secure the *kidnappers* [emphasis in the original]." Heeding Lockwood's advice, next Haines and Lewis met with Ephraim Carsons. The meeting was revelatory, as Haines realized that the letter had been a hoax devised by a local "dealer in Blacks"; this hoax, while perhaps rare, exposed another unpredictable variable in the search for kidnapping victims. Comity remained a hope, not an assumption one could take for granted.[49]

Emphasizing the sprawling geography of kidnappings, on June 8 Haines received a letter from Georgia signed "Henry Hudson." Hudson wrote that he had been kidnapped, smuggled to Georgia, escaped, and confined to jail in Savannah. He requested that Haines forward his freedom papers to Savannah lawyer Richard W. Habersham. Haines sent Hudson's certificates to Habersham and his associate, Robert Campbell. Campbell wrote Haines and explained that he was the victim of another hoax: "some one of more meanness than wit" hoped to embarrass Habersham for his membership in the local colonization society. "Although we are a Slave Holding people," Campbell wrote, "and do not know when we shall be otherwise, yet assure yourself, that there are very few in this place who would not have promptly attended to your letter had it been addressed to them." Legal categories and comity, Campbell suggested, mattered, as he tried to distance legal removals from kidnappings.[50]

After months of searching, perhaps Haines began to lose faith in finding Hudson, for when he received another letter from Bucks County, immediately north of Philadelphia, written by another man claiming to be Hudson,

Haines did not pursue this lead. This Hudson wrote, "I Take this opportunity to let you Know where I live. I was informed by John Coons that you expected I was Kidnapped. I am very much oblige[d] to you for the trouble that you have taken. I am verry [*sic*] well at present and I hope that this letter will find you all the same." Again, unwilling to succumb to a third hoax, Haines did not respond to this letter. Ripped from honest toil in Philadelphia, smuggled into the Slave South, and victimized at every turn by hoaxers, Haines may have assumed that Hudson was lost forever.[51]

Two weeks later the real Henry Hudson appeared in Haines's yard "well clothed and apparently well fed." Hudson told Haines with "a great deal of simplicity and apparent candor" that he had left Wyck Farm on his own voli- tion: he wandered away, got a job as a hostler in Bustleton for one month and worked on a farm in Bucks County. Now back at Wyck, Hudson agreed to work for Haines for a month without pay. After working "industriously" for that time, Hudson returned to farm work in Bucks County.[52]

The case of Henry Hudson underscored several important ideas bound to the process of rescuing kidnapping victims. First, Haines's assumption that Hudson was kidnapped indicated the ubiquity of the kidnapping phenome- non in Philadelphia, a paranoia that by 1820 produced narrative tropes. The truth was that Hudson exercised more freedom than whites expected a Black man could exercise. Perhaps the early parts of his travail pushed Haines to discuss the incident with his influential politician friends and thereby encour- aged them to cite the Hudson case during the 1820 liberty law debates. Second, Haines's efforts to retrieve Hudson and the subsequent confusing process in- verted the way in which slaveholders retrieved fugitives from slavery. Haines enlisted local law enforcement, harnessed Pennsylvania state power, and ex- pected comity with other whites across the country, slaveholders or other- wise. Furthermore, Haines and his allies generated an extensive search party that problematized the North-South divide, as it included helpers in the form of the slaveholders Lockwood, Habersham, and Campbell, white men of so- cial standing who believed in the legal categories bestowed by state and fed- eral law. If anything, Hudson's tale highlighted how kidnapping rumors were powerful narratives. In 1820, Pennsylvania lawmakers cited the Hudson case (but not its unlikely conclusion) to build support for legislation to revise the state's kidnapping law. That lawmakers likely knew the true circumstances of Hudson's ordeal (as discussed below) meant that white politicians' political scruples did not preclude them from protecting Pennsylvania Blacks or revis- ing kidnapping legislation by any narrative necessary.

The Case of Sarah Hagerman's Daughter

The Hudson case represented the assumptions Americans made about the disappearance of African Americans, and with good reason. Besides dangers on the streets of Philadelphia, kidnapping gangs who operated out of nearby Maryland and Delaware terrorized the city's African Americans in the decades prior to the 1820 debates. Pennsylvania politicians discussed the case of "Hagerman's daughter" to emphasize the need to protect African Americans in the state, especially those in Philadelphia, from such gangs. The case of Hagerman's daughter also presented powerful undercurrents, namely, the fact that this girl was both unnamed and never found. All we know is the brief description supplied by *Poulson's* newspaper: "the child was born in this city, is about 11 years old, has a scar on her forehead, and on one of her knees." The brief details reminded readers that kidnapping victims were real, and not forgotten, people ripped from their homes and lives in Philadelphia.[53]

This case began in April 1819, when Margaret Flannery, alias Peggy Ward, hired the daughter of an African American widow, Sarah Hagerman of Philadelphia. Similar to the aforementioned cases, a kidnapper offered Hagerman's daughter work and labor in a precarious economy. Given the unexceptional nature of child labor during the era, Sarah Hagerman might not think anything unusual about such an offer. Within a week, both Flannery and Hagerman's daughter disappeared; rumors spread that Flannery kidnapped the girl and sold her in Delaware. Around the same time Hagerman's daughter vanished, Flannery lured a free woman of color from Philadelphia named Betsey Everson to meet two "interested" gentlemen, James Welsh and John McKee. Again, the vulnerability of those most susceptible to kidnapping, children and women, made Flannery's work all the easier.[54]

Nevertheless, as to exactly why Betsey agreed to join the men, the sources were mute. Soon enough Betsey found herself drinking with the men; one man became "extremely sociable with her" and convinced her to follow them to Almond Street wharf. This particular wharf hosted hundreds of vessels each day, with one lowly schooner blending in with the larger ships that carried passengers to all places international, not to mention the large crowds that flowed up and down the docks during the day. One schooner called the "Nancy or Bright's Phoebe," contained the unconscious body of Betsey Everson. She later told the PAS that she "was so drunk that she scarcely knew what she was about" and awoke the next morning to find herself in Wilmington, Delaware. Everson realized that Welsh and McKee kidnapped her and at her first opportunity somehow escaped their clutches. The men pursued her, but with the help of "some white person," Everson returned to Philadelphia.[55]

The Acting Committee worked diligently to track down Hagerman's daughter as well as Welsh and McKee. Committee member Robert Murphy submitted a short piece to *Poulson's* in May 1819 in which he warned African Americans about Flannery and urged the slave states to "do an act of humanity by inserting this advertisement." "An act of humanity" appealed to readers' sense of morality, and from a political lens, appealed to their sense of maintaining comity. Whether these specific advertisements helped remains unknown, though by June 15 Delaware authorities had apprehended McKee and Welsh and Maryland authorities jailed Flannery in Baltimore. These arrests exemplified what abolitionists and politicians expected of each other when rescuing kidnapping victims: interstate comity. After these arrests the Acting Committee applied to Governor Findlay to bring the kidnappers to trial in Pennsylvania.[56]

Harnessing state power to combat the illegal abuse of federal power, on June 22 Findlay appointed Philadelphians George W. Campbell and John Dolbert to serve as agents of Pennsylvania to retrieve the kidnappers. Campbell served as Philadelphia's high constable and later collaborated with the PAS to rescue an African American man named John Johnson, who was kidnapped in Bensalem (directly north of the city) and confined in a house near Pine Street; in that case the kidnappers skipped their bail, court date, and of course, justice. Dolbert served as sexton of Swedes' Church and lived in Southwark, which as mentioned above, abutted Cedar Ward; that he interacted with the Black community on a daily basis seems quite probable. Findlay also requested that the governors of Delaware and Maryland use "all convenient dispatch" to expedite the process and return the kidnappers to stand trial in Pennsylvania as soon as possible. Such requests did not lack precedent: a year earlier Findlay extended the same courtesy to deliver a kidnapper named Orange Bush to the state of Maryland. In July Campbell traveled to Delaware and Dolbert to Maryland; the PAS paid the travel expenses for these missions and later the office of the governor reimbursed them.[57]

Welsh and McKee were brought before Philadelphia mayor James Nelson Barker on kidnapping charges. Educated by his father and former mayor John Barker in the art of gentlemanly etiquette, including dueling and "firmness," the younger Barker was elected mayor by the city's "democracy," a code word for supporters of those politicians whose allegiance flowed from Jefferson to Madison and eventually to Van Buren and Jackson. Barker emphasized his love for the "perpetual" Union not only by delivering electrifying speeches at July 4th events in Philadelphia but also by participating in a large and "most respectable" gathering of Philadelphians, including many influential politicians and (white) abolitionists, who resolved that the spread of slavery into Missouri represented a great "moral and political transgression."[58]

Barker listened as defendants corroborated Everson's testimony. He found Welsh and McKee guilty and set their bail at $1,000. Neither man being able to afford the payment, Barker confined them to prison. Meanwhile, Flannery was convicted for kidnapping Hagerman's daughter, sentenced to one year in prison, and fined $100. "S.T." wrote to *Poulson's* pleading for an "*honest* slaveholder" who may have purchased the girl to return her to her family in Philadelphia and attributed Flannery's "diabolical game" of kidnapping to the omnipresence of slavery in America. Flannery attracted willing kidnappers, north and south: she confessed that her gang involved at least eight people, "most of whom have been long in the trade." Like Rush before and Findlay soon enough, S.T. argued for "enlightened Pennsylvania" to amend mild punishments for kidnapping, as "Twelve months in confinement and [a] 100 pound fine" were not commensurate to lifetimes lost through kidnapping activities.[59]

Before the PAS discharged the case of Hagerman's daughter, Acting Committee member John H. Willits received word from James Welsh in November 1819 that he (Welsh) had sold the girl to Jesse Cannon of Maryland. Welsh suggested Willits leave immediately to rescue the girl before Cannon sold her farther south. Welsh's sole motive here seemed to be self-preservation, though perhaps he encouraged the PAS to travel down South to face the wrath of the kidnappers. "This duty having devolved upon me," reported Willits with an alacrity that obscured any sense of fear, "I prepared without delay to fulfill it." As with the Hudson case, the geographical scope of kidnapping did not just mean taking victims to the closest slave state: victims could and at times did end up in any slave state.[60]

Similar to Haines, Willits hoped to enlist the support of Southerners in his search. Accompanied by a man named Miller, Willits traveled to Maryland and attempted to procure help from the sheriff of Caroline County. The sheriff lacked jurisdiction but recommended that Willits apply to the Maryland abolitionist Anthony Wheatley, a man "well-acquainted" with Cannon's gang and who often rescued free African Americans. Willits and Miller then met with Wheatley, who told them that while ordinarily he would "cheerfully" accompany them, he doubted that they would find the girl. Did Wheatley ex-press doubt due to the efficacy of the gang or their penchant for violence—or both? Wheatley recommended that Willits and Miller meet with a potential ally, Hatfield Wright, who lived near Jesse Cannon and recently had a falling out with him over "stolen property."[61]

Cannon, his wife Patty, and their son-in-law Joe Johnson had operated as kidnappers in Delaware, Maryland, Virginia, and Pennsylvania for almost a decade by the time Willits ventured south in 1819. Tales of their misdeeds, including murder, were legion, which required Willits and Miller to take extra precautions not to alert the gang of their presence. The confluence of these three slave states later abbreviated to "Delmarva" was no place of comity, let alone any whisperings of abolition: for now the abolitionists found themselves "among the friends of Cannon [and] surrounded by persons engaged in the same trade." Hatfield Wright told them that approaching Cannon's house would be "needless," as the gang's multiracial informants lurked everywhere. Instead, Wright hired an agent to surveil the kidnappers' house. This agent reported seeing a girl who matched the description of Hagerman's daughter husking corn on the premises.[62]

The possible sighting of Hagerman's daughter lifted Willits's spirits, for as a white American he expected slave state officials to honor comity. In this case, he obtained a search warrant from Delaware authorities and the assistance of two constables, who "expressed much apprehension of the violent opposition which we should probably have to encounter." These constables knew the Cannon-Johnson gang often brandished guns in the face of law enforcement as well as abolitionists, and therefore, cared little about upholding interstate comity. Given Johnson's reputation as a "most desperate ruffian" and Cannon's "savage ferocity," everyone agreed to recruit reinforcements from the towns of Georgetown and Bridgeville: only two men volunteered to help the rescue party.[63]

Willits's party proceeded with caution. They divided into two groups in order to surround the hideout and prevent "the retreat of any negroes who might attempt to escape or conceal themselves." Johnson often terrorized kidnapping victims by telling them that any strangers who came to the house were slave traders from the Deep South, which prompted the victims to hide from potential liberators. Not surprisingly, none of the young Black girls at the front of the house responded to Willits's inquiries, and one girl who looked like Hagerman's daughter ran into the garden upon seeing the abolitionist. Miller pursued the girl but when he rounded the corner Joe Johnson leapt into action, placed a gun to Miller's head, and promised to "blow his brains out" if he did not identify himself. Seeing the rest of the would-be rescuers in his midst, Johnson told them not to lift a single latch in the house. When one constable began reading the search warrant, Johnson interrupted and said that it had expired because the sun had already set. The constable agreed, but Willits insisted upon a search because the sun did not set before the party's arrival. Foolhardy or not, Willits's demand to search a well-known and quite dangerous kidnapping hideout was bold. In this case, the notion of adopting a Black heart here seems insufficient when explaining how white Americans empathized with Black Americans. Willits and his party embodied an interracial abolitionism in which one risked one's life to ensure the freedom and future of another person, often a stranger who looked nothing like them. Interestingly enough, Johnson relented and allowed Miller and a constable to enter, provided "no questions should be asked of any negroes." Johnson and Jesse Cannon accompanied the pair, pistols in hand.[64]

The pair searched through the gang's horrifying hideout: the attic contained five chained Black women; outside the house was a hut and garden attended by a group of Black children and a couple of inebriated African American men, the latter of whom refused to go with the rescue party. "[We are] very well contented," the pair explained, prompting Johnson to boast, "You see gentlemen, I treat my slaves so well, that they would not leave if it were in their power." Were these men actually "content," given the omnipresent threat and reality of violence? Or was Johnson being truthful: perhaps the pair were decoys for kidnapping ploys and were truly content as members of the kidnapper's household. The dispirited party left the hideout without finding the girl, a tragically poignant moment that no doubt haunted the rescuers. Admitting defeat by this "den of thieves," Willits wrote, "When I came to reflect on the character of the people we had to deal with, that any further prosecution of the search would result only in an unprofitable sacrifice of my own time . . . [and] not doubting that as their suspicions were now excited, they would have ample opportunity before the next day of removing the girl to the houses of some of their accomplices, where she would be effectually secreted, even admitting that she was now in their possession."[65]

Similar to the Hudson case, the search for Sarah Hagerman's daughter required rescuers to cross borders and enlist slave state resources to find and liberate a kidnapping victim. Like Black and white abolitionists, the kidnappers understood how kidnapping free African Americans commodified them and transformed them into human beings without futures. Despite the best efforts of anti-kidnapping forces, punishing kidnappers required increasing penalties through state intervention.[66]

The 1820 Liberty Law Debates

The aforementioned kidnappings in Philadelphia revealed the difficulty of reconciling local and national politics through exploitable dictums pertaining to the removal of fugitives from slavery and kidnapping. State legislators addressed Pennsylvania's role in this confounding process on January 5, 1820, when Pennsylvania state legislator William Wilkins proposed fixing the punishment for kidnapping "not less than two nor more than ten years." A freshman representative, Wilkins promoted internal improvements, defended Governor Findlay against accusations of corruption, and opposed the spread of slavery into Missouri. Wilkins's colleague Josiah Randall of Philadelphia, who had presented the petition to investigate Findlay, replied that ten years would be too lenient. Most kidnappings were committed in his native Philadelphia, where "prejudice existing in the minds of the citizens against the perpetrators of it" could furnish jurors who bore no scruples against imprisoning kidnappers. Randall's words may have provided cold comfort to Philadelphia's African American community, who often experienced a local "prejudice" that exacerbated efforts to disrupt kidnappings. Prior disagreements notwithstanding, Wilkins and Randall recognized the scope of the crisis and agreed to stiffen the penalty for kidnapping.[67]

Assuming that local "prejudice" would ensure African American freedom required redefining the role and potential punishment of "petty" state officials: the aldermen and justices of the peace who relied on local law enforcement (i.e., constables) to surveil African Americans. These petty officials, it will be remembered, often issued certificates to slaveholders, their agents, and at various times and in ambiguous ways, kidnappers, too. Each removal that stemmed from their judgment, which at points seemed arbitrary, spoke to the need to ensure that a trained jurist handled such cases.

Further weakening the power of local law enforcement, those Philadelphia constables who harassed African Americans frequently disguised kidnappings through plausible deniability. Wilkins argued that punishing state officials for abuses of power would decrease the number of kidnappings. James Thackara of Philadelphia agreed, so long as the punishments provided a "variety of optics" through which anyone would be able to comprehend the penalties for kidnapping. Citing the Hudson case, Thackara commented that "it was well known that justices do co-operate with those who are daily engaged in this most outrageous practice of man stealing." Randall knew the competing, ironic, and true narrative of Hudson's disappearance and not the tale of his kidnapping. He exonerated the magistrate from "improper conduct." In the end, the legislature voted against an amendment to punish state officials directly for issuing illegal removals. Eventually the final bill increased fines for kidnapping to no less than $500 and no more than $2,000.[68]

While Pennsylvania legislators exacted heftier fines for kidnappers, they still grappled with a Federal Constitution that required Pennsylvanians to facilitate the removal of fugitives from slavery that occurred where local circumstances upheld slaveholders' property rights. State legislator William Duane acknowledged that African Americans and their white allies complained about overzealous law enforcement officials but that Pennsylvanians could do little in a context of a Federal Constitution that permitted removing "fugitives" from across the United States. Some lawmakers agreed that Pennsylvania could modify the duties performed by state magistrates, a clamoring for Pennsylvania states' rights. Besides, Duane reasoned, the Federal Constitution did not "authorize Congress to confer power upon persons deriving their authority from the individual states." Rather than hazard African American freedom or encourage unscrupulous local officials, Pennsylvania politicians used the kidnappings of Black Pennsylvanians as a way for state power to supersede federal power: the final bill deprived justices of the peace and aldermen the right to remove fugitives from slavery and dictated that only state judges and city recorders possessed this power.[69]

Over the next two months, Pennsylvania lawmakers deliberated a few more times on the subject of kidnapping to modify the wording of the provisions. Unfortunately, neither the records of these final debates survive, nor do we know exactly which legislators voted for or against the act. Yet state representatives Wilkins, Duane, Thackara, and Randall, men whose political loyalties to Findlay stood counterpoised, in a way exercised a political brinkmanship in order to satisfy their own political agendas. By adopting the general antislavery tone of federal representatives and employing state laws to countermand or at very least overcomplicate the removal process, Pennsylvania politicians balanced both comity between states and their state's relationship with federal guidelines outlining proper rendition. Their efforts were the final stage of a struggle that began with ordinary African Americans' lived reality on the streets of Philadelphia. The 1820 liberty law protected free African Americans in Pennsylvania; its ultimate effect would disrupt comity and initiate future struggles over slavery and freedom. Not coincidentally, the same day, March 21, 1820, when the legislature passed the "act to prevent kidnapping," it followed the vote with another resolution to address what it termed the "national disgrace": the spread of slavery into Missouri. The synergy of that moment revealed how local kidnappings brought slavery to the statehouse within the context of a national debate over the freedom to extend slavery across the United States.[70]

Governor Findlay signed "An Act to Prevent Kidnapping" into law on March 27, 1820. The first two provisions declared the kidnapping of "any negro or mulatto" a felony. Any person who "by force or violence" carried away "any negro or mulatto" for sale outside of Pennsylvania would be fined no less than $500 and no more than $2,000, "one half whereof shall be paid to the person or persons, who shall prosecute for the same, and the other half to this commonwealth." Those found guilty faced a sentence of no less than seven and no greater than twenty years hard labor. In addition, anyone who knowingly sold "any negro or mulatto" out of Pennsylvania would be subject to the same fines and sentences. These harsh punishments designed to protect free Blacks complemented the next two provisions, which threatened slaveholders who hoped to fast-track removals.[71]

The final provisions of the 1820 act limited the power of Pennsylvania state officials. No alderman or justice of the peace had the right to hear cases of fugitives from slavery nor the power to grant any certificates of removal. Only state judges or recorders maintained their power to remove "any negro or mulatto claimed to be a fugitive from labor" and required them to certify and record the "name, age, sex, and a general description of the person of the negro or mulatto." By severely limiting the number and type of Pennsylvanian officials allowed to assist in retrieving fugitives from slavery under federal law and increasing the safeguards against illegal removals, including recording the "general description" of the person to be removed, Pennsylvania legislators succeeded in crafting legal protections for free African Americans in Philadelphia. As the historian William R. Leslie showed, Pennsylvania's 1820 act was "the first in the United States to prohibit state officials from enforcing the national fugitive slave act." In doing so, Pennsylvanians set the stage for future contests over slavery and freedom in the state, in particular, the city of Philadelphia.[72]

The cases discussed above that inspired this legislation connected local, state, and national concerns over kidnapping and enslavement: kidnappings and retrieving fugitives from slavery in Philadelphia, politicking in the Pennsylvania state legislature, and roiling debates within Congress became as one. Thus the 1820 liberty law redefined Pennsylvania states' rights as a means to address the abuse of federal rights to enslave. These rights mutually constituted each other but not without answering the lingering question of who was the final arbiter of freedom. Did the federal government reign supreme through the Fugitive Slave Act? Did the states reign supreme through state liberty laws? Those larger forces, while important, ought not to obscure the street-level realities experienced by African Americans and their allies; for after all, these ordinary individuals acted together in extraordinary ways to precipitate meaningful political change.

Conclusion

Despite this victory, several tensions underlay African American freedom in Pennsylvania. Although Pennsylvania secured stronger safeguards to protect African Americans and prevented state officials from upholding the 1793 Fugitive Slave Act, state officials still had to find ways to honor the claims of slaveholders in neighboring states. Furthermore, the 1820 act did not prevent constables from working with slaveholders nor impinged upon their zeal for anti-Black violence. In a way, Pennsylvania politicians preferred to truncate rather than outright violate or deny the right of slaveholders to enslave within Pennsylvania and pursue fugitives from slavery across the North. Pennsylvanian politicians preserved interstate comity by allowing the 1793 act to refine the 1820 act, though the presence of African Americans, whose freedom was subject to questioning, forced Pennsylvanians to consider their place within the federal compact. The dynamic, contested, and dialectical relationship between local, state, and federal power through a comity bound to the freedom or enslavement of African Americans evolved through conflict over the course of the Early Republic.

Yet legislative actions depended upon bringing to light the precarious nature of African American freedom, a mission embraced by ordinary Blacks and white abolitionists. Against heavy odds, these forces pushed Pennsylvania politicians both to reconsider their state's relationship to the federal compact with slavery and to reconstruct how Pennsylvania punished kidnappers who passed over illusory borders. Each of the cases mentioned by Pennsylvania legislators during the 1820 kidnapping crisis revealed the perilous freedom experienced by Philadelphia's African American community, which in many ways mirrored the terrifying experience of any African American living in a "free" state. If Pennsylvanians struggled to overcome their status as a free state enslaved to a slaveholding republic, which other free state in the Union stood a chance of defending freedom?

Returning to the cases, one sees how the spectrum of kidnappers limited Black freedom in the service of terror and slavery. Professional kidnappers such as the Cannon-Johnson gang, known quantities to law enforcement and African Americans alike, exercised little wariness when confronted by the laws of Pennsylvania or the federal government. And what of Sarah Hagerman's daughter? She represented the kidnappers' hopes: silent in the archive, anonymous to the slaveholder who purchased her, and lost to the lash of American slavery as just another bound human deprived of a future.

Similarly, the case of William Young, a light-skinned African American man, exposed yet again the mysterious fates of many kidnapping victims: where exactly did John Wood, John Dorden, and Benjamin Bennet end their days? Pushed further, how many other African American kidnapping victims fell prey to the same artifice—human empathy—due to the actions of people like Young, never returning to their lives and futures in Pennsylvania? Young's motivations matter, as he strategically employed his phenotype to bind free people to bondage. Perhaps Young embodied an open secret in the African American community: the profit motive superseded racial alliances.

Reuben Haines's rescue party persisted in a search complicated by slaveholders who hoaxed him and in doing so revealed the extent to which whites employed all their resources to scour multiple states to search for kidnapping victims. Pennsylvania legislators glossed over Hudson's role in his own quasi-kidnapping because they adopted any-means-necessary politicking to protect African Americans. These same defenders of Black freedom bore fruit in Pennsylvania with the passing of the 1820 act, which in light of the Missouri crisis, brought together the reality of coordinating the fight against slavery at the local, state, and national levels. Yet expanding slavery west via the Missouri Compromise no doubt elicited the shaking of heads among Black Philadelphians, whose own fears of the omnipresent reality of slavery in their own neighborhoods meant, in short, that slavery under the guise of kidnappings crept north, right under the noses of Pennsylvanians.

Finally, the most stereotypical of the five cases—Frisby's assault and kidnapping by George Alberti—appears as predictable then as it might appear now. But George Alberti was not a typical slave catcher: as mentioned in the introduction, the vice president of the PAS, Thomas Shipley, was Alberti's uncle through marriage. Bound to each other as human beings with futures, these men worked against each other for decades in order to free or enslave

African Americans, whose futures bound them to the precarious freedom of living in Philadelphia. Against heavy odds and by no means a linear nor teleological set of steps on the road to freedom, African Americans and their allies pushed white politicians both to reconsider their state's relationship to the federal compact with slavery and to reconstruct how Pennsylvanians should resist slaveholders, slave catchers, and kidnappers who passed freely over geographic and racial borders. Pennsylvania's 1820 anti-kidnapping law sparked new contests over slavery and freedom in Philadelphia in the coming years under the guise of what I call "street diplomacy."

CHAPTER TWO

Street Diplomacy

An African American woman named Ann Chambers left her Philadelphia home on Arch Street to go to work one morning in September 1822. No sooner had she arrived at the house of her employer, James Beatty, when three men burst through the door and dragged her out into the street. The men—John Weisener, Lewis Gale, and James Clarke—threw her into a carriage and drove to the District Court judge Richard Peters, Jr.'s residence outside of the city. Chambers's friends alerted the PAS Acting Committee, who then sped to Peters's home. The Acting Committee arrived as Gale swore to Peters that Chambers was the property of his relative P. Raisin Gale of Chestertown, Maryland. Understanding the stakes of an enslaved future, Chambers made "the most solemn assurance" to Peters of her freedom. Surrounded by abolitionists, slave catchers, and a resolute African American woman, Peters gave Chambers's allies time to gather evidence and ordered her confined to prison.[1]

Ironically, Peters entrusted the men who had assaulted and kidnapped Chambers to escort her back to Philadelphia. As Chambers and the men approached the city, Gale wavered about whether Chambers was in fact a fugitive from slavery. He debated with his colleagues, who suggested devising "promises and threats to induce her to say that she was the slave of some person." Nearing South Philadelphia, Gale changed his mind again. He decided to leave Philadelphia and told Clarke to drive into town for him. The PAS noted that "Clarke proceeded down Arch street in the carriage and when it arrived near the house of the girl's residence, told her to dry her tears, wipe her face, and not tell any of the damned Quakers anything about his conduct

PHILADELPHIA
1820-1850

N
W E
S

Vine St.

33
41

Mulberry (Arch) St.
17
44

Chestnut St. 29
20
49
5
24
14
51
43
23
39
18
32
7
27
Walnut St.
28
25
35 50

S 10th St.
S 9th St.
S 8th St.

6
Spruce St.
2
22
40
31
Pine St.
37
38
30
Lombard St.
13 46
15 19
42 11
3
Cedar (South) St.
45
47
48
12
Shippen St.
21
10
Fitzwater St. 8

S 7th St.
S 6th St.
S 5th St.
S 4th St.
S 2nd St.

Delaware River

Schuylkill River

26

PHILADELPHIA
COUNTY

Downtown
Philadelphia

34
36
Christian St.
16
Carpenter St.
1

Moyamensing Rd.
S Front St.

Area of map

NJ

PA

Delaware River

0   1000   2000 feet

9

People
1   George Alberti
2   Richard Allen
4   Samuel Breck
5   David Paul Brown
6   Ann Chambers
7   George Dallas
8   Michael Donnehower
9   Betsey Everson
12 James Forten
14 Ezekiel Freeman
16 Perry Frisby
17 Samuel Garrigues

18 Jacob Gilmore
19 Stephen Gloucester
21 Sarah Hagerman
22 Eli Harman
23 Joseph Hemphill
24 Frederick Hinton
25 Joseph Hopkinson
26 Henry Hudson
27 Charles Ingersoll
28 Edward Ingraham
29 William Morris Meredith
31 James Parker
34 Richard Peters, Jr.

35 James Frisby Price
36 Robert Purvis
37 Abraham Quomoney
39 Emory Sadler
40 Samuel Scomp
41 William H. Scott
43 John Sergeant
44 Thomas Shipley
45 Cornelius Sinclair
47 Robert Ralston Stewart
48 William Still
49 John Swift
50 John Upton

Places
3   Benezet Hall
10 First "African" Presbyterian
11 Flying Horses Carousel
13 Fortress on St. Mary's Street

15 Friends Meeting
20 Grand Union Meeting
30 Mother Bethel AME
32 Pennsylvania Abolition Society
    Headquarters

33 Pennsylvania Hall
38 Red Row
42 Second Presbyterian
46 Smith's Beneficial Hall
51 Independence Hall

or they would make him sweat for it." Terrified and free, Ann Chambers was shoved out of the carriage in the middle of Arch Street.[2]

This episode illuminated the stakes of slavery and freedom on the streets of Philadelphia. Ann Chambers went from being free to being kidnapped to being accused of running away from slavery and back to her precarious freedom within a matter of hours. Her trials did not end there: the PAS and James Beatty took Clarke and Weisener (an erstwhile Philadelphia constable) to court for assault and battery. The day before Clarke and Weisener were to appear before the Mayor's Court, Clarke presented the PAS with a witness who swore that Chambers was a fugitive from slavery from Baltimore. The PAS tested this witness by placing him in a room with Chambers. The plan backfired when he immediately recognized her as the missing person. The PAS then sought to compromise with Clarke: they would drop the charges against him and in exchange stipulated that Clarke pay $200 toward emancipating Chambers within six months. However, Clarke moved from Philadelphia to Delaware by the end of 1822 and never paid for Chambers's freedom. Meanwhile Chambers remained in Philadelphia, a woman neither free nor fugitive.[3]

This chapter explores how the 1820 kidnapping law played out on the streets of Philadelphia. While Pennsylvanians believed that the 1820 law worked in tandem with the 1793 Fugitive Slave Act to prevent kidnappings and protect African Americans, the seizing of African Americans after 1820 stimulated new crises. According to the historian Thomas D. Morris "people tried to provide, at the state level" a balance between respecting slaveholders' so-called rights to property and the freedom of free African Americans, a balance unachieved by the federal government. Ann Chambers's harrowing encounter brought the changes created by the 1820 act into sharp focus. Slaveholders still recruited anti-Black allies, like constables, from Philadelphia, but instead of taking her to a state official, they brought her directly to a *federal* judge. Federal and state powers soundly conflated, slaveholders, kidnappers, and ordinary African Americans and their allies enacted struggles on the local level in such a way as to propel this continued ambiguity over Black freedom. Both federal and state-level politicking on these matters ought not to overshadow the power of people on the streets to make such existential distinctions. At street level, then, witnesses to the arrest of a supposed fugitive from slavery or kidnapping victim possessed mere moments to decide whether to

(opposite) Philadelphia, 1820–1850, with locations for persons and places discussed throughout this work. Map by Bill Nelson

facilitate the arrest under federal law or disrupt the arrest under state law. Black Philadelphians and their allies manipulated this ambiguity through what I term "street diplomacy" when they interposed themselves between slaveholders and kidnappers who profited from hunting African Americans.[4]

Defining Street Diplomacy

Street diplomacy involved ordinary people's experiences with kidnappings and fugitives from slavery, experiences that influenced the trajectory of legislation and legislators, and initiated intimate contests between freedom and slavery at the local level that heightened concerns over preserving the Union at the national level. While not a prescriptive formula for all cases of kidnappings and fugitives from slavery, street diplomacy considers the geography, time, and perspectives of those who lived through these events. Philadelphia hosted these battles over street diplomacy, the moments where one's future freedom hung in the balance and the maneuvers employed by participants to secure freedom or slavery. African Americans and their allies in particular practiced street diplomacy in novel and improvisatory ways, including purposefully conflating federal and state law, injecting plausible deniability and thus confusion into the struggle, tapping into informal networks to organize escapes or rescues, and at times, collaborating with elite whites. Their efforts across Philadelphia forced slaveholders and kidnappers to engage in similar strategies and take increasingly desperate measures to secure their enslaved property in Pennsylvania. And when street diplomacy broke down, participants resorted to violence.

The cases discussed in this chapter provide a crucial contextual backdrop to the ways in which Pennsylvania's 1820 anti-kidnapping act functioned in practice, namely, how struggles at the street level and legislative debates mutually constituted each other. These cases reveal how African Americans and their allies resisted removal by accusing slaveholders of kidnappings under Pennsylvania state law and in doing so limited the ability of slaveholders to implement legal removal under federal law. Fed up with years of failed legal removals, the state of Maryland sent representatives to the Pennsylvania legislature in 1826 to amend the 1820 law. White and Black abolitionists responded in kind and dispatched their own emissaries to sway state lawmakers against undoing the 1820 anti-kidnapping act. In sum, Maryland slaveholders resorted to "interstate diplomacy" only because African Americans and their allies actualized street diplomacy time and again in Philadelphia.[5]

Street diplomacy emerged throughout Ann Chambers's tale. First, Chambers relied on her personal relationship with James Beatty and his abolition-ist allies to protect and eventually liberate her. Second, slave catchers knew where to find her and where to take her and reflected their knowledge of the law and extralegal measures they might take to ensure Chambers's removal. Not wanting to be charged as kidnappers, they brought her to a federal judge who needed to weigh the evidence of their claim and Chambers's resolve while respecting comity. There lies an inherent difficulty in extracting the truth from such events because both sides had an interest in conflating matters: slaveholders conflated federal law with comity, and abolitionists conflated the removal of any fugitive from slavery with an attempted kidnapping. Decou-pling these ideas contained the potential to disrupt the Union.

Understanding these battles as incidents of street diplomacy revealed the extent to which African Americans and their allies contested, blurred, and exposed the limits of state and federal law. In doing so, they drove the legis-lative debates among white politicians over interstate comity. At the street level, however, comity became contentious, and appeared in the form of tense standoffs: street diplomacy epitomized the dynamic relationship between slav-ery in a nominally free state and freedom in a slaveholding republic, as well as the local, spontaneous, and improvisatory contests over whether Americans would respect slaveholders' rights guaranteed by the Constitution.

The State of Pennsylvania Politics in 1820

Pennsylvanian politicians could not avoid integrating the national debates over slavery and freedom into state politics. In light of the ongoing Missouri crisis in the national Congress and the passage of the kidnapping bill in the Pennsylvania state legislature in March 1820, the Pennsylvania gubernatorial election of 1820 between William Findlay and Joseph Hiester was primed to feature debates over Pennsylvania's role as a free state in a slaveholding re-public. Seemingly inconsequential prima facie, these crises in Philadelphia reminded Americans of the stakes of freedom and slavery, especially in Penn-sylvania.

By 1820 two political coalitions had firmly rooted themselves in the state: the "Old School" Democrats and the "New School" Democrats. The Old School Democrats claimed to represent traditional Jeffersonian views but in reality consisted both of men who desired to regain public office and of for-mer Federalists. Led by agitator-cum-editor William Duane of Philadelphia's newspaper *Weekly Aurora*, the Old School espoused egalitarianism in the form of anti-caucus sentiment, supported a popular convention system to nominate candidates, lambasted James Monroe, and favored hard currency during the Panic of 1819. When its candidate and Revolutionary War veteran Joseph Hiester lost the 1817 gubernatorial election, the Old School did everything in its power to wreak havoc on William Findlay's administration and tarnish the governor as the "spurious child of a corrupt system," up to and including holding impeachment proceedings against him in the state legislature.[6]

Unlike their Old School opponents, New School Democrats supported the caucus system, paper currency, and Monroe. They forged a coalition known as the "Family Party," which consisted of Philadelphians George Mifflin Dallas, Secretary of the Commonwealth Thomas Sergeant, Richard Bache, and William Wilkins of Pittsburgh, all of whose families had intermarried. These politicians quickly became Findlay's closest allies in the state during his administration. Under Bache's editorship the *Franklin Gazette* operated as the organ of the party. The paper trumpeted the respectability of the caucus system while at the same time castigated the Old School as "fragments and patches of faction." Both schools renominated their candidates from 1817 again in 1820.[7]

While slavery was not necessarily on the forefront of voters' minds in an economic depression—the Panic of 1819 threw nearly 12,000 Philadelphians out of work, and wages declined about 80 percent from 1816 to 1819—Philadelphia newspapers displayed their candidate's experiences with slavery and African Americans. In July 1820 the pro-Hiester *Pennsylvania Gazette* claimed that Findlay still owned an enslaved a woman named Hannah, whom he inherited from his father-in-law but never emancipated. The *Harrisburg Republican* and the *Franklin Gazette* denied this accusation and stated that "some informality" had prevented him from emancipating the woman but he nevertheless did so as soon as he caught the registration error. The *Franklin Gazette* went further and published the manumission papers of "George," an enslaved man the governor inherited from his father and whom Findlay manumitted in 1807. The newspaper presented a table that compared the candidates' principles on this "great question" of slavery (table 2.1).

This table displayed the stakes of freedom and slavery in terms that ordinary Pennsylvanians would understand before they cast their ballot. The personal nature of each man's experience with slavery—Hiester the slaveholder and Findlay the liberator—acted as useful motifs to judge the candidate's moral views. Whereas Hiester perpetuated the second middle passage, separated families, and voted against acts that benefited African Americans, Findlay came from a family that did everything it could to keep African Ameri-

TABLE 2.1.
Table published in the *Franklin Gazette* in 1820.

Hiester and Slavery *VS* Findlay and Freedom	
• Joseph Hiester voted to continue the *slave trade.* • He voted to continue the cruel practice of separating husband and wife, parent and child, *to any distance,* without their consent. • He voted against the punishment for *manstealing* and *selling* him into bondage. • He was a *slave holder* in 1804, and was probably a slave holder in 1788, and voted against the abolition law, because he wanted to retain the offspring of his slaves in slavery. • *Quere*—Is not Joseph Hiester at this time a slave holder?	• In 1804, Wm. Findlay's father purchased a slave, to prevent him from being taken out of the state. • In 1807, this slave had become the property of Wm. Findlay, the present governor, *who liberated him from bondage,* as will appear from the following manumission which shows the principles of Mr. Findlay, as tested by a sacrifice of his interest.

cans together and manumit them, with evidence to boot. The morality of these political actions also revolved around the "interest" of the candidates: Findlay's sacrifice "of his own interest" connected the moral, political, and economic consequences of slavery. The fact remained that Pennsylvania politicians whose personal experiences with enslaved African Americans inside and outside of the state represented a morality test for voters.[8]

Hiester's opponents criticized his voting record in the state senate and the national Congress. As a state legislator he voted against the state's 1788 abolition law, which among other provisions prevented enslaved families from being separated by more than ten miles and penalized kidnappings. As a congressman, Hiester avoided voting to restrict the further introduction of slavery into Missouri. The *Franklin Gazette* argued that these "cruel and unjust votes" should not exalt Hiester nor deliver him to the governor's chair. As the historian Andrew K. Diemer showed, Hiester's Democratic critics embodied the shifting views on the politics of race when they charged him both with indifference to "manstealing" as well as securing votes from "negroes who were runaway slaves." These contradictory critiques buttressed the politics of slavery in a state where African American lives and futures hung in the balance.[9]

The PAS, and one would presume many African Americans, saw no reason to divide these issues relating to freedom in Pennsylvania, and from May to June Pennsylvania abolitionists distributed 500 copies of the 1820 kidnapping bill, 750 copies of John Sergeant's speech on the Missouri Question, and

200 copies of an essay written by PAS members honoring the "preserving and virtuous support" of justice from those congressmen who voted against spreading slavery into Missouri. These documents circulated in and around Philadelphia and reminded voters of the link between protecting African Americans at home in Pennsylvania and preventing the spread of slavery into new territories.[10]

That October Pennsylvanians took to the polls in record numbers and elected Joseph Hiester by a mere 1,605 votes. Approximately 72 percent of the city and 53 percent of the county of Philadelphia voted for Hiester. Historians have pointed out that issues such as corruption and the economic depression contributed to Hiester's victory. Although those issues may have had a greater impact, Pennsylvania politicians appropriated the issues of kidnappings and fugitives from slavery to fit their own political needs and revealed how the politics of slavery seeped into the state. The temporary flare-up of a politics of slavery did more than spotlight the candidates' positions on slavery: it magnified the streetborne struggles of African Americans and their allies in Philadelphia.[11]

Street Diplomacy in Philadelphia

African Americans and their allies negotiated federal and state law by practicing street diplomacy. Unlike forms of comity that existed within the realm of white politicians, street diplomacy confronted ordinary people, white and Black, with the dilemma of African American freedom. Philadelphia's pivotal location as the cultural center of free Black life in America intensified this dilemma and heightened tensions. While African Americans found jobs in and around the city, they remained in an economically marginal position and therefore vulnerable to kidnapping. African Americans who resided in or around Cedar Ward would soon feel the push into South Philadelphia due to the growing "commercial core" in the center of the city. The coming decade would see Irish immigrants endure a similar "push" out of the center of Philadelphia into Southwark and Moyamensing, Philadelphia neighborhoods that bordered Cedar Ward. Despite growing white resentment, the city of Philadelphia projected numerous lures for African Americans as a site of cultural formation, appreciation, and protection premised upon the potential for economic stability. Given that slavery and the possibility to enslave through kidnapping always lurked in the background, the city's African Americans became prime targets and the subjects of the ongoing debate over freedom in Pennsylvania.[12]

Attempted seizures of African Americans on the streets of Philadelphia forced witnesses to choose between interfering with a legal removal under federal law and allowing a kidnapping under state law. African Americans did not stand idle during these incidents; they employed a host of strategies to resist removal regardless of federal or state law. African Americans enacted less aggressive forms of resistance without sacrificing efficacy, such as recruiting white allies to implement legal means to prevent removal. These allies, often PAS members, relied upon networks of informants within the Black community to alert them of potential kidnappings. These networks employed more aggressive forms of resistance, including rescue attempts. However, some individuals seized by slaveholders or potential kidnappers did not necessarily wait for those networks to assist them; rather, they freed themselves, typically in improvisatory ways, when given the slightest opening. Finally, when street diplomacy failed, African Americans resorted to physical violence, rioted, and in certain cases, even killed those who attempted to remove them from Pennsylvania. These cases act as illustrative examples of street diplomacy and in doing so, remind historians of the nonlinear paths toward freedom, the dynamic and at times unpredictable interactions between Americans at the street level, and how these contests fused local, state, and national politics.

"It is life for life": The Case of John Reed

An African American named John Reed employed a surefire method to overcome confusing circumstances involving slaveholders and kidnappers: he armed himself. In December 1819 Reed escaped from Samuel Griffith of Baltimore, Maryland, and relocated to West Chester, Pennsylvania, where he found work as a farmer. Griffith's attempt to capture Reed from Pennsylvania epitomized the conflated nature of retrieval and kidnapping, a state of confusion promoted by African Americans willing to fight and kill in order to live free—a troubling vision of comity to slaveholders to say the least, especially those living in Maryland. The connections between local, state, and national politics within the person of John Reed spoke to the fraught and extemporaneous decisions made by parties present in a removal attempt.[13]

On December 14, 1820, Griffith, his overseer Peter Shipley, and two other men ventured to Reed's house "on the business of taking the Black." The group demanded that Reed open the door; Reed refused. While the slave hunters argued outside, Reed placed a cider barrel on his side of the door to prevent a break-in. After pounding on the door, the men grabbed a rail and lifted the door off of its hinges. The door fell over the barrel, and Reed exclaimed, "It is life for life!" Griffith entered the house brandishing two pistols and ran face-first into the flashing muzzle of Reed's musket; Griffith died instantly. Shipley rushed in next; Reed attacked him with his "oaken club." With one Marylander dead, another mortally wounded sprawled out on the floor, and the other two men running for their lives, Reed went to a neighbor's house to tell them what happened. Reed claimed that he did not know who they were, and he assumed (like his neighbor) that they were kidnappers "as there were handcuffs found at the door." Lying to maintain one's freedom highlighted, in this case, how African Americans willingly conflated slaveholders with kidnappers and viewed them as one and the same. Street diplomacy broke down when Reed took the lives of two men.[14]

Reed went to trial twice for murder. In May 1821, Judge John Ross of the Chester County court of Oyer and Terminer in West Chester told the jury that Griffith was a kidnapper according to the 1820 law only if they found that Griffith did not plan on taking Reed to a Pennsylvania state judge for a certificate of removal prior to leaving Pennsylvania. The jury thus found Reed not guilty of murdering Griffith, as he had acted in self-defense. Perhaps the jury privileged Reed's status as a Pennsylvania resident over the rights to retrieval exercised by Griffith and company, whom they may have viewed as slave-hunting interlopers.[15]

In November 1821 Reed went before Judge Isaac Darlington for the murder of Shipley. A writer for the *West Chester Village Record* claimed that Reed "was the child of Muria, formerly an African queen," and had no proof of his manumission. Alexander Duer, speaking on behalf of the Commonwealth, contended that Griffith had a right under the law of Congress to seize Reed "at any time and place, and at any hour." Reed's regal African heritage marked him as a human being with a questionable freedom and future, one whom a "free state" lawyer from Pennsylvania justified removing under a federal law that considered any attempt to resist slave catchers as proof of one's enslavement. In other words, Reed practiced street diplomacy when he resisted arrest and, by doing so, proved that he knew Griffith as a slaveholder and not a kidnapper. By making this distinction, the prosecutor for the state of Pennsylvania offered a crucial point: the 1820 act applied only to kidnappers, not slaveholders. Reed and other African Americans like him in Pennsylvania became trapped by their drive for freedom. If they resisted arrest, the law viewed them as an enslaved person, and if they went willingly with the slaveholders, they condemned themselves to slavery: a unity of enslaved opposites.[16]

Darlington modified the prosecution's terms in a lengthy discourse on the 1820 kidnapping act and explained how the previous court erred in its interpretation. According to Darlington, a slaveholder could not be penalized for a legal federally sanctioned removal, even if there was no "conclusive proof" that Reed knew that Griffith and Shipley intended to remove him. Finally, although Darlington advised the jury to disavow Reed's neighbor's testimony that Reed confessed to beating "the deceased 'till he thought him quite dead," they found Reed guilty of manslaughter and sentenced him to nine years in the penitentiary.[17]

African Americans and their allies interpreted and then implemented the 1820 law to transform legitimate slaveholders into kidnappers, and in doing so, their actions on the ground allowed them to implement state law to nullify a federal guarantee. Abolitionists hoped that the 1820 act would prevent anyone, including slaveholders, from retrieving fugitives from slavery in Pennsylvania. Such a development troubled the neighboring slave state of Maryland, as Andrew K. Diemer argued, because Maryland slaveholders felt stymied by the inability to control the "movement of Black bodies" across the border and into Pennsylvania. While slaveholders possessed claims to fugitives from slavery through the Federal Constitution, the 1820 law could be implemented by African Americans on the street in such a way as to make the slaveholders appear as attempted kidnappers and therefore make their actions illegal.[18]

The significance of the Reed case lay within the way African Americans faced down the threat of removal. African Americans like Reed actualized street diplomacy by injecting plausible deniability when confronted with the person who formerly "owned" him, his agents, or kidnappers, and forced white Pennsylvanians to make harrowing distinctions between legal and illegal removals. African Americans who practiced street diplomacy proved that white Americans lacked the final say on the legality of removal attempts. Put another way, while racial animosity and the law consigned all African Americans to potential removal, they nonetheless created novel strategies to disrupt these potentialities.

The Case of "Hezekiah Cooper"

Two years after the Reed trial another case illustrated the fundamental tensions of federal versus state power exposed by Pennsylvania's 1820 liberty law. In 1823, Marylanders "Mr. Corbin" and Peter Case seized a man who identified himself as a free man named Hezekiah Cooper in Huntingdon County, Pennsylvania (about 200 miles west of Philadelphia). The arrest originated from a witness who stated that Cooper told them that he was owned by Edward Williams of Maryland. Instead of following the 1820 law, Corbin and Case removed Cooper from Pennsylvania and confined him to jail in Hagerstown, Maryland. As a result agents from Pennsylvania arrested Case for kidnapping Cooper. Case claimed that Cooper belonged to Williams and that Cooper's real name was Peter Berry and that Williams paid them to retrieve him. The slave catchers found Berry living as "Hezekiah Cooper," who was a free Black man who had died sometime prior. This unique form of passing illuminated all of the potentialities of street diplomacy, that sometimes free or freed Blacks who passed away in Pennsylvania "passed on" their freedom to living African Americans who were still susceptible to enslavement or kidnapping. Berry's counsel argued that the 1820 act did not distinguish between whether the kidnapped person was free or enslaved; the crime "was the same" in both cases, and thus Case deserved the harshest punishment under the 1820 law: a $2,000 fine and twenty-one years imprisonment.[19]

Cooper's case revealed how Pennsylvania state law might be rendered unconstitutional in view of the 1793 Fugitive Slave Act. In this trial, "probably the first under the act of 1820," according to *Niles' Weekly Register,* the presiding judge Charles Huston's interpretation of the case exposed these flaws. He disagreed with the liberating potential of the 1820 law because it opposed the 1793 act. To Huston, all that mattered in this case were the "laws" of the land: Pennsylvania's 1780 act for gradual emancipation of slavery, the 1788 anti-kidnapping act, and the 1820 anti-kidnapping act, all of which protected both slaveholders who sought fugitives from slavery in Pennsylvania and, ironically, free Black Pennsylvanians. The 1793 Fugitive Slave Act outlined the procedure by which slaveholders could claim fugitives from slavery, and as a supplement, Tilghman's ruling in *Wright v. Deacon* stated that no state could revise this federal procedure. Like Tilghman before him, Huston claimed that interstate comity depended upon "every good citizen" of Pennsylvania aiding slaveholders in reclaiming fugitives from slavery. In reality, Huston stressed that the 1820 act upheld prior state, federal, and judicial precedents on retrieving fugitives from slavery, and buttressed the eleventh section of the 1780 act, which stated that slaveholders possessed the right "to demand, claim and take away his slave or servant" in Pennsylvania.[20]

Cooper's testimony amounted to a confession of his former enslavement and ensured that the jury would find Peter Case not guilty. At first glance this ruling reinforced and expanded the power of the 1793 Fugitive Slave Act to the detriment of the 1820 act. Huston argued that an enslaved person could and should be removed at once without recourse to a judge if they "did not *pretend* [emphasis in original] to be free." Pretending to be free placed the burden of enslavement on the accused, a paradoxical bind similar to that of John Reed: African Americans who pretended to be free were to be treated as though they were enslaved, and those who did not pretend to be free were also to be treated as if they were enslaved: an ontological crisis to say the least. Factoring in the woefully limited time given to African Americans to decide how to act or pretend when faced with enslavement—and considering how this time was inversely proportional to the enslaved future that awaited them if their performance did not convince slaveholders, kidnappers, abolitionists, judges, or politicians—African Americans' dilemma warped time and rendered spaces of freedom in Pennsylvania an open question.[21]

Slaveholders who came to Pennsylvania needed only to present a certificate of removal from their home state, an extraterritorial legal document that empowered slaveholders to maintain comity and avoid the consequences of their victims exercising their power as street diplomats. However, street diplomacy efforts were unpredictable at times, especially when the accused claimed their freedom, for now slaveholders needed to abide by the 1820 law and appear before a state judge. In sum, Cooper admitted his enslavement and therefore Corbin and Case had the right to transport him to Maryland without appearing before a Pennsylvania judge.[22]

African Americans in Philadelphia understood the lesson exposed by the case of Peter Berry alias Hezekiah Cooper when they practiced diplomacy on the streets, a bitter lesson fraught with tension and contest. Not only did claiming one's freedom, regardless of the veracity of the claim, lay at the heart of street diplomacy, but enacting such a claim meant that African Americans and their allies often tried to make any attempted legal seizure appear like a kidnapping. Injecting plausible deniability into chaotic battles over slavery acted as a vital stratagem within the African American community. Street diplomacy in Philadelphia after the passage of the 1820 law meant interfering with both the federal compact to compromise on the slave issue and the peaceful relations between white politicians across the country.

The Case of Ezekiel Freeman

Street diplomacy in Philadelphia collapsed the local, state, and national politics of slavery. Kidnappers and slaveholders confronted both a vibrant and well-connected "white" community as well as the country's most powerful free African American community. This reality greeted the Maryland slaveholder Solomon Lowe when he came to Philadelphia to retrieve a Black man named Ezekiel Freeman in March 1821. A man who owned ten enslaved people in 1820, Lowe recruited another man named William Flint and a man known only as "Dardin" and seized Freeman in the city. Lowe called upon the US district attorney Charles Ingersoll, who along with his brother Joseph frequently represented slaveholders who traveled to Philadelphia in search of fugitives from slavery. Ingersoll advised Lowe to take Freeman to the city recorder, Joseph Reed, because the 1820 liberty law listed city recorders as state officials who could oversee cases of fugitives from justice. Ingersoll told Lowe to obey the law and thus preserve comity.[23]

Seeing Freeman walking down the streets of Philadelphia shackled and humiliated made an impression on passersby. Not finding Reed at home, Lowe visited a friend in another part of Philadelphia and left Freeman with Flint and Dardin. As the two slave catchers strolled down Spruce Street with the handcuffed Freeman, two African American men who happened to pass by the trio stopped and asked them what they were doing with the man. The open secret of stealing African Americans from Philadelphia moved these two men, complete strangers really, to interpose as street diplomats and challenge Flint and Dardin: their question spoke to the life and death consequences of passing by an accused fugitive from slavery. The two men might walk by with their future intact, while a third man who looked like them saw his future dissipate into oblivion. Flint and Dardin explained that Freeman was a fugitive from slavery and must be kept in custody until a judge would hear them. They respected the queries of two African American men by answering them, and in doing so, reiterated how all parties knew the laws of the land. Legal knowledge begat legal fiction, for the two African American men could have taken the slave catchers' answer at face value and kept walking. Yet that plausibility was matched by the two Black men asking the question in the first place: was Freeman free, fugitive, or a victim of kidnapping? All participants assumed that they knew enough federal and state law to interpose, and in doing so, positioned themselves to either contest or uphold Freeman's enslavement.[24]

Soon two other "gentlemen" (whether white or Black, the sources remain silent) appeared on the scene and along with the African American men insisted that they needed to take Freeman to a magistrate and obtain a warrant before meeting with a judge. Perhaps the four men hoped that the slave catchers would incriminate themselves; after all, under the 1820 liberty law aldermen were not permitted to issue certificates of removal under the 1793 act.

This potential ruse notwithstanding, Flint and Dardin agreed and proceeded to Alderman Abraham Shoemaker. In heeding this advice Flint and Dardin bought Freeman valuable time and allowed Black and white bystanders to work together, gather information, and plot his escape. Soon Lowe rejoined the trio, but as they neared the alderman's office they saw a large crowd awaiting their arrival. Finding that the alderman had gone to dinner, Lowe and the other men decided to wait on the office doorstep. With their backs to the crowd, the slaveholder Lowe and his slave-catching associates formed a human shield in front of Freeman and waited patiently for Shoemaker's return.[25]

Meanwhile, several African Americans ran and informed the abolitionist Isaac Hopper of the situation. Hopper had joined the PAS in 1796 and assisted as many as 1,000 fugitives from slavery in his forty years of work. The zealous Hopper wasted no time when he arrived at Shoemaker's office and asked Lowe, "Who can tell whether he is thy slave or not? What proof is there that you are not a band of kidnappers? Dost thou suppose the laws of Pennsylvania tolerate such proceedings?" When Lowe turned to argue with Hopper, he created a precarious opening in the wall of slave hunters, giving Freeman all the space he needed to make a daring escape. Lowe and his men shouted, "Stop thief!" and along with the crowd ran after Freeman. This interpellation of law and order echoed James Forten's thoughts on the Philadelphia constabulary cruelly shouting "Halloa!" at random Black Philadelphians: Lowe and his men assumed that bystanders might assist them in catching a "thief." Ironically, of course, human beings like Freeman stole themselves from slavery.[26]

Freeman fled into the shop of the watchmaker and PAS Acting Committee member Samuel Mason, Jr., who locked the door just as Lowe, Flint, Dardin, and the crowd reached the entrance. Simply put, Mason assumed that Freeman was indeed a free man and therefore Mason tacitly exercised the letter of the 1820 law, which did not discriminate between kidnappings and retrieving fugitives from slavery. Freeman escaped out the back door of the shop and was never recaptured. Mason opened the door to Lowe, who asked him for Freeman. Mason replied, "He is not on or about my premises, and I do not know where he is."[27]

Lowe sued Mason for the loss of Freeman before Judge Richard Peters, Jr. of the federal Eastern District of Pennsylvania in June 1822. Peters's lengthy decision reflected a Southern slaveholder's view of federal power and comity: while Pennsylvania abhorred slavery, this feeling did not justify ignoring the rights of neighboring slave states. Retrieving fugitives from slavery represented "the great ligament" of comity, and therefore the 1793 act remained crucial to this bond of Union. If "we are equally bound to guard against abuses attempted to be practiced under [the 1793 act]," Peters argued, Pennsylvania should, "from a sense of justice and legal obligation, restore those of an opposite character." Mason "knowingly and willingly" disrupted comity through street diplomacy: he used the pretense of the 1820 act, i.e., that Freeman was being kidnapped, to violate the 1793 act, i.e., that Freeman was being arrested as a fugitive from slavery. Peters fined Mason $500 for his split-second decision to lock the door, a decision that allowed Freeman to escape his supposed kidnappers and therefore violated the bonds of the Union.[28]

Mason's role does not overshadow the actions of the two African American street diplomats who questioned the slave catchers, actions that judge Peters castigated as the "violent and intemperate conduct" of Black Philadelphians. These unnamed men felt no qualms about violating the 1793 act. According to Peters, these men and their allies spared "no means in their capacity and power to dry [the fugitive's] tears." The men who questioned Lowe interposed as Pennsylvanians and human beings by contesting Lowe's claim to Freeman in a public space. Other Black Philadelphians concentrated their resources by seeking out Isaac Hopper. The help of a well-known white ally with a proven track record for assisting Blacks regardless of whether they were fugitives from slavery lent credence to the open and empathetic hearts of some white Philadelphians. The crowd that assembled in front of Shoemaker's office warranted mention because of how fast they acted to distract and intimidate the slave catchers. The public spectacle of Freeman's arrest and escape no doubt changed the lives of bystanders and prompted them to make history, a free future for Freeman, through street diplomacy.[29]

Peters condemned the entire display as a sop to sentimentality over constitutionality, in that "naturally and sympathetically colored people crowd around the victim, and do not 'let the stricken dear go weep.'" Taking Peters at his word, Philadelphians Black and white well understood the "natural" human inclination to help others. Crowds formed by "sympathetic" people of color and their allies highlighted street diplomats' symphony of resistance efforts. Peters's insensitive, possibly sarcastic mention of weeping crowds at such scenes overlooked how an emotive exhibition of loss reminded African Americans of their precarious futures and became a diplomatic strategy to utilize anti-kidnapping resources and liberators.[30]

While Freeman unfortunately disappeared from the historical record, Mason's struggle did not end with a $500 fine. He appealed Peters's ruling on a writ of error and in October 1822 went before the Circuit Court for the

Eastern District of Pennsylvania, presided over by Judge Bushrod Washington. Nephew to the first president, Washington was championed by contemporaries as a legal mind who possessed "an uncompromising firmness." This firmness included a deep love of a Union free of African Americans, as evidenced by his selection as the American Colonization Society's first president. As the historian Andrew K. Diemer has noted, Washington was chosen because of his stature, which "transcended the sectional and the partisan," an insightful comment in that enslavement and kidnappings transcended both the sectional and the partisan, too. As a wealthy planter who inherited his uncle's estate, Washington once promised the enslaved people living in Mount Vernon that they would never be freed—and when some of them balked at his firmness, Washington sold the most restive of his "family" to the Deep South.[31]

His atrocious behavior toward African Americans notwithstanding, Washington reversed Peters's decision on Mason through what amounted to semantics. He cited a strict construction of Section 4 of the 1793 act, namely, the portion that identified the actual moments when a person obstructed the law: "that any person who shall knowingly and willingly obstruct or hinder such claimant, his agent, or attorney, *in so seizing or arresting* such fugitive from labor, or shall rescue such fugitive from such claimant, his agent or attorney, *when so arrested* pursuant to the authority herein given and declared." Washington understood this language to mean that one could obstruct the seizure only before or during an arrest, and not after the claimant made the arrest. Once a claimant initiated the arrest, Washington argued, "no subsequent obstruction, whilst the custody continues, although it should afford an opportunity for an escape or be a restraint upon the free will of the claimant, can constitute the offence of obstruction, or hindrance mentioned in the fourth section of the act." If a claimant desisted in making the arrest and abandoned "all attempt to make a new seizure" they could not then charge an outside party with obstruction.[32]

This "obstruction" highlighted how moments mattered to street diplomats like Mason. Washington's technicality asserted that Mason indeed obstructed Lowe, but did so outside the scope of the act: not before or during but "after" Lowe and his group made the arrest. Mason also obstructed Lowe when he did not immediately allow him to enter his shop; but after Mason opened the door, Lowe made the decision not to pursue Freeman any further, thus abandoning his claim. As a result, Washington sent the case back to Judge Peters in the District Court. The semantics of decisions made in mere moments mattered because these words and choices dictated the freedom or enslavement of African Americans in Philadelphia.

Two intertwined questions guided the parties when they reconvened for the third trial in the District Court in Philadelphia in November 1823. First, how would Pennsylvania protect claimants who hoped to retrieve their human property, and second, since obstructing claimants depended upon spur of the moment decisions, how could Pennsylvanians protect African Americans in a lawful manner? To apply contradictory state and federal laws and a convoluted removal process to the mere moments before, during, and after created confusion in the minds of African Americans vulnerable to slaveholders and kidnappers alike. These fears of an unremitting future under slavery became imprinted onto the entire process of answering these questions, as each "legal" pursuit contained the potential seed of illegal action. Ordinary people thrown into street diplomacy had little time to decide whether the removal they were witnessing was legitimate, illegitimate, or both.

Freeman and Mason's struggles were very grave because they showed how once again, ordinary people's street diplomacy dictated and pushed local fights over slavery into the orbit of national political figures. Charles Ingersoll and his brother Joseph represented Lowe. As mentioned, the Ingersolls fought valiantly for slaveholders throughout the nineteenth century, especially Charles, whose staunch support of the Democracy and Southern slavery sustained a contorted comity. Charles felt that it behooved "the great central zone" of Mid-Atlantic States like Pennsylvania to ensure comity between the slave South and "the slave-hating northeast." The Ingersolls sided with comity and claimed that Mason obstructed Lowe's pursuit. Moments mattered: despite briefly harboring Freeman, Mason broke the law.[33]

The US congressman, lawyer, and loyal PAS ally John Sergeant represented Mason and retorted that his client had no connection with the crowd chasing Freeman. Yes, Mason locked the door to his store, but he did so to protect insentient property, not property in human beings. Ironically, in claiming that he was protecting his property from the crowd, Mason freed the supposed property of Lowe, which allowed Freeman to seize the moment and free himself, a point ignored by the court. Sergeant explained that Lowe never gave Mason notice of his pursuit and thus Mason did not need to assist Lowe at all. The Ingersolls objected to Sergeant's suggestion: Mason should have presumed Freeman to be a fugitive from slavery. After all, Freeman was a Black man in the custody of white men, white men who claimed to have contacted Mason previously to ask for his assistance in retrieving Freeman! If the men did in fact contact Mason previously, they did so to protect themselves and their freedom, not Freeman's. Nonetheless, Peters agreed with the Ingersolls that Mason received some form of notice from the slave catchers and that this notice complied with the 1793 Fugitive Slave Act, which superseded Mason's right to prevent Lowe from entering his shop. Yet while Peters admitted that "no person is legally bound, however from comity it may be done, to assist in arresting a slave," in reality, Lowe's right as a slaveholder to give notice and enter a shop or dwelling overrode Mason's right to protect himself, his property, and those human beings like Freeman whom they presumed to be free.[34]

Street diplomats were beholden to what Peters called the "transaction of a moment" to enforce, modify, or break either a state law that prohibited kidnappings or a federal law that permitted removals. The jury met and debated this moment for five days before asking Peters to acquit Mason. Lowe, meanwhile, went bankrupt as a result of the case. The success of increasing fines for kidnappings under the 1820 law obscured the fact that the law was by definition difficult to enforce. Street diplomats encountered a multiplicity of variables, improvised, legal, temporal, or otherwise, that prevented a clear-cut distinction between kidnapping victims and fugitives from slavery.[35]

The 1826 Liberty Law Debates

White politicians also struggled to distinguish between "legal" removals and illegal kidnappings. The 1793 Fugitive Slave Act protected the former, while the latter emphasized a state's right to protect its citizens. Slaveholders believed that their property rights as members of the Union enshrined particular laws of their states with federal power, namely, the right to enslave. As the above cases (and countless others no doubt) proved, slaveholders and their allies assumed that the Black Americans whom they pursued were fugitives from slavery; if this assumption required artifice, intrigue, and criminality to make a free person a potential enslaved person, then so be it. Their opponents, Black and white, believed precisely the opposite: any form of slavery or removal was akin to kidnapping. These local conditions on the streets of Philadelphia forced Pennsylvania politicians to act and answer a lingering query: to what extent could these same politicians uphold the guarantees of the Federal Constitution, protect their own state's residents, and preserve peaceful interstate relationships? The cases described above epitomized what slaveholders perceived as the inadequacy of Pennsylvania state law to affirm their federal rights to property. These cases stemming from incidents involving Maryland slaveholders venturing into or near Philadelphia connected the local to the state and national, and in so doing, they and their consequences reified street diplomacy.[36]

In light of the passage of the 1820 anti-kidnapping law and numerous incidents involving Maryland slaveholders and African Americans, Marylanders insisted that Pennsylvania aid in recovering fugitives from slavery. In 1821 the Maryland state legislature presented its case to the national Congress and requested that it force Pennsylvania to devise new legislation friendly to slaveholders' rights. However, their demands failed to gain traction in the House of Representatives. As the historian William R. Leslie has written, "It had become apparent that Congress was not at that time the proper arena in which to improve legislation on reclaiming runaways." Marylanders could find comfort in Chief Justice William Tilghman's 1824 Pennsylvania state supreme court decision in *Commonwealth v. Case*, which preserved the "general right of reception" guaranteed slaveholders prior to the 1820 liberty law. Such confusion over state and federal powers illuminated the place of ordinary people striving for future freedoms in and around Philadelphia.[37]

Inaction at the national level forced the state of Maryland to take its protests to the state of Pennsylvania. The PAS preempted Maryland slaveholders and enlisted PAS Acting Committee stalwart Thomas Shipley to draft a letter to Pennsylvania governor Joseph Hiester imploring him to interfere on the behalf of "individuals kidnapped and held in slavery," and not slaveholders hunting human "property." Shipley urged Hiester to strengthen the 1820 law and "to arrange and reward the detection" of kidnappers who came into Pennsylvania, the possible confusion between kidnappers and slaveholders notwithstanding. Hiester also received a letter in March 1822 from Maryland governor Samuel Sprigg, "respecting the encouragement given to, and harboring and employing negroes absconding from this state." African Americans who fled Maryland often found work in the Pennsylvania hinterland and even more so in the burgeoning urban spaces of Philadelphia, which again hinted at the precarious borders between states. The "encouragement" Sprigg mentioned pertained to Philadelphia abolitionists and more importantly, acknowledged how the African American community partnered with these same abolitionists to protect fugitives from slavery. These sources of encouragement acted as pull factors, attracting African Americans to Pennsylvania, though one cannot ignore the major push factors of slavery, namely, violence and terror.[38]

In 1822 Sprigg requested that Hiester push the Pennsylvania legislature to protect the rights of Marylanders to retrieve fugitives from slavery in Pennsylvania. A slaveholder himself, Sprigg owned at least seventy-three enslaved people, had posted numerous "runaway" advertisements in the preceding decade, and may have fathered at least one child with an enslaved woman. Hiester delivered the letter to the Pennsylvania House of Representatives and asked that it adopt measures to "prevent the evil complained of." In response, the PAS drafted a memorial the next year (1823) noting that while the 1793 act proved sufficient for slaveholders to retrieve their property, "every man is presumed to be free, until it is duly proved that he is a slave, as every man is presumed to be innocent till legal proof of his guilt." Here again the PAS remarked on the general assumption of abolitionist street diplomats: human beings were free and any hampering of that freedom represented a form of kidnapping. While the PAS respected the rights of its "sister state" under the Federal Constitution, they and their Black allies believed that Pennsylvania possessed the right to modify its state's kidnapping laws.[39]

The Maryland state legislature formed a delegation to visit with the Pennsylvania state legislature in early 1826. Maryland governor Joseph Kent explained in a letter to Pennsylvania governor John Shulze in January that this delegation would address "the immense losses sustained by the citizens of [Maryland] by the absconding of their slaves, and the great difficulties experienced in recovering them." This ensemble delegation, comprising the slaveholder and state senator Ezekiel F. Chambers and the state representatives Archibald Lee ("a gentleman of distinguished reputation") and wealthy planter Robert H. Goldsborough, first met with the Delaware state legislature in December 1825, where they secured a stronger fugitive slave act that made preventing rendition a crime. Pennsylvania need not "disgrace" itself like Delaware by pleasing the Maryland delegation, explained the *Genius of Universal Emancipation*. As residents of the Keystone State, Pennsylvania abolitionists asserted the unique and liberating potential of their state while acknowledging how Pennsylvania, like other states leery of slavery, was tethered to a national compact that demanded comity.[40]

The Maryland delegation arrived in Harrisburg on February 2, 1826, accompanied by none other than federal judge Richard Peters, who hoped that he could learn how to cultivate their "merits and talents" toward aiding free Blacks in Pennsylvania. He found the Marylanders to be humane and even sympathetic to African Americans in Pennsylvania, and he stated that one could find no "firmer or more ardent friends to the abolition of slavery in the United States, upon proper and *Constitutional* principles." Here Peters blended slave state concerns with free state concerns and appealed to the Constitution to maintain comity. Figures like Peters embodied the connection between the local and the national, too: as in the case of Ann Chambers, slaveholders and their agents often brought their victims to Belmont Mansion, Peters's home on the edge of Philadelphia, in order to secure removal certificates as well as avoid the wrath of African Americans and their allies. As a longstanding member of the PAS, Peters understood the intimate dynamics of the politics of slavery, having interacted with elite white abolitionists and, within his home, an indentured African American woman named Cornelia Wells. His role as a federal official lent the imprimatur of federal responsibility toward upholding comity, a comity derived from Peters's personal experiences with slaveholders, white abolitionists, and ordinary African Americans.[41]

The Maryland agents presented their bill to the Pennsylvania state legislature on February 2. This bill established a hierarchy that privileged slaveholders and subordinated African Americans living in Pennsylvania. Marylanders sought to implement Pennsylvania state law and strengthen local enforcement to modify the Fugitive Slave Act of 1793 and therefore manipulate the Constitution to protect slaveholders. The proposed bill authorized claimants to file an affidavit with any justice of the peace in Pennsylvania, who would then issue a warrant. This warrant entitled the claimant to the aid of constables to bring supposed fugitives from slavery to justices of the peace, whose summary judgment could result in a certificate of removal. These provisions worked to the detriment of the 1820 act, which prevented petty officials like justices of the peace from drafting certificates of removal. The PAS wrote in an open letter to Philadelphia's *National Gazette* that these provisions ignored the "abuses of thirty years" from petty state officials who were integral to the legal and illegal removal of African Americans from Pennsylvania.[42]

The bill's infamous sixth provision proposed to punish those who obstructed the rendition process with a fine of $500 to $1,000 and three to twelve months in prison. This provision served multiple purposes. First, it hoped to protect slaveholders and their "assistants" (whether fellow Southern slaveholders or protodoughfaces, those northern politicians who sympathized with the South and slavery, like some Philadelphia constables) from bodily harm during rendition, i.e., rescue attempts. Second, the bill shifted the threat of a fine from state officials to the rescuers, which preempted abolitionists from claiming plausible deniability when they witnessed the seizure of a supposed fugitive from slavery. In sum, the sixth provision targeted those Pennsylvanians most likely to disrupt rendition: ordinary African Americans and their white allies who engaged in street diplomacy in Philadelphia.[43]

Pennsylvanian proponents of the Maryland bill, such as writers from Philadelphia's *Weekly Aurora,* believed that the proposal "would be humane to the slave; enable the Maryland slaveholder to recover his property in a peaceable and legal manner; prevent the scenes of outrage and tyranny which often occurred in the capture of colored person[s] within our borders, and protect the sovereignty and the feelings of Pennsylvania from violation upon such occa sions." These scenes of "outrage and tyranny" came part and parcel with street diplomacy; on just which Pennsylvanians felt this "violation" most keenly, the paper was mute, though one doubts it considered African Americans' views on the matter. Richard Peters wrote a lengthy dispatch to the *Easton Gazette,* claiming not only that the bill reaffirmed Pennsylvania's responsibility to comity and the Constitution but that, when put into effect, might "produce the entire abolition of slavery" in Maryland and elsewhere because slaveholders would no longer be tempted to punish enslaved people by sending them to the Deep South. Better to place accused African Americans under "guardianship and protection of one of our officers" within Pennsylvania than deliver them to a Southern slaveholder "excited to resentment." However the bill's proponents framed their rationales, African Americans and their allies could not ignore the potential for violence inherent in removal, not to mention the fines and jail time for disrupting the removal process.[44]

Opponents of the bill remarked that Philadelphians "have witnessed extraordinary things within the few years past" but even they were surprised by the audacity of the Maryland bill. The sixth section interfered with "just and humane interposition," rights possessed by Pennsylvanians who disrupted "groundless" arrests on the streets of Philadelphia. Although Marylanders hoped to recover fugitives from slavery legally, a writer to *Poulson's* explained how the bill made it *"much easier for unprincipled men to kidnap and drag away free Blacks."* The kidnapping of one free person by a "mercenary manstealer" under the new bill represented a greater affront to Pennsylvanians than if Maryland failed to retrieve "a single runaway." "VERITAS" wrote an open letter to *Poulson's* that contained a grave prophecy: in the not-so-distant future Pennsylvanians would stand idle while slaveholders seized "any poor Black," "a freeman like ourselves, borne off triumphantly . . . doomed to Slavery and bondage that will only be terminated by death." Pennsylvanians needed to prevent this "sad reality" by recognizing the omnipresent dilemma of free Black lives and futures: Blacks and their allies assumed any form of removal was a kidnapping, while slaveholders and their allies assumed that their rights to own human beings destroyed geographic borders and entitled them to reap the benefits of a slave society.[45]

Black Street Diplomats in Harrisburg

The bill served as a clarion call for Philadelphia's African Americans to teach white politicians about street diplomacy. Not only did they send memorials "praying that no further legislative act may be passed relative to run-away negroes," African American leaders Richard Allen and Stephen Gloucester ventured to Harrisburg and cornered state senator Jonathan Roberts. As the historian Andrew K. Diemer has explained, this "most direct political action undertaken" by a pair of free African Americans demanded that white politicians consider how the bill might surrender African Americans to kidnappers and slavery. Allen confronted Roberts with a barrage of questions and opinions, and while we do not know the exact content of these conversations, it is hard to believe that Allen would omit how a wayward slaveholder–cum–slave catcher accused him of being a fugitive from slavery earlier in his life.[46]

Personal stories about slave catchers and kidnappers made removals more than just abstract legalistic grandstanding: Allen and Gloucester exposed the terror of living as free Blacks in a free state. Explaining their experiences to white politicians in the hopes of forging bonds of empathy was essential to their actions as street diplomats. Regardless of Allen's enthusiasm (or maybe because of it), Roberts believed that Allen remained "entirely ignorant" about the bill and in a letter reassured his wife that "he kept the fanatics in check" while in Harrisburg. Union-minded Northern politicians like Roberts who termed freedom-minded African Americans as "fanatics" placed Black and white abolitionists on the subversive side of contemporary politics. Allen and Gloucester's presence mattered and shook Roberts because these men served as visual, visceral reminders to Pennsylvania and Maryland politicians about just whose freedom was in danger.[47]

News of the kidnapping of free Black children from Philadelphia sparked controversy in the midst of the 1826 debates. (This episode will be discussed more in chapter 3.) Mayor Joseph Watson received letters from Mississippians John Hamilton and John Henderson in January and published them in several Philadelphia newspapers. Henderson wrote that Ebenezer Johnson offered to sell them three boys and two girls the previous fall. Johnson was brother to Joseph Johnson and related to Patty Cannon, the notorious "corp[s] of little negro stealers," in the words of the Delaware abolitionist Thomas Garrett. No doubt the mention of the Cannon-Johnson gang incited Black Philadelphians and their white allies, for after all, the 1820 anti-kidnapping bill featured one of the gang's victims: Sarah Hagerman's daughter. Thomas

Shipley wrote that the abolitionist delegations to Harrisburg cited these cases to "enlighten the minds" of Pennsylvania and Maryland politicians.[48]

Given these recent kidnappings, the PAS held emergency meetings in Philadelphia in February to draft a memorial to the state legislature. PAS president William Rawle advised that the memorialists object to Pennsylvania "enforcing and even extending the provisions of a law of the U.S. in favour of a subject so revolting to us." The memorialists then questioned the value of comity: Why must Pennsylvania "do more than submit to the execution of those Laws which the Government of the Union may think proper to establish" and "join . . . with the slave holding States, in concurrent acts of legislation on this subject"? The PAS expressed disgust at the provision, which addressed recovery, because it "might make benevolent individuals the companions of convicts": PAS Secretary Samuel Mason, Jr. could relate to this potentiality, and he affixed his name to the memorial. Maryland slaveholders had no right to dictate state policy to Pennsylvania, nor did they have the right to further implicate Pennsylvanians in facilitating the "odious traffick" of the domestic slave trade. In sum, the PAS called upon politicians to redouble their efforts to preserve the integrity of the state within a Union bound to slavery.[49]

The legislator who worked the hardest to resolve this impasse over comity was William Meredith, a recently elected state representative from Philadelphia City. As a member of the city's "elite nexus," Meredith received letters from prominent Philadelphia abolitionists like PAS member Roberts Vaux, who warned Meredith that the sixth provision would "never be submitted to by the freemen of this Commonwealth" and, if the bill passed as stated, might result in the arrest of some of Meredith's abolitionist friends. Vaux's point was that African Americans and their white allies were street diplomats willing to disrupt any type of removal and face arrest. While Vaux avoided condemning the Union outright, he did assert Pennsylvania states' rights when he asked Meredith whether Pennsylvania was "bound to legislate for the South." Vaux walked the comity tightrope and answered his own question: "I say no: the law of Congress may have its course throughout Pennsylvania [and] we will do nothing to impede it, but in the name of Mercy spare us from the disgrace of lending such assistance to the merciless slave keeper and dealer in human flesh and rights." At issue were slave states pronouncing their right to property as synonymous with abiding by the Constitution, an extraterritorial right exercised to the expense of what Vaux and his allies understood as the extraterritorial guarantee of freedom across the Union. Like white politicians, white abolitionists like Vaux struggled to respect a comity that favored slave state interests at the expense of Pennsylvania states' rights.[50]

Meredith's father, William Sr., informed his son that the "most violent" opposition to the bill in the city came from "uninformed" abolitionists. The "public feeling being so strong" in Philadelphia prevented the elder Meredith from debating with the bill's opponents, who remained in "absolute ignorance." This group astonished him when they insisted that they were "not bound by the Const. [and] consequently not by the Act of Congress to do anything in order to give [the 1793 act] effect." Such a strident assertion made by abolitionists in defense of freedom, whether the moral high ground of principle or the state right of Pennsylvania to protect residents, impinged on comity. Ultimately, the elder Meredith counseled patience toward the "hurricane" unleashed by the delegation from Maryland and the abolitionists in Philadelphia so that cooler heads might render an "expedient" solution.[51]

Richard Allen did not mince words in his letter to the younger Meredith: passing the Maryland bill would be "bad." Allen explained in detail how two decades prior a Maryland slaveholder came to Philadelphia, recruited a constable, claimed Allen as a fugitive from slavery, and brought him before Alderman Alexander Todd. Fortunately for Allen, Todd knew him to be a free man. The slaveholder "supposed that he was mistaken" and offered Allen one dollar for his trouble, which Allen refused. Speaking to the timing of this incident, the slaveholder and constable waited until dusk to seize him in order to prevent Allen from "calling upon any of [his] friends" to disrupt the arrest. A similar occurrence happened in recent weeks, Allen explained, when a Philadelphia constable arrested a man on his way to work, claimed him as a fugitive from slavery, and imprisoned him for several hours. "Finding that spectators began to get numerous," the constable conceded, gave the supposed fugitive from slavery five dollars, and released him.[52]

To Allen and other Black Philadelphians, slaveholders, constables, and kidnappers straddled the line between legal and illegal removals and in effect made both forms of removal one and the same. A veteran street diplomat, Allen made it clear to Meredith that while some African Americans benefited from friends or crowds coming to rescue them, there were many more cases in which a person's liberty vanished in moments absent any support. His larger point was that all African Americans in Philadelphia faced the threat of having their freedom questioned by whites and could be kidnapped with ease. He drew Meredith's attention to Watson's open letter on the kidnappings of Black children in Philadelphia newspapers, and he stated how "we"—i.e., the African American community and its allies—"frequently receive letters from Kentucky, Alabama, New Orleans, etc." In other words, kidnappers and their victims traversed the Union, visiting numerous waystations of the internal slave trade before arriving at the terminus of the cotton economy of the Deep South.[53]

The incoming correspondence to the PAS lent credence to Allen's claim. Barely a month before meeting with Meredith, Allen received a letter from Adam Brown of New Orleans informing him that a woman named Hettey Gibbins, also of New Orleans, owned a girl who claimed to be from Philadelphia. This girl told Brown of her father's affairs in Philadelphia and noted how a minister named Glasgow frequented her parents' house. Brown begged Allen to send proof of the girl's freedom but to be careful when selecting the person who would send the documents, in order to prevent them from "being destroyed" in transit. James Forten received a similar letter from a lawyer on behalf of an African American boy named Amos, who was kidnapped from Philadelphia and now languished in a New Orleans jail. Whether or not Allen and Forten were able to assist these victims remains unclear, though the point of these tales was clear: slaveholders and kidnappers possessed an ability to enslave that transcended borders.[54]

"Black founding fathers" Allen and Forten were among the most famous African Americans in Philadelphia, men whose prestige and influence left indelible marks on African American kidnapping victims who survived the horrors of the second middle passage. Allen and Forten, along with other notable "history-minded" Black Philadelphians, used their public platforms as a means to craft a support system for African Americans, north and south. This support system included not only making public addresses defending African American culture and life in the city, as Allen, Forten, and other Black activists were wont to do across their illustrious careers, but also writing letters and browbeating white politicians and even more subversively, creating the basis for what would become the Underground Railroad. That the victims' letters survived the trip north and found the eyes of either man was a remarkable testament to the work of victims and their defenders. In a word, the kidnapped African Americans who wrote letters while incarcerated, their allies who delivered these letters, and their allies who read and acted upon them demonstrated bravery as an essential element of street diplomacy.[55]

Returning to his letter to Meredith, Allen projected a grim future. If the bill passed, Allen speculated that "five freemen to one slave" would be taken from Pennsylvania and sold south. The bill disrupted street diplomacy because it punished those who assumed the freedom of African Americans and assisted fugitives from slavery, even those abolitionists who might use plausible deniability to protect a potential kidnapping victim. Allen asserted that "it is unknown to you how many depredations are committed upon our race by persons from the South"; too many futures hung in the balance. Fittingly, Allen signed his letter with a postscript indicating that he spoke for a "large body of Coloured persons" from Philadelphia.[56]

A Compromised Protection or a Protected Compromise?

Meredith presented a compromise package to the Pennsylvania state legislature on February 13. The stiff fines and punishments as well as the measures preventing petty magistrates, state officials all, from enforcing the 1793 Fugitive Slave Act remained intact. Meredith argued that allowing claimants to apply to a state judge ensured "equal protection" to African Americans. Perhaps Meredith viewed state judges as representatives of an elite white male culture more prone to release fugitives from slavery than petty state officials like constables who stalked Philadelphia. Judges like Peters sought to preserve comity through federal removal despite the potential to conflate legal removals with kidnappings, a calculated but acceptable risk to whites who did not have to fear anyone asking for their freedom papers.[57]

Meredith's "equal protection" provision acknowledged the limits of empathizing completely with African Americans, and from a Constitutional standpoint, modified the 1793 law, which allowed "any person . . . without oath, warrant, or officer" to seize an African American and bring them before a judge "under pretense of [them] being a fugitive slave." Meredith justified the new provision with a strict construction of the phrase "shall be delivered up" within the 1793 act: "A paramount power may come and *take* him, but surely it is the *State* alone that can possibly *deliver him up*." Since only Pennsylvania could "deliver" supposed fugitives from slavery, Meredith asserted that his proposal maintained state sovereignty through its own removal process, ensured comity with slaveholders, and protected free Blacks from "arbitrary seizure." Meredith hoped his bill would make the federal law "fall into comparative disuse" because only legitimate claimants would go through the complicated and legal state process rather than risk seizing African Americans without state approval.[58]

While Pennsylvania legislators reconvened on February 14 to discuss Meredith's compromise, street diplomats Thomas Shipley and fellow PAS member

Caleb Carmalt went to work polling and conversing with "most prominent members of the House." The "Quaker" amendments advocated by Shipley repealed Section 11 of Pennsylvania's original 1780 gradual abolition act, which allowed slaveholders "residing in any state . . . the right and aid to demand any" African American living in Pennsylvania. The suggested repeal therefore denied slaveholders' federal right to property in Pennsylvania. Shipley then suggested an amendment that disallowed the oath or evidence of the slaveholder or other interested party during hearings involving fugitives from slavery. Instead, the claimants or their agents would need a certified affidavit from their place of residence. Abolitionists like Shipley and Carmalt synthesized their experiences of street diplomacy in Philadelphia to devise amendments to inconvenience slaveholders and would-be kidnappers, assert that Pennsylvania state law need not assist slaveholders, and most importantly, protect African Americans with whom they shared bonds of struggle, empathy, and friendship.[59]

The combined street diplomatic forces of Allen, Gloucester, Shipley, and Carmalt struck a chord with Meredith, whose influence among his Democratic colleagues, many of whom came from Philadelphia County as well as other counties that bordered Maryland, allowed these same legislators to cross party lines in a Democratic-controlled house and senate vote for the new kidnapping law. As Andrew K. Diemer has argued, Meredith's essential contribution was his insistence in promoting comity between whites living in Maryland and Pennsylvania. Crafted through compromise, the bill, including the amendments recommended by the PAS, passed the Pennsylvania house by a vote of 44 to 39 on February 15, and Governor John Shulze signed it into law on March 25, 1826.[60]

The 1826 act changed the 1820 act in numerous ways, starting with the name of the bill. Rather than simply "an Act to prevent kidnapping," the new act, entitled "An Act to give effect to the provisions of the Constitution of the United States, relative to fugitives from labor, for the protection of free people of color, and to prevent kidnapping," crystallized the struggle between states' rights, federally sanctioned removal, and illegal kidnappings. Much like their colleagues at the national level, Pennsylvania politicians confronted slaveholders' demands through an evolving sense of Northern states' rights, a sense that permitted antislavery actions instead of abolition. Rather than a top-down set of changes, abolitionist groups and, most importantly, African Americans like Allen and Gloucester, injected their experiences into the debate, and forced white politicians to consider the basic concern of street diplomacy: African American freedom was a freedom made and not begotten, a precarious freedom subject to questioning, harassment, and violence.[61]

The question of who in Pennsylvania had the right to remove fugitives from slavery reflected concerns over comity. Although both acts prohibited state officials from issuing removals under the 1793 federal Fugitive Slave Act, the 1826 act now permitted state officials to issue removals through a complicated process within Pennsylvania state law. This process helped slaveholders by increasing the number of Pennsylvanians who could legally participate in removal but at the same time prevented slaveholders from practicing "self-help" efforts of removing African Americans under the 1793 act. Significant to the long-term trajectory of African American freedom in Pennsylvania, this amendment modified federal retrieval and portended future conflicts over a state's right to protect its citizens while abiding by the Constitution. Ultimately, this 1826 law acted as a through line to the 1842 *Prigg* decision and the 1850 Fugitive Slave Act.[62]

From the abolitionists' perspective the purpose of the act was to prevent the kidnappings of African Americans, whether fugitive, freed, or free. One solution came through the 1826 act's threatening state officials with a hefty fine if they failed to make a record of a removal. Another way to prevent such a misunderstanding came from a nod to both the PAS and more importantly, the experiences of Philadelphia's Black community: the 1826 act disallowed slaveholder testimony, coming full circle from protecting a slaveholder's right to retrieve under the Federal Constitution to denying their proof of ownership in Pennsylvania. Here the slaveholders' freedom to own human beings became made and not begotten. In sum, what made the 1826 neither Northern nor Southern but American was that it seemed to have something for everyone: slaveholders could exercise their federal right to remove supposed fugitives from slavery so long as they went through Pennsylvania's byzantine removal process, while abolitionists and the African American community could exercise their right to live free in the state by employing every trick in the street diplomacy arsenal to shirk federal guarantees to human property.[63]

Conclusion

The case studies in this chapter reveal how the force and efficacy of the 1820 act ebbed and flowed, not unlike the precarious freedom experienced by African Americans in Pennsylvania in general and Philadelphia in particular between 1820 and 1826. African Americans and their allies interpreted the

1820 act in such a way as to confirm their deep-seated belief in assuming human freedom: the act allowed them to purposefully conflate moments of "legal" retrieval with kidnappings. These moments occurred on the local level in Philadelphia, spawning what I have termed street diplomacy. Street diplomacy facilitated and exacerbated contests over freedom and slavery at the local level that influenced political action at the state and national levels.

Since federal apparatuses lacked the manpower to enforce the 1793 Fugitive Slave Act directly, slaveholders relied on themselves and their allies in Philadelphia to enforce federal fugitive retrieval at the local level. Slaveholders and kidnappers traveled around, to, and within Philadelphia to hunt African Americans like John Reed, Hezekiah Cooper, and Ezekiel Freeman and, in doing so, exercised their right to remove supposed fugitives from justice under the 1793 act. Perceiving these local efforts as insufficient and Pennsylvania as dilatory on matters of "removal," the state of Maryland sent a delegation to convince the Pennsylvania state legislature to respond to these affronts to comity.

Pennsylvania state politicians like William Meredith worked with other elites in the PAS to reach a legislative détente with the Maryland delegation. African Americans and their PAS allies brought street diplomacy into the Pennsylvania state legislature. Their actions epitomized the blend of strategies employed by street diplomats, from PAS members like Shipley and Carmalt lobbying white lawmakers to Allen and Gloucester confronting politicians face to face with personal tales of terror that they experienced while living as African Americans in Philadelphia.

The combined efforts of African Americans and their white allies supported the long-term vision of freedom for African Americans in Pennsylvania and the United States through an improvisatory set of actions on the street level. Street diplomats impugned slaveholders' motives time and again not only by disrupting the removal process but by forcing slaveholders and bystanders to make risky choices, namely, whether they could or should honor federal or state mandates to enslave or protect African Americans. Their activities as street diplomats forged inextricable links between the local, state, and national politics of freedom and slavery.

No clear picture of a free-soil Pennsylvania emerged when Pennsylvania state politicians passed the 1826 act. True, the act complicated removal as a way to stave off kidnapping and refused to honor slaveholders' testimony. However, the act acknowledged that Pennsylvanians, whether specific state officials or cautious onlookers, must in some way help facilitate the removal and therefore potential kidnapping of African Americans. The fact that the debates over the 1826 act passed as a compromise meant not only that Northern politicians listened to those African Americans and their allies who sought protection from illegal and legal removals but also that Black freedom still represented an ongoing question rather than an assumption—perhaps especially—in Pennsylvania. Finally, the 1826 act became a through line for later dire episodes in the history of slavery and freedom in the United States, namely, the 1842 *Prigg* decision and the 1850 Fugitive Slave Act.

CHAPTER THREE

Fugitive Freedom in Philadelphia

A free African American boy named Eli Harman wandered along south Philadelphia's wharves on his way home from school in the spring of 1822. Seeing
a boat drifting toward him, Harman ran to tie the vessel's rope to the dock.
As he leaned over to pick up the rope, hands seized him, gagged him, and
took him below deck. The boat sailed to Maryland, where the kidnappers
sold Harman to a man named John Martin, who worked him "bear headed
[sic] and half naked till the sun burned his skin so yellow that he was able to
sell him." Slave traders sold Harman twice more before Lewis Wimberly of
Bibb County, Georgia, purchased him. Harman told his story to an anonymous Bibb County resident, who wrote the PAS asking for their help: "Tho' I
know not your name, I have taken the liberty to write to you on a subject that
ought to concern every man that [possesses] one spark of humanity." The
writer stated that Harman claimed to have lived in Philadelphia and that his
father worked as a ship carpenter for a "Capt. Grot." The writer remained
apprehensive that Harman came from Philadelphia but trusted him enough
to request that the PAS publish Harman's account "so that his friends may
hear of him." The letter concluded with an ominous postscript: "The boy has
made one attempt to escape to get home." The combined efforts of the PAS
and the African American community came to no avail. No one ever found
out what happened to Eli Harman.[1]

This chapter explores the multiplicity of threats faced by Philadelphia's
African American community both outside and inside the city. As with the
previous case studies, I analyze the relationships between kidnappings, fugitives from slavery, abolitionism, and street diplomacy. Kidnappings of free

This depiction of the Chestnut Street wharves alongside the Delaware River, circa 1850, hints at the haunted, terrified realities of Black life in the city as wharves served as prime locales for African American laborers, kidnappers, slave catchers, and slaveholders alike. Courtesy of the Library Company of Philadelphia

Blacks in Philadelphia represented a breach of state law due to the street-inspired legislative efforts passed by the Pennsylvania state legislature. Yet the difficulties inherent in distinguishing kidnapping victims from fugitives from slavery remained in force. Philadelphia abolitionists and the Black community worked with local and state politicians to retrieve both the kidnappers and the victims in a stunning display of interstate comity. Even if multiple state law enforcement officials did not catch the kidnapper, at least Pennsylvanians could rely on slave states to help facilitate the victims' rendition. Over time, however, cracks in interstate comity began to appear in Philadelphia through diplomatic activity on the streets, as free and slave states confronted Black and white activism.

Practitioners of street diplomacy, many if not most Black Philadelphians and their white allies presumed that any seizure of an African American person represented an attempted kidnapping, regardless of the victim's back-

ground. Their opponents, who included most white Philadelphians, thought the exact opposite and worked to quell street disturbances caused by African Americans, namely, when they rescued other Blacks in the custody of slaveholders and constables. These riotous actions undertaken by Black Philadelphians faced a brutal response from white Philadelphians and showed the consequences of a breakdown in comity. The increased motivations for preserving law and order in a country ensnared in a whole host of revolutions—revolutions in markets, transportation, abolitionism, work, leisure, and the law itself—helped catalyze the belief that pitting slavery against freedom on the streets of Philadelphia epitomized a threat to the Union itself.[2]

"A dishonored corps of little Negro stealers": Philadelphia, 1826

> In the years 1826–1827 there were frequent alarms in relation to
> kidnapping colored children, which created much excitement.[3]

As mentioned in chapter 2, the kidnapping of Black children from Philadelphia by what one abolitionist called a "dishonored corps of little Negro stealers" influenced Pennsylvania lawmakers during the course of the 1826 liberty law debates. Mississippians John Hamilton and John Henderson alerted Philadelphia mayor Joseph Watson in January 1826 that Ebenezer Johnson offered to sell them five African American children the previous fall. Fourteen-year-old Samuel Scomp, 9-year-old Enos Tilghman, and 8-year-old Alexander Manlove explained that they were kidnapped from Philadelphia by a "yellow" man named John Purnell, who in passing as a sympathetic ally offered them work carrying fruit to the south Philadelphia docks. Once aboard the ship, Purnell and Joseph Johnson bound and gagged the boys. The kidnappers and the ship's captain, Thomas Collins, transported their victims to Delaware before sailing for Norfolk, Virginia. The group then traveled by wagon more than 600 miles to Rocky Spring, Mississippi, and into Hamilton and Henderson's world. These accounts horrified the men, who demanded that Johnson produce a bill of sale for these "slaves." Johnson did so, though he claimed plausible deniability if his brother Joseph or Collins "delivered these negroes to him . . . if they were stolen." Despite being apprised that Blacks could not give testimony against whites in Mississippi, Johnson panicked, left the "slaves" with Hamilton, and promised to return after he obtained proof of ownership.[4]

Hamilton and Henderson grew increasingly suspicious of Johnson's motives and implored Watson's aid so that "the coloured people of your City and other places may be guarded against similar outrages." These Southerners appeared to value comity and, in doing so, respected the freedom of Blacks upheld by Pennsylvania state law. Watson wrote an open letter to his fellow Philadelphians in *Poulson's Daily American Advertiser.* Not only did he urge "reputable Blacks" to submit depositions and inform the families of the missing children, he condemned the open secret of kidnappings in the city. The characters involved in kidnapping were "not unknown to the Police" and no doubt Mayor Watson, and quite often included Philadelphia constables like George Alberti and John Weisener.[5]

Watson practiced street diplomacy to extradite both the victims and the kidnappers. His antislavery stance derived from his membership in the Society of Friends. He attended the Philadelphia monthly meeting and engaged in debates over the moral sanctity of slavery alongside august abolitionists Thomas Shipley and James and Lucretia Mott. Quaker meetinghouses in Philadelphia were in a sense sites of resistance that, while racially segregated, still consisted of whites willing to desegregate their moral efforts to help African Americans. That these antislavery activists met, prayed, and conversed with each other meant that Watson was, in a way, primed to confront the kidnappings of African Americans within Philadelphia.[6]

Philadelphia African Americans and the PAS assisted Watson by gathering evidence from the streets. Black and white abolitionist efforts on the street paired with Watson and Pennsylvania governor John Shulze's politicking bore fruit: Watson sent the Mississippians more than thirty pages of depositions supporting the kidnapping victims' claims as well as warrants for the arrest of the kidnappers. Watson wrote Hamilton in March 1826 to assure him that he would secure Johnson by encouraging Shulze to respect comity and "demand Johnson from the Governor of your state, as a fugitive from the justice of ours." Hamilton followed Watson's instructions and escorted Tilghman and Scomp to New Orleans, where they boarded a ship to Philadelphia. The boys arrived in the city on June 29 and met with Watson, where Scomp confirmed that "a small mulatto man" named John Purnell kidnapped the children.[7]

This correspondence between Watson and Hamilton revealed how African Americans embodied the tensions at the heart of comity. Extraditing white and black kidnappers promoted Black freedom while leaving the institution of slavery relatively unscathed. Citing the extradition clause of the Constitution, in late March 1826 Watson wrote to Shulze, who permitted Watson to appoint Samuel P. Garrigues to retrieve the kidnappers from the states of Virginia, Alabama, and Mississippi. Mississippi attorney general Richard Stockson contacted Watson around that time to pledge his support in the hunt for "those infamous miscreants who thus deal in human suffering." However, by that point the kidnappers appeared to have fled the Deep South and returned north, possibly to the Cannon-Johnson gang.[8]

Having gleaned vital information from Black and white street diplomats in Philadelphia, Watson practiced comity by enlisting the help of the governors of Delaware and Maryland. While his contact in Delaware seemed wary of engaging the kidnappers, Maryland governor Joseph Kent reported to Garrigues that he would assign the sheriff of Talbot County to assist in the arrests. Back in Philadelphia, on January 25, 1827, Watson pledged a reward of $500 for information leading to the capture of any member of the Cannon-Johnson gang. "Instances of such high-handed and atrocious villainy," he wrote, required that the public must pay "most watchful attention of all classes of the community to prevent its repetition." Watson's willingness to assist kidnapping victims served as a high point for protecting Philadelphia's African American community by charging Philadelphians with the task of ferreting out kidnappers who threatened African American freedom.[9]

Watson and Garrigues never caught any of the white members of the Cannon-Johnson gang. The Delaware abolitionist Jesse Green alerted Watson in March 1827 that the gang had returned to "their old business of kidnapping ... [and] will have as usual some Blacks to assist and decoy etc." As previously mentioned, African American decoys operated as a fifth column within the slave states and Philadelphia itself. Green qualified the use of decoys, kidnappers all, by writing "as usual" and reified this ever-present fear: African Americans took a leap of faith when accepting offers for work in a kidnapper's world. Green recommended sending Garrigues to Concord, Delaware, to intercept the gang but warned of Johnson's "army [of] little rascals"—Black and white informants—"that will give him information of the approach of any officers." Most likely fearing for his own safety, Garrigues did not travel south to Delaware. Nonetheless, the exploits of the Cannon-Johnson gang came to end in 1829, when Delaware authorities indicted the Johnson brothers and Patty Cannon for a slew of murders on their property. The brothers fled to parts unknown, and Cannon committed suicide in jail after confessing to the murders of eleven people.[10]

Fortunately, the efforts of Black and white Philadelphians to pursue comity were not in vain, for in June 1827 Garrigues apprehended Purnell in Boston, Massachusetts. Having traveled hundreds of miles between Pennsylvania, Maryland, Mississippi, and Louisiana over the course of the previous year, Garrigues brought Purnell back to Philadelphia to stand trial in both the Mayor's Court and the Quarter Sessions Court. Purnell appeared before Watson with Philadelphian Henry Carr, a Black oyster shop owner. The Mayor's Office was "crowded to excess" with members of the Black community, the most important of whom were Purnell's actual kidnapping victims. Despite the testimony of the recently freed victims Cornelius Sinclair and Alexander Manlove, Purnell and Carr were found not guilty.[11]

Henry Carr's Oyster Shop

Purnell's second trial offered insights into how kidnappers who ignored borders operated in the heart of Philadelphia. Purnell did not have such luck at the Quarter Sessions Court: this time the boys' testimony worked to great effect. Sinclair testified that Purnell stole him at Second and South Streets in broad daylight, a public spectacle of violence and theft at a bustling metropolitan intersection. Scomp explained how Purnell asked him to carry watermelons to the dock, which the boy considered a "marvelously good joke." Scomp laughed at his treatment in such a way as to make the audience laugh along with him—such levity seems strange, but understandable, given that Scomp probably reserved more laughter for the potential fate awaiting his captors.

A site of Black and white interaction below the city's streets, oyster shops may have proved "bon-ton" for some Philadelphians, but they certainly became life-altering for African Americans when kidnappers colluded with shop owners like Henry Carr. Courtesy of the Library Company of Philadelphia

The Quarter Sessions Court found Purnell guilty, fined him the maximum $1,000 for each kidnapped boy, and sentenced him to forty-two years in prison. Desiring a harsher sentence, the Philadelphia-based abolitionist newspaper the *African Observer* commented that "the prisoner might have been prosecuted by the laws of the United States [i.e., death by hanging], but those of the state were preferred, probably from the motives of humanity." Purnell died in prison six years later.[12]

In reality, the Black community of Philadelphia received the harshest punishment: the trial forced Blacks and their allies to consider the kidnappers who already infiltrated their city and community. An African American man named Simon Wesley Parker testified that he first met Purnell in the oyster shop of a Black Philadelphian named Henry Carr in 1825. Parker witnessed Purnell ask an African American boy in the shop to leave the shop with him. Purnell returned shortly thereafter without the boy and warned Parker that "if he ever mentioned anything of this he would blow his brains out." A moment later the boy returned to the shop and he and Purnell then left a second time. Carr ran after Purnell, perhaps to inquire whether they should include Parker in their ruse. When Carr reentered his shop, he told Parker that Purnell was going to kidnap and sell the boy. Parker pondered taking a cut of the kidnapping proceeds when Joseph Johnson entered the shop. After meeting with Johnson, Carr insisted that Parker not tell anyone about the boy; Parker obliged. Carr and Parker then went to the docks to rendezvous with Johnson aboard his boat. The men shared a drink, at which point Johnson said to Parker, "I had like to have taken you for one." In other words, Johnson thought Parker would make a good kidnapper. Johnson then told Carr that he expected him to "fetch" a few more boys, so Parker and Carr left the boat in search of victims. Carr called to a few children on South Street, but they fled. Later Carr and Parker met with Purnell on Shippen Street, where Purnell gave Carr $25 for helping kidnap the boy in his shop. Carr split the money with Parker.[13]

The next day Parker helped Purnell carry a trunk to Johnson's house on Race Street, an embedded kidnapping den in the middle of Philadelphia. Purnell told Parker that Carr had cheated him and that he wanted Parker "to go partners with him in kidnapping." Purnell seemed to have grand designs for this partnership, even sharing a grisly family anecdote in which his father, also a kidnapper, slit his own throat rather than be taken by the authorities. Regaling Parker in such a casual way acted like a "trust exercise" akin to the kidnappers' strategy of quizzing their victims. According to Scomp, Johnson would send fake buyers to purchase kidnapping victims. These buyers would feign sympathy and ask how they were "procured." When the victims revealed their freedom, Johnson would beat them, sometimes to death. In this way, kidnappers seasoned their victims; "this discipline is continued at intervals until they become so completely *drilled,* that a stranger, whether the professed owners is present or not, can scarcely obtain from them, by any means whatever, any other account than the false one which has been prepared for them." Parker's own testimony remained unclear as to how he replied to these stories and the proposal.[14]

Parker's testimony exposed the terrifying realities faced by street diplomats in Philadelphia. First, Purnell's ability to move in and around the city, steal human beings, and purchase or rent property to detain victims spoke to the lack of borders perceived by kidnappers. After all, kidnappers broke the law and, therefore, borders could matter only so long as they were useful. Second, Purnell exploited this ease of movement by loitering around the docks and in doing so, exploited people on the economic margins: vulnerable Black children. Finally, the casual nature in which Purnell attempted to enlist Parker as a kidnapper in the oyster shop of another Black kidnapper suggested that at times economic motives overrode racial solidarity when it came to the kidnapping of African Americans. The existential threats that emanated from Henry Carr's oyster shop in the heart of the Black community warranted vigilance from Black and white street diplomats.[15]

The Protecting Society

Eliding messy street-level realities of Black-on-Black kidnappings, abolitionists heaped praise upon those involved in bringing the kidnappers to justice. The *American Convention* for Promoting the *Abolition* of Slavery and Improving the Condition of the African Race offered resolutions in 1827 and 1828 thanking the "unwearied and successful exertions" of Watson and Garrigues. "A number of citizens of Philadelphia" sent Henderson and Hamilton two silver pitchers to commemorate their "disinterested, spirited and benevolent" actions to free those "who had by force or fraud been taken from their homes." The African American victims themselves failed to receive such plaudits, even though they lived through these vicious circumstances and offered vital testimony that exposed the kidnapping network plied by the Cannon-Johnson gang within their own city.[16]

Despite these selective praises, white and Black abolitionists reminded themselves that hundreds of kidnapping victims still suffered in the Southern states due to many cases that were never brought to light or if brought to light never solved; the case of Eli Harman, for example. Street diplomats did not fail to connect these lost lives and futures to the ongoing brutality and tragedy of the million and a half enslaved people living in the South. The difficulties inherent in finding anyone willing to travel great distances to rescue kidnapped African Americans meant that free people were often "doomed to irredeemable slavery." Besides travel distances, the mere fact that these diplomats faced local violence at the hands of slaveholders and kidnappers alike was enough to discourage such journeys.[17]

No doubt responding to the omnipresent threat of kidnapping–cum–"fugitive retrieval," in 1827 Black Philadelphians organized a "Protecting Society" auxiliary to the PAS. While it remains unclear exactly how the Philadelphia Protecting Society defined "auxiliary," if it meant "auxiliary" as a part of the PAS, then again the PAS integrated much earlier than historians have supposed. It should be noted that this society's public pronouncement of its work in no way meant that other covert societies operated before, during, or after this society's creation—the public pronouncement of a society dedicated to blending covert and overt means to protect Blacks epitomized the creativity and bravery of street diplomats. No surprise that street diplomacy was multigenerational in scope: Richard Allen's son John acted as secretary of the society, which published the following advertisement in *Freedom's Journal* on April 25, 1828:

> NOTICE. The Protecting Society of the city and county of Philadelphia, for the preventing of Kidnapping and man-stealing, auxiliary to the Abolition Society of the above city, deem it expedient to inform their Coloured brethren generally, that this Society was formed in the year 1827; hoping that all will use their best endeavors to carry the benevolent views of the Society into operation. Of the many evils to which we as fallible creatures are liable, none is more to be dreaded and execrated than the system of kidnapping free persons of Colour, which has been carried on even in this city by a set of unprincipled men, for some years past. Persons desirous of assistance in the recovery of their friends who have been kidnapped, must make application personally or by letter post-paid, addressed to the Secretary of the Society. JOHN ALLEN, Sec'ry. Philadelphia, April 24, 1828.[18]

This society represented an example of grassroots immediatism practiced by African Americans. Little is known of the society's anti-kidnapping exploits—perhaps that was the point! Portending and in many ways informing the activities of the Underground Railroad, such resistance strategies spoke volumes of the efforts made by Black activists in the decades prior to 1850. In its capacity to prevent kidnapping and man-stealing the group likely supplied the PAS with informants and witnesses to aid in recovering friends or family who disappeared. Then again, perhaps offering to assist "their Coloured brethren generally" meant that it also took on cases of an unofficial character independent of the PAS. In either case (or both), the Protecting Society's formal announcement exemplified how African American street diplomats liberated human beings on their own terms and actualized the emancipatory goals they shared with the PAS.[19]

Interstate Intermediaries:
Emory Sadler and Governor John Shulze

Kidnapping victims and their white and Black allies pushed white politicians like Mayor Watson and Governor Shulze to disrupt kidnapping efforts. Pennsylvanians' demands for slave states to requisition kidnappers and their victims typified the expectation of reciprocity and therefore comity between states. Praised for his piety, patriotism, "great prudence and good judgment," Shulze assisted the PAS in the liberation of Emory Sadler, an African American man who was stolen from Philadelphia in 1825. The slaveholder Ebenezer Massey of Kent County, Maryland, sold Sadler to Arnold Jacobs (also of Maryland) under the stipulation that Jacobs would not sell Sadler out of state. Jacobs went a step further with his promise to Massey and told Massey and Sadler that the latter would be hired out to earn his freedom, not in Maryland, but in Pennsylvania. This hiring-out agreement in effect allowed for slavery to cross the border into Pennsylvania. Thus Sadler arrived in Philadelphia in 1825 as what can only be described as an enslaved free man.[20]

Sadler easily found work at a tannery owned by a South Philadelphia leather dealer named William Pritchett. A few months later Jacobs appeared in Philadelphia to collect Sadler's wages, at which point he offered Sadler his freedom. Jacobs claimed that Sadler would need to return to Maryland to file the manumission papers. Suspicious, Sadler contacted the PAS for multiple reasons: he wanted to know the manumission process and consequently betrayed his obvious and realistic fear that he might face consequences for "stealing himself" and risking permanent enslavement by not abiding by the proper procedure to become emancipated. The PAS, as well as Sadler's wife and mother, remained skeptical to Jacobs's intent, yet Sadler agreed to his offer. Sadler accompanied him back to Maryland, where Jacobs promptly chained and sold him.[21]

Although confined to a jail in Warwick, Maryland, Sadler enacted street diplomacy and fought kidnapping-cum-reenslavement by writing to those best positioned to help him: his white employer, his PAS allies, and his family. Working together under the auspices of the PAS, Sadler's friends and family contacted Governor Shulze, who then wrote to Maryland governor Samuel Stevens, Jr. multiple times in late 1825 requesting that Stevens extradite Jacobs to Pennsylvania to stand trial for kidnapping. Shulze's first letter combined state and national precedents: he cited Pennsylvania's 1820 anti-kidnapping statute as well as the extradition clause of the Constitution. Stevens refused to deliver up Jacobs because Sadler's freedom was unproven. The PAS and Sadler's supporters soon tired of Stevens's "apparent contradiction of the Constitution and laws of the United States" and gathered depositions, which they then sent to Stevens, who ignored their pleas. In early December 1825 the PAS brought the case to the Philadelphia Court of Oyer and Terminer, which declared Jacobs guilty of kidnapping, thus making him an official fugitive from justice. Equipped with this new knowledge, Shulze responded to Stevens's rebuff by sending him a second missive in December in which he declined to withdraw his demand for Jacobs.[22]

Stevens's intransigence and refusal to reciprocate defied any clear-cut sense of Southerners willfully assisting free Blacks or their allies. To wit, we lack any evidence that Stevens ever sent an official response to Shulze's second letter. Taking Black freedom seriously on the basis of a flawed comity, Shulze appointed John Thompson, Jr., the sheriff of Philadelphia, to extradite Jacobs; the PAS paid him $50 to defray travel expenses. Thompson delivered the requisition request to Maryland's new governor, Joseph Kent, who issued a warrant to a Maryland sheriff to work with Thompson to arrest Jacobs. This sheriff refused to execute the warrant, so Thompson journeyed to Jacobs's house alone. Jacobs "received [Thompson] politely," even after Thompson explained the nature of his visit, and told him to stay the night so that they could discuss the warrant the next morning. Upon waking Thompson walked into the parlor, where Jacobs sat with two loaded pistols pointed directly at him. Jacobs threatened to "shoot [Thompson] dead on the spot" if he mentioned the warrant; Thompson left and returned to Philadelphia empty-handed.[23]

Thompson explained his encounter with Jacobs to the PAS. Dissatisfied, the PAS remained vigilant in the search, a vigilance that stemmed both from its work with Black Philadelphians as well as its expectation of comity between states. The PAS ordered Thompson to return to Maryland. Thompson refused and found someone else to go for him. At the same time, Governor Kent, who seemed more sympathetic and receptive to working with Pennsylvania, received word of Thompson's meeting with Jacobs and summoned a posse comitatus to assist the new agent from Pennsylvania; a handful of men joined the posse. Like before, the Maryland sheriff refused to aid the Pennsylvania agent, stating that "Jacobs was constantly provided with weapons of defence which he had publickly avowed it to be his determination to use to the fullest extent in resisting any attempts to arrest him under that warrant." Moreover, somehow Jacobs heard of the posse's mission, likely through local informants. When the posse arrived at Jacobs's house, he shouted from inside that he "would not be taken alive." The posse scattered, and like Thompson, the second agent from Pennsylvania returned home.[24]

The 1826 Pennsylvania anti-kidnapping bill became law by the time Thompson reported his encounter with Jacobs to the PAS in late 1826. Months earlier Thomas Shipley negotiated with Maryland commissioners Ezekiel Chambers and William Welch for Sadler's freedom during the 1826 debates. Welch wrote

PAS president William Rawle in February 1826 to propose dropping the case against Jacobs in exchange for Sadler's return to Philadelphia, "if he would be purchased for anything near the usual price of such persons in the country." It was unclear whether Welch or the PAS would foot the bill, but Rawle's eagerness to agree to these terms suggested that Welch would pay for Sadler's freedom. However, once the debates over the liberty law were settled, Welch ignored several letters written by the PAS in June 1826 that requested updates on Sadler's recovery.[25]

Almost two years into the struggle, the PAS and Sadler's family remained determined to find Sadler and contacted Governor Shulze a third time in late 1826. In February 1827 Shulze forwarded to Governor Kent "certain depositions and other authentic documents," which most likely attested to Sadler's character and freedom as well as Jacobs's subterfuge. The content of these documents convinced Kent to issue a proclamation and a $200 reward for the arrest and delivery of Jacobs to Thompson "for the crime of kidnapping a certain negro man, called Emory Sadler." Several Maryland newspapers (as well as the *Genius of Universal Emancipation*) published this proclamation in May and June 1827. Despite the reward and tenuous cooperation between Pennsylvania and Maryland, Jacobs was never arrested for the kidnapping of Emory Sadler.[26]

Slaveholders' need for laborers in the sprawling cotton economy fueled kidnappers' opportunism and drew Sadler into their orbit. William Rawle received word in July 1827, perhaps from an actual Alabamian, the sources do not say, that Sadler was enslaved hundreds of miles away in Athens, Alabama. Rawle advised sending certified copies of the laws of Pennsylvania to the unnamed Alabamian. The PAS negotiated the release of Sadler over the course of the next two years. Unfortunately, nobody recorded these debates. In 1829 Sadler finally made it back to Philadelphia, mainly through the efforts of a Tennessee abolitionist named Ezekiel Birdseye, who spent $150 of his own money to liberate him. William Pritchett, Sadler's former employer, paid for most of these expenses, and in March 1831, Sadler himself paid the final $25 to the PAS.[27]

Sadler's ordeal showed how Black and white Philadelphians worked together with politicians to secure the freedom of kidnapping victims. Unlike Watson's experiences with slaveholders, the unpredictability of comity between politicians appeared in the person of Maryland governor Samuel Stevens, whose Democratic politics matched his overall distrust of African Americans. His refusal to assist Governor Shulze represented a crack in the bonds of comity and Union, bonds restored when Stevens left office and Joseph Kent lent his aid. The weight of evidence gathered by street diplomats in Philadelphia bore down differently from governor to governor, Northern or Southern. Nonetheless, Sadler's kidnapping and subsequent rescue marked a turning point, with Southern slaveholders and politicians cherry-picking legitimate from illegal seizures of free African Americans in the North.[28]

The Elections of 1826 and 1828

The ever-present fears of kidnappings in Philadelphia forced Philadelphia politicians to consider how the national politics of slavery functioned at the local level. Two hotly contested elections epitomized the effects of such a politics: the 1826 campaign to fill former Federalist Joseph Hemphill's seat in Congress and the 1828 presidential election itself. Hemphill synthesized the local and national politics of slavery. In the previous decade he spoke on the Missouri question in Congress, stating that Congress had the right "to arrest [slavery's] farther progress" into the new territories and that Pennsylvania stood at the forefront of the "glorious cause" of gradual emancipation. By 1826, however, Hemphill offered a conciliatory approach toward Southerners on the slavery question; he viewed Pennsylvanian interference with slavery as impolitic. This interference derived from the success of street diplomats in Philadelphia, whose actions inspired liberty laws. "The more I see and become acquainted with southern gentlemen," Hemphill explained, "the more I am convinced of the inutility of propositions from the non-slaveholding States on the subject of emancipation." He remained mute to the opposite phenomenon, that is, slaveholders dictating the laws of Pennsylvania a la Maryland's interstate diplomats. Hemphill's disapproval of tampering with slavery served as an early example of what would later be called "Doughface-ism," and his move from the Federalist Party into the ranks of Jackson supporters cemented his place in the Democracy.[29]

If Hemphill's shifting alliances mattered to national partisans intent on maintaining federal support of slavery, so too did his views impact African Americans in Philadelphia. Hemphill served as the District Court judge in Philadelphia from 1811 to 1818. In that capacity he presided over at least one case involving the notorious George Alberti in 1815. Working with an accomplice, Alberti tore up the freedom papers of a free African American man named Richard Keen and incarcerated him somewhere in Philadelphia for seven weeks. Hemphill fined Alberti and his partner $250. In another more personal incident, the son of one of Hemphill's African American coachmen was kidnapped by the Cannon-Johnson gang. White politicians in Philadelphia remained intrinsically linked to the fate of freedom in Pennsylvania because of their regular interactions with African Americans. Although we do not know how Hemphill reacted to the kidnapping of his coachman or the nature of their relationship, we might assume that, like many white politicians of his era, he consciously separated illegal and legal removals, the latter of which upheld comity and exposed the competition between state and federal law over protecting slavery.[30]

Most of the candidates in the 1826 election had direct ties to the politics of slavery. While candidate Henry Horn's relationship to slavery remained unclear, he served as secretary for a "large and respectable meeting of the democratic citizens [of Philadelphia] friendly to the election of Gen. Andrew Jackson" in May 1826. John Sergeant's involvement with the PAS and Federalist Thomas Kittera's defense of free Blacks in court made them the "antislavery" candidates. As for Hemphill's contested seat, the 1826 election ended in a tie between Horn and Sergeant. The candidates returned to the field the next year, 1827, this time with Hemphill coming out of retirement to compete. Like the first election, candidates were not above linking the national and local politics of slavery. Writing for the *Genius of Universal Emancipation*, Benjamin Lundy noted that Hemphill "wandered away from what he knew were the wishes of his constituents," when he abandoned a recent set of resolutions made by Pennsylvania congressman Charles Miner to gradually emancipate enslaved people in Washington, DC. Furthermore, when PAS supporter John Sergeant won the election, Lundy criticized pro-Jackson editor Duff Green for his comments that only the election and popularity of Jackson could stave off abolitionism. To Lundy, Green and Jackson represented a "Negro Aristocracy" hell-bent on precipitating a conflict between the "slaveites" and abolitionists and their allies like Sergeant. This attitude toward the powerful "slaveholding combination" breathed fire into the 1828 presidential election.[31]

The buildup toward the 1828 presidential election burned the issue of slavery into the minds of Pennsylvania voters. The Philadelphia newspaper editor John Binns distributed broadsides that reproduced Josiah Wedgwood's "Am I Not a Man and a Brother?" medallion with text proclaiming Jackson "a trafficker in human flesh, a Buyer and Seller of Men, Women, and Children." The broadside called on voters to support John Quincy Adams, who abhorred "the foul trade." Lundy, too, attacked Jackson's proslavery credentials, calling him a "SOUL-SELLING, SLAVE-DRIVING, SOUTHERN COTTON-

PLANTER." Slaveholders and politicians like Virginian John Randolph conceded that Southern interests would be secured by "white slaves of the north,"
in particular middle state voters in Pennsylvania, who helped propel fellow
slaveholder, Andrew Jackson, to the presidency.[32]

Little is known of how Philadelphia's African American community reacted to Jackson's election. Of course, they were aware of the election results,
as Jackson won by a two-to-one margin in Philadelphia and Pennsylvania. As
the historian Andrew K. Diemer has argued, Black Philadelphians were more
drawn to local and state concerns, rather than national political figures who
in many ways were no friendlier to them than Jackson. Slaveholding presi-
dents and politicians reminded Black activists of the perils of anti-Black views
and actions espoused by Jackson's supporters at the local level. The abolitionist *Freedom's Journal* did not come out directly against Jackson, though its
pages often informed readers of pro-Jackson sentiment. Citing a question
posed by a Kentucky newspaper of whether or not Jackson participated ac-
tively in the domestic slave trade, *Freedom's Journal* mocked Jackson by stating that if the claims were true, then they would surely "add to the fame of
the Hero of Orleans." *Freedom's Journal*'s critique of Jackson would have resonated with Philadelphia's African American community. Bombarded with
anti-Jackson tropes that laid bare the general's support for slavery and slave
trading, African Americans must have questioned their freedom amidst the
riot culture that defined so-called Jacksonian democracy.[33]

Rioting in Its Philadelphia Setting, 1829–1830

Hardly a year passed before Philadelphia witnessed its first riot during Jackson's administration. This riot set a precedent in its intensity and motives,
and it ushered in a period in which African Americans confronted those who
associated freedom with violence. On November 22, 1829, a group of whites
ambushed African American worshippers as they left the Second African Presbyterian Church on St. Mary's Street in South Philadelphia. Like other African American churches of the era, the church was a symbol of Black achievement in Philadelphia. The church's congregants sustained Black potential and
upward mobility, which some whites interpreted as a threat to racial inequality. Jeremiah Gloucester, eldest son of John Gloucester, founder of the First
African Presbyterian Church, and brother of the abolitionist and 1826 liberty
law street diplomat Stephen Gloucester, organized the church in 1824.[34]

Like his brother, Jeremiah Gloucester epitomized Black achievement and
used his position (and church) to resist the connected issues of kidnapping

and slavery. In a speech to the congregation of Mother Bethel in 1823 he denounced the slave trade and kidnappings and called for Blacks to maintain their respectability because "the blissful period is just at hand, when we shall be elevated to an equal stand!" In 1828 John Gloucester, Jr., who assumed leadership of the church after Jeremiah's death, purchased the property that would become the Second African Presbyterian for $1,000 and renovated the building for the sum of $3,000. The new church housed over 400 worshippers and at the time of its destruction by a white mob in 1842 was valued at over $10,000.[35]

The 1829 riot grew from a quarrel into "an immense gang of Blacks and number of white men and boys" fighting each other outside the church. The latter group consisted of poor white Irish immigrants from Philadelphia County, who struggled for social standing amidst the relative wealth and prestige of Philadelphia's African American community. The whites soon found themselves overwhelmed. Some Blacks ran to a nearby "board yard" and began hurling pieces of wood at the mob. Isaac Kennedy, constable of Cedar Ward, implored bystanders not to rush into the fracas. Like Alberti and other Philadelphia constables, Kennedy connected the local brutality of Black life to slaveholders' drive to kidnap and enslave human beings. Six months earlier a supposed fugitive from slavery stabbed Kennedy in the face during an attempted arrest; the blade broke off in Kennedy's "jaw or cheek."[36]

As the acting law enforcement agent on the scene of the riot, Kennedy defied his own advice and apprehended a Black man he thought was the ringleader. When Kennedy brought the man before Philadelphia mayor Benjamin Wood Richards, the mayor released him as "the constable stated that the Black fellow [looked] so much like himself that one might easily be mistaken for the other." The *Philadelphia Chronicle* noted that although all Black Philadelphians deserved protection from mistaken identity, African Americans in South Philadelphia "think themselves above all restraint," and called their "insolence . . . intolerable." This "insolence" acted as a catalyst to excuse the violence of the whites, plain and simple, and would incite further riots in the decade. Further, cases of mistaken identity, especially Black identity, dovetailed with plausible deniability during the arrest process and thus spoke to one of the central thrusts of street diplomacy: bystanders made split-second decisions to determine if they were witnessing a kidnapping.[37]

Pennsylvania representatives, all PAS members, defended this supposed "insolence" at the American Convention in December 1829. They asserted that the current political context prevented whites in Philadelphia from appreciating "the merits of one whose hue is deeper than his own." These thoughts echoed a pamphlet written by Thomas Shipley earlier that year in which he recommended that African Americans maintain their "virtuous and industrious conduct" to avoid negative reprisals from whites. Pennsylvania abolitionists pointed out that poor Blacks in Philadelphia were less depraved than their poor white Irish counterparts. Considering that many Blacks immigrated to the city from the South, where they had been forced into the "debasing" effects of slavery, one could not "wonder at their helpless, though not hopeless condition." Interestingly, the convention also looked westward to American expansion into Mexico: this movement would increase the domestic slave trade "as well as the practice of kidnapping in the more eastern parts of our own country." Once again, Pennsylvania abolitionists had no qualms connecting kidnappings and seizures in Philadelphia to the fear of slavery spreading into new territories.[38]

Struggling against perceived insolence from the public as well as the best hopes of white abolitionists, ordinary African Americans refused to surrender their freedom to choose who was a kidnapping victim on the streets of Philadelphia. Street diplomats strategized and ultimately exercised their absolute freedom to make this choice, which became, at times, the only true freedom they could enjoy in Pennsylvania within a time of slavery. When African Americans attacked would-be kidnappers, including law enforcement officials, they did so on the basis of resolute individual choices that always contained the potential to metastasize into collective and, at times, direct action.[39]

On March 16, 1830, a crowd of two hundred Black Philadelphians attacked Philadelphia County constables in an attempt to rescue a supposed fugitive from slavery outside of the Franklin Institute Hall. The court had decided for the slaveholder, prompting several African Americans in the courthouse to approach the accused man and speak with him privately. After their talk, the constables and the accused made their way to the building's exit when the latter stopped at the door and refused to move any farther. The accused man chose to stop a "legal" kidnapping and to give his rescuers time to execute their plan: African Americans waiting outside then rushed the man and started dragging him away from the constables, who tried to put him in a waiting carriage.[40]

Torn between freedom and slavery, an African American doctor named Henry Washington lunged at the man and tried to rip a mace out of the hands of a county constable. Washington's daring prompted a constable "Dunhart" to level a pistol at Washington's face. Fortunately, someone bumped into Dunhart, who discharged his pistol just above Washington's head. The constables managed to bring the accused man inside the courthouse and fled out the back door. Washington appeared before the Mayor's Court on the charge of attempting a rescue. Several respectable witnesses spoke against Washington and hinted at Washington's pretense, but the doctor handled his accusers with "coolness." Washington denied precipitating a rescue, he merely wanted the man to go before Alderman Badger to "answer the Overseers of the Poor" for two unidentified, possibly licentious charges. The court ended up releasing Washington.[41]

Several themes emerged from these riots. First, some white Philadelphians felt threatened by Black mobility and attacked symbols of Black achievement. Second, Black and white abolitionists redoubled their efforts to ensure that African Americans continue to strive to maintain themselves as virtuous citizens. Finally, the daily reality of retrieving fugitives from slavery highlighted how African Americans used riotous behavior to enforce freedom, often using extralegal means to do so: every unsuccessful rescue confined one to slavery. Street diplomacy erupted into violence because unlike the anti-Black denizens of Philadelphia, African Americans and their allies assumed the freedom of Blacks arrested by constables and slaveholders.

The Convention Movement

African Americans' street diplomatic efforts in Philadelphia to prevent the national forces of slavery from kidnapping them resulted in yet another link between the local and the national: the convention movement. African American leaders met in Philadelphia in September 1830 to debate hosting national conventions in the city. Henry Zollificker, a Quaker and "friend of the Blacks" attempted to dissuade Hezekiah Grice, a Black tradesman from Baltimore and the guiding force of the convention, from holding the meeting in Philadelphia. Zollificker feared the consequences that might follow if the convention succeeded, and "deep injury" if it failed. The recent riots indicated a fundamental lack of respect for Black uplift, let alone a convention designed to project the respectability of African Americans across the nation.[42]

African Americans viewed these local-as-national conventions as vital to political activism. Grice met with Bishop Richard Allen at Mother Bethel AME Church on September 20, 1830; soon thereafter more representatives from Pennsylvania, Maryland, and New York arrived in the city. The Pennsylvania representatives included some of Philadelphia's most prominent Black businessmen, sans James Forten, which suggested his reluctance to engage in "community politics" that augured radical possibilities or threats to his person or property. While not identified as the first "official" Black convention, this group crafted an "Address to the Free People of Colour of these United States," which lambasted conditions that restricted social advancement, especially in cities like Philadelphia. It asserted that "our forlorn and deplorable situation earnestly and loudly demand of us to devise and pursue all legal means for the speedy elevation of ourselves and brethren to the scale and standing of men." These means included dignifying African American labor, with attendees urging Blacks across the country to embrace "agricultural and mechanical arts." When it came time to select officers, the Philadelphia representatives dominated the leadership positions and in so doing linked their freedom struggles in Philadelphia to African American struggles across the nation.[43]

The First Annual Convention of Black abolitionists met from June 6 to 11, 1831, at the Wesleyan Church on Lombard Street in Philadelphia. Attendees spoke out against the "many oppressive, unjust, and unconstitutional laws" that abridged the rights of free people of color. The main address did not identify the 1793 Fugitive Slave Act or the 1826 liberty law, but these laws may have weighed on the minds of many representatives as much as they did their less resourceful Black constituents outside the convention. The address encouraged African Americans to seek skilled professions that would serve the dual purpose of ennobling their status as citizens of their "native land" as well as attacking racist whites who viewed "accidental diversities of colour" as an excuse to exploit free Blacks. Finally, the convention also hosted a number of important white abolitionists, including Arthur Tappan, Benjamin Lundy, William Lloyd Garrison, and Thomas Shipley. One hesitates to assert how many of the Black organizers' goals mirrored those of white abolitionists, whose "gaze" may have influenced the moderate courses of action espoused by the organizers. More importantly, this amicable convention integrated abolition under the auspices of the African American organizers. Black freedom in Pennsylvania required a concerted multiracial effort.[44]

"Sleeping on gunpowder": Turner's Rebellion in Philadelphia

In August 1831, news arrived in Philadelphia of Nat Turner's rebellion. This bloodletting in Southampton, Virginia, represented the inevitable consequences of enslavement across time and space. Turner's group wreaked havoc across southeastern Virginia, killing any white person they could find. Although Turner ultimately failed in his plans to capture rifles and arm his allies, he eluded authorities for several months. By the end of August 1831, Turner's group scattered after skirmishing with a posse; the final death toll consisted of nearly sixty whites and an estimated 200 African Americans, who faced deadly reprisals for direct or presumed association with Turner.[45]

Rumors of Turner's whereabouts circulated around Philadelphia as many residents assumed that their city, buttressed by a powerful Black community and dedicated abolitionists, would be the rebels' obvious destination. The fears of some white Philadelphians may have derived from projecting upon themselves the senseless violence they inflicted upon African Americans. Whites in South Philadelphia took no chances and attacked a group of Black Methodists returning from a meeting in Wilmington, Delaware, in the week following the insurrection; one African American was killed during the fracas. These Blacks were attacked, beaten, and even murdered due to guilt by phenotypical association. The *Philadelphia Inquirer* published extracts from the *Baltimore Chronicle* that heightened fearmongering in Philadelphia: "insurrectionary movements among the people of colour should cause precautionary measures to be adopted *everywhere.*" Like the interstate diplomats from Maryland in 1826, a slave state resident tried to force the hand of Northerners to restrict African American freedom.[46]

William Lloyd Garrison's newspaper, *The Liberator,* founded the same year as the Turner revolt, responded to these attacks by stoking controversy, and labeled the recent violence enacted upon white slaveholders as a kind of declaration of Black independence. Like his Black counterparts, Garrison assumed human freedom and equality and argued that whites must bear the costs of depriving liberty from those born "both *free* and *equal.*" Philadelphia newspapers at first reported on the *Liberator* in a balanced manner. The *Philadelphia Inquirer* framed Garrison as "a gentleman somewhat noted for excessive zeal as a philanthropist, but a man of unquestionable talents." After Turner's revolt, however, the paper performed an about-face and claimed that the *Liberator* prayed for an emancipation premised "on the extermination and murder of whites." The writer suggested that the mayor of Boston research whether he could suspend Garrison's paper. Like many Southerners, the *Philadelphia Inquirer* hoped to gag voices that might deprive an imagined community of American slaveholders' loyal subjects: Northern whites who pursued, arrested, or rioted acted as racist shock troops. These same "plain Republicans" of Philadelphia who attacked African Americans reified Martin Van Buren's political vision of the Second Party system: "festive and obscene" street spectacles projected a nationalism based upon the legitimacy of inflicting violence upon Blacks across the United States. Garrison and his Black and white allies who attempted to undermine slavery were affronts to this nationalism.[47]

The power of race and rumor linked Philadelphia's African American community to Turner. A Philadelphia correspondent named "Sidney," wrote to the *Liberator* complaining that Virginia expelled many Blacks from the state who had nothing to do with Turner, and doubted that these refugees could rely on Northerners receiving them with open arms. "I grieve to say it," Sidney lamented, "that the northern people, though not openly abettors of slavery, are in their hearts as warm in the cause as the most violent slaveholder." Furthermore, Sidney admitted that while Northern whites detested oppression, they understood freedom as the purview of "whites only." Like human beings in pursuit of their own freedom or criminals in pursuit of new victims, racist perceptions defied borders.[48]

Preexisting racist ideas and Turner's rebellion motivated a large group of white Philadelphians to meet at John Upton's Hotel on Dock Street in November 1831. Upton hosted numerous gatherings of journeymen and pressmen; the former participated in rioting against African Americans, the latter operated newspapers like the Democratic-backed *Pennsylvanian* as well as meetings of the American Colonization Society. Clearly Upton possessed influence in Philadelphia, as his hotel served as a site where whites could galvanize anti-Black conspiracies. Attendees resolved to deal with "base and brutalizing" African Americans in Philadelphia. They claimed that free Blacks in the Northern and Southern states sent or received incendiary publications across borders that inspired Turner's "insurrectionary spirit." In order to protect Pennsylvania and preserve the "moral principle, religion, of our very union"—comity—participants agreed that all African Americans within the United States must be removed. In the words of the historian Andrew K. Diemer, this colonizationist screed emphasized "the national threat posed by Black Philadelphians." Willing to expel on the slightest of racist pretexts, influential whites like Upton worked with attendees to christen African Americans, especially those of Philadelphia, as existential threats to their freedom and their sense of comity.[49]

Philadelphians at the Dock Street meeting identified the presence of abolitionists and the supposed arrival of Southern Blacks in the city as disruptive to the Union. Fanatics like Garrison, they argued, "alienate[d] [Southerners'] affections from their countrymen of the north." The group chastised the "anti-national" laws passed in some Southern states to expel African Americans and force them north, "hence subjecting us to the demoralizing influence" of Black emigrants on Northern whites. This local-as-national anti-Black sentiment fueled attendees' vision of a non-Black America. In a bold paean to the African American community, the *Liberator* doubted that Philadelphia whites "could have resisted the pressure which has rested up on the Blacks, and shown one half the number of persons rising superior to adverse circumstances, and conquering the difficulties which prejudice and tyranny have thrown in their way." When it came to the American dream of overcoming one's circumstances, African Americans seemed more American than white Americans.[50]

Those at Upton's meeting perceived African American emigrants as "burning with hatred and revenge, and . . . may, in the event of war, be employed against us in the field." That the group would assign blame for the current crises—Turner's revolt and Black emigration—to abolitionism, African Americans living in the North, and Southerners' expulsive efforts made for strange bedfellows. The fact was that attendees addressed national anti-Black concerns in such a way as to shove the spotlight toward Philadelphia. African Americans' successful movement in, around, or to Philadelphia not only destabilized the city but, according to Upton's attendees, acted as a microcosm for the duties of comity and therefore reified the subversive effects of Blacks living in the Union.[51]

Debating Black Emigration

Given Pennsylvania's geographical position as a state that bordered three slave states, African Americans crossed its southern border with ease. Pennsylvania politicians considered exclusionary measures toward potential Black emigrants from the South in the wake of Turner's revolt. Here Pennsylvania followed the trend of Ohio, Indiana, and Illinois, all states that had, at their time of admission into the Union, either explicitly banned Black emigration or required Blacks to forfeit an exorbitant bond proving their independence. In late 1831 Philadelphia Democrats presented memorials requesting that Pennsylvania representatives in the national Congress support removing African Americans from the country. Philadelphia County Democratic state representative Franklin Vansant speculated that perhaps as many as 123,000 Blacks might flee north in the wake of Southampton. To Vansant, these "ignorant, indolent, and depraved" African Americans represented dangers to the "peace, rights, and liberties of the citizens" of Pennsylvania. He and other lawmakers presented House Bill 446 to the Pennsylvania state legislature on January 9, 1832, a draconian measure to impede African American movement into or around Pennsylvania. The bill required Black emigrants to post a $500 bond and Black Pennsylvanians to register in their local counties as proof of their freedom. Another addendum to the bill proposed to assign a committee to investigate repealing the 1820 and 1826 Pennsylvania liberty laws and to give "full effect" to the 1793 Fugitive Slave Act.[52]

Philadelphia's African American community did not sit idly by, and in January 1832 it held "a numerous meeting of the people of color." African American leaders James Forten, William Whipper, and Forten's son-in-law Robert Purvis crafted a memorial to the state legislature that discussed the emigration proposals and the repealing of the state's liberty laws. Pennsylvania's attempts to extinguish slavery within its borders and the lack of any "instance of insurrection" by Black Pennsylvanians made memorialists wonder why the state now wanted to devise "iron borders" to exclude a "banished race of freeman" from the South. The group credited this shift to white Pennsylvanians' unfounded claims that African Americans in Pennsylvania encouraged Turner's rebellion. This accusation was false, explained the memorialists, for as citizens of Pennsylvania they shared mutual ancestors with the very same politicians who moved to limit their mobility and evict them from the state. Furthermore, the memorialists added that they viewed the legislature as a "guardian and a protector" of a goal shared by all Pennsylvanians, Black or white: to ensure law and order for "the promotion of the common weal." The "common weal" depended upon uplifting Blacks, and so the memorialists included an addendum that provided evidence of their uplifted condition, citing property ownership, beneficial societies, and the marginal number of African Americans in Philadelphia almshouses. While these strategies may have convinced some white politicians of the benign existence of African Americans in Pennsylvania, many of their constituents did not agree with this framing and viewed the mere presence of African Americans as an insult to white racial pride.[53]

The memorialists criticized the legislature for debating any modification to Pennsylvania's 1820 and 1826 liberty laws, both of which represented their work as street diplomats. Eliminating either law represented "far too great a concession for the spirit of slavery." Pennsylvania moved past those "flagrant" injustices in recent years, and the matter should rest solely with Pennsylvania judges. Moreover, judges already had the difficult choice as freemen to condemn African Americans to permanent servitude. The memorialists boldly

suggested that Pennsylvania should place itself in the vanguard of states willing to give jury trials for fugitives from slavery. However, the writers of the
memorial ended on a conciliatory note that spoke to the power of African
American Philadelphians to uphold comity. Instead of revoking slaveholders'
rights to enslave, the memorialists made it clear that they did not wish "to interfere with those rights of property which are claimed by our fellow citizens
of other states." By ending the memorial in this ironic fashion, Philadelphia
African Americans placed themselves not only on the same level of citizenship
as white Pennsylvanians but also deemed themselves equal citizens willing to
maintain comity with Southern slaveholders.[54]

This memorial caught the notice of white Philadelphians who still linked
Turner to African Americans living in the city. "A Pennsylvanian" wrote to
the *Philadelphia Inquirer* and warned readers that they had witnessed the "for-
wardness and upheadedness" of ordinary Philadelphia Blacks who tried to
defend a small group of African Americans recently arrived from Virginia,
possibly from the Southampton area. The "horror" of African Americans defending themselves stunned this writer, who feared that the city was "sleep-
ing on gunpowder." Stoking these fears, the writer added that a recent Black
émigré who worked as a carpenter in Southampton assured him that at least
500 other Blacks followed him to Philadelphia. "A Pennsylvanian" asked
readers if they would "continue to fold our arms and cry a little more sleep
and a little more slumber, until we are aroused up by our newcomers from
Southampton?"[55]

African Americans and their allies quickly responded to the "gunpowder"
accusations. The *Liberator* quoted a rebuke from another Philadelphia newspaper, the *United States Gazette:* maybe a dozen and not 500 Southampton
Blacks immigrated to Philadelphia. The paper instructed readers to ponder
the reality of the situation: "how much less, then, will [African American
émigrés] attempt anything of the kind *here* [in Philadelphia], surrounded by
whites?" Acknowledging how whites attacked African Americans at random
bolstered the fact that whites enjoyed a near monopoly of violence when it
came to forcibly removing African Americans from Philadelphia. The *National Gazette*, another Philadelphia newspaper, echoed the *United States Gazette* and cited the *Richmond Whig*, with the latter paper stating that "*A Pennsylvanian's*" account was not an "honest mistake . . . [but] a *mistake*" and a
purposeful one at that. But the damage was done, for injecting the notion
of Black Philadelphians rising up a la Turner fed the violent imaginations of
some whites in the city. Thus, from Northern and Southern papers alike, the

thought that free Blacks might follow suit and rebel in the North remained unfounded, despite the subtle hint that these African Americans might have good reason to terrorize Northern whites.[56]

Legislators in Harrisburg continued to debate House Bill 446 throughout early 1832. This bill contained four sections designed by lawmakers to limit African American movement into and around Pennsylvania. The first section stated that any Blacks entering the state must post a $500 bond within twenty days of their arrival. The second section stipulated that if they failed to post the money in the allotted time, constables like Alberti, Weisener, or Kennedy could use their own means or "information of any other person" to arrest the offender for vagrancy and bring them to a state official. This stipulation would open the floodgates for kidnappers and slave catchers, a not so subtle way of assisting the slave states and slavery. According to section three, African Americans who could pay the bond received a notarized certificate from the court. However, any person who harbored or hid a Black migrant without reporting them to the court faced a fine of $50, with half going to the informant and the other half to the overseers of the poor. Finally, the fourth section required "all negro and mulatto persons" to register with their local ward or township. This census would list the names and "complexions" of Black residents and acted as a means to track African Americans as they moved around the state. In practice, the bill would strengthen the proslavery provisions of the 1826 liberty law as well as the federal Fugitive Slave Act of 1793. Most importantly, the bill encouraged Pennsylvanians to believe that African Americans did not belong in the state, and it epitomized the limits of African American freedom in Pennsylvania, a freedom questioned rather than assumed, circumscribed rather than exercised, and burdensome rather than emancipatory.[57]

Pronouncing their freedom more "precarious" than in any other period since the Declaration of Independence, Black leaders lambasted legislative efforts by Pennsylvania lawmakers to freeze "the streams of humanity" coming into the state. At the Second Annual Convention of the People of Color held in Philadelphia's Benezet Hall June 4–13, 1832, these leaders linked House Bill 446 to the recent anti-Black outcry raised by Turner. As the historian Christopher Bonner wrote, the middle class and elite African Americans who attended this and similar meetings understood the perilous balance of proving themselves "valuable members in their communities" without encouraging white backlash, including violence. These "valuable members" may have earned nods of agreement from their allies, though at the same time, proslavery zealots literally believed all Black lives were valuable because they could be converted into commodities and money. According to these leaders, African Americans would endure if they heeded the dictums of the closing address, which encouraged them to "personal and moral elevation by *moral suasion alone.*" Such suasion did little to fend off proslavery forces prowling Philadelphia. Despite the best efforts of Pennsylvanian legislators to close the border between slavery and freedom, African American activists, fugitives from slavery, and emigrants continued to poke holes in the already porous border and made every effort to resist (re)enslavement on Pennsylvania soil, "the home of the Black man."[58]

In early 1833, Black Philadelphians assembled a "large and respectable" meeting to draft a memorial to the state legislature in which they asserted that their rights as US citizens and African Americans were one and the same. As African American citizens they had rights to "free ingress and regress" as stipulated by Article IV, Section 2 of the Constitution, the text of which read "that the citizens of each State shall be entitled to all privileges and immunities of citizens in the several States." The memorial defined comity through examples of citizens moving between Northern states, though not the open secret of human beings between Southern slave states and Northern "free" states. The movement of African Americans to, through, and around Philadelphia served as the model of mobility across the Union, a model that states ought to recognize as their duty to uphold. Philadelphia Blacks equated this comity as a form of protection and security in Pennsylvania, especially when their freedom was hazarded by the bill's gloomy underbelly, which linked emigration debates to registering free Blacks and eliminating Pennsylvania's liberty laws. Registering free Blacks equated to legislating on racial differences, the memorialists argued, and placed them in an "intermediate state of social being," a liminal space between citizens and noncitizens. In the case of defining African Americans as noncitizens, the memorial suggested querying their political enemies to find one example in which the Constitution declared them as such. African Americans were neither Northern nor Southern: they were American.[59]

The most dangerous and demeaning feature of the house bill consisted of the sections that at first circumvented and then outright nullified the major success of street diplomacy: the 1826 liberty law. First, the bill encouraged constables to arrest any African American "without previous oath." This measure made all Blacks susceptible to legal removal, if not continual harassment from law enforcement. Fears of deportation weighed on the minds of the me-

morialists, given the variety of means employed by constables to remove supposed fugitives from slavery from Philadelphia. Secondly, the bill suggested
voiding the 1826 law by depriving any African American a right to trial, a
right guaranteed to "vagrants." Here the memorialists acknowledged the rationale of white racism. Many African Americans "who have struggled long
and anxiously with public prejudice" now faced Northern whites rejuvenated
by the assumption that any Black—rich, poor, middling, or otherwise—was
a fugitive from slavery or unregistered person of color subject to removal by
a Northern anti-Black law of more immediate consequence than the federal
Fugitive Slave Act or the 1826 law, the latter of which at least complicated legal
removals by slaveholders from the South.[60]

Ultimately, House Bill 446 died in committee. While the content of the
conversation pertaining to the bill in its waning days remains unclear, state
senator Samuel Breck seemed best positioned to speak for Philadelphia's African American community. In 1822 none other than James Forten stopped
Breck on the streets of Philadelphia to tell him that Breck owed him a "debt."
This debt, as Breck found out, consisted of Forten taking fifteen white men
to vote for Breck in the recent congressional election. Breck shook Forten's
hand, a street diplomatic action that cemented Breck's friendship with Black
Philadelphians. A National Republican from Philadelphia, Breck headed a
committee formed to determine whether "the land of Penn" and "distinguished philanthropy" faced an upsurge of Black emigrants. Breck's motives
for forming this committee may have stemmed from the Pennsylvania National Republican Party's unease with and suspicion of Southern influence
within the Jackson administration as well as the president's war on the Second Bank of the United States, the latter issue key to the economic lifeblood
of Philadelphia and Pennsylvania. In what amounted to a miscount of freed
people, Breck and his committee explained that the current Black:white ratio
of forty to one in the eastern half of the state meant that monitoring Pennsylvania Blacks or restricting Blacks from entering the state—both provisions of
the House Bill 446—represented a deluded notion.[61]

Shutting out Blacks from "philanthropic" Pennsylvania, argued Breck, dis-
couraged slaveholders from bringing them to the state to free them. Closing
borders made "every citizen within our borders" assume responsibility for
the blood of perpetual slavery. In effect, Breck buttressed the points made by
African American memorialists in the previous month: freedom of movement between and within Pennsylvania permitted slaveholders and enslaved
people to cross the so-called border from slavery to freedom. In a paradoxical

twist, the same pressures faced by Pennsylvanians to assist slaveholders in returning fugitives from slavery also required Pennsylvanians to search their "philanthropic" roots and allow slaveholders to enter into the state to free enslaved African Americans. On top of these intertwined tensions lay House Bill 446, a bill designed to register, surveil, and expel Blacks from the state. Although the memorialists and Breck's committee reinforced each other and succeeded in fending off House Bill 446, the ambitious scope of the bill inspired a wave of anti-Black sentiment and represented a decline in support for Philadelphia's African American community.[62]

Conclusion

African Americans living in Philadelphia experienced a fugitive freedom in the wake of the 1826 liberty law. Their lives were "fugitive" in the sense that their "freedom" could be questioned at any time for what seemed like any reason. Questioning an African American's freedom at the local level immediately escalated into state and national concerns over slavery. Preserving freedom or ensuring enslavement meant confronting the law, which writ large meant honoring the compact of the Union and thus comity. However, Black and white street diplomats in Philadelphia questioned exactly which laws they were to follow: the laws of Pennsylvania, the laws of slave states, or the 1793 Fugitive Slave Act. Each choice threatened comity. Abiding by Pennsylvania law might alienate the slave states; abiding by slave state law might alienate Pennsylvanians; abiding by the 1793 Fugitive Slave Act alienated stolen African Americans. In answering that question, then, street diplomats employed a number of strategies, including working with local, state, and national politicians. When diplomatic efforts failed, Black and white Philadelphians did not eschew violence. The catalyst for all of these actions stemmed from individual African Americans who sought to live or already lived free in Pennsylvania.

The comity realized by Northern and Southern in the case of the 1826 kidnapping crisis might lead one to conclude that this blatant disregard for all law, state or national, rendered a favorable outcome for the victims and thus, the Union. Yet it seemed that slave state citizens, especially elected officials like Maryland governors Stevens and Kent, did not provide a linear path to freedom: witness the case of Emory Sadler. Scanning the cases with a microscope, one finds a constant undercurrent of anti-Black thought and action in Philadelphia, too, whether in the form of kidnappers and constables–cum–slave catchers, African American informants–cum–oyster shop owners, and

zealous proslavery and pro-Southern lawyers and politicians. Comity became further disrupted when Pennsylvanians debated Black movement into
and around the state. The fear that Turner's followers would embed themselves
in places like Philadelphia for the sole purpose of plotting to terrorize and kill
whites did nothing to help race relations in the city, state, or nation.

Rather than remain passive, African Americans and their allies in street
diplomacy redoubled their efforts at the national, state, and street level. Delegates to the American Convention, especially the Philadelphia cohort, emphasized the national implications of local kidnappings. Turner's revolt bridged
the gap between racist words and actions in Pennsylvania, Philadelphia in
particular. It showed how white Americans leapt at the chance to equate any
violence committed by African Americans anywhere justified violence against
them everywhere. At the state level, African Americans and their allies labored
profusely to confront white politicians and remind them not only of their
status as free(d) people but also their identities as free Pennsylvanians. The
emigration debates in the Pennsylvania state legislature spoke to the impos-
sibilities of both eliminating African American presence within the state and
walling off Pennsylvania's borders to African Americans, slave catchers, and
kidnappers alike.

Finally, the actions undertaken by African Americans and their white allies at the local level reiterated the improvisatory nature of street diplomacy.
Scomp's words and experiences, Sadler's skills and mobility, Black and white
leaders' interracial activism, ordinary African Americans who knew the law,
and John Allen's protecting society represented effective decisions made on
the street level to hamper kidnappings, resist enslavement, and in the best
cases, ensure freedom. Whether that freedom remained fugitive depended
on the work of Philadelphians who understood how the burden of the Union
rested firmly upon the backs of African Americans.

CHAPTER FOUR

Domestic Sanctuary

An elderly African American woman named Maria Congo hustled her daughters to the attic of their employer's residence on Sixth and Lombard Streets on a warm night in June 1835. At least ten African American men and women ruthlessly pursued them up the stairs and finally grabbed Congo when she found herself cornered. Seeking "vengeance," the group of Black men and women clung tightly to Congo as they debated what to do with her. Should they bring her to a local Philadelphia law enforcement official or magistrate? Should they contact their friends in the PAS to sort out Congo's fate? Or should they simply continue to beat Congo? Ultimately, they dragged Congo from the attic down to the street below. Such drastic considerations begged the question: why did this group of Black men and women attack Congo and her daughters that night?[1]

Some days earlier Maria Congo informed the Maryland slaveholder Robert Aitken that she saw a girl who looked quite similar to one who ran away from him a decade earlier. Implementing a slaveholder's view of comity, Aitken partnered with a Baltimore constable and Congo and tracked the girl to a Philadelphia bakeshop owned by the African American baker Jacob Gilmore. After dismissing the opinion of the Baltimore constable, who told Aitken that he did not recognize the supposed fugitive at all, Aitken continued with his view of comity, placed his trust in Congo, and arrested the girl, Mary Gilmore. The ten Black men and women who attacked Congo exacted a willful, desperate justice predicated on viewing any seizure of an African American as tantamount to a death sentence. The resulting trial over Mary Gilmore's freedom or potential (re)enslavement inspired the aforementioned group of ten African Americans to "riot" and assault Congo.[2]

This chapter explores two major race riots that broke out in Philadelphia in 1834 and 1835. Historians have proffered numerous reasons for the riots of the Jacksonian Era, including fighting over economic inequality, establishing boundaries of "hard" and "soft" racisms, shifting demographic patterns, and developing schisms between North and South. As the previous chapter showed, the 1829 riot on St. Mary Street and the 1830 rescue attempt outside of Franklin Institute Hall reflected white fears of Black achievement and the "flood" of African Americans crossing borders into Pennsylvania. When analyzed through the lenses of fugitives from slavery and would-be kidnapping victims, one finds white rioters justifying their activities due to the mere presence of African Americans in the city, a community whose "guilt" consisted of living and being socially mobile and politically active in Philadelphia. In many ways, too, these riots stemmed from the work of street diplomats, interracial abolitionists who purposefully complicated clear-cut distinctions between free Blacks and fugitives from slavery. Their diplomatic efforts connected local threats to freedom in Philadelphia to the national compact with slavery as well as linking the violent experiences of enslavement across borders. These street diplomats assumed that any seizure of an African American represented a kidnapping, plain and simple. In a word, street diplomacy threatened comity between states because it complicated retrieval attempts made by slaveholders and helped to spur the "Great Riot Year" of 1834–1835.[3]

The rise of immediate abolitionism in Philadelphia buttressed ongoing interracial activism and placed resentful white Philadelphians on notice. The 1834 "Flying Horses" riot began at an interracial meeting place, transformed into an armed struggle, and ended with thousands of African Americans evacuating their homes and fleeing to the countryside. The trial of Mary Gilmore, which occurred the next year and precipitated the riot against Maria Congo, put Philadelphians on edge, in that Gilmore herself complicated geographic, political, and racial borders. An 1835 riot featured a "deranged" African American man named Juan, who attacked his "master" in a fit of rage and thereby initiated both a major riot and an opportunity for some white Philadelphians to pledge their support for Southern slavery. Even though it appeared as though the mixed blessings of the 1826 liberty law had faded into the background, street diplomats who inspired the law continued to place African American freedom at the forefront of their concerns.

The Rise of Immediate Abolitionism in Philadelphia

By 1832, Black Philadelphians remained the strongest and most besieged of all Northern Black communities. Their successes were legion, and more importantly they showed no compunction explaining them to Pennsylvania state legislators in an 1832 memorial entitled "Conditions of Free Blacks in Pennsylvania." The memorialists refuted the "false and exaggerated accounts" of Black degradation in Philadelphia. Citing a report published by the guardians of the poor, the neglect of tax assessors to assess black property, the "labor and industry" that allowed Blacks to become "freeholders," and the increase of the schooling of Black children, the memorialists submitted these proofs to a "candid public" in the middle of the crises over Turner's rebellion and Black emigration. At no point in the memorial did the authors request that the state reconsider kidnapping legislation or the role of fugitives from justice— two realities they faced every day in Philadelphia. Did these memorialists forget the stakes of freedom and slavery? Not at all, as the willingness for African Americans to advocate for themselves, contact white lawmakers directly, appeal to ordinary whites, and work with white activists existed as a crucial subtext. This drive for an interracial abolitionism proved to be the most lasting success of the Black community, an ironic success that bore no mention in the "Conditions" memorial but, at the same time, undergirded the entire struggle for freedom on the streets of Philadelphia.[4]

The street diplomacy practiced by Black and white Philadelphians linked local struggles to a national drive for a continued interracial activism. In December 1833, sixty abolitionists from across the United States convened in Philadelphia to form a national organization premised upon the immediate emancipation of the enslaved and chaired by William Lloyd Garrison. Convention delegates drafted a "Declaration of Sentiments," an updated moral and race-conscious version of the original Declaration of Independence. Unlike the patriots of the American Revolution, who spilled blood while waging war against Great Britain, the sentiments promised "moral purity" in the face of morally corrupt "Man stealers" whose affronts to the laws of God made a mockery of a Divine will designed to provide and promote the same privileges to all human beings regardless of skin color. The convention asserted that human law and the law of the land—namely, the Constitution—both empowered slaveholders to launch raids into the free states and prevented Congress from emancipating the enslaved. The fettered landscape of the South bled easily into the free states, argued the abolitionists, and this national compact "must be broken" by their efforts.[5]

The Pennsylvanians who attended the convention represented a blend of abolitionists old and new, with old PAS stalwarts such as Thomas Shipley combining their efforts with passionate youngsters like Robert Purvis and James Miller McKim. Purvis was a mixed-race Philadelphian whose mother was a freedwoman and whose father was a wealthy English émigré to South Carolina. Light-skinned, well-educated, and married to James Forten's daughter Harriet, who also plied her skills as a poet and activist, Purvis embodied the perpetual beauty of a multiracial United States. Consequently, he embodied the potential to undermine ossifying racial dichotomies, which made him a target for white fury in the coming years. A white man, McKim lived in Carlisle, Pennsylvania, where as a youth he made inroads into the Black community by joining the local all-Black abolition society. He was the youngest delegate to the convention, and his role was limited, though what he observed there inspired him to serve as a "traveling agent" of immediate abolitionism for the next three decades. Such were the qualities of the men who gathered in Philadelphia in December 1834: persevering immediatists who viewed interracial cooperation as vital to ending slavery.[6]

Anti-abolitionist newspapers latched onto the abolitionists' controversial new strategies and demographics. The *Richmond Inquirer* claimed that the goal of the meeting was to raise a panic in the South, while the *Boston Courier* excoriated the participants for breeding "hatred" between the different sections of "our common country." Perhaps most damning for the abolitionist community in Philadelphia, the *Philadelphia Inquirer* called the convention a "conclave" of "visionary fanatics." That paper lamented that a sole police officer guarded the door to the Adelphi Saloon, where the convention first met late at night on December 3, and thus prevented a "body" of Pennsylvania citizens from delivering a "true expression of public opinion" to the abolitionists: an anti-abolitionist, anti-Black riot. The "wild and visionary schemes" of race mixing would undo the Union in practice as much as emancipation would in theory. Interracial abolitionism thrived in Philadelphia to the chagrin of those white Philadelphians who made it clear that these activists were neither safe nor welcome in the city.[7]

Four months after the convention, on April 18, 1834, Black and white abolitionists redoubled their efforts and founded the Philadelphia Anti-Slavery Society (PASS). Again, a who's who of abolitionist stalwarts served as managers for this local auxiliary to the American Anti-Slavery Society: President

David Paul Brown, a lawyer who had for decades worked pro bono for the PAS, Thomas Shipley, and Joseph Cassey, an African American entrepreneur who served as an agent for the *Liberator* and also owned extensive property and a notable hair salon in Philadelphia. While some historians labeled Cassey's appointment as manager "symbolic," Cassey, like other African American abolitionists, served an indispensable role as a purveyor of immediatism in Philadelphia by bringing more Blacks and their experiences to bear on the meeting. In the words of the preamble to the PASS Constitution, members pledged to peacefully abolish "the operation of a system which enters so largely into our domestic relations": Philadelphia's African Americans lived in a context in which their future hopes were often dashed by kidnappers and slavecatchers who invaded their city.[8]

These bold words and actions were not rarified fantasies of freedom's plight in Philadelphia. When the PASS reconvened at the College of Pharmacy in late April 1834, an incident involving a Virginia slaveholder, local constable, and African American boy occurred barely half a mile away at the state house, Independence Hall. The slaveholder claimed the boy as a fugitive from slavery and brought the case to Judge Archibald Randall of the Court of Common Pleas. Randall was no stranger to such cases, as the PAS recorded him presiding over at least a dozen similar trials. But was Randall prepared to address the crowd of at least 300 African Americans and their allies who crowded the court and spilled out into the street? Clearly, African Americans and their allies did not eschew shows of force, which to many white Philadelphians was a disconcerting affront to public order within Philadelphia and comity across the nation. Just as African Americans did not fear traveling to Harrisburg to pressure elected officials, their presence in the court room no doubt intimidated judges like Randall, local law enforcement officials, and racist whites.[9]

The African American boy brought before Judge Randall may have felt relief seeing a mixed-race crowd of approximately 300 abolitionists in attendance. While little is known of the testimony from Black and white witnesses, Randall quickly declared the boy to be "property" of the Virginian slaveholder. The African Americans in attendance reacted with "great excitement" to the ruling, forcing the officers who held the boy in custody to believe that a rescue was imminent. Constable Michael Donnehower handcuffed himself to the boy and declared that "if they carried off the slave, they should take him along with them." Sure enough, the crowd pounced on Donnehower and his fellow officers as they exited the courtroom. The officers pushed the boy into an awaiting carriage, one surrounded by "several hundred Blacks," who quickly cut the harnesses connecting the horses to the carriage. The officers fought off the rioters and arrested seven of them. Coincidentally, these rioters were tried by Judge Randall, who witnessed the entire scene from the safety of the second-floor window of the courthouse. True to form, the *Philadelphia Inquirer* lamented that while "we [Philadelphians] may regret the existence of slavery in this country, the laws must be enforced." Enforcing laws on their own terms through street diplomacy dictated that any "retrieval" effort represented a kidnapping attempt. Street diplomacy further engendered African American freedom by employing the resources of white abolitionists and thus promoting interracial activism. Both aspects of street diplomacy contributed to the outbreak of riots in Philadelphia in 1834 and 1835.[10]

The Flying Horses Riot, 1834

The Philadelphia riots of 1834–1835 were illustrative of anti-abolitionist and anti-Black backlash across the United States. As the historian Kellie Carter Jackson has noted, the 1830s in general were in fact the most violent decade in US history prior to the outbreak of the Civil War. One such riot erupted in New York in July 1834, when the abolitionists Arthur and Lewis Tappan worked with other activists in the city to launch their own immediatist campaign. Anti-abolitionist groups in New York sparked rumors that Tappan and his allies planned on promoting interracial marriage and rallied angry whites, mostly Irish immigrants, to defend New York against abolitionist "incendiarism." The *Journal of Commerce* wrote that the mob of young men launched their attacks on July 7, and it noted that the rioters "shamefully" beat Black men outside their places of employment. Meanwhile, another group used bricks and rocks to smash the windows of Black churches, a few of which were set ablaze during the four-day melee. By July 11, seven churches and more than a dozen homes, including Arthur Tappan's, had been heavily damaged or demolished by the mob. These bellwether events in New York ushered in the "great riot" year of 1834–1835, the effects of which infected cities and towns across the United States, not least of all Philadelphia.[11]

Philadelphia's uniqueness as the hub of interracial activism and the preeminent destination for African Americans made these riots different, both in scope and intensity. Whereas the historian David Grimsted has argued that Northern rioters destroyed property and Southern rioters attacked human beings, no clear "north-south" divide characterized the Philadelphia riots: rioters in Philadelphia destroyed property and lives. The scale of these riots makes one shudder in disbelief: entire blocks of Black Philadelphia were burnt down and hundreds, perhaps thousands, of African Americans fled the city. Furthermore, the omnipresent slaveholders, kidnappers, and constables found new allies in the waves of Irish immigrants arriving in the city. Seduced by the Democracy's race baiting and "whitening" through violence, many young, poor Irish men became willing accomplices to authorities who made a living hunting Black people.[12]

The hardening of racial categories overtaking the city and country begat many whites' assumptions of seeing African Americans solely as potential "fugitives" and therefore "dangerous." Again, the real "danger" came from the work of street diplomats who brought about effective change from the streets to the state legislature and beyond. In the eyes of some anti-Black zealots, these victories promoted "amalgamation." In addition, Philadelphians rioted in the past to prevent race mixing. In March 1828, for example, about 200 young and well-dressed African Americans held a "fancy ball" on Fourth Street. The *Pennsylvania Gazette* relished the fact that a group of "boys and idlers" felt offended by the ball and attacked the Black attendees and their white footmen attending to their carriages. With the racial hierarchy inverted, with "masters and servants" changing places, the mob wreaked havoc.[13]

Blacks and whites willing to work together to rescue anyone they saw being kidnapped blended with whites willing to view any Black as a "fugitive" in their own city and set the stage for the riots of 1834–1835. Stoking fears of African Americans, race mixing, and the violence they inspired in whites, the *Pennsylvania Enquirer* stated that "no public journalist in [Philadelphia] would, under existing circumstances, give place to a call for a meeting of abolitionists," even adding that force should be used to prevent any distribution of handbills calling for such an event. Yet interracial mingling took place every day in Philadelphia, as residential patterns prevented any semblance of racial or economic segregation, and while not defined as "abolitionist" meetings, certainly these events were interracial in scope.[14]

The "Flying Horses" carousel in Philadelphia epitomized the fears of such interracial mingling. With constituents Black and white, male and female, young and old, this location represented open "amalgamation." Little is known about the venue other than that it was a place of "low," "illegal," and therefore popular amusement owned by a white man. On August 8, 1834, a group of Blacks left the carousel to attack the nearby Fairmount Engine Company and steal a hose. As the historian Ric N. Caric has argued, the culture of fire companies in Philadelphia during this time period blended firefighting with gang violence, with any affront to the company's fire hose symbolizing an attack on the firemen's collective identity. The firemen from this company responded by encouraging fifty or sixty men to attack a symbol of African American collective identity and prosperity: James Forten's son Thomas. A white neighbor came to Forten's aid and noted that he overheard the attackers debate returning to the same location later. Philadelphia mayor John Swift arrested some of the men who rendezvoused near the Forten home in the hopes of ambushing the family. During the afternoon of the 11th, another group of men and boys hurled racial insults at Flying Horses' customers, calling them "Yorkers," that is, amalgamationists like Tappan. Making matters worse, several Philadelphia newspapers alluded to several "respectable" women engaged in interracial hobnobbing at the Flying Horses.[15]

Amalgamation rumors and Mayor Swift's sympathy toward the Fortens inspired hundreds of young men to descend upon the Flying Horses on August 12 with one purpose: destruction. Armed with clubs and paving stones, this "detachment of boys and very young men" demolished the Flying Horses. This group acquired bricks from the rubble and began vandalizing Black-owned homes on South Street, spreading violence down Bedford and Mary Streets and into Moyamensing. According to the *Pennsylvanian,* the city and county police mustered the courage to try and overtake the mob and arrest the ringleaders a few hours later, around 9 p.m. Unfortunately, the chaos mounted and the crowd 500 strong began chanting "down with the police!"[16]

Numbering about forty officers in a city of 80,000, Philadelphia's police force—i.e., the sheriff, police, constabulary, and night watch—was ill equipped to handle the rioters. Officers including the likes of Michael Donnehower entered the fray and suffered grievous injuries. These constables wrested John Cox's "Diving Bell" from the grip of the rioters, a location supposedly regarded as the "veriest brothel in the country," and another site of race mixing, but the riot did not end there. Panicked, Alderman Robert L. Loughead swore in special constables, who rushed the mob and apprehended eighteen culprits. City authorities arrested at least another forty Irish men. As the historian John Runcie has pointed out, further research into the Prisoners for Trial docket revealed many of them were poor working-class apprentices and repeat offenders for charges such as "disturbing the peace, assault and battery, drunkenness, and larceny." Alderman Loughead detained the rioters and fended off assaults on his office "with a pistol in each hand." By 11 p.m., the joint efforts of the Moyamensing and Southwark police forces had restored order to the vicinity.[17]

Despite these protective measures, rumors arose the next day that the riots would resume. Dissatisfied with attacking interracial hotspots, the rioters targeted African American households that symbolized Black social mobility. Mayor Swift ordered the city police to stand guard at the border between Philadelphia City and Philadelphia County, the latter outskirts more rural than urban, where most of the rioters lived. Swift and his men "tarried in the neighborhood" until 11 p.m., at which point they decided to return home. What the police and mayor did not know, however, was that several rioters from the previous day had warned white residents along South Street to place candles in their windows that night to spare themselves the fury of the mob. No one warned the African American community, and so when the riots recommenced after the police and mayor retired, they suffered the reinvigorated fury of the rioters.[18]

The attacks on Black homes began on Seventh Street between Shippen and Fitzwater Streets, where "windows and doors were dashed to pieces, the furniture demolished, and the inhabitants dragged from their beds and dreadfully beaten." The rioters then made their way to Baker Street, destroying at least twenty houses in their wake. The next target was the First African Presbyterian Church, a place of worship founded by Reverend Archibald Alexander and the freedman John Gloucester, father of the street diplomat Stephen Gloucester. This church symbolized civic pride and community longevity, and it boasted a number of wealthy African American congregants. No doubt this fact resonated in the minds of rioters, who scorned any pretense of Black achievement.[19]

While Mayor Swift and the police returned and quelled the riots by 2 a.m., the second day of riots devastated the African American community. The *Pennsylvanian*, the leading Democratic organ of the city, avoided sympathizing with the African American victims and reported that most of the property destroyed to "vent the animosity to the negroes" belonged to their white landlords. "The negroes owned nothing except a little furniture," added the *Pennsylvanian*, suggesting that the source of the riot lay in African Americans frequenting the Flying Horses carousel. The "little property" owned by the victims revealed the precarious right to property enjoyed by Black Philadelphians. Among other examples, Daniel Williamson, a 95-year-old African American and one-time "servant of General Washington," lived at Baker's Court; rioters laid waste to his property: "not even a chair or glass" remained intact. The extent of property damage ensured that these Black Philadelphians would not advance in society.[20]

Those who observed the riot's epicenter would have agreed with the *Pennsylvanian*'s comment that the aftermath represented "only part of the whole mischief perpetrated." Edward Strutt Abdy, an English lawyer who visited Philadelphia a few weeks after the riots spoke with many Black victims, including James Forten. Although Forten's son faced the initial wrath of the rioters, Philadelphia police officers defended his property and family from further assaults. Other Philadelphians interviewed by Abdy were not so lucky. One elderly Black woman hid in her closet while men in masks ransacked her home. This woman recognized the voice of one of the men and complained to Mayor Swift. The accused party appeared before Swift's court, though when the proceedings began a "well-dressed man" whispered in the mayor's ear. Swift then ordered all of the African Americans present to leave the courtroom. This maneuver served the dual purpose of preventing Black voices from being taken as evidence and the presence of Black Americans from threatening a riot. Influential whispers equated to evidence, and Swift dropped the charges against the rioter. Abdy queried Swift about this anecdote, who responded matter of factly, "You have not seen one-tenth of the horrors that are constantly practiced here." Perhaps Swift's admission weighed on his conscience during the riots, for he sheltered about a dozen African Americans in his house until the terror died down.[21]

Pennsylvania political leaders steeled themselves to prevent the violence from resuming on August 14. President Judge of the Court of Common Pleas Edward King and State attorney general George Mifflin Dallas ordered Philadelphia sheriff Benjamin Duncan to summon a posse comitatus and restore order to south Philadelphia. This posse represented order, stability, and in a way, the Union itself, as this body was charged with protecting Philadelphians' lives and property. Duncan entrusted the posse to Peter Arrell Browne, a Philadelphia lawyer who in the past worked on a few cases for the PAS. In addition, Duncan issued a curfew, called out a troop of cavalry stationed in the city, and assembled the entire police force. The posse gathered at Pennsylvania Hospital by midday, while the military stationed itself at Independence Hall. This force numbered anywhere from 200 to 5,000 armed men. Although the crowds around South Street grew larger than the previous two days, the posse contained them. This show of force protected Black Philadelphians as well as the property of white landlords. Black property enjoyed no such protection: that night a group of whites burnt down a Black place of worship near Wharton's market. By the time the posse arrived on the scene, a smoldering pile of rubble remained of what the PAS identified as a "fine" meetinghouse in Southwark.[22]

This third day of rioting on August 14 perpetuated the chaos in Philadelphia. First, even though white authorities mustered a posse, their efforts could not prevent the destruction of Black property. Second, a massive crowd lingered around Black Philadelphia to hunt African Americans and surveil the area for any sign of Black resistance. Finally, the lack of a Black presence on this third day remained striking, as newspaper reports stated that "the negroes of the devoted section have nearly all abandoned their dwellings." Hundreds, perhaps thousands, of African Americans fled Philadelphia between the 12th and 14th, choosing to "bivouac" in the fields outside the city; others crossed the Delaware River to take refuge in Camden, New Jersey. Violence, fear, and a survival instinct drove many in Philadelphia's African American community to take this unprecedented step and abandon the city en masse.[23]

Not all African Americans left Philadelphia. Late on August 14 a group of African Americans from the "Incorporated Colored Benezet Society" asked Mayor Swift for his protection. Swift informed them that they had the right to protect "themselves and their property." African Americans made use of Swift's political position as mayor as a means to both nullify the extralegal power of the rioters and wage a defensive war against white Philadelphians. This group and about sixty others returned to Seventh and South Streets and fortified Benezet Hall from "cellar to garret." Rioters gathered outside this building after hearing rumors of African Americans arming themselves, which was true to a point: at best they possessed "swords, sword canes, and clubs." The crowd growing rowdier, a few African Americans "made a sally" outside the hall and dispersed the mob. Thomas Shipley witnessed this scene, and fearing the worst, quickly caught up to his Black allies and convinced them to return to the hall. The crowds soon resurfaced, pelting the building with rocks and making it well known to civil authorities that they intended to shed blood that night.[24]

Rioters, civil authorities, and African Americans amassed together set the stage for a showdown at Benezet Hall. As the crowed continued to grow, Mayor Swift brought the police to the area. He dispatched one of the heroes of the 1826 kidnapping crisis, high constable Samuel Garrigues, to negotiate with the besieged. The African Americans who dispersed the rioters now clamored for another charge into the larger crowd, composed of young men, mostly Irish laborers. The sources conflict as to who dissuaded the African Americans from taking the offensive. The PAS and Abdy alluded to Thomas Shipley as the arbitrator, the official report on the riot commended Garrigues, and contemporary historians credited Mayor Swift with assuaging the group in Benezet Hall. In reality, the sixty armed African Americans within the hall, who were no doubt prepared to fight and even die for their freedom, took matters into their own hands and stood down from the fracas. In a word, they concluded the struggle on the street by acting diplomatically. In the end, police guarded the hall while these courageous African Americans shepherded themselves out the backdoor of the building, fugitive in their own city, yet free.[25]

Civic leaders held a town meeting a month later to discuss the Flying Horses riot. The assigned committee included politicians, members of law enforcement, and abolitionists like James Mott. The committee identified two major causes for the riot. Historians have paid attention to the first cause, "white right to employment." The young Democratic men of Philadelphia often clashed with their Whig employers over hiring African Americans. The committee argued that white unemployment encouraged poverty and hatred toward Black Philadelphians, though it refused to legislate on hiring practices so as not to disrupt relationships between white employers and white employees. Instead, it suggested that African American victims display "a respectful and orderly deportment" to prevent further mob activity. Acknowledging the burden of comity that came with street diplomacy, the committee noted that "the peace and welfare, not only of [Philadelphia], but of the whole United States," depended on African Americans behaving themselves in the face of oppression.[26]

The committee identified a second cause of the riot: the open secret of fugitives from slavery and their white and Black allies within the city. "When any of their members are arrested as fugitives from justice," explained the report, Philadelphia's African American community "forcibly attempted the rescue of [the] prisoners." True, African Americans involved in rescue attempts epitomized the bonds between local, state, and national compromises over freedom and slavery; these bonds became frayed whenever African Americans or their allies practiced street diplomacy. To the committee members, helping fugitives from slavery promoted lawlessness, aroused the "unfriendly feelings" of whites, and ensured riots in the city. Nonetheless, the committee pledged to collect money for the victims, though according to Abdy, many whites agreed to donate so as long as the funds went toward removing African Americans from Philadelphia. This solution encouraged those white politicians who in recent years hoped to restrict Black emigration in general.[27]

This lack of empathy for Black Philadelphians persisted in the months following the riot. Thomas Shipley complained in November that nobody informed the PAS of cases involving fugitives from slavery that transpired in the city. He recommended distributing circulars to Philadelphia judges requesting that the PAS receive six hours' notice for all such cases. Judicial indifference robbed the accused and their allies of the time needed to construct a defense and in doing so, deprived African Americans their freedom. Regardless of the judges' intentions, all parties understood how time equated to potential freedom and, when pressed, African Americans believed that they possessed a right to riot, rescue, and defend themselves. Now more than ever African Americans and their white allies needed to work together to uncover "fugitive" cases and kidnapping incidents.[28]

African American leaders praised the patience of Black Philadelphians at the Fifth Annual Colored Convention held in Philadelphia in June 1835. Such patience represented a "most successful refutation of the pro-slavery arguments" propagated by slaveholders. The attendees resolved that human rights trumped property rights in human beings and called upon Black Americans to "peaceably bear the punishment" of breaking the law. Attendees declared that they "cheerfully enter[ed] on this moral warfare in defence of *liberty*, *justice*, and *humanity*." Much like the fugitives from slavery, slaveholders, and kidnappers who crossed borders with ease, the delegates pledged themselves to a revolutionary freedom that transcended geography.[29]

"Malicious spite" for those "not entirely white": The Mary Gilmore Case

Race mixing, abolitionism, and fugitives from slavery wove together in the person of Mary Gilmore, a white woman accused of being a "fugitive" from slavery in 1835. This case highlighted how white skin did not equate to freedom but given the proper circumstances, could guarantee slavery. Describing a person as "yellow," "mulatto," "brown," or "Black" often acted as proof of one's assumed fugitive or enslaved status, and as such, the charges brought against Mary Gilmore put "white slavery" on trial. This case constructed race in real time and enabled her to pass as both white and Black. While her case may seem atypical, it began like any other: a slaveholder claimed her as their property. The resulting trial required implementing street diplomacy through interracial cooperation and placed the burden of the Union on the back of a supposed fugitive from slavery.

Maryland slaveholder Robert Aitken arrived in Philadelphia on June 12, 1835, accompanied by Baltimore constable William Swift and an elderly African American woman named Maria Congo. Congo informed Aitken that earlier in the year she saw an enslaved girl who ran away from him some years past in a bakeshop located at Sixth and Spruce Streets. Aitken believed that the fugitive from slavery was Emily Winder, the daughter of a mixed-race woman named Amelia (nicknamed "Milly"), whom he had freed a decade earlier. When Emily disappeared after Aitken emancipated her mother, he suspected that Milly Winder smuggled the girl to Baltimore. Congo insisted that the child grew up in Philadelphia and changed her name. Mary lived with Jacob Gilmore, a wealthy African American man who owned the Sixth Street bakery. Aitken told constable Swift to accompany Congo to Gilmore's bakery. When Swift peered through the shop window, he found that he did not recognize Mary as Emily. Aitken dismissed Swift's opinion and had Mary arrested the next day.[30]

Although the seizing of Mary Gilmore seemed "ordinary," according to the *Philadelphia Inquirer* it possessed an "unprecedented circumstance, of the complexion of the Respondent being to all appearances *entirely white*." Notable here in the newspaper's account was the use of the adverb "entirely." It is unclear whether the writer qualified Mary Gilmore's whiteness to suggest that perhaps other whites risked being kidnapped. Nonetheless, her trial and physical appearance added curiosity and complexity to her case, for after all, while many Philadelphians would have acknowledged the open secret of interracial mingling in the city, they had never witnessed a white woman defending her freedom in court.[31]

African Americans and their allies lost little time in disputing Aitken's claim. Jacob Gilmore paid Mary's $1,000 bail soon after her arrest. The parties appeared in court on June 15. George Griscom, David Paul Brown, and Charles Gilpin represented Mary and peppered Swift and Congo with questions. Swift alleged that he saw Mary's mother, Milly Winder, in Philadelphia but could not find her. The PAS lawyers and Aitken's counsel John W. Williams agreed that Milly Winder's testimony would prove Mary's true identity, as she would be able to recognize her daughter. Congo admitted that she had known of Mary residing in Philadelphia for the last two years but chose not to tell anyone. Like Swift, Congo did not know of any "*particular mark*" to

TEN DOLLARS REWARD.
STRAYED, or as it is supposed taken away by some coloured persons, on Tuesday after-noon the 26th of last month, and by them har-boured, a small girl named Emely, about 8 or 9 years of age, nearly white, very black eyes and hair; her mother is a yellow woman, known by the name of Milly Winder; any person giv-ing information to the Subscriber, so as to ena-ble him to get her again, shall receive the a-bove reward, and if taken out of the State and brought home, a reward of $20 will be paid.— All person or persons from this date, are for-warned harboring the said girl.
aug 24—d4t   R. AITKEN.

Robert Aitken's reward advertisement for Mary Gilmore that aided Gilmore and her allies' efforts to secure her freedom. Courtesy of the David M. Rubenstein Rare Book & Manuscript Library, Duke University

identify Mary as Emily. When court adjourned that day, both sides had posed a simple question: who could find evidence to convince presiding judge Archibald Randall that Mary was Mary and not Emily?[32]

Court proceedings on June 16 fleshed out Aitken's claim and Jacob Gilmore's version of Mary's life in Philadelphia. Aitken's lawyer presented two pieces of evidence to Randall: the will of Aitken's father, which listed both mother and daughter as enslaved people, and a notice that Robert Aitken placed in the *Baltimore Commercial Chronicle* on August 24, 1825, which described Milly as "nearly white." Given that the 1826 liberty law prevented slaveholders from contributing testimony, the PAS counsels argued against including the notice. Randall permitted it as evidence, either because it furnished the only description of Emily, or perhaps because Aitken published his testimony prior to 1826. Pushed further, when Randall allowed the advertisement as evidence, one may speculate that he did so in the interest of comity, thereby threatening Mary's freedom.[33]

Jacob Gilmore explained his relationship with Mary to the court. In 1819 a "poor" old Irish woman appeared on his doorstep with a 3-year-old girl. The woman pleaded with Gilmore and his wife to take the girl, but Jacob hesitated because of the girl's skin color; the woman assured him that the girl "was a very light mulatto, and not entirely white." The child's whiteness presented Jacob with a problem: could he face kidnapping charges? Perhaps Jacob was convinced that the girl could pass for white or Black, as the 1830 census taker listed one free African American female about Mary's age living in the Gilmore household. Jacob explained that, having no children of their own, they accepted Mary into their home. The Gilmores saw the woman once more, when she returned to his bakery drunk. Jacob removed her from the premises; she died a few years later, leaving a "profound mystery" as to the identity of Mary's parents. Gilmore attacked Congo's credibility, too. He claimed that Congo acted as Aitken's "spy [and] informer" out of "malicious spite." Congo was related to Gilmore's wife, who had recently passed away. When Congo asked Jacob for some of her relative's clothes, he refused. Congo then broke into his house several times to steal "money and goods" from him. Gilmore concluded his account by stating that ever since that time Congo remained determined to "annoy" him. In this case, "annoy" meant sending his adopted daughter into slavery. The court adjourned until the next day, June 17.[34]

Clearly Mary touched the Gilmore family and Jacob in particular, as he made her his heir. Such an intimate relationship made Mary part of the African American community, regardless of her phenotype or background, one who deserved protection at any cost. Jacob Gilmore's friends acknowledged this essential fact when they attacked Congo the night before the court could reconvene. Maria Congo left court on the 16th and returned to John Hill's house located at Sixth and Lombard streets, where she and her daughters lived at the time. That night a group of African American men and women sought "vengeance" against Congo, charged into the house, and began beating the inhabitants. Congo ran to the top floor, but the group pursued her. They dragged her down from the attic and continued to beat her until a group of constables arrested ten of them and broke up the "riot." At court the following day, Aitken's lawyer applied for a postponement, given these events. He also claimed that an unnamed newspaper had encouraged the riot in the first place because it "directed the public attention" to the case. Mary's lawyers argued against the postponement, but Randall agreed with Williams and rescheduled the trial for June 29.[35]

Philadelphians linked the attack on Congo to questions of comity. The *Philadelphia Inquirer* admitted that "the feeling in this section of the country is decidedly adverse to slavery—but it is far more adverse to any improper interference with the slave question." The newspaper's phrase "improper interference" reminded readers of the stakes of maintaining comity, even if it meant sending a white girl to interminable slavery. The phrase also encouraged readers to remind Black Philadelphians like Jacob Gilmore to keep in their place. Rioting to prevent removal created disorder within the city that might spread to other places across the country. If Congo's assailants persisted "in their efforts to produce riot, and again attempt to interfere with the police . . . heaven only knows what results may grow out of such unwise, imprudent and censurable conduct. The riots of the last summer should not be forgotten."[36]

The Black men and women who assaulted Congo did so not only to protect a young woman whom they no doubt knew personally but also because, even if Mary happened to be a "fugitive," any kidnapping of anyone in the Black community represented an affront to their sense of innate human freedom. The former reason may have hinted, too, that these Black men and women had witnessed so many arbitrary and illegal removals in Philadelphia that the odds of Mary being kidnapped and enslaved seemed very high indeed. Nonetheless, the ten men and women charged with assaulting Congo appeared before the Mayor's Court on June 26. Despite the efforts of twenty-nine witnesses, including Jacob Gilmore and Mayor Swift, the grand jury declared six of them guilty; their punishments ranged from one month to two years in prison. Soon thereafter Congo left Philadelphia for Wilmington, Delaware. A crowd of over 200 African American residents of Wilmington who knew of the case gathered at her house and threatened "vengeance" before constables broke up the riot. Similar to slaveholders' tracking fugitives from slavery, African Americans' frustrations crossed borders and showed that they could also hunt people like Congo, people from within their own community who leveled falsehoods that could result in permanent slavery.[37]

Both sides gathered witnesses before the court reconvened. Much like other kidnapping and fugitive from slavery cases, the defense team employed interracial, and thus street diplomatic, means to search Philadelphia for credible and respectable witnesses who knew Mary prior to 1825. Eventually a multiracial group of more than a dozen people promised to testify for her defense, which again showed the strength of Black and white collaboration. While Aitken's claim rested mainly upon Congo's testimony and his decade-old advertisement, he secured additional witnesses who claimed to remember Mary. The *Philadelphia Inquirer* pondered "how far a person may be able to identify the features of another, after a lapse of ten years." These speculations swirled within a courtroom packed with hundreds of African Americans and their

allies, for possessing "white skin . . . entirely devoid of any indication of African extraction" may not protect one from slavery.[38]

Excitement and curiosity reached a fever pitch when the trial resumed.
Blood had been shed, and more importantly, Mary embodied another hall-
mark of street diplomacy: the paradox of differentiating a fugitive from slavery from a free African American. This paradox of differentiation was at the
crux of comity. Philadelphians experienced how comity could and did kidnap
and enslave free human beings, with both acts supported by law, depending
on which law one chose to implement, where they implemented it, and who
they were and who they were with when they implemented it. Pushing the
matter further, Mary's skin color and all of the assumptions therein begged
the question whether a phenotypically white woman could be declared a fugitive from slavery in order to uphold comity.

The parties reconvened on June 29, fully prepared to sort out the question
of Mary's race and how that answer related to her freedom. Jacob Gilmore
reiterated his story to David Paul Brown and Aitken's new attorney, Edward
Ingraham, a lawyer who often defended slaveholders who came to Philadelphia looking for fugitives from slavery. When he took Mary into his house in
1820, Gilmore concluded, he thought she was "entirely white" and added that
he "expected Congo to come again and take her away." Aitken's first witness
was George Witman, a bricklayer who lived just outside of Philadelphia. Witman testified that, while he knew of Milly Winder, he did not know that she
had a daughter until his wife told him so. When Mrs. Witman appeared before the court the next day, she admitted that she did not recognize Mary. All
of Gilmore's witnesses provided solid evidence that they knew Mary prior to
1824; most were ordinary African American street diplomats whose lives in a
city constantly visited by slaveholders and kidnappers alerted them to the
consequences of Mary's case.[39]

Gilmore's Black and white friends' search produced an individual vital to
Mary's case: her supposed mother, Amelia, alias Milly, Winder. Winder denied ever having seen Mary, adding that she looked "older and larger than her
child would now be." Furthermore, Winder put a spin on Aitken's story: she
accused him of selling her daughter. Here Winder exercised street diplomacy
in court and turned the tables on the slaveholder. Even if the trial did not end
in Mary's favor, Winder's claim brought the proceedings to a standstill when
she bravely announced how Aitken, like countless other slaveholders, sold off
family members to slavery. No doubt many of the Black spectators in the audience could relate to this reality. One wonders how white attendees reacted

to Amelia's words: did they sit in stunned silence, nod in approval, feign ignorance, or simply turn away? Winder reminded the court that the only reason she went to Philadelphia after Aitken emancipated her was to find her
daughter, Emily. While her decade of exertions proved futile, she explained
that she continued asking around for Emily whenever she met a person from
the South. With the assistance of Black and white street diplomats, Milly
Winder's testimony established Mary neither as a freedwoman nor a fugitive
from slavery, but as a free woman.[40]

Despite hearing the closing testimony from both sides, Judge Randall allowed Aitken to present two witnesses on July 1. Perhaps Randall viewed the
outcome of the trial as riotous at best: if Mary went free, Randall might appear
to violate slaveholders' comity; if Mary was enslaved, Randall might maintain
comity but witness the wrath of the Black community, much as he did in 1834
(see above). David Paul Brown initially protested Randall's action, but then
realized that he would have no problem finding witnesses of his own to support Gilmore. Perhaps Brown drew them directly from the multitude of African Americans present in court; some may have volunteered on the spot.
"The excessively crowded state of the spacious hall, testified the general so-
licitude with which the proceeding was upon by our citizens, of every class"
as street diplomacy attracted an audience. After hearing the witnesses for
the defense, Randall allowed Williams to summarize Aitken's claim. Instead,
Williams harangued "with extreme severity, some of the 'coloured' witnesses"
brought forth by Gilmore's legal team. He finished by attacking "busy" Thomas
Shipley's "real, or 'affected' philanthropy" as well as the designs of the press to
"aggravate the public sympathy." Having heard enough, Randall announced
his decision.[41]

Randall defined Mary Gilmore's case as a "question of property," which in
effect represented the promises and perils of comity. On the one hand, Aitken
exercised his right as a slaveholder to claim Mary under the 1793 Fugitive
Slave Act. If his testimony stood as evidence for his claim, Mary would have
been sent back to Maryland. On the other hand, Randall explained, the case
"does not rest here" because Pennsylvania's 1826 liberty law prevented slaveholders' testimony from being acknowledged in court. Furthermore, although
Aitken's witnesses swore that Emily disappeared in 1825, they did not recognize Mary as the missing girl. Opposed to the spotty memory of the prosecution's witnesses, the defense culled witnesses from among Black and white
Philadelphians, who presented overwhelming evidence that they knew Mary
as Jacob Gilmore's daughter prior to 1825. The efforts of this multiracial group

cast "a very strong doubt upon" Aitken's claim and for that reason, Randall announced that he could not grant her removal. "The vast concourse" of Mary's supporters burst with thunderous applause and, not taking any chances, accompanied her out of the courtroom.[42]

Local newspapers praised the outcome of the case. Prior to the 1826 liberty law, stated the writer for the *Downingtown Standard*, "wicked and mercenary" magistrates granted removals with little proof. As a result, "many free Blacks have thus been carried off into slavery. Some have returned to tell the tale of their sufferings and sorrows, while others have died in bondage." The *Philadelphia Inquirer* thanked the unremitting work of Thomas Shipley, yet overlooked the fact that Black testimony, namely Maria Congo's and Jacob Gilmore's, proved just as valuable to the outcome of the case. African Americans' words were one thing, but their actions, namely, attacking Congo in Philadelphia and then in Wilmington(!), represented the consequences not only of making false claims against other African Americans within the Black community, but in a way how these false claims and promises of comity betrayed the innate human freedom espoused by street diplomats.[43]

Abolitionists flouted the supposed safety of a comity that assumed Black enslavement. A few weeks after the trial, the *Liberator* reported that almshouse records identified Mary's parentage as Irish and invited nonbelievers to visit Mary and see her "perfect whiteness." These pieces of evidence, written documents and Mary herself, "set at rest the question of her freedom, unless those who dispute it shall contend that the offspring of Irish fathers and mothers are subject to slavery under the laws of this Republic." In Mary's case, her near kidnapping and enslavement represented too close a call that resonated with African Americans living in Philadelphia. Black Philadelphians identified with Mary's plight and lived in fear that at any moment a slaveholder might invade and, in the words of a poet for the *Liberator*, "scatter ruin" in their "happiest homes." Comity worked in the Black community's favor this time, but the open question remained whether comity might ensure future freedom.[44]

The Founding of the Philadelphia Anti-Slavery Society

Shortly after the Gilmore case, Black and white Philadelphia abolitionists emphasized their street diplomat credentials by forming the interracial Philadelphia Anti-Slavery Society (PASS) on July 4, 1835. The board of managers elected David Paul Brown president and included a leadership core of veteran street diplomats, among them Thomas Shipley and James Forten. This interracial organization proclaimed that its cause supported a "harmonious and perpetual" Union, even while their opponents castigated it as a threat to the United States. In reality, Black and white abolitionists stood alone as the "true patriot[s]." Rather than dissolve the Union, they would cement the bonds of Union upon "the immutable principles of justice and the rights of man." The safety and perpetuity of the Union required ending "heart-rending separations" and incorporating Blacks into the "body politic." In doing so abolition would alleviate fears of servile insurrection and usher in a golden era of peaceful relations between North and South, Black and white. This group firmly believed that interracial, immediate abolition actualized interstate comity through racial comity.[45]

The PASS went further and drafted a public address that explained how porous borders wreaked havoc on the Union. The internal slave trade extended into contested spaces like the streets of Philadelphia and proved that "there can be no such thing as local disease in the American system." The Federal Constitution that upheld the American system risked spreading that "detestable traffic" into any new states admitted in the Union. In fact, the whole system represented "one continued series of unmitigated cruelties, sparing neither age, sex, nor condition" and it would be in the best interests of politicians to end the slave trade and guarantee immediate emancipation. The address ended on a conciliatory note, with the abolitionists identifying themselves as "friends of order and of public peace." Yet order and peace could be assured by tampering with the Union between slavery and freedom—and tampering meant immediate abolition. The aggressive tone of the address matched the abolitionists' passion to disseminate the document, as the PASS distributed 1,500 copies of this address throughout the Philadelphia region.[46]

The Juan Riot, 1835

These attempts made by the PASS to assuage its fellow Philadelphians over portents of a Union destroyed by emancipation failed in the week following the public address. While the address may have acted as one of the immediate causes of the 1835 riot, the lingering effects of the Gilmore case as well as the PASS meeting put many Philadelphians on edge. The spark that lit the fuse of the riot came on July 12, 1835, when a young Igbo African "servant" named Juan tried to murder Robert Stewart, the former American consul to Cuba who had brought Juan from Cuba to Philadelphia.

Philadelphia newspapers claimed that Juan attacked Stewart because local Philadelphia African Americans ridiculed Juan's clothing. When Juan asked

Stewart for new clothes, Stewart consulted his wife, Rachel, who told him that Juan already owned trunks of clothes valued at $100; Stewart refused Juan's request. Upset, Juan purchased clothes behind Stewart's back and charged them to Stewart, who returned them. While Stewart napped during the afternoon of July 12, Juan snuck into his room and began hacking at Stewart's head with an ax and a knife. Thinking that he killed Stewart, Juan ran from the room, informed the cook of Stewart's murder, and sat on the front steps of the Stewart house. Stewart's groans and screams drew the attention of the other household members, including his son and coachman. Juan told the boy that "your father scolded me this morning, and I have killed him." Hearing Stewart fighting for his life, Juan told the coachman, "Me begin to kill Mars' Stewart—now me go back finish him!" Before he could do so, the coachman and Stewart's son-in-law chased him out of the house and down the street, where he was quickly arrested and detained. Stewart survived the attack but lost the use of his right hand and one of his eyes.[47]

Not only did contemporary newspapers believe the Stewarts' version of events, they connected Juan's motives to the "hardening" of racial categories. The *Philadelphia Gazette* stated that Juan's Igbo pedigree betrayed a partiality for "suicide" and "revengeful acts." Juan's "gloomy" disposition emerged when he left Cuba, and the family grew apprehensive that Juan might "make way with himself," i.e., commit suicide. Prior to the attack, Juan seemed loyally "attached" to Stewart, according to the *Philadelphia Inquirer.* When Philadelphia African Americans supposedly mocked him as a "Guinea negro," Juan pleaded with Stewart to send him back to Cuba. Perhaps Stewart reminded Juan of the benefits of living with his family in Philadelphia, a reminder of how some white Americans living in the North expressed paternalism toward Black Americans. These accounts of Juan's demeanor and behavior represented the power of newspapers to essentialize racial traits, as if to argue that Juan's innate character made the attack inevitable.[48]

The simplest way to explain Juan's motives would be to consider that Stewart still "owned" Juan and treated him as an enslaved person. Such confusion spoke once again to how claims to enslave African Americans like Juan conflated fugitives from slavery and kidnapping victims: Juan embodied both conditions of freedom. According to the *Liberator* and the PAS, despite Stewart's claims that he emancipated Juan in Cuba and hired him as a servant, no copy of Juan's manumission papers surfaced during or after the ordeal. This was a clear violation of Pennsylvania's 1788 anti-kidnapping law, which required slaveholders to register enslaved people with the PAS. Stewart may have ignored this law and therefore faced the consequences at the hands of Juan, especially if Juan knew about Pennsylvania's anti-kidnapping laws. In other words, if Juan was informed of these laws, perhaps he accused Stewart of kidnapping him or just harbored this view until the opportunity arose to change the situation. In keeping with the notion that Stewart held Juan illegally, the *Liberator* contradicted other newspapers and indeed claimed that Stewart "struck" Juan for asking him to buy new clothes. The logic then followed that because Stewart hit Juan, Stewart still "owned" Juan. Regardless of the reason for striking Juan, Stewart normalized violence against an African American in his home, an African American whose freedom status was in no way assured. Likewise, the claim that some anonymous Black Philadelphians teased Juan about his clothes might suggest another motive for Juan's request for new clothes: maybe Juan needed a disguise in order to escape from Stewart. Unfortunately, Juan did not escape; he went before the Mayor's Court as "John Price" and was charged with assault and battery "with intent to murder." Juan/John was sentenced to seven years in the penitentiary, after which time he disappeared from the historical record.[49]

Juan's attack on Stewart, a white man, acted as a pretense for white Philadelphians to usher in a new wave of riots against Black Philadelphia. A large number of whites held vigil outside of the Stewart house the night of the attack. There they conspired to riot and, in the meantime, began attacking any African American in the vicinity. Mayor Swift dispatched the police to break up this gathering, which they did without incident. Tacitly supporting the whites, the *Philadelphia Inquirer* cautioned the city's African American population that "the slightest offence on the part of the Blacks would at this particular time be visited with the severest penalty." In other words, Blacks needed to stay in their place. Even worse, rumors persisted that some form of violence would take place on Monday in the southern part of the city, the same area that was rocked by anti-Black riots the year before. Fearing the worst, Swift sent the entire police force to keep order in South Philadelphia. Swift himself led a mass of "one hundred efficient men" to Sixth and Lombard Streets. Standing at this intersection these men would have seen vital institutions of African American life, including multiple Black churches as well as some 1,500 white Philadelphians "of the very lowest classes," arrayed for battle. The mayor's men dispersed this crowd, which then rendezvoused farther down Lombard Street.[50]

Still seething from the beating of a respectable white man by a young Black man, this crowd launched an all-out assault on Black Philadelphia that night.

The destruction did not lack focus, as the rioters selected Black institutions and homes as targets for their fury. Shouting "to Small Street!" the crowd ran down Sixth and Seventh Streets, stopping to deface Black-owned homes along the way. Many houses were still deserted due to the riots from the previous summer, providing another sobering reminder of how riots produced long-term damage: the African American community had yet to recover. The crowd continued hunting and beating any African Americans they found in the neighborhood. These sadistic acts added texture to the historian David Grimsted's study on mobs, which posited that unlike Southern riots, which focused on assaulting people, Northern riots focused on destroying property. What made the riots of 1834 and 1835 unique was that white property was to be protected at all costs, at the expense of Black property, and that violence was expected to be exacted upon Black Americans and their futures. The arrests and kidnappings of Black Philadelphians and vicious riots against this same community synthesized terror as the "ruling principle" of a slave system that transcended borders.[51]

The rioters took pleasure in terrorizing African Americans, some of whom they targeted, others whose skin color engendered arbitrary assaults or worse. Attacking young Black men at random and chopping down doors to Black dwellings, the crowd moved up Small Street and broke into a house on Shippen Street in the hopes of finding a Black barber, "an object of peculiar animosity." According to the *Philadelphia Inquirer*, "not a colored person was to be seen within three or four squares" of Cedar Ward, the heart of Black Philadelphia. Similar to the previous year, many African Americans fled Philadelphia to sleep "in the open air" of farms and forests outside of the city. The rioters set fire to a block of Black-owned homes on Eighth Street known as "Red Row." Firemen attempted to extinguish the flames, but the rioters cut their hoses. The rioters then proceeded to the neighborhood of Fitzwater Street and Passyunk Road, where they damaged more than two dozen houses. By midnight the firemen gained control of the fire at Red Row and the mayor and police force dispersed the crowd. City newspapers warned Black and white Philadelphians, especially the children and apprentices of the latter, to avoid the riot area in the interest of "peace and order." Once again, African Americans who "did not give the slightest offense" were at the center of maintaining stability within the city.[52]

The disturbing enthusiasm with which the Philadelphia rioters hunted Blacks was eerily reminiscent of slaveholders, slave catchers, and kidnappers pursuing African Americans across the North and the South. The resemblance to Southern slavery was further evidenced by a crowd numbering more than 1,000 that reassembled the next night on Sixth and South Streets, "eager for the renewal of the sport." Not willing to resume this "sport," nearby about sixty Black Philadelphians armed with "knives, bludgeons, and pistols" garrisoned a house on St. Mary Street. Rioters received word of this fortress and would have attacked it had it not been for Mayor Swift, City Recorder William Blayney, and City Solicitor Edward Olmstead, who headed off the mob at the corner of St. Mary Street and prevented anyone from approaching the building. Blayney and Olmstead entered the house and found a lone African American man on the main floor while the others remained on alert upstairs. The two officials held a long "parlay" with the man and persuaded the African Americans to leave the dwelling through the back door. Once again, African Americans made the diplomatic choice to not attack the mob. The mayor addressed the crowd and stifled rumors that armed African Americans were ready for battle. The crowd disbanded, but the damage was done: several African Americans were hospitalized, many fled Philadelphia, and at least thirty homes were destroyed in Cedar Ward. A week later arsonists burnt down the rest of the Black-owned homes on Red Row, a terrifying coda to the riots.[53]

Violence directed toward African American lives and property in Philadelphia mirrored the terror of Southern slavery. In both cases, many whites viewed African Americans as malleable objects whose futures were not their own. Deprived of the opportunity to engage in a world with other human beings, Black Americans faced violence and terror, an omnipresent reality. Yet African Americans like Juan and the Black men who fortified buildings inverted this reality: their own precarious position as potentially free people under Pennsylvania law and more importantly, the street diplomat view of inherent human freedom, legitimized the former's attack on Stewart and the latter's defense of their lives. The actions of these Black men and women drove white politicians to respond. The local contests over freedom in Philadelphia reflected the broader national concerns over the innate disorder of living in a slave society, one that projected benevolence but in actuality consisted of separation, violence, and terror.[54]

These riots drew the attention of Pennsylvania Democratic governor George Wolf. In his 1835 address to the state legislature, Wolf lamented how "the domestic sanctuary was entered by violence, the obnoxious individual sought for, and if found, fell victim to an infuriated mob; if not, his property became a sacrifice to a phrensied [sic] populace." Here Wolf decried mob violence against all Americans without specifically naming the true victims: African Americans, north and south, who daily experienced the "lawless violence" feared most by Wolf. Yet as a stalwart of President Andrew Jackson, Wolf then linked the riots to abolitionists, those fanatics of "the most dangerous and alarming character." The forces of this surging interracial abolitionism, with Philadelphia as its capital city, "may prove fatal to the Union." Once again, African Americans willing to fight for freedom alongside white allies before, during, and after the riot demonstrated the efficacy and thus threat of interracial abolitionism, a foundation of street diplomacy. Finally, Wolf suggested that the state legislature deliberate over whether to "impose an immediate check and restraint" on abolitionism in Pennsylvania, a portentous recommendation that coincided with these same abolitionists' "Great Postal Campaign."[55]

The Late Philadelphia Mails

The American Anti-Slavery Society's Great Postal Campaign to disseminate one million abolitionist tracts met with a vociferous response from Southerners and proslavery elements in Philadelphia. When Southern newspapers accused Northerners of supporting immediatism and endangering slaveholders' right to property, the *Philadelphia Inquirer* responded that the "vox populi" of Northern cities, Philadelphia in particular, felt "agreement and fraternity with the South, which no innovation can shake or endanger." The *Inquirer* hoped that Philadelphians would awaken to the "unwarrantable and criminal interference of northern fanaticism with southern interests." In short, Philadelphians would strengthen comity by reserving the right to terrorize their native-born abolitionists, Black and white.[56]

Meanwhile, Philadelphia abolitionists took an ambivalent approach to meeting after the riots. On the one hand, the Philadelphia Young Men's Anti-Slavery Society held "interesting [and] well-attended lectures" that encouraged Pennsylvanians to form abolition societies, thus ignoring both Governor Wolf's pleas and the wishes of slaveholders. David Paul Brown cancelled the August 14 meeting of the PASS for fear of riots; the PAS canceled its monthly meeting, too. Speaking to the power of rumor, word of the proposed PASS gathering spread throughout Philadelphia. A rowdy crowd assembled to demolish Brown's house, because he had "rendered himself particularly obnoxious" by spending his career aiding African Americans. Luckily for Brown, foul weather dispersed both the crowd and the proposed abolitionist meeting.[57]

SOUTHERN IDEAS OF LIBERTY.

Sentence *passed upon one for supporting that clause of our Declaration viz All men are born free & equal* " *Strip him to the skin! give him a coat of Tar & Feathers!! Hang him by the neck, between the Heavens and the Earth !!! as a beacon to warn the* Northern Fanatics *of their danger!!!* "

NEW METHOD OF ASSORTING THE MAIL, AS PRACTISED BY SOUTHERN SLAVE-HOLDERS, OR

ATTACK ON THE POST OFFICE, CHARLESTON, S.C.

While Southern in scope, illusory borders between Pennsylvania and the Slave South collapsed when outrages against abolitionists, Black and white, as well as the "new method of assorting the mail," bled easily into Philadelphia. Courtesy of the Library Company of Philadelphia

Brown's public defense in the *Philadelphia Inquirer* illustrated the tensions within street diplomacy. He denied being involved in the postal campaign and disapproved of it because of the potential to disrupt comity. While he refused to make "undue concessions" to slaveholders, Brown knew not to "encroach upon their rights, privileges, or security." Even so, Brown's professional duty was to defend those claimed as fugitives from slavery in Philadelphia, a duty protected by the Constitution and Pennsylvania law. Here Brown privileged a pro-Black view of comity premised upon innate human freedom. He claimed that it would be "unmanly for me to withhold my humble aid from a fellow creature" and that he had no problem experiencing "personal inconvenience or peril" in the course of such a career. For example, most recently Brown argued for the release of Mary Gilmore, "a hapless orphan Irish girl." Brown's rhetorical strategy of combining comity, race, and enslavement reminded Philadelphians of the impenetrable link between all Americans living within a slave society: "the course of human proscription has not always a *color* for its excuse." After the proposed razing of his home, his own "domestic *peace*" became the reward for his service to liberty and defense of humanity.[58]

Other than his storied career, the crowd's immediate issue with Brown was that he spoke before the Young Men's Anti-Slavery Society the previous week. This radical interracial organization was founded in 1835 as an auxiliary to the American Anti-Slavery Society. Members of the society included relatives of PAS members, including William Garrigues and Edward Hopper as well as rising stars like James Forten, Jr. The younger Forten possessed dazzling oratorical talents. His 1836 speech to the Philadelphia Female Anti-Slavery Society outlined much of their shared immediatist philosophy as a "desperate struggle . . . between freedom and despotism—light and darkness." The latter society, interracial and female-led, featured his sisters Margaretta and Sarah Forten, both of whom wrote for abolitionist newspapers and fundraised to bring about immediate emancipation as well as comfort impoverished African Americans in Philadelphia. Forten, Jr. would no doubt agree with Brown, who ended his open letter to Philadelphians with dark prophecies regarding the future: "The evils now complained of, the turbulence and tumult of the times originate much deeper than their ostensible cause, and will ere long embrace wider mischiefs, if not promptly subdued, than those which as present we deplore. In the language of Talleyrand, 'This is but the beginning of the end.'"

Philadelphia's abolitionist community echoed the existential dangers to the

Union that mirrored the threats of interracial alliances forged through street diplomacy to ensure Black freedom throughout the Union. Public debates over interstate comity, immediate and interracial abolitionism, the kidnapping of free Blacks, and the crisis over fugitives from slavery, all of which Philadelphians negotiated through street diplomacy, drew the ire of many Philadelphia residents, who gathered to pledge their support to a Union with slaveholders.[59]

The "Young Men of the City and County of Philadelphia" called for "FRIENDS OF THE UNION" to attend a town meeting on August 24 to discuss the "RECENT INCENDIARY MOVEMENTS OF THE IMMEDIATE ABOLITIONISTS." Although the group gathered more than 1,000 signatures in support of preserving a Union with slavery, the *Philadelphia Inquirer* estimated that thousands of men participated, with thousands more unable to obtain tickets to the event. This "noble demonstration of public opinion" for the Union and against the abolitionists would have a "salutary effect" on the South. These Philadelphians, many of whom participated in the recent riots, would prove that they were not "soft" on race, slavery, or the Union and vowed to support Southerners through a "hardening" of racial categories.[60]

The speakers conflated their alliance with slaveholders with their devotion to the Union. Philadelphia grocer William C. Patterson, whose in-laws included the wealthy slaveholding Orr family of South Carolina, called the meeting to order and nominated the Jacksonian Democratic alderman Morton McMichael as president. McMichael delivered a "truly eloquent and highly appropriate" address that likely referenced sustaining comity and avoiding the excesses of abolitionism. Next on the dais was Robert T. Conrad, an anti-Jacksonian lawyer and former editor of the *Philadelphia Gazette.* Like McMichael, Conrad gave a speech that "elicited frequent bursts of applause from the audience." State senator Dr. Jesse Burden, a "bank Democrat" who, as the moniker suggested, opposed Jackson's veto of the Second Bank of the United States, spoke next. Born and raised in Southwark, Burden formed part of the powerful Democratic political machine in Philadelphia. In his speech he pointed out that "humanity shudders" at the thought of emancipation, a fate more "galling" than slavery itself: freed African Americans would turn the United States into Haiti. Only the South could solve the problem of slavery, and the North need not interfere with that region's necessary evils.[61]

These men agreed that preserving the Union meant preserving slavery and slaveholders' rights to property, all the while glossing over how the recent riots perpetrated by their supporters nearly created a race war in Philadelphia. Upholding a Union with slavery meant ignoring the precarious freedoms enjoyed by African Americans in the North. Joseph R. Ingersoll spoke last. As a member of one of Pennsylvania's political dynasties, Ingersoll had a reputation "throughout the Union" that lent gravitas to the meeting and to the role of Philadelphia within the national debate over freedom and slavery. Those who labored to preserve the Union need not see their work die in vain: Northerners needed to work to correct the South's misperception that the "whole North is united in one array against them."[62]

Ingersoll's speech, noted the *Philadelphia Inquirer*, "diffused a flood of light" upon these topics. He began by meditating on the abolitionists' recent postal campaign. "Subterranean fires" of abolitionism may produce salutary effects in the long term, but short-term agitation would cause an "unquenchable rage" dangerous to all. Ingersoll asserted that the Founders envisioned a republic that compromised over slavery. They ratified a Constitution based upon comity "extending to all and over all," thereby necessitating cooperation between states to ensure "the prompt and effectual restoration" of fugitives from slavery. Pennsylvania respected comity for the most part. Recently, however, "*ultra abolition*" brought comity to a breaking point. Ingersoll pronounced that now was the time for the many to rise and "put [the abolitionists] down" for disrupting the bonds of Union. While not all abolitionists projected disunion, "when they wear the appearance of incendiaries and do their deeds, they must be content to bear the opprobrium." Any violence that resulted from such agitation "is not by our hands," though devotees to the Union who exercised violence prevented the "atrocious *consequences*," of immediate emancipation. Ingersoll in effect absolved himself, his colleagues, and his constituents of any responsibility to protect abolitionists, let alone African Americans.[63]

Ingersoll believed that interracial activism disrupted comity and threatened the Union. Calling African Americans and their white allies "ultras" and "scattered agitators," Ingersoll hinted that their affronts to stability could and would pop up anywhere across the state and nation. Interestingly and perhaps reflecting his elite status, Ingersoll was more charitable to members of the PAS, whom he identified as the "legitimate, genuine friends of abolition" and thus abolitionists who respected comity. Yet the ambitious actions of Black and white Philadelphia abolitionists, not to mention ordinary African Americans who resisted kidnapping and enslavement by providing intelligence to the PAS Acting Committee, belied Ingersoll's notion that the PAS was somehow more moderate. If anything, the PAS projected moderation in public while working behind the scenes to do anything in its power to protect Philadelphia's African American community. Among other examples of these interracial ties, the budding friendship and collaboration between Robert Purvis and Thomas Shipley embodied how interracial harmony promoted, not disrupted, comity and the Union. So even though Ingersoll hoped to mark "ultras" and their allies as enemies of the Union and therefore subject to violence, actions undertaken for decades by Philadelphia abolitionists in the Union-"friendly" PAS betrayed a clear-cut distinction between radical and moderate or "conservative" abolitionism.[64]

After Ingersoll spoke, the committee drafted resolutions that epitomized how street diplomacy eroded comity. One resolution sought to take measures to "rescue" slaveholders from "the incendiary efforts" of Pennsylvania abolitionists. "Obnoxious measures" such as the postal campaign might require state legislation to limit abolitionist mailings and monitor their movement within Pennsylvania. The ordinary Philadelphians who attended the meeting could do their part by rooting out and aiding in the arrest of Pennsylvania abolitionists. The North was "sound to the core on the subject of slavery": should a domestic insurrection erupt in the South, "the young men of the North [were] prepared to meet the danger, shoulder to shoulder . . . by the ready sacrifice of their blood, their devotion to the peace and the rights of all the parts of our beloved Union."[65]

The power of slavery to motivate these Philadelphians and their resolutions met with the liberating power of the written word. The day after the meeting a steamboat arrived in Philadelphia carrying among its cargo a large wooden box labeled "dry goods." When the dockworkers read the recipient's name, William H. Scott, president of the Young Men's Anti-Slavery Society, they "*accidentally* forced open" the box; out poured "*incendiary pamphlets and newspapers*" addressed to slaveholders across the South. Anticipating Postmaster General Amos Kendall's rationale for censoring mails—that Americans "owe an obligation to the laws, but we owe a higher one to the communities in which we live"—the *Philadelphia Inquirer* called these materials a "gross and daring violation" of comity: these documents were "calculated to excite and inflame the mind of the slave." The large crowd gathered at the dock included a few of the city's "most respectable citizens," and this latter group visited Scott.[66]

Scott's role as president of the Young Men's Anti-Slavery Society (YMASS) proved his willingness to forge interracial bonds with African Americans. His

position also epitomized the changing character of Philadelphia abolitionism, a community torn between the public gradualist intentions of the PAS
and the immediatist persistence of the American Anti-Slavery Society. Accepting that the YMASS leaned more toward radicals like Garrison, Scott's
defense likely masked his complicity. When confronted by the deputation of
"respectable" Philadelphians, Scott pled ignorance regarding the box's purpose and contents. Had he known that someone would send him such a box
in the midst of such contentious times, he would consider it his "duty" to
surrender it to the city of Philadelphia, which he did. Satisfied with Scott's
alibi, the delegation returned the box to the transportation office.[67]

A crowd of more than 100 "respectable citizens" gathered at the transportation office and voted on what to do with the box, and in doing so, communicated how many white Philadelphians understood street diplomacy. They
had two options: support the abolitionists or stand with the South and slavery. The group chose the latter course and dumped the box into the Delaware
River. They carried out their plan accompanied by cheering throngs of Philadelphians, who witnessed street diplomacy in action. Given the volatility
of the times, the *Philadelphia Inquirer* described this display as the "proper
course." The newspaper concluded its account by stating that "Philadelphia is
perfectly tranquil, and is likely to continue so."[68]

Conclusion

Many Philadelphians did not take kindly to street diplomacy practiced by
abolitionists in the city. Innately interracial, well connected, highly effective,
and willing to drop diplomacy and defend themselves if necessary, these
abolitionists moved in tandem with the rise of immediate abolition that
in many ways began in Philadelphia. This new wave of abolitionism gave
a stronger voice to the plight of Black Americans, though their opponents
viewed these words and actions as threats to their alliance with slavery they
called the "Union." Anti-abolitionist and anti-Black meetings held in the wake
of Turner's revolt and the 1834–1835 riots themselves all but confirmed the fact
that many Philadelphians deemed interracial abolitionism unworthy of safety
and domestic sanctuary.

Fugitives from slavery and the ongoing kidnapping of free Blacks remained
crucial to understanding the 1834–1835 riots. Contemporary complaints of
rescue attempts and Blacks assembling in courtrooms as a show of force
spoke to the deep-seated fears of whites, especially those living in Philadelphia
and across the North. Distinguishing a free person from a supposed "fugitive"

in Philadelphia inherently threatened comity and therefore the Union—a point that everyone understood and more than a few were willing to point out. These riots were an all but necessary consequence of Americans' failure to confront the Union with slavery in all its guises, from gang labor to the kidnapping of free Blacks. Ironically, the riots subsided just as the wave of immediate abolitionism crested upon the great postal campaign, a poorly timed measure that pushed white Philadelphians interested in promoting interstate harmony into the open arms of the Union-friendly slave states.

The fierce determination of Black and white abolitionists on the streets became an all-too-real and riotous specter that haunted some white Philadelphians, especially those aligned with slave-hunting constables like Michael Donnehower, politicians like Pennsylvania governor George Wolf, and acclaimed proslavery lawyers like Joseph Ingersoll. The anti-Black "friends of the Union" who frequently held large meetings in Philadelphia and who pledged to fight with the South to suppress enslaved African Americans gave license to attacks on African Americans living in the North. Here the border between freedom and slavery crumbled in the minds of these whites much as street diplomats' views of fundamental human equality encouraged them to assume any arrest of a Black person as tantamount to a kidnapping. When faced with the decision over whether to assist Black Philadelphians or stand with the South, many white Philadelphians chose and acted upon the latter course. In doing so, the burden of maintaining the Union remained not on whites who hoped to succor positive relationships with slaveholders but on the backs of African Americans and their allies in Philadelphia. These struggles by ordinary people, ordinary Black people in particular, forced whites, politicians or otherwise, to consider the value of sustaining a Union tied to slavery.

CHAPTER FIVE

A Theatre of Scenes

The Philadelphia lawyer and PAS stalwart David Paul Brown delivered the keynote address at the opening of Pennsylvania Hall on May 14, 1838. Calling liberty "far, far more precious" than life, Brown began with an anecdote intended to chart a course between immediate and practical abolitionism. In 1808 two Black men, John Joyce and Peter Mathias, were hung in Philadelphia for the murder of Sarah Cross, a "harmless, industrious old woman." A decade later the Philadelphia abolitionist Isaac Hopper called upon Brown to defend an alleged fugitive from slavery. When Brown asked the man his name, he replied, "Peter Mathias." Astonished, Brown related the story of Peter Mathias to the man. The man nodded and replied, "Come nearer, and I'll tell you about it." This man, John Johnson, explained that he shared a prison cell with Mathias in 1808. Just before Mathias was executed, he told Johnson, "John, you are a slave, I am free; here are my freedom papers; I am going where I shall not want them." Ever since that day Johnson assumed the identity of Peter Mathias: an accused man with a dead man's name and a dead man's freedom. Johnson and Mathias brought together the immediacy of freedom with the pragmatism of a political exchange of identities: freedom was made, not begotten, in Philadelphia. To Brown and his allies, no American could ignore "this inhuman traffic in undisguised abhorrence."[1]

Battles over street diplomacy continued to rage in Philadelphia following the "long" riot year of 1834–1835. These everyday conflicts over freedom and slavery between 1836 and 1843 made Philadelphia, in the words of Pennsylvania governor Joseph Ritner, a "theatre of scenes." These scenes manifested themselves in large part due to Philadelphia's continuing status as a hotbed of activity for slaveholders, fugitives from slavery, and political activism. Illusory borders between North and South enabled slaveholders and their African American targets to influence the political and racial strategies adopted by Black and white abolitionists. In doing so, these competing groups reinforced the dialectical relationship between physical violence arising from the streets and top-down political actions in the state and nation. The burden of the Union and comity rested firmly on the backs of African Americans and their allies and showed how white politicians lacked a clear solution to contests over slavery and freedom in the state. By the time of the 1842 *Prigg* decision, the stakes of African American freedom in Philadelphia, Pennsylvania, and the nation seemed higher than ever.[2]

Politicizing Philadelphia, circa 1836

By 1836 Philadelphia had become a city in transition, economically, demographically, and politically. No longer simply a cosmopolitan port city, Philadelphia solidified its reputation as one of the preeminent manufacturing cities in the United States. Irish immigrants arrived in search of work throughout the 1830s, the peak decade of immigration to the city. Many immigrants settled in South Philadelphia, which was the center of African American life in the city. The influx of Irish immigrants led to income insecurity within the African American community, as both groups competed for jobs. Similar to Black Philadelphians, the Irish formed beneficial societies, created fire companies, joined the police force, and built churches, and they learned that they were "white" through attacking African Americans and supporting the Democratic machine. No wonder, then, that the patterns of Irish settlement in Philadelphia County (which incorporated South Philadelphia) yielded Democratic victories in local, state, and national elections.[3]

The Second Party system in Philadelphia underscored how each party's relationship with African Americans influenced political loyalties. Unlike Philadelphia County, Philadelphia City itself maintained a Whig core throughout the 1830s and drew support from Philadelphia's abolitionist community, especially those who benefited from the market revolution and hated Jackson. Philadelphia Whigs such as John Sergeant and Josiah Randall vigorously supported public education, the expansion of public works, and the defense of the "monster" Bank of the United States, located in Philadelphia. Democratic stalwarts and Jackson campaigners such as Charles Ingersoll and Thomas Earle espoused the hard money ethos and the destruction of the bank. These same Democrats encouraged their Irish constituents to attack and terrorize

the Black community as if it were their birthright. Such partisan loyalties reflected the broader truths of the rise of the Second Party system in the United
States to the extent that, on the surface, the economics of the era glossed over
debates pertaining to slavery.[4]

One would be hard pressed to separate economics from racial politics in
1836 Philadelphia. Some grand colonial mansions once occupied by merchants
became overcrowded tenements filled with Irish immigrants while others became bustling factories forbidden to Black labor: both transitions promoted
a precarious existence for African Americans. By 1838, the PAS observed that
many Blacks found it difficult "to find places for their sons, as apprentices, [or]
to learn mechanical trades"; a decade later the PAS found that many dwellings in Cedar Ward—the dynamic heart of the Black community—consisted
of "the lowest and most degraded of the coloured population, whose occupa-
tions were ragging, boning, and prizing." In short, the Second Party system
had little to offer Black Philadelphians: Whig programs for social uplift failed
to extend to them, while overzealous Irish Democrats employed in the city's
factories forced many African Americans into "pauperism." "That many of
them have been held as slaves" led to an increase in crimes committed by
African Americans, argued the PAS in 1838. Here the PAS linked the ongoing
effects of Southern slavery to poverty and acts of desperation within Black
Philadelphia. The legacy of slavery, the perpetual discrimination and violence toward African Americans, and the presence of fugitives from slavery
in Philadelphia collided with the Second Party system. The local politics of
slavery forced Philadelphians and their state and national allies to grapple
with how Americans should conceive of African American freedom and comity in a country where slaveholders possessed the right to own and hunt
human beings.[5]

The Death of Thomas Shipley

The loss of a single abolitionist meant the loss of a street diplomat, and the
abolitionist community of the United States suffered such an inestimable loss
in the death of Thomas Shipley on September 17, 1836. Shipley's career embodied street diplomacy. He had served on the PAS Acting Committee, interviewed and befriended countless African Americans, confronted politicians,
reconnoitered and negotiated during the recent riots, and was elected president of the PAS shortly before his death. The *Centennial Anniversary of the
PAS* mentioned Shipley in the same breath as Benjamin Franklin when it
spoke of the society's "rich inheritance of renown." His lifelong involvement

in bringing justice to African Americans defied exaggeration, a point acknowledged by his white and Black colleagues. All the more remarkable, Shipley accomplished these deeds fully knowing that his stepnephew, the notorious slave catcher George Alberti, undermined his efforts in Philadelphia for decades.[6]

Black Philadelphians recognized that Shipley contributed to abolitionism by promoting interracial harmony. Upon hearing of his death "thousands collected in the vicinity of his dwelling," anxious to "mingle their tears and lamentations at the grace of one whom they had loved and revered as a protector and a friend." His friends James Forten, Charles Gardner, and Robert Purvis presided over a "numerous and respectable meeting of the people of color" to honor him after his death. This meeting affirmed that Shipley's "unwearied exertions contributed much to the melioration of the long-neglected condition of our people," and his loss represented a "void which time can never fill." Black Americans lost a genuine friend in Thomas Shipley.[7]

Purvis's tribute to Shipley pointed to the "broken hearts made whole" by their friend. All abolitionists owed a debt to the "principles of *Shipley*" (emphasis in the original). His principles were "our principles": "love their neighbors as themselves and secure a practical recognition of natural and equal rights amongst men." These same principles dictated that any attempt to arrest an African American as a fugitive from slavery was tantamount to a kidnapping. Securing these principles required "willing, active co-operators in the great work of Abolition," which Purvis and his allies actualized. Finally, these principles were premised upon respect, adoration, and intimacy between African Americans and whites and revealed how street diplomacy bred hope for an emancipatory future for all Americans.[8]

The Rise of Robert Purvis

Purvis vowed to continue the work of street diplomacy. In his eulogy to Shipley, Purvis outlined the perils faced by Black Philadelphians: "the wife of your bosom, the child of your heart, the friend of your confidence, may fall a victim to the hellish talons of a northern kidnapper, be thrown into the presence of a prejudiced judge, and without an intercessor, doomed to hopeless, hapless, interminable bondage." Such day-to-day realities haunted Purvis, who as a light-skinned elite Black man shuddered at the plight of poor Black Philadelphians who struggled against institutionalized slave catching. As a conductor on the fledgling Underground Railroad, Purvis matched his actions to his words: he delivered caustic speeches attacking slavery in public, and he

Robert Purvis's role in securing the freedom of hundreds of African Americans and overall work to promote liberty in the United States defies words, as he perpetually agitated against enslavement through his words, works, and compassion. Courtesy of the Boston Public Library

protected fugitives from slavery and accused Blacks by hiding them in his Lombard Street home. These actions produced grave consequences for Purvis and made him a target for violent rioters in Philadelphia. As the historian Christopher J. Bonner has asserted, African Americans like Purvis helped popularize "lawbreaking" activities such as these and, in doing so, worked to redefine their legal relationship with local, state, and national governments. Purvis persevered as the new face of street diplomacy and abolitionism at the risk of becoming a victim of the violence he so deplored, and he went to great lengths to secret hundreds of Blacks into and out of Philadelphia for decades.[9]

The case of the Dorsey brothers left the deepest impression on Purvis and spotlighted his skills as a street diplomat. Brothers Basil, Thomas, Charles, and William Dorsey arrived in Philadelphia looking for work in the summer of 1836. Their father, a recently deceased Maryland slaveholder named Sabrett Sollers, promised to free them upon his death yet omitted that guarantee in his will. The brothers, now "finding themselves slaves" in Maryland, fled to Pennsylvania. Purvis hired all but Thomas to work on his farm in Bucks County, north of the city. Basil's wife, a free woman in Maryland, and her brother-in-law, also free, soon joined the Dorseys at Purvis's farm. The brothers worked and lived in freedom for about a year and a half. In 1838 the Dorseys' "false and treacherous villain" of a brother-in-law worked with a "notorious slave catcher" to contact Sabrett Sollers's son, Thomas Sollers. Like other Black kidnappers, the Dorseys' brother-in-law lived and surveilled within Purvis's home as a means to gather information and ultimately, transform the brothers into money. The brother-in-law, slave catcher, and Sollers tracked Thomas Dorsey to Philadelphia, seized him in the street with the help of a constable, brought him before a judge, and carried him back to Baltimore. While Purvis and other Philadelphians raised $1,000 to purchase Thomas's freedom, the other Dorseys were far from safe in Pennsylvania.[10]

Thomas Sollers and the slave catcher sought to avoid street diplomats like Purvis and Pennsylvania state law when they returned to Bucks County to apprehend Thomas's brother, Basil Dorsey. Instead, these men relied on illusory borders: the 1793 Fugitive Slave Act that permitted "removal" across the country and willing accomplices, in this case an unnamed constable and a group of slave catchers, who viewed removing and kidnapping as their constitutional right and livelihood. The slave catcher, an unnamed constable, and Sollers apprehended Basil while he was working outside of Purvis's home. Basil struggled with the men, who carried him off to Bristol (also in Bucks County). An "excited" crowd of Bristol residents formed outside the market house where the slave catchers had imprisoned Basil, which to anyone present portended a rescue attempt, a riot, or both.[11]

Purvis negotiated with Sollers to release Basil. When the negotiations broke down, Purvis agreed to go with Sollers to Judge Fox of Doylestown the next day. When Purvis returned to his farm, he was alarmed to find Charles Dorsey at the doorway holding a "double barreled gun heavily charged." Whether a coincidence or not, it is not too much to speculate that Sollers took Basil to

Bristol to divert attention from a second group of slave catchers charged with taking Charles. Unwilling to risk bloodshed, Purvis secreted Charles and William to his brother's farm a few miles away, after which point the pair traveled to New Jersey, and from there to freedom in Canada.[12]

Even with one set of brothers safe, Purvis rose early the next morning to secure Basil. On his way to Bristol a woman informed him that she saw the slave catchers taking Basil to the courthouse a full hour earlier than was agreed upon at the previous day's "parley." "Go tell Mr. Purvis, they are taking me off!" Basil screamed as he passed by the woman. This extemporaneous cry of freedom found refuge in this stranger's heart, an anonymous street diplomat who did not need to tell Purvis anything. Purvis raced to the courthouse with Basil's family in tow and surprised the slave catchers by arriving early to court. "Doubtless the judge was deeply impressed by the appearance in the court-room of the delicate and beautiful wife and the young children clinging to the husband and father," Purvis recalled. A common but overlooked practice endemic to cases involving fugitives from slavery, bringing Basil's family to court made it clear to everyone that lives and future freedoms hung in the balance. The judge's sympathy for the Dorsey family convinced him to postpone the trial.[13]

In the meantime, Purvis concocted a plan to combine the immediatist and "practical" impulses of this new abolitionism. From the outset, Basil well understood the potential consequences of the trial and declared to the packed courtroom that "if the decision goes against me, I will cut my throat in the Court House, I will not go back to slavery." Moved by Basil's conviction, Purvis "resolved that no effort should be spared to secure Basil's freedom." Purvis planned to "arouse the colored people to rescue [Basil]" and organize "in squads about the three leading roads of the town." These "desperate measures" ultimately proved unnecessary, according to Purvis, for he had also enlisted the support of David Paul Brown. "I am always ready to defend the liberty of any human being," Brown told Purvis. Noteworthy here was Purvis's dual and complementary strategies: he recruited African Americans on the scene and a well-known white lawyer from afar in order to protect Basil. Purvis and other street diplomats like him did not depend upon a "white savior" strategy as much as they implemented every means available to ensure Black freedom.[14]

Now it was Brown's turn to exercise street diplomacy. He unloaded the full fury of his moral and legal sagacity onto Sollers's young lawyer, Mr. Griffith, who had never appeared before the bar. Brown demanded that the plaintiff show that "Maryland *is* a slave state" (emphasis in the original). "Why Mr.

Brown," Griffith responded, "everybody knows Maryland is a slave State." Brown retorted "everybody is nobody"—to which Griffith obtained a copy of the Laws of Maryland, though the book "was not considered authority" according to the judge, who promptly dismissed the case. Basil almost breathed a sigh of relief until the judge then suggested that Sollers could secure Basil's "re-arrest" by implementing Pennsylvania state law and obtaining a warrant from another magistrate, a typical strategy employed by slave catchers when things did not go their way. This time Purvis improvised and rushed Basil out of the courthouse, only to be met by Sollers and his slave hunters waving this new warrant. They attempted to pull Basil off of Purvis's horse, but Purvis cracked the whip and the horse rode out of town. The African American crowd outside the courtroom exploded with applause at Purvis's and Basil's bravery, leaving Sollers empty-handed. Basil resettled in New York, and with the help of the abolitionist editor of the *Emancipator* Joshua Leavitt, spent the rest of his life in Connecticut.[15]

While Purvis may have spoken with aplomb in the safe haven of 1883 America, his words and actions in 1838 actualized street diplomacy. Purvis's open-armed acceptance and sheltering of the Dorsey brothers in 1836 was at the time an illegal act, one that could have resulted in Purvis's own arrest for kidnapping enslaved "property." The hypothetical arrest of Robert Purvis on charges of kidnapping in 1836 would result in a hefty fine and jail time, to say nothing of the violence that Sollers and the quasi–law enforcement officials who hunted the Dorseys exacted upon African Americans like Purvis. The same process of street diplomacy that saved Purvis and the Dorsey brothers not only required navigating state and federal law but, more importantly, meant combining the traditional legal efforts of the PAS with the immediate impulse of African Americans and their allies to assemble and organize rescues. The willingness of abolitionists like Shipley and Purvis to mix these strategies matched the bravery and resolution of ordinary African Americans like Basil Dorsey, who viewed the horrific public spectacle of slitting their own throats more appealing than living out their existences in an enslaved future.

Pennsylvania Governor Joseph Ritner, Anti-Mason and Antislavery

Philadelphia street diplomats tapped into their personal experiences to pressure Pennsylvania politicians to support trial by jury for fugitives from slavery in Pennsylvania. In late 1836 the interracial and immediatist Young Men's Anti-Slavery Society submitted a memorial before the Pennsylvania state legislature that would make "all who live in the land of Penn . . . feel secure that justice will be done to them and theirs." The PAS adopted a resolution to call for jury trials, too, while a state antislavery convention held in Harrisburg urged all abolitionists in Pennsylvania to unite as one voice and speak to politicians about this important issue.[16]

Philadelphia abolitionists knew that the campaign to pass this bill might garner more political support because of the current governor of Pennsylvania, the Anti-Mason Joseph Ritner. Born on a farm in Berks County, Pennsylvania, Ritner was bound out by his father at the age of 13. Largely self-taught, Ritner married into the Alter family, a renowned household that supported the Democratic Party. Although he supported Jackson for president twice, Ritner left the Democracy for the populist politics of the Anti-Masonic Party in 1829. The Anti-Masons would go on to nominate him for governor three times, with his sole victory occurring in 1835. Statewide Ritner won a plurality of nearly 30,000 votes over his Democratic rivals (who experienced a temporary party schism) and carried the Whig strongholds of Pittsburgh and Philadelphia. Ritner's chief ally in the state legislature was Thaddeus Stevens, who, lauded by abolitionists for his fierce antislavery arguments, forged an alliance between the Anti-Mason and Whig Parties in Pennsylvania, giving the governor's office to Ritner.[17]

Ritner's inaugural address castigated those who attacked comity and "the doctrines of the people of this state." Noting how the history of emancipation in Pennsylvania ought to be "written in letters of gold," he reiterated the tireless efforts of Pennsylvanians to expel "the evil from her own borders." While Ritner acknowledged that Pennsylvania respected "the Constitutional rights of the other States," it now seemed as though comity had devolved into sister states "imposing terms and dictating conditions" on Pennsylvania, including attacks on free discussion—an obvious critique of the congressional gag rule, which the US House of Representatives instituted in May 1836 in order to table antislavery petitions—and possibly even the censoring of abolitionist mailings. Ritner chided those who would silence Pennsylvania's history of rebuking slavery in the state and, in doing so, brought to the fore a fear of unconstitutional subjection by other states. By identifying comity as subjection to and not friendship with neighboring states, Ritner applied to state and national politics that which fit squarely into the local conflicts experienced by Black and white Philadelphians who engaged comity through street diplomacy.[18]

Pennsylvania's abolitionist community praised Ritner's speech. The Young Men's Anti-Slavery Society published a statement about Ritner, calling him a

"true Pennsylvanian" unafraid to defend "our right to think and act for ourselves." The PAS noted at its general meeting in December 1836 that it, too,
approved of Ritner's address. The poet-abolitionist John Greenleaf Whittier
composed a poem entitled "Ritner." Whittier called Ritner the "one spirit un-
trammeled" by the "Traitors to Freedom, and Honor, and God, / Are bowed
at an Idol polluted with blood." He pondered "will that land of the free and
the good wear a chain?" "No, Ritner!" Whittier replied: the "friends" of freedom and truth will stand as one and proclaim "Our Country and Liberty!
God for the Right!" Whittier's poem to Ritner reflected the hope abolitionists
placed in the governor, so much so that they felt emboldened enough to publish a list containing hundreds of names of Pennsylvania abolitionists within
the Young Men's Anti-Slavery Society's memorial to Ritner.[19]

Despite having an antislavery, pro–Pennsylvania states' rights governor
and a fractured state Senate, the trial by jury bill failed to pass. While details
as to precisely why the bill did not pass remained scanty in the newspapers
of the time, the *Harrisburg Reporter* noted that the bill engendered "consid-
erable discussion" in the state Senate. Perhaps Philadelphia's state senators,
Democrats all, who voted against the bill influenced their colleagues with the
not-so-hidden transcripts of race baiting, those "harvests of insults and injuries to human dignity" as explained by the anthropologist James C. Scott, so
prevalent in legislative debates of the time period (e.g., see the debates over
disenfranchising African Americans in Pennsylvania below). This Second
Party moment reasserted the power of the Philadelphia Democracy and exposed its recalcitrance toward helping Black Pennsylvanians. Part and parcel
with these Democratic senators, the final vote of 20–10 against trial by jury
reflected the fact that despite tripartisan support for the bill—i.e., Whigs,
western Pennsylvania Democrats, and Anti-Masons—accused fugitives from
slavery in Pennsylvania, and Philadelphia in particular, continued to endure
a precarious freedom.[20]

The Pennsylvania Constitutional Convention

The ongoing debates over comity and Black freedom in Pennsylvania dovetailed with the drive for a state constitutional convention. Competing political factions in Pennsylvania clamored for a new convention ever since the ink
had dried on the state's Constitution of 1790. Riding the tide of Andrew Jackson's victory in Pennsylvania in 1824, reform-minded Democrats, typically
from the northern and western parts of the state, tried numerous times to
democratize state government. An 1835 state referendum to amend the state

constitution passed by more than a 10,000-vote margin, and within a year, the Democratic majority in the state senate finally passed a bill calling for a convention to revise the state's Constitution in 1837. The convention began in Harrisburg on May 2, 1837, and the Whig–Anti-Mason alliance capitalized on its slim one-vote advantage over the Democrats to elect the Philadelphia native, prominent Whig, and antislavery sympathizer John Sergeant to the position of president of the convention.[21]

The 1790 state Constitution gave the vote to "every freeman, of the age of twenty-one years, having resided in the State two years next before the election, and within that time paid a State or county tax, which shall have been assessed at least six months before the election." Thus freedom, residency, and tax assessment defined the franchise in Pennsylvania, and in doing so elided the issues of race and enslavement, at least temporarily. Historians have shown how African American voting rights declined across the United States throughout the 1830s and 1840s. African Americans who demanded voting rights projected their own notions of citizenship rather than the amorphous suffrage distinctions promoted by the Pennsylvania state Constitution. Voting rights exposed the feedback loop "between laws on the books and decisions at the polls." Philadelphia's Black elite were crucial to the fight for voting rights and became emboldened precisely because they were mired in the ambiguous freedom afforded them in Philadelphia. In the words of the historian Ira Berlin, "by choice and of necessity," these elite African Americans pushed for their city and state to honor their conception of voting equality.[22]

Indeed, African Americans technically possessed the right to vote in Pennsylvania prior to 1837. Their supporters at the convention articulated how "prejudice or design"—i.e., voter intimidation and physical violence—prevented most, if not all, African Americans in Pennsylvania, especially those in Philadelphia, from voting. In addition, the historian Van Gosse has reasoned that a lack of tax assessment, again, especially in Philadelphia, prevented Blacks from being placed on voting rolls. Even such an established figure as James Forten could vote only indirectly, as revealed by his street conversation with Samuel Breck (see chapter 3). On the other hand, Forten left the notion of Black voting rights, in the words of the historian Julie Winch, "untested." Despite visiting Harrisburg multiple times in the early 1830s, Forten never pushed for the franchise; he believed "these slumbering privileges," i.e., voting rights, "need not be awakened now." In a sense, then, politicians braced themselves for two hypothetical situations: Black Pennsylvanians voting en masse and fugitives from slavery, inspired by Nat Turner, transgressing geographical borders to assault a whites-only political border known as the franchise.[23]

Whether or not African Americans actually voted in Pennsylvania elections, the issue over Black voting reminded white politicians of the political power of fugitives from slavery. Barely a month into the convention Black Philadelphians gathered at Mother Bethel on June 5, 1837, to strategize over how best to handle the issue of suffrage. The participants wrote that "the price of liberty is unceasing vigilance," which, to buttress a point developed by the historian Stephen Kantrowitz, meant a vigilance that connected local issues like voting to national issues like slavery. The attendees prepared a memorial that emphasized the "improvement of our colored brethren" in Philadelphia and the nation and tasked a delegation composed of Black abolitionist stalwarts Frederick Hinton and Charles Gardner to deliver the memorial and speak before politicians in Harrisburg.[24]

The anti-Black emigration disputes that permeated Pennsylvania political discourse were foundational to how delegates debated Black voting rights. White delegates to the constitutional convention equated Black emigration into the state with the ongoing crisis of fugitives from slavery that erased the border between slavery and freedom. When delegates broached the topic of Black emigration on June 9, they bolstered a perceived rather than actual threat to white, especially Irish, employment in the state. The convention resolved "that a committee be appointed to enquire into the expediency of so amending the Constitution of Pennsylvania, as to prohibit the future emigration into this State, of free persons of color and fugitives from slavery, from other States or territories." Thaddeus Stevens moved for the resolution to be postponed "indefinitely," because "it could reflect no credit on the head or the heart of this body, to give any countenance to a proposition so totally at war with the Principles of the Declaration of Independence, the Bill of Rights, and the spirit of our free institutions." When Sergeant opened the resolution to a vote, the delegates agreed to continue to debate the matter.[25]

Motivated by their colleagues' antislavery sympathies, other Pennsylvania Democrats injected racist vitriol into the debate. John Cummins, a Democrat from Juniata County, rebuked his fellow Democrat William Darlington's suggestion to replace "of free persons of color and fugitives from slavery, from other States or territories" with "of all foreigners." Echoing anti-Black invective from the Turner rebellion, Cummins argued that unlike "the Blacks," recent immigrants like the Irish did not come "as beggars." Darlington then recast the voting issue as an immigration issue by stating that, similar to the

problems of preventing the Irish from entering Pennsylvania, a clear "difficulty would stand in the way" of Black emigration. Furthermore, Darlington
reasoned, "it was well known that in some of the States, free persons of color
were put on the same footing of all other free citizens, and entitled to vote as
such." These opening moves by Stevens, Cummins, and Darlington revealed
early in the debate how their racial presuppositions reflected the fear of Black
aspirations to white equality, an aspiration that Darlington, a white man,
crystallized in his retort to Cummins.[26]

Proponents of Black disenfranchisement trumpeted the manufactured danger of Black freedom throughout the convention. Concerns over Black mobility and equality spread like a contagion amongst the convention's Democrats, especially on June 19, when Democrat John B. Sterigere of Montgomery
County (directly north and west of and neighboring Philadelphia) sought to
change the language of voting rights to "free white male citizen." Although
the delegates initially voted 61–49 against adding "white" to qualify for the
vote, E. T. McDowell, a Democrat from Bucks County and a "principal cham-
pion" of the Democracy during the convention, wondered, "If a negro is a
human being, and not a *baboon,* as some contend—if he is born in Pennsylvania—is twenty-one years of age, and is not a slave then he is a freeman and
a citizen, and is entitled to vote. Sir, is it not so? A free negro is the freest man
on earth—his freedom is unrestrained and irresponsible—unmixed with a ra-
tional intervention or Constitutional limitation. Are we seriously asked thus
to enlarge the ballot boxes?" McDowell conceded that perhaps at "best 50"
Blacks out of a statewide population of nearly 40,000 might have the "mental
and moral condition" to qualify as voters. However, he feared that enfran-
chisement would encourage Black Pennsylvanians—"degraded and debased,
as nine tenths of them are"—to storm polling places on Election Day; he
theorized that as many as 5,000 African Americans could vote in Philadelphia alone. Yet McDowell ignored how Philadelphia Blacks faced both the
"soft" racism of friendly whites discouraging them from voting and tax assessors who refused to add their names to voter rolls and the "hard" racism of
violence on Election Day. Instead, McDowell and his Democratic allies believed that they alone could stave off the "impending doom" of enfranchising
African Americans.[27]

The Black Vote in Practice

Democratic delegates credited street diplomacy for the supposed flood of
Black voters and fugitives from slavery. After all, street diplomats collaborated

across racial lines and, despite the omnipresent terror of "legal" arrests and kidnappings, enacted a variety of strategies to create a safe and welcoming environment for African Americans living in Philadelphia. It is no surprise then that Benjamin Martin, a Democrat from Philadelphia County, feared that Pennsylvania would continue to act as a beacon of liberty for Black Americans. His push to deny suffrage conflated free and "fugitive" Black emigration: Martin bemoaned how African Americans saw Pennsylvania as free soil at best and, at worst, a terrifying waystation between the Slave South and Canada—a mixed success of street diplomacy. "The great increase of the colored population" in Philadelphia during recent years, argued Martin, portended an all-out explosion if African Americans gained the vote. African American voters were the first step along a dangerous path, as Martin feared that Black-majority wards would go completely for the "Black" candidates, who might "distribute all the offices" to their African American constituents. Martin's overriding concern was to prevent disrupting the status quo, a normalcy whites expected to enjoy in Philadelphia and Pennsylvania: "there always must be an inequality." Whether this inequality manifested itself in voting, crossing borders, or unwarranted violence, Martin's words underscored the interconnected dangers African Americans faced in Pennsylvania.[28]

A number of significant developments regarding African American voting rights occurred across the state before the convention reconvened in January 1838. In July 1837 the Pennsylvania Supreme Court decided on a case from Luzerne County, *Fogg v. Hobbs,* in which an election official named Hiram Hobbs had turned away a property-owning, taxpaying African American man named William Fogg in October 1835. Although Fogg won at the county level, Hobbs appealed to the state Supreme Court, which overturned the county court's decision. Justice John Gibson believed that one could not successfully divide sovereignty between the states and the federal government. At both levels, these entities possessed a sovereignty that expected and demanded comity. Gibson therefore argued that enslaved African Americans held in the South should not be treated as Pennsylvania freemen or citizens, but he spoke nothing of the opposite situation that permeated daily life in Black Philadelphia, i.e., free people being identified as fugitives from slavery. "Slavery is to be dealt with by those whose existence depends on the skill with which it is treated," asserted Gibson, whose words epitomized a comity friendly to slaveholders.[29]

Further complicating matters, in October 1837 "thirty or forty" African Americans voted in an election in Bucks County, the results of which were immediately challenged in court. The African Americans who had voted then drafted a petition, which sparked a fierce debate among the delegates when the convention reconvened in Philadelphia in November 1837. Recognizing the petition meant acknowledging the fragile nature of comity. George Shellito of Crawford County argued that allowing Blacks to vote as stipulated by the Bucks County petition was tantamount to "amalgamation to the fullest extent" and sure to face opprobrium from the "southern states of the confederacy." "Would not such a state of things result in the dissolution of this Union," he asked and concluded that "Pennsylvania had better withdraw from the Union at once, than venture upon an experiment of this kind."[30]

The judge in the Bucks County case was John Fox, a known Democrat and opponent of Black suffrage. Fox reviewed the 1776 state Constitution and the Gradual Abolition Act of 1780. Pennsylvanians who supported Black voting conflated these two documents because they believed the latter granted political rights to Black citizens on par with whites and, more importantly, gave Blacks "all privileges and immunities of citizens in the several states." Fox upheld the Democracy's comity: "Could any one of the slaveholding states have supposed that they were making a compact, by which a free Negro of another state would have the right to pass into a slave holding state, and there be entitled to all the privileges and immunities of a citizen of that state?" Put simply, had the Southern slave states known that Pennsylvanians would interpret African Americans in their state as citizens, they would have never ratified the US Constitution. Blacks were not entitled to a comity that protected them, and Fox did not differentiate free from enslaved African Americans. In December 1837, Fox ruled against the African American voters.[31]

Changed Venue, Unchanged Minds

The convention reconvened in Philadelphia in January 1838, an appropriate location to discuss African American freedom. The delegates returned to the suffrage question on January 17, when Benjamin Martin proposed inserting the word "white" before "freemen" to determine eligible voters. Calling Black voting rights "a violation of the law of nature" and amalgamation, Martin believed restricting the suffrage to white Pennsylvanians would prevent "a war between the races." Rehashing arguments from the previous fall, Martin declared that African American suffrage would make Pennsylvania a "receptacle" of fugitives from slavery. As matters stood, fugitives from slavery possessed the dual effect of threatening "honest and industrious" white workingmen and inspiring abolitionists' "fanaticism." Martin concluded that Pennsylvania's "destiny" depended upon a whites-only suffrage commensurate with a whites-only freedom. Viewing these debates through Martin's fears, one observes how politicians interpreted street diplomacy: as Americans, they could never separate the fate of African Americans from the fate of Pennsylvania as well as the fate of Pennsylvania from the fate of the Union.[32]

Moderate politicians familiar with the plight of Black Pennsylvanians could not extricate themselves from the voting rights debate. On January 18 Philadelphia Whig William Meredith of the 1826 liberty law debates spoke to the convention. He admitted that, while he knew a few African Americans who "possessed strong intellect," the mass of them "could not be considered as advanced in education, or in a knowledge of political principles." Giving them the right to vote would be "impolitic" at best. Besides, Meredith explained, "as long as the Constitution of the United States remained in force, we were bound rather to guard the rights of the south, than to do anything to impair them." Despite his hope that the South would abolish slavery, Meredith believed that Pennsylvania should not ratify a constitution that disrupted comity. His conciliatory approach to Southern slavery produced the opposite effect, for his words revealed how even political moderates wavered in the face of anti-Black racism, which pervaded Northern political discourse and threatened Pennsylvania's rights as a state in the Union.[33]

Democrat John Sterigere campaigned against Black suffrage across the state between the sessions, promoting the views of Pennsylvanians threatened by the Black vote. He told the convention that proposing the franchise meant proposing racial equality: political rights engendered human rights— an "insult" to white men. Black voters would "join one of the greatest political parties, or be controlled by some political demagogue, or modern abolitionist, and must become the umpire between the two great political parties in the state." Placing so much power in the hands of Black Pennsylvanians would no doubt make the state a true bastion of liberty. Protect white Pennsylvanians, i.e., their political, employment, and racial superiority, Sterigere argued, or else "tens and hundreds of thousands of this base and degraded caste, [would be] vomited upon us."[34]

The Pennsylvania Constitutional Convention represented a microcosm of the Union. Democrats stoked fears of Black equality while at the same time claiming, in the words of Democrat George Woodward from Luzerne County, that a lack of political equality helped Blacks "enjoy the blessings of freedom without prejudice." Channeling arguments made by Roger Taney barely two decades later, on January 20, Democrat Hiram Payne from McKean County moved further and sought to deprive Pennsylvania Blacks of their citizenship for a simple reason: the Pennsylvania Constitution could not define African Americans as citizens because it would be foolish, not to mention a gross violation of the Federal Constitution, to venture to Pennsylvania to recapture their "citizen" fugitives.[35]

While these Democrats preached vitriol, Democrat William Darlington from Chester County alluded to the forfeiture of Pennsylvania states' rights. Quaker-born and known as a "scorner of cant, bigotry, and hypocrisy," Darlington reminded the delegates and the audience in the gallery how in recent years the Southern states demanded that Pennsylvania deliver up African Americans to face enslavement under Southern laws. Now these states called on Pennsylvanians to vote with slavery against their own best interests, "be his color what it may." The true threat to the Union came from slaveholders and their allies in Pennsylvania, not from Black emigration, voting rights, or most importantly, interracial abolitionism, which flourished in the very city where the convention took place.[36]

Darlington's rousing speech brought the hall to a fever pitch and incited a major disturbance in the gallery from Black Philadelphia street diplomats. African Americans John P. Burr, Thomas Butler, James Forten, Jr., and "another highly respectable and worthy colored man" were violently ejected from the proceedings, not coincidentally right before the vote. Burr, the son of Mary Emmons, an East Indian woman and Aaron Burr, Jr., served as a member of the Vigilance Committee within the Pennsylvania Anti-Slavery Society. Butler, an affluent barber, made a name for himself in Philadelphia as a member of the Black elite. These men resisted their rough removal and served as a provocative reminder of street diplomacy: real people outside the hall who looked just like these men were constantly subjected to arbitrary arrests and kidnappings—denying them voting rights acted as another attack on fundamental human equality. What impact these removals had on the delegates remained unclear, but when they cast their final vote on including the word "white" as a qualification for voting in the state of Pennsylvania, the proposal to disenfranchise Blacks passed 77–45. The amendment would come up for the statewide constitutional ratification vote later that year in November 1838.[37]

Black activists gathered in March 1838 to draft an "Appeal of Forty Thousand Citizens, Threatened with Disenfranchisement, to the People of Pennsylvania." Purvis led the committee and linked the issue of voting to Black

freedom and comity. Neither the 1776 nor the 1790 Pennsylvania Constitu-
tions included the word "white" as a voting qualification. Ignoring this fact
risked "reimposing the chains" of slavery upon Black Pennsylvanians. Purvis
saw behind the veil of comity and found only white "free state" political aspi-
rants bowing to the "dark spirit of slavery." He argued that the "inconsider-
able" number of Blacks in Pennsylvania might force the slave states to "demand that a portion of the white tax-payers [be] unmanned and turned into
chattels." Would new racist demands for comity include enslaving Northern
whites?[38]

    While Purvis may have exaggerated the threat of white slavery, he cer-
tainly projected this future into the minds of whites to earn their support and
empathy. At the heart of this appeal lay the omnipresent fears experienced
by African Americans, who at any time could be "exposed to be arrested as
a fugitive slave." Here, on February 2, Purvis returned to the issue of trial by
jury for fugitives from slavery, a last-minute motion proposed at the convention by James C. Biddle, a leader of the Whig–Anti-Masonic coalition. Biddle
conceded that Pennsylvania must abide by the federal Fugitive Slave Act and
that slaveholders must respect the 1826 Pennsylvania liberty law, but he stated
that "nobody in the commonwealth of Pennsylvania presumed another to be
a slave . . . every man, at least *prima facie*, was a freeman." Here Biddle sounded
very much like a street diplomat, one who also assumed freedom when he
saw a Black person. Such a claim flew in the face of many white Philadelphians, who assumed the opposite when they saw constables or slaveholders
arresting African Americans. Biddle's words spoke to the assumptions made
by Black and white street diplomats, who considered themselves free by nature of their humanity. This assumption led to an obvious consequence to
street diplomats like Purvis and his Black and white allies: all "legal" removals
were kidnappings.[39]

The Rise and Fall of Pennsylvania Hall

Fed up with riots, anti-Black rancor, and flawed comity, and left with few
meeting places in the city, abolitionists convened in Philadelphia in 1838 to
solicit donations to fund their own hall "wherein the principles of *Liberty*,
and *Equality of Civil Rights*, could be freely discussed, and the evils of slavery
fearlessly portrayed." The Pennsylvania Abolition Society coordinated its
efforts with those of local Black leaders, the interracial Philadelphia Female
Anti-Slavery Society, and the recently formed Pennsylvania Anti-Slavery

Society to raise $40,000 for the task, and on May 14, 1838, the Pennsylvania Hall Association threw open the doors to Pennsylvania Hall. Three days later, rioters reduced the building to a smoldering pile of rubble.[40]

Pennsylvania Hall struck fear into the hearts of white politicians as a "fiery fulfilment" of interracial abolitionism. Philadelphia Democrat Charles Ingersoll viewed Pennsylvania as "the great central zone" that bound together the Union of the slaveholding South and the "slave-hating northeast": figuratively and literally Pennsylvania acted as the bond of Union between increasingly hostile regions. What disrupted comity more than allowing "slave-haters" to construct a "temple of abolition" in Philadelphia? Ingersoll saw folly in placing abolition and Pennsylvania in the same sentence, for according to him, there were "no slaves to be freed" in the state. While this was not completely true, as the 1830 and 1840 federal censuses counted 403 and 64 enslaved people in Pennsylvania (respectively), Ingersoll represented slaveholders at trial numerous times, people who could transform free Black Pennsylvanians into enslaved kidnapping victims. Ingersoll ignored such abstractions and proposed a solution to the menace of Pennsylvania Hall: once filled with abolitionist "traitors to the American Union," the building "should be desecrated to the demon of national discord and destruction." Ingersoll's views of Pennsylvania Hall reflected many white Philadelphians' prejudices and, in effect, all but encouraged Philadelphians with similar views to destroy the building. As a national political figure with ties to the South, Pennsylvania, and the intimate relationships forged through defending slaveholders in Philadelphia, Ingersoll brought together the local, state, and national dilemma of protecting African Americans in the antebellum North.[41]

Although abolitionists did not know that they were operating on borrowed time, in the three short days in which the building stood, activists, Black and white, male and female, deliberated numerous social issues and of course, listened to David Paul Brown's opening lecture. "Like life," Brown explained, liberty is "to be enjoyed, not to be defined, and it is improved in proportion as it is diffused." Listeners no doubt understood how Pennsylvania politicians permitted slavery to diffuse through political backchannels and outright violence directed toward African Americans in Philadelphia. "Am I a fanatic when I decidedly condemn kidnapping, man-stealing, trafficking in human flesh, disfiguring and destroying the mind of man, the miniature resemblance of the Deity?" Brown asked the audience. The real fanatics, Brown argued, were those whom Ingersoll encouraged to riot, the "last and lowest" class of citizens who were "always brawling about liberty without understanding it." The solution to this chaos lay within practical abolition, comity, and "every possible effort with the government, and with the free and slave states to abolish [slavery]." In short, Brown combined the liberating actions taken by ordinary people at the street level with his networking with political elites, and therefore he believed that maintaining the Union required working with slaveholders.[42]

In the speech's first half, Brown suggested that the ends justified the means. Street diplomacy necessitated employing multiple resources to ensure African American freedom, including working within the political system. According to William Lloyd Garrison (who spoke after Brown), the second half of Brown's speech, which sought "discretion" when dealing with the slave states, "neutralized all the good that had been said; it contained poison enough to kill all the colored men on earth." Garrison insisted that abolitionism in Philadelphia would not prosper and slavery throughout the nation would not end without "a most tremendous excitement"—disunion was the ultimate political means to an emancipatory end. Garrison's ally Charles C. Burleigh agreed and noted that the latter part of Brown's oration was a "surrender of fundamental principles." Garrison and Burleigh thundered for a "popular tumult" that went hand in hand with the pitched battles over street diplomacy that Brown had witnessed and worked to alleviate in Philadelphia for decades. Brown's views sounded obsolete to younger abolitionists like Garrison and Burleigh, who hoped to eclipse Brown's practical methods through perpetual agitation up to and including disunion. So while Garrison complimented Brown on his longstanding support of African Americans, he abhorred how Brown "preferred the perpetuity of slavery to a dissolution of the Union."[43]

These disputes over abolitionism and comity resonated with those who viewed Pennsylvania Hall and its supporters as a threat to maintaining a Union with slavery. Protestors, some of whom were Southerners, posted placards around Philadelphia that warned residents about how this abolitionist gathering planned to foist immediate emancipation upon Americans. The text on the placards encouraged Philadelphians to "interfere, *forcibly* if they *must*, and prevent the violation of these pledges [to the Union]." These anonymous protestors' public words and actions had in a way already received permission from Ingersoll and other Pennsylvania Democrats: the protesters and their allies trusted Philadelphians as Pennsylvanians and Americans to destroy the hall, defeat abolitionism, and maintain the Union all at once. One suspects that many white Philadelphians did not need additional pretexts to set fire to the building or attack African Americans; hundreds of concerned citizens heeded these incitements and gathered outside Pennsylvania Hall while the abolitionists inside presented their cases to an audience of more than 3,000 people.[44]

Public pronouncements of the hall's impending doom and the day-to-day threats to their lives, homes, and families forced the hall's board of managers to seek protection from the highest-ranking local politician, Mayor John Swift. Not only did Swift work as a lawyer for the PAS in the past, his actions during the Flying Horses riot were instrumental in protecting Black Philadelphians. The hall's board of managers asked Swift to defend the building from the crowd the day of the riot. Swift replied that "there are always two sides to a question—public opinion makes mobs and ninety-nine out of a hundred of those with whom I conversed are against you." He suggested that the managers shut down the building and give him the keys; the board of managers agreed to the proposal. When the riot erupted later that night, Swift urged the crowds to disperse by stating that the abolitionists did not plan to hold another meeting that night. Interestingly, Swift told the crowd that he would "*never call out the military here!*" because he considered this crowd of "fellow citizens" his "police." Trusting an unruly crowd to transform into sober law enforcement officials produced the opposite result, as the attacks on Pennsylvania Hall escalated soon after Swift departed. A group of dockworkers, who worked at the South Philadelphia wharves, lived beside African Americans in Cedar Ward, rubbed shoulders with slave-catching constables, and rioted against African Americans numerous times in the previous five years, broke into Pennsylvania Hall and set it ablaze. Some 15,000 people watched the "beautiful temple dedicated to liberty" burn to the ground.[45]

Spurred on by Democratic politicians, the presence of abolitionists, and a preconceived right to attack African Americans, the rioters all but declared an open season on Black Philadelphia. Rumors abounded that the meeting featured white women strutting around arm in arm with Black men and enraged the hostile crowd assembled in the streets outside the hall, who pelted the building with rocks and bricks and "pummel[ed]" a number of African Americans who had just left from that last fateful session. The rioters then attacked the nearby Shelter for Colored Orphans, Mother Bethel AME, and the office of the *Public Ledger*. PAS members rushed the children out of the shelter and face to face with the rioters; while likely, it is unknown whether they physically attacked the children. Mother Bethel of course represented a mainstay of Black life and achievement and unlike the shelter survived the riot intact. The crowd attacked the *Public Ledger* for promoting "free discussion," a mission shared by the supporters of Pennsylvania Hall. A May 18 editorial in that newspaper remarked that the perpetrators of this "scandalous outrage against law and decency" deserved quick and severe punishment. The rioters made their point clear to Black Philadelphia and their allies: those who supported Black lives and freedoms would face their wrath. The courts were of no help after the riot, either: while dozens of rioters were arrested, none of the rioters were convicted of rioting. It would take the hall's board of managers a decade to recoup part of their losses. No one rebuilt Pennsylvania Hall.[46]

The Aftermath

Despite its brief existence and yet much like the state Constitutional Convention, Pennsylvania Hall became a microcosm for the Union in 1838. The successes and consequences of street diplomacy, namely, interracial abolitionism premised upon assumptions of innate human freedom, pushed both ordinary and more politically connected whites to actualize a violent racism that eroded geographic borders. Attacking or defending the hall under a variety of pretexts, Philadelphians struggled over comity and what it meant to live in a Union with Southern slaveholders. Southerners "exulted" over the hall's destruction because they successfully gagged abolitionists at the local level just as they had at the national level. However, abolitionists who witnessed the carnage also used this local-as-national framework to work together. Robert Purvis spent the night of the riot trying to protect William Lloyd Garrison from the mob. Purvis reenacted an extraordinary rendition that would have resonated with a fugitive from slavery: he smuggled Garrison to Bucks County and directed his safe passage back to New England. Purvis's actions as a street diplomat on the local level ensured that Garrison would continue to agitate on the national level.[47]

The destruction made Philadelphia abolitionists even more resolute in their work. According to Daniel Neall, Jr., a white member of the Philadelphia Anti-Slavery Society, the destruction of Pennsylvania Hall ensured that "the slave has now friends in [Philadelphia] where ears were deaf to the Truth." In June 1838 Philadelphia abolitionists formed the Junior Anti-Slavery Society of Philadelphia, with Black and white members as young as the age of 15 vowing to use every "honorable means to affect [the] speedy overthrow" of slavery.

They organized a committee of "lectures and addresses" and held numerous meetings in and around Philadelphia. Clearly these young abolitionists had no intention of remaining silent in the face of threats to Black freedom.[48]

Older African American abolitionists redoubled their clandestine activities, too. Robert Purvis began reorganizing the Vigilant Committee of Philadelphia, which since its founding in 1837 had lapsed into a funding quagmire due to the costs of assisting large numbers of fugitives from slavery and kidnapping victims, which included legal, advertising, travel, food, and lodging expenses as well as a charity for victim's families. This committee formed an auxiliary wing, the Female Vigilant Association, led by Elizabeth White, Sarah McCrummell, and Harriet Forten Purvis. The fifteen-woman committee pledged to assist "the poor and oppressed of our country" in concert with the Philadelphia Vigilant Association. By 1839 Purvis had streamlined the Vigilance Committee by reassigning positions, refinancing expenditures, and interviewing fugitives from slavery to reduce the risk of "imposters" infiltrating what was a shadowy operation. By 1839, the day-to-day operations of both Vigilant Committees numbered at least three cases per week and revealed the numerous successes in spite of anti-abolitionist backlash that could have hampered their efforts from the get-go.[49]

Abolitionism, the state Constitutional Convention, and the recent burning of Pennsylvania Hall came back to haunt politicians during the October 1838 gubernatorial and congressional elections. Incumbent Anti-Mason Joseph Ritner ran against Democrat David R. Porter for the office of governor, and Democrat Charles Jared Ingersoll against incumbent Whig Charles Naylor for Pennsylvania's 3rd district seat located in Philadelphia. Generally sympathetic toward Pennsylvania Blacks and abolitionists, Ritner posted a $500 reward for information leading to the arrest of those responsible for the burning of Pennsylvania Hall. As the historian Andrew K. Diemer has noted, Ritner's critics "mocked" him for portraying himself as an abolitionist, while Ritner's allies denied that he was an abolitionist. Such a contorted political identity meant that politicians like Ritner who appeared "soft" on slavery therefore appeared to be enemies of the South, of comity, and the Union. His opponent, David Porter, latched onto Ritner's "abolitionism" and critiqued him for speaking out against the "gag rule" and for supporting jury trials for fugitives from slavery. Porter enlisted the help of Pennsylvania senator James Buchanan, who stated that Ritner's reelection "will be hailed as a victory by the abolitionists everywhere, [and] will be felt to the extremities of the Union as a most portentous omen of its dissolution." Pennsylvania once again stood at the precipice of dissolving the Union because of its citizens' views on comity and slavery.[50]

The contest between Ingersoll and Naylor also pivoted on these issues. Naylor's allies denounced Ingersoll for calling Northern workingmen "slaves in an equal degree with the negroes of the South" at the recent Constitutional Convention. This "disdainful" regard for Northern white labor complemented Ingersoll's derisive treatment of African American rights. Ingersoll's supporters retaliated by claiming that a vote for Ritner and Naylor meant a vote for Black suffrage and, thus, Black political equality. Ingersoll lost his bid, as did Ritner, yet the referendum to disenfranchise African Americans passed, albeit by a slim margin of less than 1 percent across the state. Ironically, more Philadelphians voted against the amendments when compared to the neighboring and western counties. Whether this reflected white sympathy toward African Americans in the city is uncertain, though perhaps African Americans and their allies campaigned more in Philadelphia than other counties, hence their local victory and statewide defeat. Regardless, Black Pennsylvanians lost the franchise in a time when their political actions as street diplomats dictated comity and national cohesion.[51]

"Evidently hurried and confused": The Case of William Stansbury

Disenfranchising Black Pennsylvanians represented a clear setback for the development of American democracy. Yet as mentioned above, such a defeat did not extinguish the drive of Black and white street diplomats. The 1839 case of William Stansbury exposed how abolitionists employed street diplomacy to combat a veteran slave catcher who relied on equally adroit, though illegal, maneuvers. The legal counsel for both sides also featured some heavy hitters, including David Paul Brown and future Philadelphia mayor Charles Gilpin representing the defense and Edward D. Ingraham representing the prosecution, men who had battled against each other for decades. Finally, no stranger to such cases and the politics therein, federal judge Joseph Hopkinson presided over the trial and added gravitas to the proceedings.[52]

William Stansbury worked as a carter and lived in South Philadelphia for decades. As with many African Americans who struggled on the city's economic margins, Stansbury's precarious freedom was subject to contest and confrontation. Unbeknownst to Stansbury, in January 1839 widow Ruth Williams of Prince George's County, Maryland, received a letter from the erstwhile Philadelphia constable and professional slave catcher George Alberti.

Alberti's contact with Williams illustrated how he and others like him performed the work of hunting human beings: they scoured "runaway" advertisements, collaborated with known slave merchants and jailers (for example, the infamous Hope Slatter in Maryland), and consulted with their Black and white informants in cities like Philadelphia. More importantly, Alberti was a known quantity to Southern slaveholders and one who utilized these methods irrespective of borders to arrest Stansbury.[53]

Slaveholders, kidnappers, and slave catchers alike relied on plausible deniability. Excuses of "mistaken identity" when hunting human beings showed not only how those groups denied accepting African Americans as individual human beings with individual bodies, lives, and futures but also how Americans would use any pretense to hunt and capture human beings, once again, irrespective of the border between slavery and freedom, law and criminality, truth and falsehood. Alberti and people like him worked to make any potential deniability appear plausible. He informed Williams that her enslaved man "Isaac" who had escaped from her in February 1816, now lived in Philadelphia. Alberti told Williams that he would "render his services for [Stansbury's] recovery for a given compensation" and send word of his arrest. In the meantime, Alberti protected himself and gave Williams a "full description" of Stansbury so that the Maryland witnesses would have an easier time recognizing him when they arrived in Philadelphia. The trap set, Alberti seized William Stansbury on the streets of Philadelphia on January 30, 1839.[54]

Understanding the efficacy of his street diplomat enemies, namely, their skill at gathering witnesses, proofs of freedom, and potential rescuers, Alberti rushed Stansbury to US district judge Joseph Hopkinson to obtain a removal certificate. Hopkinson reviewed Williams's claim from William W. Hall, Williams's grandson and acting claimant, and her attorney, Edward Ingraham, both of whom presented Hopkinson with an affidavit from Williams that stated that Stansbury had escaped in February 1816. Stansbury's lawyers, David Paul Brown and Charles Gilpin rejected Williams's affidavit because it violated the 1826 Pennsylvania liberty law, which made ex parte testimony from slaveholders inadmissible in court. Ingraham retorted that regardless of what Pennsylvania law said, the 1793 Fugitive Slave Act was clear: the presiding judge determined the proof of enslavement. Hopkinson disagreed with Ingraham, but not federal law, and suggested interpreting the clause in terms of the proof of ownership, which according to the act of Congress, "must be 'to the satisfaction of the judge.'" Dissatisfied by the slaveholder's evidence,

Hopkinson believed the question of Stansbury's freedom remained inconclusive. Significantly, Hopkinson's words symbolized the precarious tightrope all of the participants tread upon, that of discerning whether state or federal law reigned supreme when identifying supposed fugitives from slavery.[55]

Perhaps Ingraham thought that distinguishing between federal and state law would goad Hopkinson into making a summary judgment and deliver Stansbury to Williams. Hopkinson was too circumspect a judge, so Ingraham relied on his witness pool. Hopkinson disallowed an affidavit from one Maryland witness but allowed the will of Ruth Williams's husband into testimony, which listed a "boy named Isaac, about ten years old, appraised at $200." While Alberti and Ingraham's plan for a speedy rendition failed, several Marylanders who all happened to be in Philadelphia at the time of the arrest testified that Isaac and Stansbury were one and the same person. These Marylanders stated that Isaac had a burn on his forehead much like the scar on Stansbury's forehead, but they admitted that they had not seen Isaac for twenty years. The testimony of Marylander Dennis Duval also weakened Williams's claim. Duval confessed that he met and conversed with Alberti and Hall about Stansbury the previous night. When asked by David Paul Brown if he recollected the topic of conversation, Duval stated he could not remember. Although Hopkinson later stated he felt Duval was "evidently hurried and confused" and in need of forbearance, Hopkinson let Ingraham's conspiracy with Alberti and the other witnesses stand because such conversations seemed plausible and "legal," especially if Stansbury was a fugitive from slavery.[56]

"Evidently hurried and confused" might as well have described many African Americans' lives when confronted by the likes of Alberti, Ingraham, or Hall, human beings who did everything in their physical and legal power to enslave them. Their power to kidnap and enslave flew right into the clutches of Black and white street diplomats, who employed their entire arsenal to protect African American freedom. Thus, while Ingraham's witnesses relied on decades-old memories of "Isaac," an 1806 inventory, and inadmissible ex parte affidavits, Stansbury's defense relied upon the reputation of African American witnesses. No witness aided Stansbury's defense more than Ignatius Beck. An African American freedman and trusted friend of Richard Allen, Beck forged a reputation in the Black community "unimpeached by a whisper against his veracity or general character." Beck, too, experienced the terror of freedom in Philadelphia in 1810, when a "respectable looking man" kidnapped him. Only the combined efforts of Richard Allen and Isaac Hopper led to Beck's liberation. Beck testified that he met Stansbury in 1810, when Stansbury helped Beck move furniture into a tenement on St. Mary's Street, and he presented Hopkinson with a number of receipts from 1810 and 1811. He also knew that Stansbury was born free in New Bedford, Massachusetts, a fact Stansbury conveyed to Beck at some point early on in their relationship. Finally, Beck and other Black witnesses told the court that they and Stansbury worked together building batteries to protect Philadelphia during the War of 1812.[57]

Stansbury's case hinged on the plausibility of arresting a free Black man, the legality of a slaveholder's conspiracy, and the veracity of Black testimony. The plausible prospects transformed Stansbury's case into a question of comity between Pennsylvania and the slaveholding states. Hopkinson emphasized comity and the power of Black testimony when he decided in favor of Stansbury on March 8, 1839. Hopkinson began by praising the "general good character" of each sides' witnesses; in other words, each side, slavery and freedom, had a claim to Stansbury's life and freedom. "On the one side we have a citizen of a sister state," Hopkinson explained, "coming here under the protection and authority of that state, claiming to have restored to her certain property, of which she alleges she has been unlawfully deprived." Alberti and Ingraham's conspiring prior to the trial was irrelevant and "no part of my business," Hopkinson decided, as the real issue of Stansbury's identity involved Williams's "right" to have her "property" delivered to her by the 1793 Fugitive Slave Act. On the other hand, Hopkinson noted that Stansbury's position in the community, his family, friends, life, and future in Philadelphia may indeed be disrupted because "the happiness of Black and white, of the freeman and the slave, is intimately, I may say in our present circumstances, inseparably connected with the maintenance of that government." In a word, comity and therefore the Union depended upon two contradictory versions of "happiness": one version allowed slaveholders to steal human beings, the other version inspired Blacks and white street diplomats to work together to preserve freedom.[58]

Hopkinson reminded the claimants that even though they brought the case to a federal judge, they still held the trial in Philadelphia, Pennsylvania, where African American testimony was both valid and on par with white testimony. "It would be a strange principle for a court of justice to adopt, in trials of this sort," reasoned Hopkinson, "that no Black witness is to be believed; that perjury must be presumed of all of them." The silencing of African Americans in the Slave South did not cross into Pennsylvania, at least in this instance. However, the ability of proslavery forces to conspire across borders without consequence represented a subtle way in which African Americans could be silenced without due process. On the other hand, African American testimony coupled with the legal expertise of two white lawyers revealed how interracial abolitionism produced a positive result during an otherwise trying time for African American freedom in Philadelphia. When Hopkinson finished reading his opinion and released Stansbury, Stansbury's friends erupted in applause, carried him out of the courthouse, and "amid the greetings and grateful feelings of hundreds," triumphantly escorted him home to his family, which "had awaited throughout the trial in tearful anxiety."[59]

Prigg v. Pennsylvania and the 1826 Liberty Law

One wonders how many people present at Stansbury's celebration of freedom connected his plight with the larger issue of Black freedom across the country. We can, of course, never know the answer to that question, though street diplomats in Philadelphia certainly understood how local trials contained national consequences. Thus, Philadelphia abolitionists agreed with the city's *National Gazette* that *Prigg v. Pennsylvania* would "decide the conflicting question of State and national jurisdiction over fugitive slaves." The case began when an African American woman named Margaret Morgan escaped from Maryland in 1832. Respecting the 1826 Pennsylvania liberty law, slaveholder Edward Prigg and several other slave catchers obtained a warrant for her arrest from a justice of the peace in York County, Pennsylvania, and seized Morgan and her children in 1837. Prigg brought Morgan before this justice of the peace, who refused to hear the case. Frustrated, Prigg defied the 1826 liberty law and Fugitive Slave Act of 1793, both of which required a certificate of removal from a judge, and carried Morgan and her children back to slavery. Two months later a Pennsylvania grand jury found Prigg and his associates guilty of kidnapping. Pennsylvania governor David Porter requested that Maryland governor Thomas Veazey extradite the men on the condition that regardless of the verdict the case would go to the Supreme Court. The Pennsylvania court found the men guilty, and the case went before the US Supreme Court in May 1840.[60]

The Supreme Court needed to answer three questions in deciding *Prigg v. Pennsylvania*. First, did citizens from slaveholding states have the right to pursue fugitives from slavery into nonslaveholding states and remove them without resorting to "judicial tribunals"? Second, did slaveholders have the right to "the produce," i.e., free state children born of enslaved parents? Third, what exactly was "the Constitutionality of the laws of Pennsylvania on the subject of fugitive slaves"? The historian H. Robert Baker has written that the second question remained unanswered by the court, even though slaveholders would argue in future cases that the 1793 act "affixed the state of slavery to fugitives no matter where they ran [and] that their children would be subject to the law of the state from which they ran, and thus counted as slaves" (see chapter 6). On the first question, Justice Joseph Story, writing for the majority, stated that slaveholders possessed the right to retrieve fugitives from slavery from nonslaveholding states like Pennsylvania because the 1793 act contained "a positive and unqualified recognition of the right of the owner in the slave, unaffected by any state law or legislation whatsoever." Consequently, Story answered the third question by striking down the 1826 Pennsylvania liberty law, which "must be declared inoperative and void" because it modified the 1793 Fugitive Slave Act.[61]

Prigg's seizure of Morgan did not qualify as a kidnapping because Pennsylvania state law violated federal law, though according to Story, seizing fugitives from slavery represented a breach in the relationship between the federal government and slaveholders. Federal judges were few and far between within all the states of the Union, and requiring slaveholders to find these officials added to the difficulty of retrieval. Story then suggested that state officials could choose to exercise the authority to deal with fugitives from slavery under Article IV of the Constitution or the 1793 Fugitive Slave Act, "unless prohibited by state legislation." This phrase left open the possibility for future liberty laws in Pennsylvania, and in doing so, ensured the continuing struggle over Black freedom.[62]

The *Prigg* decision elicited mixed reactions from abolitionists. Some, like William Lloyd Garrison, stated that "the enormity of this decision of the Supreme Court cannot be exhibited in words." Conjuring fears that resonated with Blacks in Philadelphia, Garrison argued that now "the slaveholding power is permitted to roam without molestation through the Northern States." The "molestation" slaveholders and their allies faced in Pennsylvania came as a direct result of the work of street diplomats, especially the 1826 liberty law, which complicated the entire removal process. Other abolitionists, such as Alvan Stewart, opined that Congress should eliminate the 1793 act and place "Canada on Mason and Dixon's line." This congressional solution would destroy slavery in the border states "in three years." Nothing would be left but for the enslaved to walk over the border between the states and make themselves free.[63]

Since creating a new liberty law in Pennsylvania seemed impolitic at the moment, street diplomats in Philadelphia took to clandestine activities to defy federal laws premised upon kidnapping and enslavement. The minute books of the Philadelphia Female Anti-Slavery Society bore testament to the increased pace of self-emancipation efforts after *Prigg*. These records matter as much as, and at times more than, opining in newspapers because they showcase human lives, however fragmented. African American women in Philadelphia lent aid to fugitives from slavery through church donations, personal assistance, and fundraising efforts, with Sarah and Margaretta Forten leading the charge. Donations and fundraising revenue went from the pockets of ordinary people and into the coffers of the Pennsylvania branch of the American Anti-Slavery Society. These ordinary yet to us anonymous street diplomats directly contributed to efforts that protected vulnerable Blacks in Philadelphia.

The street diplomats in the Vigilant Committee also experienced a resurgence in fugitives from slavery after *Prigg*. Led by Black dentist James Mc-Crummell, the Vigilant Committee, which frequently met at Robert Purvis's home, handled more than twice the number of cases in the six months following *Prigg* than in the previous year. The auxiliary Female Vigilant Association, led by Elizabeth White, assisted with cases, too, and furthermore raised money to celebrate West Indian Emancipation, an event that ended in ignominy in 1842. Nonetheless, these committees did not merely spur the growth of the Underground Railroad in the region: the Philadelphia Vigilance Committees were the preeminent organizations dedicated to Black freedom in the country. In essence, the vigilance of street diplomats in Philadelphia created, inspired, and enshrined the Underground Railroad in the United States. Ironically, the successes of street diplomacy transformed Philadelphia into a waystation instead of a terminus for fugitives from slavery and suggested that while the city maintained an efficient network of interracial activists willing to assist them, their final destination, Canada, proved safer.[64]

Three days after the *Prigg* decision, Philadelphia lost one of the guiding lights of the Black community: James Forten, who passed away on March 4, 1842. Robert Purvis and Stephen Gloucester memorialized Forten in two speeches before an interracial audience numbering in the thousands. "The Life and Character of James Forten," stated Purvis, consisted of "benevolence." Forten rescued kidnapping victims personally on at least two occasions, and his petitioning and pamphleteering efforts often reproached white politicians for their treatment toward Blacks in Pennsylvania. To Purvis, reflecting the interracial cooperation so vital to Philadelphia abolitionism, Forten "was a *model*, not . . . for what is called 'colored men,' but for all men." Like Shipley, as a street diplomat, James Forten transcended the color line and though cautious at times, proved effective in his ability to galvanize and support the Black and white community.[65]

Gloucester took a more theological approach to Forten's life, and he began by discussing Forten vis-à-vis the biblical Solomon's conduct as a man and as a servant of God. As a man, Forten displayed intelligence, punctuality, and energy, traits that he utilized to help free Gloucester's own family from slavery decades before. As a servant of God, Forten dedicated himself to God's will, and "Providence seemed to smile on him, and prospered him in all he did, and withersoever he turned himself." The prosperity of an elite Black man working with white allies to free other Blacks seemed self-evident, and Forten's passing in a way promoted the prosperity of his son-in-law Purvis, whose vim and cunning as a street diplomat borrowed heavily from Forten and, in so doing, overcame some of the conservatism Forten displayed during his life. Purvis and Gloucester delivered their eulogies not only to commemorate the passing of a powerful and noble ally: as Philadelphia Vigilant Committee members and street diplomats, they channeled their own hopes and aspirations into the ongoing project of protecting the Black community irrespective of the law; freedom was that important.[66]

Mary Louden Interprets the Local, the State, and the National

National decisions like *Prigg* did little to prevent the flow of African Americans and slaveholders going to Philadelphia. The streets of the city remained a battleground because street diplomats challenged slaveholders and, therefore, federal law. Street diplomats made life-altering decisions that promoted innate human freedom and bore the consequences of comity and Union. These men and women understood how they could implement legal knowledge and collaborate with allies to prevent enslavement from extinguishing an individual's life and future. The case of Mary Louden that rocked Philadelphia a month after Forten's death showed how street diplomats confronted slaveholders in the wake of *Prigg*.

The incident began in 1833, when an African American woman named Mary Scott fled Virginia for Philadelphia. Scott married Jabez Louden in 1835 but never revealed to her husband that she had escaped slavery, even when her former "master," a Mr. Watson, came to visit the couple every spring. On May 27, 1842, an African American woman informed the Loudens that Watson wished to meet with them at the United States Hotel on Chestnut Street. The pair obliged and after a brief conversation with Watson, the Virginian told Louden to meet him downstairs in the hotel bar to share a drink. When Watson failed to appear, Louden returned to the room and found the door locked. "They have laid a plan to kidnap me," Mary screamed from inside the room, prompting Louden to "give the alarm" and raise some friends to help rescue her from Watson and James Crawford, a Philadelphia constable Watson enlisted to kidnap Mary. Not having found any help, Louden returned to the hotel to find Watson and Crawford loading Mary into a carriage. Louden's public cries of "kidnapper" and "murderer" brought a large number of people to the hotel, including several watchmen and policemen. Meanwhile, Louden got word that the carriage was en route to Moyamensing prison. He trailed the vehicle, which instead of heading to the prison, left the city. The Delaware abolitionist Thomas Garrett helped Louden track the carriage to Wilmington, Delaware. When the pair confronted Watson, he promised to "shoot anyone who attempted to wrest his property from him." Fearing for their lives, Louden and Garrett watched Watson shove Mary aboard a train for Baltimore.[67]

The failure to rescue Mary Louden from that train symbolized the failings of the removal protocol established by the 1793 Fugitive Slave Act and reaffirmed by *Prigg*. As a slaveholder, Watson did not have to obtain a warrant for Mary's arrest, which begs the question as to why he obtained one from Philadelphia alderman John Binns in the first place. The most likely answer was that all of the players involved, from Watson to Mary and later the PAS, needed to interpret federal and state laws on the streets of Philadelphia, taking care to act as meticulously as possible when faced with obscure and obscuring legal questions. That is to say, like Black and white street diplomats in Philadelphia consulting local, state, and government officials, slaveholders protected themselves by conducting removals that respected federal law in the form of the Constitution and state law in the form of an alderman's warrant.[68]

Now lacking the protection of the 1826 liberty law, the PAS could only press charges against constable Crawford and alderman Binns for kidnapping Mary. Jabez Louden and the PAS castigated constable Crawford for his role in "this abominable transaction." The Philadelphia city recorder, Richard Vaux, met and listened to the depositions gathered by the PAS and confirmed that

Crawford would be bound over to the courts. When Crawford went before the Court of General Sessions, the grand jury "ignored all the bills growing out of the Mary Louden case" and dismissed the charges. Louden and the PAS contacted Philadelphia mayor John Scott and urged him to arrest Binns for a misdemeanor in office for failing to keep a record of this warrant; Scott told them to gather the necessary depositions, which they did. Interestingly, when Louden and the PAS presented the depositions to Scott, they did so with the hope that they would "at least [prevent] a similar circumstance from again occurring in this city." While there was no record of Scott's response to these depositions, a silence that may have meant that the deponents somehow lacked credibility, he did agree with the PAS that the carriage driver who helped Watson abduct Mary be bound over to the criminal court. Perhaps believing that the charge against Binns was a nonstarter, the PAS instead shifted strategies not by its own accord: Mary Louden took matters into her own hands.[69]

Mary attempted to free herself by implementing the logic of *Prigg:* she appealed to circuit court judge James Herbert Gholson, a Virginia federal judge. While in prison in Petersburg, Virginia, Mary wrote in a letter to the PAS that Gholson "had seen or knew something of the written permission given her by Watson" to leave Virginia and settle in Philadelphia. When the PAS contacted Gholson about this claim, he declared to "have no knowledge of the transactions of which you write and it would be alike inconsistent with my personal feelings and official duties to have any conversation whatever with the subject." Whether or not Gholson knew Mary (or received a letter from her) remained unclear, but Mary's connection to a federal court judge exposed how ordinary African Americans clearly understood how to use elite whites to free themselves.[70]

The failed attempts to rescue Mary offered crucial insights into how *Prigg* promoted a comity favorable to slaveholders that linked local, state, and federal officials. Despite offering to listen to depositions from Black and white Philadelphians, Mayor Scott did not seem eager to enlist the help of the governor in arresting Watson and rescuing Mary. State officials like Binns received a slap on the wrist for not recording his issuing of a warrant to Watson for Mary's arrest, a warrant that would precipitate enslavement. Federal officials like Gholson pled ignorance about Mary's letter, going as far as to say that he did not "wish to know anything about" her situation. The product of these interconnections enslaved Mary Louden.

Mary's street diplomacy clearly frightened Watson. Like countless other slaveholders who purposefully sold African Americans as far away from

This ironic "View of the City of Brotherly Love" from 1843 demonstrates the seemingly omnipresent cacophony of conflict within the city. In particular, the lithograph depicts scenes from the 1842 Lombard Street riots that laid waste to Black Philadelphia. Courtesy of the American Antiquarian Society

their families as possible, Watson did not send her home to Virginia: he "let his brother take her with him to Arkansas." To add insult to injury, Watson claimed he did not fear "the excitement" caused by the case in Philadelphia, and he cared little about separating Mary from "her broken-hearted husband." Watson dictated Mary's future, sundering her family ties in the interest of slavery. A hard-wrought consolation to the case of Mary Louden came from the fact that even when Black and white street diplomats knew she was a fugitive from slavery going into the trial, they still tapped into available local, state, and federal resources. They failed to rescue Mary Louden, an African American woman who had admitted to her "fugitive" status, but the larger failure occurred through the unwillingness of white politicians at all levels of government to recognize the burden of freedom placed on African Americans in Philadelphia.[71]

The Lombard Street Riots

Constable James Crawford of 2 Wager Street, Philadelphia, provided a through line between Mary Louden and the 1842 Lombard Street riots. As previous chapters have revealed, a single person, whether Black or white, male or female, rich or poor, old or young, possessed the potential to bring together local, state, and national issues that contested slavery and freedom and, indeed, their actions shaped the futures of countless others. So when the PAS castigated the Philadelphia grand jury that met to determine the origins of the 1842 Lombard Street riots, it did so because that same body accepted testimony from constable James Crawford, who "presented the colored Temperance Hall as a nuisance."[72]

Throughout the summer of 1842, rumors spread within Philadelphia that a major attack on the Black population was imminent. One anti-Black commentator from Philadelphia spoke for many disgruntled whites when they despaired that African Americans would "take the city" if they continued to promote Black achievement and protect themselves from slaveholders. In effect, anti-Black thought reached the point in Philadelphia where any attempt by African Americans to live or dignify their own existences may face a brutal reprisal. As previous riots demonstrated, young, white, working-class Irish men took great umbrage at the successes of the African American community in Philadelphia. Recent developments in the Black community heightened white paranoia. The Black entrepreneur Stephen Smith built his Beneficial Hall in early 1842 as a replacement for Pennsylvania Hall, that temporary temple of liberty destroyed by rioters in 1838. Such a display of liberty from an elite Black man reaffirmed the work of both the male and female Vigilant Committees, who organized a parade to celebrate the anniversary of the emancipation of the British West Indies on August 1, 1842.[73]

Black Philadelphians' show of force overwhelmed white Philadelphians. Holding aloft banners displaying present prestige and future freedoms, over 1,000 African American members of the Black-led Young Men's Vigilant Association marched down Lombard Street in South Philadelphia on August 1. A few blocks into their march a crowd of white men and boys began pelting the procession with rocks and bricks. When a Black man punched a white boy for hitting one of his fellow marchers, South Philadelphia erupted into a "war," according to one witness. Hundreds of Blacks and whites fought viciously in the streets, with "missiles of every description" flying about the fracas. Streams of whites who caught word of the battle poured into the melee in the hopes of destroying the banner that the Vigilant Association used to lead its march. These whites believed a rumor that the "much talked of banner" featured an emancipated person with the words "Liberty or Death" written above them while a ship burned on the horizon. In reality, the banner portrayed an emancipated African American with the word "liberty" in gold letters. On the reverse side of the banner was this "pacific inscription":

The Young Men's Vigilant Association of Philadelphia
Instituted July 23, 1841
How grand in age, how fair in truth,
Are holy Friendship, Love, and Truth.

The perceived and actual meanings of the banner mattered for a number of reasons. First, one gets the sense that the Vigilant Committee cast the die by marching in force with the banner. To make such a point does not blame the victim as much as it argues that African Americans were willing to march because they were disgusted with the state of the country they built, bled, and died for: they were disgusted with their country. And as the historian Kellie Carter Jackson has made clear, by the 1840s many Black abolitionists shifted from moral suasion to physical violence as a means to liberate; what better example of such liberation than a banner that depicted an emancipated African American? Second, white rioters used any pretext to unleash their fury toward African Americans: parades celebrating Black achievement, replete with 1,000 African American Vigilant Committee members and a throng of thousands more Blacks and no doubt friendly whites seemed to confirm racist rioter's fears of Black Philadelphians and their allies' expression of street diplomacy. Finally, it was no stretch of the imagination to conclude that the actual meaning of the banner, which celebrated a past emancipation in the West Indies, presupposed the purpose of street diplomacy: a future emancipation in the United States, a point not lost on anyone involved in the parade or riot.[74]

White rioters eventually overwhelmed the marchers, who by this time began to scatter to all corners of the city. Once again, as slaveholders, kidnappers, and constables purposefully conflated the freedom and enslavement of the African Americans they hunted, the white rioters went about inflicting indiscriminate violence upon any African Americans they could find, especially those of "desperate character." This "desperate" group made a number of sallies into the ranks of the rioters, fighting for their lives and using any rock, brick, or club to do so. Many African Americans retreated to Sixth and Lombard Streets in the heart of Black Philadelphia, where superior numbers of white rioters again drove them from the streets. Similar to the 1834–1835 riots, hundreds of African Americans fled Philadelphia and the "summary justice" of the mob, choosing instead to lodge "in open air in the woods" and swamps of New Jersey. Meanwhile, the rioters now had the streets to themselves, and made good on their promise to burn down Smith's Beneficial Hall as well as Stephen Gloucester's Second Colored Presbyterian Church on St. Mary Street, two beloved symbols of Black freedom intrinsically connected to street diplomacy: Smith had hosted dozens of meetings there with other street diplomats and Gloucester had conducted crucial work on the 1826 liberty law. By the end of August 1, police had arrested merely two dozen rioters, while Black Philadelphia remained a ghost town.[75]

The rioters moved from destroying specific symbols of Black achievement to targeting specific street diplomats. A group of Irish men surrounded Robert Purvis's house at 270 Lombard Street the next day, August 2. Purvis sent his wife and children to the second floor, sat down on the stairs with a loaded rifle, prepared to fight to the death, and waited for the rioters to burst through the door. One wonders what nightmares swirled in Purvis's mind as he sat there waiting with his rifle; fortunately, the rioters spared the Purvis family. Later that day Philadelphia sheriff Henry Morris sent officers to Black Philadelphia, but the rioters repulsed their assault. This final action forced Mayor Scott to call out seven militia companies to restore order. Despite a few "light skirmishes" on the night of the 2nd, including a mob that threatened to burn another symbol of Black freedom and street diplomacy, Mother Bethel, the police and militia finally brought quiet to Philadelphia.[76]

African Americans began returning to Philadelphia on August 3. A theater of horrific scenes welcomed them: broken glass, bricks, buildings, weapons, and human beings strewn across an urban battlefield. The *Public Ledger* reported that across Cedar Ward, the heart of Black Philadelphia, there was "scarcely an alley or street, lane or avenue where the colored population lives but bears testimony to the fury of the mob." Robert Purvis, Charles Gardner, and Daniel Payne issued a joint statement defending the righteousness of the parade and catalogued the atrocities they witnessed, including assaults, theft of their property, and fires that enveloped Smith's Beneficial Hall and the Second Colored Presbyterian Church. One building that survived the destruction was the Colored Temperance Hall of Moyamensing: the "instigator" of the riots, according to constable Crawford.[77]

Returning to Crawford and the grand jury, the latter group convened on August 3 to inspect the damages in South Philadelphia. With callous eyes the grand jury scanned the devastation that was Black Philadelphia. Taking Crawford's advice, the jury called the Colored Temperance Hall of Moyamensing a "nuisance," and the cause of the "present excited state of feeling." Compounding these findings, the jury asserted on August 4 that the riot had been caused by "the display and parade of part of the colored population." It offered two solutions to avoid future riots in Black Philadelphia. First, city officials needed to devise and enforce a curfew for Black Philadelphians, especially when they left church service. This recommendation to limit Black mobility in Philadelphia smacked of the Black emigration debates of recent years, and never came into fruition. The second solution was to tear down the Colored Temperance Hall, which was carried out immediately.[78]

Thus, a parade that began as both a celebration of Black achievement and a show of force by the Black community ended in chaos. White rioters assumed that any display of Black achievement, from churches to "fancy" balls to marches and liberty halls, assumed the consequences. That is, whites viewed Black success as something that automatically denigrated their own self-worth, especially if the whites in question lived near and suffered with and competed with African Americans on the same economic margins. The other compounding factor, and an inspiring one at that, derived from 1,000 African American street diplomats (and no doubt some whites) marching together as one. This show of force provoked many Philadelphia whites to violence in the same way slaveholders and their allies committed violence against African Americans, North and South. African Americans wielded tremendous strength across the United States, not least of all through their street diplomatic efforts, which synthesized emancipatory strategies, transcended the color line, and viewed any assault on them as an affront to the entire Black community.

Conclusion

The street diplomat Robert Purvis could barely put into words the "most ferocious and bloody spirited mobs" he witnessed rampaging through Philadelphia in early August. Writing to his friend and fellow abolitionist Henry Clarke Wright, Purvis stated, "I am convinced of our utter and complete nothingness in public estimation." This "nothingness" manifested itself in various ways: the disenfranchisement of the state's Black population, the loss of Shipley and Forten, the destruction of Pennsylvania Hall, the *Prigg* decision, and of course, the riots themselves. White disdain seemed unending, increasing even, especially when political forces—namely, the Democracy—outright encouraged violence against Black Philadelphians. The cunning of street diplomats like Purvis and his allies lay within their ability to act and ensure that all African Americans enjoyed their freedom unhampered by terror, racism, and enslavement.[79]

Yet ordinary people–cum–street diplomats who fought against proslavery and anti-Black zealots continued to make informed and often extemporaneous existential decisions that spoke to their will to live in freedom: from Peter Mathias to the Dorsey brothers, William Stansbury, Margaret Morgan, and Mary Louden, these individuals collapsed the politics of slavery into a real and material set of possible futures, futures that disrupted comity and threatened the Union, futures that aspired to but did not guarantee freedom. This group of human beings, marked by struggle and hope in an amorphous present, emerged as the key players and playwrights in this theater of scenes, as they were neither Northern nor Southern, but simply American.

In the embers of the 1842 riot, while elite Black Philadelphians like Purvis had the means to relocate outside the city, most Blacks lacked that ability, and again, one wonders of the terrors that haunted this larger, latter group in the wake of the riots. For Charles Black, an African American man and longtime resident of Lombard Street; a man who fought in the War of 1812 after refusing to fight for the British while impressed and in chains aboard a British gun ship; a man whose father fought at Bunker Hill; and a man whose grandfather fought "in the old French war," the physical injuries that he sustained from a mob of angry whites who rushed into his house, dragged him down the stairs, and beat him "so unmercifully," reflected just one example of the pain suffered by African Americans during the riot, the pain that they carried every time they walked down the streets of Philadelphia.[80]

CHAPTER SIX

Interlocking Opportunities

The executive committee of the Pennsylvania Abolition Society (PAS) considered the following confluence at its August 1846 meeting in Philadelphia: "It having been intimated that in view of the excitement occasioned by the alteration of the Tariff, and the indignation so warmly expressed against the South, thro' whose influence that measure is mainly to be attributed, the present would be a favorable time to lay before the people the great power which the slaveholding interest exerts in Congress to the detriment of Northern labor."[1]

Philadelphia abolitionists viewed the summer of 1846 as a set of interlocking opportunities designed to establish the status of freedom and slavery in Pennsylvania. Debates over a national tariff that benefited the Slave South to the expense of Northern states, particularly Pennsylvania, presented a convergence by which abolitionists exploited comity borne from their work as street diplomats. The current US vice president George Mifflin Dallas, a Philadelphia Democrat, held the fate of the tariff in his hands. Pennsylvanians wondered whether Dallas or other "native sons" would work against their own state's interests to maintain the Union. The open question of comity, that is, if a state like Pennsylvania would continue to support demands of slaveholding states, was in fact the fatal flaw of comity. Street diplomacy reflected this reality, as any attempt to arrest an African American in Pennsylvania automatically ushered in state and national conflicts over slavery and freedom. These conflicts defined comity, a striving premised upon maintaining slavery as the national status quo. Comity continued to fracture during 1846 due to the outbreak of the Mexican War in April and Pennsylvania congressman David Wilmot's proviso in August, both of which foisted the question over slavery's expansion onto the nation.

While these issues festered among politicians at the state and national level, the *Prigg* decision hung over the heads of Black and white street diplomats. On the one hand, *Prigg* was, to date, the fullest expression of federal power over retrieving fugitives from justice, in that states could not modify the protocol of federal rendition under the 1793 act. Yet on the other hand, Justice Joseph Story's belief that state legislation could prohibit state officials from cooperating with federal removals created a space through which states could act to protect their citizens and prosecute slaveholders for kidnapping attempts. Street diplomats drew from their experiences with fugitives from slavery in Philadelphia and initiated the process by which Pennsylvania officially ended slavery in the state, the 1847 Pennsylvania liberty law.

Pennsylvanians' struggle to address the frightening reality of free Black life in the state spoke to the larger problems inherent in the Federal Constitution. More often than not, applying the Fugitive Slave Act of 1793 to local cases in Philadelphia reignited debates over whether states, free or otherwise, could ensure the freedom of their citizens. The Federal Constitution acted as a Southern states' rights document in the sense that it protected slaveholders' freedom to cross geographic borders to retrieve their property in nominally free states like Pennsylvania. Slaveholders' freedoms produced inevitable clashes in Pennsylvania, a state whose emancipatory potential developed through African Americans and their allies defining themselves as innately free through street diplomacy. Battles over street diplomacy highlighted these dueling ways of defining freedom—a slaveholder's comity that assumed Black enslavement versus a street diplomat's comity that viewed any form of slavery as a kidnapping. By 1847, Pennsylvanians rebuked the Federal Constitution and outlawed slavery in the state.

"The largest negro": Abraham Monroe and the People of Newport

Justice Story's attempt to demarcate federal and state power in *Prigg* did little to change the porous border between Pennsylvania and Maryland. Not long after *Prigg*, another court case wound its way through the Pennsylvania courts and onto the national stage: the Circuit Court of the United States for the Eastern District of Pennsylvania. In October 1842 Abraham Monroe and others were called to Philadelphia on charges made by the brothers John and

George Hall of Maryland that Monroe's group prevented him from "arresting a fugitive slave, and aided and abetted the escape of the slave, after having thus opposed his arrest and detention." Monroe's improvisatory decisions, namely, his maneuvering as a street diplomat, protected African American fugitives from slavery.[2]

At first, the catalogue of participants and the hunt for the men in this case seemed like nothing unusual. A state official, Abraham Monroe worked as a justice of the peace and toll collector in the small town of Newport, Pennsylvania, about 130 miles west of Philadelphia and 30 miles north of Harrisburg. John and George Hall hailed from Harford, Maryland, and according to the 1840 census, John owned seven human beings, while George owned thirteen. In July 1841 a "good servant" named Alick owned by the Halls' father escaped with the help of two enslaved men owned by John. One of these helpers was a man named Ben, "the largest negro" of the group, according to Jonathan McVay, a fellow slaveholder recruited by the Halls to pursue the men to Newport. Now in Pennsylvania, George Hall (John did not accompany them) and McVay tapped a Pennsylvania resident named Richard Black as an additional slave hunter. At this point George Hall left to return to Maryland, but before doing so, he transferred the power of attorney given to him by his brother to McVay and Black. These men learned that the fugitives from slavery had just left Newport and headed for the locks located on the outskirts of the town. With the help of a man named Toland, McVay and Black caught up to the men at the locks. When one of their pursuers fired a pistol into the air to scare the men, Ben threw himself into the river "in a fit of nervous fear" and drowned. McVay and the others brought Alick and the other man back to Newport to await the coroner's inquest regarding Ben's death.[3]

McVay and Black's night in Newport featured several hallmarks that attested to the inherent difficulties in apprehending fugitives from slavery, and in a larger sense, how these difficulties translated into street diplomacy. The citizens of Newport appeared to have been on high alert and on watch for slave catchers in the community; here the hunters were already being hunted from the moment they stepped into town. A pro-Black, anti–slave catcher welcoming party formed upon their arrival, which suggested that a network of informants lurked in Newport; at the very least these residents made their presence felt when confronted by the agents of slaveholders. The crowd grew larger as the slave catchers traveled in and around the town, constantly surveilling them while the coroner completed the inquest, which attributed Ben's death to drowning and not the firing of the pistol. This "mob" contained armed "men of wealth, character, and standing," willing to threaten and even commit violence upon "these men entrusted with the recovery of the negroes" should their show of street diplomatic force fail.[4]

While McVay and Black undoubtedly expected resistance from the men they hunted, they expected comity from Pennsylvanians. The allies of the "fugitives" in Newport shattered this expectation. Spooked by the ever-growing crowd, McVay and Black rushed Alick and the other man to the Newport justice of the peace, Abraham Monroe. On the way to Monroe, the crowd continued to harass the men. Like other slaveholders before them, McVay and Brown claimed the African Americans were thieves; the lie did not sway the crowd. When McVay and Black arrived at Monroe's home, they admitted to him that the men were fugitives from slavery. Monroe refused to give them a warrant to detain the men, but McVay and Black brought the pair back to the hotel anyway, which seemed very much akin to kidnapping.[5]

The words and actions of ordinary people like Alick and his unnamed companion mattered to Abraham Monroe, especially if these words and actions resulted in trying slaveholders for the murder of Ben, a man who freed himself. Monroe hoped to subpoena the African American men as witnesses, and he visited them at their hotel the next morning. There Monroe took the African Americans into custody as "witnesses" to Ben's murder and placed them on a boat headed for the scene of the crime to perform the inquest. The coroner having already declared Ben's death a drowning, Monroe, McVay, and Black accompanied the pair back on the boat to Newport. Yet again, a crowd formed to welcome all of them, a visible threat to the slaveholders. Seeing the danger, McVay offered to take Alick and the other man back to their hotel; the pair refused, perhaps anticipating a rescue attempt. At that point a man named "Mr. Bosserman" emerged from the crowd and pointedly told the slave catchers that, "you will never be allowed to take these negroes out of town; you shall not take them from this spot." McVay and Black immediately left town, and Bosserman and the crowd retired to a local tavern with the now-free men.[6]

John Hall charged Abraham Monroe and several residents of Newport with "arresting a fugitive slave, and aided and abetted the escape of the slave, after having thus opposed his arrest and detention." The lawyers in the case were veterans in the long war over comity. Hall was represented by Ovid Johnson, the state official and Pennsylvania attorney general who had recently argued before the Supreme Court in the *Prigg* trial that "the acts of Congress and Pennsylvania form together a harmonious system." Johnson stated that

Monroe's refusal to grant McVay a warrant in his position as a state official violated that "perfect right" of slaveholders or their agents under the Constitution to "come into Pennsylvania, and seize their slaves, as they would seize their horses or cattle." To Johnson, now was not the time to second-guess *Prigg* and though he himself preferred "a contrary result" to the recent ruling, state officials needed to "aid the recovery of fugitive slaves by their owners, instead of advising and aiding their escape." Making matters worse, Monroe's position as a respected member of Newport reinforced the zeal of the crowd to use "open and daring violence in resisting the enforcement of a right," that is, a slaveholder's right to retrieve fugitives from slavery anywhere in the United States.[7]

The federal official and US attorney for the Eastern District of Philadelphia William Meredith represented Monroe and his fellow defendants. Meredith, it will be remembered, labored for the 1826 liberty law, a street diplomatic measure designed to protect Blacks in Pennsylvania regardless of their status of "servitude," while maintaining comity with slaveholders. According to Meredith, Justice of the Peace Monroe would have violated Pennsylvania's 1820 anti-kidnapping law if he issued a warrant to McVay and Black. Instead, Meredith stated, Monroe "anticipated" the recent *Prigg* ruling and acted as a "state magistrate," whose responsibilities as defined by the state government did not include "the performance of a United States duty." For that reason, Meredith argued, Monroe was innocent.[8]

Yet Meredith also claimed that *Prigg* "aimed a fatal blow at the right of the South, at the principles of Southern Institutions." Part of the "fatal blow" derived from how *Prigg* left open the possibility for states like Pennsylvania to continue to legislate on fugitives from slavery; the other part of the blow came as a result of a slaveholders' comity that embarrassed Pennsylvania on the national stage. The *Prigg* trial, Meredith complained, "dragged" Pennsylvania "before the supreme tribunal at Washington—she is dragged before her sister States—she is exposed to their contempt—she is stamped as an abolition State, [where] slave owners in pursuit of a fugitive within her borders, are put forthwith, within the walls of the penitentiary." Blending national and state concerns in the interest of comity elided threats to African Americans at the street level, living, breathing human beings who not only acted as potent catalysts for political change but were also at times literally "dragged" before tribunals. Ironically, the Supreme Court struck down an act (the 1826 liberty law) that, according to Meredith, helped slaveholders who took advantage of an act they believed promoted comity. In a complicated exercise of legal legerdemain,

Meredith reasoned that Monroe was innocent because he refused to abide by the 1826 act and therefore anticipated the unconstitutionality of the act, in other words, the 1826 act declared unconstitutional by the Supreme Court in *Prigg*.[9]

The closing arguments for each side revealed the extent to which slaveholders demanded federal protection to retrieve fugitives from slavery at the expense of comity. Johnson reminded the jury that he had defended the 1826 Pennsylvania law before the Supreme Court, a law that had become obsolete because of the changing "feelings" of the country, i.e., the growing anti-Black racism. *Prigg* merely reflected the "great change" that took place "in the feelings, if not in the institutions of our country, since the law of '26 was enacted." The litany of discord stemming from street diplomacy, namely, interracial abolitionism, scattered threats of "disunion" across Pennsylvania and the nation, which to Johnson kept the public mind "in a state of continual agitation on the subject of slavery." Given these circumstances, the proceedings against Monroe and his associates jeopardized "the rights and property of thousands" of slaveholders. Any state interference in the retrieval process amounted to a breach in the federal compact. In a telling line of argument premised upon comity, Johnson in effect sought to protect a federal right to human property at the expense of his own state's power.[10]

Questioning both the legitimacy of slavery and the property rights of slaveholders disrupted comity, according to Johnson. Pennsylvania "proved herself the Keystone of the Arch" by acquiescing to Southern demands in *Prigg* and upholding slaveholders' comity, including assisting in removing fugitives from slavery. "If you hold the conduct of the defendants blameless," Johnson warned, "Pennsylvania will become a city of refuge for all the runaway Blacks from the Southern States." Here Johnson echoed the paranoia of Pennsylvania state legislators from the Black emigration debates of the previous decade: failing to uphold the federal right to retrieve fugitives from slavery would encourage African Americans to venture into the state and inexorably lead to more clashes between states over Black freedom.[11]

While Johnson and Meredith debated the finer points of state and federal power and shared the common view that both sides did not work together well enough to prevent the escape of an enslaved person, the figure at the center of the trial, Alick, had already slipped through the cracks created by these very same overlapping and confused powers. Self-emancipated people like Alick confronted the Gordian knot of comity by becoming swords of freedom and sundering the ball of twine. The sword of freedom became the sword of Damocles, which Alick and others who looked like him lived under in Pennsylvania. Alick, Ben, and the other unnamed African American man's self-emancipation seemed irrelevant to the slaveholders and their lawyers in the courtroom. These latter groups of elite white men hoped to eliminate street diplomacy's emancipatory potential by extending slaveholders' constitutional right to retrieve "property."[12]

Extending this right to slaveholders' agents meant that anyone could pursue supposed fugitives from slavery across the US. These attempts to reenslave and kidnap permitted slavery to cross borders and at times even encouraged willing accomplices from Pennsylvania to participate in hunting African Americans, "fugitive" or free. According to Johnson, the logic behind this extension, that "McVay and Black were merely the hands by which [Hall] grasped his own appropriate rights and property," paralleled the projected fantasies of the slaveholder by extending the dominating status of slaveholder, not only to the enslaved people they owned and their agents tasked with retrieving fugitives from slavery but also to those Pennsylvanians who might project "threats of intimidation." Slaveholders believed that the Constitution extended "mastery" to Northerners. Northerners' sense of "mastery" relied on racism and anti-Black violence, especially when white rioters fought against Blacks and their allies. "Noisy mobs" like those of Newport that facilitated rescue attempts were accountable to the law, Johnson reasoned, given how the Supreme Court recently "decided that the owner's right to his fugitive slave is without restriction or limited, without restraint or control." Indeed, Johnson argued that "deceit and stratagem" were the only "proper means of recovering a fugitive slave." Enslaved people like Alick must have, at a certain point, applied the reverse logic to their own enslavement: an enslaved human being's right to freedom was without restriction, and stratagems that would produce the intended result, i.e., freedom, were the only proper means to escape.[13]

Faced with the possibility of sending another case involving a fugitive from slavery to the Supreme Court, the Philadelphia jury brokered a compromise between the Maryland slaveholders and the accused Pennsylvanians. The jury found Bosserman and three other defendants guilty of "trespass vi et armis"—i.e., "a wrongful interference" that caused "unlawful injury to the plaintiff's person, property or rights, involving immediate force or violence"—and fined them $350, far less than the $2,000 suggested by Johnson. Monroe, on the other hand, was acquitted of all charges.[14]

The outcome of the trial served the needs of comity, in that, like other compromises of the Antebellum Era, there was something for everyone. Fining

Bosserman placated slaveholder John Hall, whose "property" had run away, and in doing so, maintained *Prigg* by upholding the right of slaveholders to pursue fugitives from slavery and confirmed this right to agents who ventured north into Pennsylvania. Monroe's acquittal was also in keeping with *Prigg*, in that a state official need not interfere with removal under the Constitution. Most importantly though, the role of Alick, Ben, and the other unnamed enslaved man remained crucial, in that they initiated what almost became another Supreme Court decision regarding slavery, a case that could have disrupted the fragile comity between North and South.

Although the Philadelphia abolitionist community avoided any direct mention of this case, the actions undertaken by ordinary African Americans like Alick broached the confluence of retrieving fugitives from slavery and a Northern state's right to protect its citizens. Thus, even if Alick and his colleagues hoped merely to escape their former enslaved lives and not bring about immediate emancipation in the United States, their choice to free themselves dovetailed with the interests of Pennsylvania abolitionists who lobbied for a new liberty law, one that acknowledged the ebb and flow of human beings and their ideas crossing borders and one that upheld Pennsylvania's place as the Keystone of the Union. But what was "free" Pennsylvania's right as a state when it came slavery? To African Americans and their allies, Pennsylvania possessed the right to end slavery in Pennsylvania.

"A continuous procession": Philadelphia Vigilance

Philadelphia abolitionists made numerous attempts to convince Pennsylvania politicians to exercise this right. In early 1843 the PAS drafted three memorials, one calling on Congress "to amend the Constitution of the United States as to exonerate the citizens of this Commonwealth from all participation in Slavery." The PAS sent two memorials to the Pennsylvania state legislature in late January "asking them to repeal all laws of this state that in any [way] uphold Slavery" and to exert their "full Constitutional Power" to eliminate any aid for slaveholders. Perhaps anticipating little movement in the state legislature, the PAS held public meetings in Philadelphia, where its members argued that while they respected comity, they believed "that our own soil ought to be really free to all that tread upon it." Placing "really" in front of the word "free" spoke to how slavery took on a number of different forms in the state, including anti-Black violence, arresting supposed fugitives from slavery, and kidnapping free African Americans. Yet while multiple bills were introduced in the Pennsylvania House of Representatives and Senate to limit state involvement in slavery and revise the kidnapping laws, no legislative action was taken throughout 1843 and 1844.[15]

The city of Philadelphia continued to attract Black migrants due to the efforts of street diplomats. By 1840 nearly 30,000 Black Philadelphians represented about 10% of the population of the city, with perhaps as high as 40 percent of African Americans being born outside the state of Pennsylvania. Many of those who composed that 40 percent came from the Slave South, which again, led to inevitable clashes between slaveholders and street diplomats in Philadelphia. African American street diplomat Pastor Charles Gardner attempted to reorganize the Philadelphia Vigilant Committee in 1843 after Purvis moved out of Philadelphia in the wake of the 1842 riots. It was now called the Vigilance Committee of Philadelphia; its members vowed to "remember them that are in bonds as bound with them." Most committee meetings took place at members' homes, where abolitionists discussed anti-slavery propaganda, wrote pieces for the *Pennsylvania Freeman* (the main organ of the PASS), criticized defamatory accusations regarding their activities, conversed about the deeds of their fellow abolitionists, sent letters to recalcitrant newspaper editors and politicians who sympathized with slavery, and most importantly, interacted with and assisted between 100 and 400 fugitives from slavery per year. Unfortunately for historians, the committee did not record the names, origins, escape methods, and final destinations in its official minutes—taking a cue from Robert Purvis, perhaps, who burnt all of his records after the 1842 riots. Regardless of the relative lack of record-keeping, the Vigilance Committee of Philadelphia, an organization subsumed by the Underground Railroad, aided, abetted, and plotted hundreds of escapes, and thus acted as a subversive counterpart to the PAS and the PASS.[16]

The Philadelphia Vigilance Committee established the framework of what became the Underground Railroad. Culling the wealth of experiences from Blacks and sympathetic whites buttressed the multiplicity of escape methods for those who stole themselves. These methods ran the gamut from African Americans traveling by rail from Baltimore or Wilmington and piloting small vessels up the Delaware River to creeping through the farmland surrounding Philadelphia. The city that greeted them alternated between idealized notions of Black social uplift, those Black community institutions that must have dazzled fugitives from slavery who had never before seen buildings and organizations owned and operate by African Americans. Perhaps, too, many of these recent arrivals were saddened by the "vice and misery" experienced by the poor and marginalized population of Black Americans in the city. Nonethe-

The Vigilance Committee of the PAS, circa 1854: James Miller McKim (*top left*), N. W. Depee (*top center*), Charles Wise (*top right*), Thomas Garrett (*center left*), Robert Purvis (*center right*), Jacob. C. White (*bottom left*), Passmore Williamson (*bottom center*), and William Still (*bottom right*). Courtesy of the Boston Public Library less, the self-emancipated arrivals had at their disposal a large number of Black and white "conductors" like Purvis, William Still, and James Miller McKim, and plenty of "stations" in the city, including churches like Mother Bethel and the residences of Forten, Purvis, Jacob C. White, and Philadelphia Vigilance Committee president James McCrummell.[17]

Philadelphia's recent history of anti-Black violence required street diplomats within the Vigilance Committee and the later Underground Railroad to work covertly within the city while at the same time make its case for emancipation to the broader American public. The PASS complained at its August 1843 meeting in Norristown that it could no longer hold major reform conventions, let alone abolitionist meetings, within Philadelphia. Discussing the recent attempt by Philadelphia abolitionists to celebrate West Indies Emancipation in 1843, a year after the 1842 Lombard Street riot, the PASS remarked, "The truth is, our city is ruled by mob violence, and kept under perpetual terror of its law." No meeting was held in Philadelphia that year to commemorate West Indies Emancipation. Vigilance committee leaders present at the annual PASS meeting could not divorce menacing and violent rioting from their overall project of helping fugitives from slavery, and so they begrudgingly acknowledged this bitter truth that "freedom cannot be enjoyed in one part of a country, in any part of which men are held as slaves." Thus, the attendees to the August 1843 meeting acknowledged the central problem within street diplomacy: the national problem of distinguishing and constructing consistent boundaries between freedom and slavery.[18]

Despite being a quasi-public organization, the Philadelphia Vigilance Committee worked on the streets to counter *Prigg*. PASS members at Norristown in 1843 praised the committee's activities while keeping mute to specific examples, which in many cases blurred the line between legal and illegal modes of protecting fugitives from slavery in Philadelphia:

> This branch of effort, to be sure, does not fall within the Constitutional purview of our society; but from its interesting nature, and the extent of its operations, and from the evidence it furnishes of anti-slavery progress, it may be properly alluded to in our review. There has been almost a continuous procession of fugitives from southern injustice to the land of freedom. We have no means of arriving at the precise number of persons of this class who have passed through our borders, but, have no doubt it might be safely estimated at several hundreds. Doubtless an equal, and perhaps a larger number, has passed through other parts of the North adjoining the slaveholding States.

Much like its New York counterparts, led by the inestimable David Ruggles, the Philadelphia Vigilance Committee served as an example of continual resistance to the laws protecting slavery in Pennsylvania and the United States in general. While its activities indeed suffered the blowback from the aggressive race riots that plagued Philadelphia during the mid-1830s and early 1840s, by December 1843 the committee officially re-formed, no doubt encouraged by its allies in the PASS, who viewed the "little prospect of abolition" in the American political Union as a barrier to overcome through the shadowy operations of street diplomats and the legislation they inspired.[19]

"The mob city": Philadelphia, 1844

The political culture of Philadelphia mirrored the volatile political realm within the city and nation. As will be recalled, Philadelphia County was composed of a diverse set of working-class communities like Moyamensing and Southwark. With the exception of the African American population who lived there, Philadelphia County often voted for the Democracy. Philadelphia City, on the other hand, featured a more robust and affluent population and typically supported the Whig Party. The heart of Black Philadelphia's Cedar Ward bordered the edge of South Philadelphia, while the settlement patterns of Black Philadelphia straddled the line between Philadelphia City and Philadelphia County. Like all cities, Philadelphia featured a population in motion, one that traversed the permeable borders between City and County, not unlike the precarious borders between North and South, with African Americans caught in the middle.[20]

This settlement pattern of Philadelphia's African American community was exacerbated by the dramatic rise in Irish immigration which swept the city between 1840 and 1850. African Americans and impoverished Irish immigrants concentrated in Philadelphia County, which experienced a 75 percent increase in population during that decade. Allying themselves with Democratic ward leaders of Philadelphia County and the national Democracy in general enabled Irish immigrants to assume law enforcement positions and establish fire companies, which were often fronts for street gangs. This alliance allowed the Irish then to eke out a precarious existence, not unlike the African Americans whom they targeted for random bouts of senseless violence. As previous chapters have shown, Irish immigrants typically made up the bulk of anti-Black rioters. In a word, Philadelphia's Irish community did not hesitate to utilize direct action to enforce the hardening lines of racism to protect what little many of them possessed in Philadelphia.[21]

While Irish-Black tensions exacerbated race relations in the city, different tensions boiled over when Philadelphia's Protestant majority, who used the King James Bible as a textbook, required Irish immigrant children to sing Protestant hymns in Philadelphia schools. Catholic Bishop Joseph Kenrick, an Irish immigrant himself, railed against these pedagogical practices, as did Philadelphia Democrats, who believed the Irish had the right to use their own bibles. Many Protestants resisted this logic and fomented an anti-Catholic wave that peaked with the formation of numerous Nativist, or "Native American," political organizations in Philadelphia. One such organization, called the American Republican Association, boasted 5,000 members in 1844, maintained that the Bible "without note or comment, is not sectarian; that it is the fountain-head of morality and all good government," and lobbied to extend the waiting period for naturalization for Irish immigrants. Making matters worse, the city's Whig elite, who again dominated the political and geographic core of Philadelphia, also supported stricter naturalization laws for political advantage and often berated the Irish for their "great faults": being uneducated, insular, drunk, lazy, and of "clannish spirit and action" when it came to voting Democratic.[22]

The dangerous mix of poverty, religion, and xenophobia touched off major riots in Philadelphia during May and July 1844. Anti-immigrant mobs spurred by Nativist "monarchs of the mob," according to the *Philadelphia Sun*, attacked Irish communities across the city. Rioters destroyed two Catholic churches, and hundreds of Irish immigrants endured random and brutal violence, not unlike the attacks they had inflicted upon Black Philadelphians in previous years. The *Liberator* noted that Philadelphia had become a "mob city" with "mob principles." The "awful scene of desecration and destruction" mirrored anti-Black riots, as did Philadelphia "public opinion," which ignored assaults on Irish immigrants. Only with the arrival of the militia did the Nativist-Irish "civil war" come to an end on July 7.[23]

As other historians have noted, the 1844 Nativist riots must be viewed in the context of pervasive anti-Black violence. An anonymous political satirist drew on anti-Black and anti-Irish riots to craft a poem called "De Philadelphia Riots; Or, I Guess it Wan't De [epithet] Dis Time," complete with a mock African American accent. The poem began by reminding "Philadelphia Folks" that African Americans were to blame for the riots of the previous years. Such an assumption relegated Black Philadelphians and Black Philadelphia to an illegal or illegitimate existence directly related to their race, which presumed a connection to slavery and permitted whites to harass, attack, or even kidnap them. The poet emphasized guilt by phenotypical association and the former enslavement of many African Americans in the city by referring to Jefferson Street, the site of one of the Nativist riots, as "Massa Street." The poem's concluding stanza commented on the political motives undertaken by newspapers to fuel the riots, and the general public's return to political indifference and quietude.[24]

Even though the anonymous satirist took care to correct the public's assumption about the source of the 1844 riots, the fact that the Philadelphia public might interpret any riot in the city originating as a result of race relations spoke to the decades of violence suffered by African Americans. Anti-Black rioting in Philadelphia depended upon racist presuppositions and the fears of abolition projected by white politicians and their allies at the local, state, and national levels. The 1844 riots reminded Americans that previous riots in Philadelphia disrupted the bonds that held the city and country together and superimposed the flaws of comity and the national compact onto street battles in the city. Many street diplomats would have concurred with the Philadelphia diarist Sidney George Fisher, who on April 28, 1844, wrote, "The Union of the country is factitious, and is becoming less real every day . . . such a Union is one of interest merely, a paper bond, to be torn asunder by a burst of passion or to be deliberately undone whenever interest demands it." Fisher wrote these words in the midst of the storm brewing over the annexation of Texas, which in the context of mid-1840s abolitionism, represented the revitalized spread of slavery under the banner of the Union.[25]

Storms over Pennsylvania

The annual PASS meeting in August 1844 reported that the "general tone of public feeling is becoming more and more modified by the element of abolitionism." Abolitionist efforts that began on the streets promoted the "real or pretended" aid of legislative bodies as well as inspired the speeches delivered by Whig orators over the question of Texas annexation. Whig leaders protested against the prospect of territorial extension, which in effect meant slavery's extension, and claimed that "bloated empires, scattered settlements, and alien people attenuated the bonds of Union." Pennsylvania abolitionists agreed, noting that the Whigs "sometimes mingle[d]" the slavery question with that of free labor when critiquing annexation, which in a way could provide a step forward for Black freedom.[26]

Pennsylvania abolitionists at their 1844 meeting noted the irony that some Democrats viewed annexation as a ploy to "hasten the abolition of slavery."

The words and actions of Pennsylvania Democrats, who boasted a two to one majority in the Pennsylvania Senate, a four-seat majority in the House and two Democratic Senators, betrayed any notion of abolition in the country. Making matters worse for the opponents of annexation, Pennsylvania Democrats abandoned incumbent Martin Van Buren after he questioned the "propriety" of acquiring Texas. These Pennsylvania Democrats transferred their loyalty to presidential hopeful James K. Polk, an advocate for annexation who curried the favor of many Pennsylvanians by promising to promote economic protectionism as well as selecting Pennsylvania Democratic leader George M. Dallas as his running mate.[27]

As an "out-and-out advocate" for Texas annexation, Dallas told his supporters that expansion represented "the high duties of our political existence," that of promoting the "genius and maxims" of the Union. Pennsylvania's Democratic senator James Buchanan, another fervent expansionist, spoke for Texas annexation in the Senate, while Pennsylvania Democratic congressman and longtime abolition antagonist Charles J. Ingersoll chaired the House Foreign Affairs Committee. In keeping with their Southern sympathies, these men used their positions as leaders in Pennsylvania's Democratic Party to aid what the *Liberator* called "the plot of the Texas plunderers" who viewed slavery as "the foundation stone of freedom."[28]

The spread of slavery as a national concern produced local consequences in Pennsylvania. As mentioned earlier, the heavily Irish Philadelphia County typically leaned to the Democracy, while Philadelphia City typically supported the Whigs. The recent anti-Irish riots of 1844 changed that climate: every single Philadelphia County Democrat lost his election bid due to his support of Irish Catholicism as well as a cunning political alliance between the Native American and Whig Parties in the state. Yet this alliance did not bear fruit in the 1844 Pennsylvania gubernatorial elections because the Native American party never galvanized support from the interior of the state. The Democrats sent their candidate Francis R. Shunk to Harrisburg. When judged by what Pennsylvania abolitionists called "a time of severe trial," the 1844 presidential election saw the Whigs' Henry Clay lose by 7,000 votes in Pennsylvania, the Liberty Party barely make an electoral dent, and Democrat James K. Polk assume the presidency. The United States would annex Texas within a year.[29]

The *Liberator* interpreted Polk's victory as a "triumph of the slaveholding oligarchy." The inevitable spread of slavery west by Southern slave interests mirrored the constant fears of African Americans, who now had to contend with more evidence that their country preferred spreading rather than limiting slavery. James K. Polk, exclaimed the *Boston Post*, "in whose hands stolen human beings are found, and who is the presidential incarnation of slavery," would usher in a new era. "The robber of the poor, the slave owner and slave-driver, the human kidnapper"—all of these names were attributed to Polk, whose "slave power" allies demanded the "*rule* or *ruin*" of the Union.[30]

Showing little sympathy for Northerners steeped in the slaveholders' version of comity, abolitionists like the Ohioan editor of the *Palladium of Liberty* David Jenkins claimed that "just raise the cry of war or disunion and the North, rather than have a fuss, jealous to the wants of the peculiar institutions, grants [rights to] Slave State after Slave State [and] things go just as they say." Using language that street diplomats in Pennsylvania could appreciate, Jenkins resolved that "it is time and high time that the North was acting for herself." Disgusted abolitionists had demands: the North should either remove slavery or dissolve the Union. More and more abolitionists opted for the latter route and made the "repeal of the Union" and "No Union with Slaveholders" their perpetual refrain.[31]

Maintaining the Union also had its adherents, as noted by the 1844 meeting of the PASS, whose members acknowledged the philosophical rift regarding abolitionists participating in politics. Calling these differences "irreconcilable" within the eastern Pennsylvania abolitionist community, the executive committee of the PASS broached the topic of possibly separating the political participation faction, which favored the Liberty Party but bemoaned its inability to win local elections, from the political nonparticipation faction, which deemed it "their duty to refrain from voting at all under our present Constitution." This rift failed to take hold at the annual meeting when attendees voted down the motion to separate these two factions "in peace and harmony and mutual good will." The inability to remove politics and politicians from emancipation strategies opened the door for street diplomats to remove slavery from Pennsylvania. Even if the spread of slavery to new lands was unavoidable, then perhaps Pennsylvania lawmakers could remove the vestiges of slavery that operated on the local level.[32]

"Quite an abolition feeling": Harrisburg, 1845

Pennsylvania state legislators revisited the notion of revoking state assistance from the federal process of fugitive retrieval shortly after a botched kidnapping took place in Harrisburg in February 1845. Alexander A. Cook and Thomas Finnegan, the latter a noted Maryland kidnapper, "knocked down in the street" an African American man named Peter Hawkins, who resided with his family in Harrisburg for several years. Cook and Finnegan bound Hawkins "within the intention of taking him South" and brought him before Judge Nathaniel B. Eldred the next day. As a judge "highly esteemed for his impartiality" Eldred released Hawkins and ordered Cook and Finnegan to be arrested for kidnapping. Slavery and street diplomacy had exploded in Pennsylvania's capital city for all to see.[33]

According to the *Philadelphia Inquirer*, the horror experienced by Peter Hawkins inspired "quite an abolition feeling" among Pennsylvania state legislators. Cook and Finnegan awaited trial mere blocks from the Pennsylvania state legislature, while the House heard no fewer than four bills regarding slavery in Pennsylvania during February 1845. The first bill sought to repeal the section of the 1780 gradual abolition act that allowed slaveholders to bring enslaved people into the state for six months unmolested; no vote took place over revising that section. The second attempt, also in the House, came from John C. Kunkel of Dauphin County on February 6. Kunkel, a Henry Clay Whig and Harrisburg native, offered a resolution for the Judiciary Committee to "inquire and report what statutory provisions exist defining and punishing kidnapping, and how far our laws relative to slavery are affected by the decisions of the Supreme Court, and what further Legislative action is necessary." The House agreed and gave the task to state senator Charles Sullivan.[34]

Sullivan's investigation of kidnapping and slavery in the state yielded a third attempt to revise state legislation. On February 7, Sullivan, a Whig from Allegheny and Butler Counties who was known to be a "pronounced abolitionist," cited a recent kidnapping attempt in Pittsburgh to bolster the resolve for Pennsylvania politicians to modify state and therefore federal law. He suggested a more radical version of Kunkel's bill: Sullivan married state and federal law in his bill "to preserve the public peace, to prevent kidnapping, to extend the trial by jury to accused runaways, and repealing certain laws which have been overruled." The first and fourth parts of this bill flew in the face of the *Prigg* ruling, as they utilized the power of the state of Pennsylvania to first define the act of kidnapping as an affront to the peace and security of the state, and second, for Pennsylvania to "preserve" this same peace, in other words, interpose and nullify federal law.[35]

Retrieving fugitives from slavery had, in a sense, now become kidnapping attempts in the eyes of Pennsylvania legislators, a position espoused by Black and white Philadelphia street diplomats for decades. Contests over freedom and slavery that removed African Americans from the state were truly Pennsylvania's "domestic insurrections." While the Hawkins case forced Pennsylvania state politicians to look upon slavery "more and more with horror," Sullivan's findings stoked minimal debate, and the bill "to punish kidnapping, to repeal the act making it obligatory upon magistrates and constables to arrest runaway slaves, and extending the right of trial to such persons" did not come up for a vote in the state legislature. Whether this lack of a vote spoke to the legislators' hesitancy cannot be known, though like other votes that related to slavery in Pennsylvania, the specter of comity always hung over their heads. Regardless, local kidnapping attempts reminded Pennsylvanian politicians of their duties to their state and humanity first, their country second.[36]

"An unholy league with oppression"

Pennsylvania politicians may have been slow to equate removing fugitives from slavery to kidnapping, though their work to ensure comity in previous decades revealed the inherently difficult position "free" state Northerners faced when grappling with the politics of slavery in an ostensibly free state. The thoughts and actions of street diplomats may have been ahead of the curve in the respect that they viewed kidnappings and removals as one and the same, though they, too, made fraught decisions from a precarious position. At their annual meeting on August 11, 1845, Pennsylvania abolitionists balanced the gains of the previous year. On the one hand, new antislavery politicians like Cassius Clay arose in Kentucky, immediatist "agitation" began to strike at national religious institutions for their tacit or outright support of slavery, and Congress rescinded the infamous gag rule—each of these moments symbolized "a forward step in the march of freedom." On the other hand, Pennsylvania abolitionists reported that even "though Pennsylvania boasts of having abolished slavery within her own jurisdiction, she is yet in close alliance with slavery beyond her borders, and is making the oppressor's every act of tyranny her own." In short, slavery existed in Pennsylvania through a slaveholders' comity that used the Constitution to transform African Americans into potential "fugitives" and celebrated the violence inherent in "removal" as fundamental to maintaining slavery.[37]

Pennsylvania abolitionists needed to "press forward" in their efforts to stop the flow of slavery south and west—those "slave power" incursions into Texas meant to extend "the area of freedom." The slave power needed Texas, Pennsylvania abolitionists reckoned, so that it could carve the territory up into "an indefinite number of slave states" and thus "strengthen indefinitely but mightily the supports of its despotic throne." Now, more than ever, argued the attendees, abolitionists must shore up their defenses against threats to freedom in Pennsylvania and Northern states' rights. As with their 1844 meeting, abolitionists debated whether or how they should support the law of the land: the Constitution itself. Delegates drafted and debated a number of anticonstitutional resolutions, the first of which labeled that document "an unholy league with oppression, virtually pledging the strength of the whole nation to the defense of slavery." Another resolution called on attendees to stop voting in elections or pledging oaths to the Constitution "so long as its pro-slavery features remain." Yet another resolution called the Constitution "contrary to the law of God" and thus neither "morally or legally binding" on abolitionists. Abolitionists therefore questioned yet again the legitimacy of a national document that protected Southern states' rights.[38]

When it came time to debate the resolutions, Pennsylvania abolitionists reorganized themselves into the same anti- and propolitical participation factions that surfaced at the 1844 meeting. William Lloyd Garrison and Charles Burleigh represented the antipolitical participation faction and voted to adopt the resolutions. Thomas Earle represented the propolitical participation faction. A lawyer for the PAS, a one-time Liberty Party vice presidential nominee, an erstwhile Jacksonian Democrat, and the vice president of the PASS, Earle presented a passionate and persuasive defense of the Constitution that the PASS consequently refused to print. Besides being too persuasive, Earle's speech was not printed for a couple of other reasons. As the motion for antipolitical participation passed 442–188, it seemed that many of the attendees had drifted more toward the antipolitical ethos of Garrison. Ironically by "gagging" Earle, Pennsylvania abolitionists could then present a united front to their members and the broader American public.[39]

Yet even after the abolitionists voted to adopt the antipolitical participation resolutions, Earle ensured that abolitionists remained tethered to the Constitution and the American political system in general. Toward the end of the annual meeting, he proposed two resolutions designed to engage abolitionists in politicking with both the national legislature and the Pennsylvania state legislature. Interestingly, attendees adopted Earle's first resolution for "the circulation of petitions to be forwarded to the next session of Congress, asking such change of the Constitution and laws, as shall abolish slavery throughout this country." The PASS rationalized its support of this resolution by highlighting how recent debates over Texas and the Walker Tariff, the latter of which is discussed in the next section, created a "favorable time" to petition Congress.[40]

Earle's second resolution—another one the attendees refused to adopt—excoriated the Whig Party at the state and national level. Earle believed that the Whigs could not be trusted for three important reasons: they refused to hear abolitionist petitions, failed to move to abolish slavery or the slave trade, and did nothing to effect "the abrogation of the law which requires the United States Officers to assist in slaveholding." This final reason was a not-so-veiled attack on the *Prigg* ruling, in which Justice Story suggested the use of federal officers to retrieve fugitives from slavery. Although attendees failed to adopt this second resolution, the executive committee of the PASS salvaged the right to petition state and national representatives, particularly Whig politicians, on the precipice of what would become in a few short months the Mexican-American War and in a little over a year a free Pennsylvania.[41]

Pennsylvania's 1847 Liberty Law: "A minimum of debate"?

The Pennsylvania state legislature passed three liberty laws between 1820 and 1847. Each law originated in the actions of street diplomats and cemented Pennsylvania's burdensome position in the Union. The 1820 liberty law pivoted on the actions of ordinary African Americans and their allies, the latter of whom successfully lobbied lawmakers to increase the fine for kidnapping and limit the role of state officials from participating in federal rendition. In effect, Pennsylvania legislators passed a law that asserted their rights as a state to legislate on slavery. The 1826 liberty law confronted slaveholders' demands for comity, i.e., that Pennsylvanians continue to assume that any arrest of a Black person was a legal rendition. The work of street diplomats in Philadelphia and Harrisburg forced lawmakers to nullify slaveholder testimony, yet these same slaveholders convinced state legislators to permit state officials to assist them in hunting African Americans. As a result of this compromise, the 1826 bill became a state law designed to protect slaveholders' rights in Pennsylvania under the auspices of the Federal Constitution. The 1842 *Prigg* decision ruled the 1826 law unconstitutional because it tampered with what slaveholders viewed as a constitutional guarantee for neighboring states to assist them in pursuing fugitives from slavery. However, *Prigg* allowed space for state legislatures to contest the ruling and slaveholders' rights, in that state legislatures retained the power to legislate nonparticipation in retrieving fugitives from slavery, thus making the 1793 Fugitive Slave Act extremely diffi-cult to enforce in Pennsylvania.

Removing African Americans accused of being fugitives from slavery was rooted in confusing and overlapping federal powers and states' rights that mired Pennsylvania in the politics of slavery regardless of its status as a "free state." Street diplomats well understood the precarious position of Pennsylvania. These Black and white allies worked to convince Pennsylvania lawmak-ers and ordinary Americans that the arrest of any Black person as a "fugitive" represented a kidnapping. Slaveholders and their minions operated under the exact opposite principle, as stated above: they desired that all Americans as-sume Black criminality and, furthermore, demanded that all Americans assist them in (re-)enslaving African Americans across the United States. This flawed comity between the "free" and the "slave" states broke down time and again due to the movement of a whole host of people—slaveholders, kidnappers, abolitionists, and most importantly, the self-liberated—across borders they rendered useless and illusory. In early 1847, the Pennsylvania state legislature passed a bill that withdrew state assistance from the federal retrieval process. This final piece of legislation turned Pennsylvania into a free state.[42]

To what extent did the 1847 bill pass, in the words of liberty law historian Thomas D. Morris, with "a minimum of debate"? Both the Pennsylvania House and Senate journals reveal scant discussion of the bill, which in a way obscured the unique relationship between slavery and Pennsylvania in the years, if not the decades, leading up to its passage. The 1820 and 1826 laws, along with *Prigg*, not only motivated the 1847 bill, they also spoke to the on-going open question of Black freedom in the state, a freedom punctuated by the terror of slaveholders and kidnappers, a freedom defended at times to the death by Black and white street diplomats. Individual African Americans who lived under these liberty laws and *Prigg* represented the burden of Union as their actions drove white politicians to legislate on slavery and freedom in Pennsylvania. In 1847, national political concerns became intertwined with the work of Pennsylvania state lawmakers and street diplomats in Philadelphia—ironic, of course, in that the individual kidnappings, or "retrieval" efforts, at the local level had always in some way represented or at least complicated state and national views of enslavement. National political concerns included not only the Mexican War and the Wilmot Proviso but also the Walker Tariff of 1846, which offered Pennsylvania's political leaders a chance to reassess and execute what they considered "Pennsylvania doctrines." The effects of these three national political events collided with Pennsylvania's interests as a state and street diplomats' views of innate human freedom, and they resulted in an upset in the 1846 state elections. The combination of these factors proved decisive, as state lawmakers made their stand against slavery in 1847, and in doing so, emancipated Pennsylvania from its enslaving responsibilities to the nation.[43]

Both the PASS and the PAS petitioned the Pennsylvania state legislature to end slavery in the state in early 1846. Reminding legislators that the 1780 Gradual Abolition Act declared slavery to be a "violation of natural rights," the memorialists argued that the state should therefore "in no manner voluntarily give countenance or aid to Slaveholding." Thus, Pennsylvania lawmakers should abandon comity by banning slaveholders from bringing enslaved people into the state, refusing to allow state officials to assist in recovering fugitives from slavery, and closing state prisons to victims of federal rendition. The PAS hesitated when it came to amending the Constitution directly, however, and preferred that the state legislature lobby the national Congress "to endeavor to obtain such alteration of the Constitution and Laws as will either abolish slavery throughout the nation or prevent the public officers of the Union from aiding in the enslavement of any portion of the Human Race." The PAS thought it best to then petition the national Congress itself with a simple request: "take such measures as will either Abolish Slavery itself, or all support given to it by the National Government." The PAS sent the petitions to both legislatures and printed 500 extra copies; it distributed 400 copies of the state petition and 100 copies of the petition to Congress across Pennsylvania.[44]

Not coincidentally, the PAS charged two Philadelphia Whigs with introducing these petitions to their respective chambers: the first was state representative Charles B. Trego of Philadelphia City, whose "knowledge of the different parts of Pennsylvania" added to his influence within the state House of Representatives; the second was state senator Charles Gibbons (also of Philadelphia City), a Henry Clay Whig who came from a family of abolitionists and thus maintained close ties with white and Black Philadelphia activists. A contemporary noted how Gibbons "represented the intensity of Republicanism. His earnest, close-knit, imperative face; his hatred of slavery and especially of [the] Democracy, as the outcome of slavery." To Whigs like Trego and Gibbons, the Democracy and slavery had become synonymous. Edward Needles, whom the PAS sent to Harrisburg to meet with the pair, reported that both men read the petitions and "in a very satisfactory [manner] assured us of their cordial cooperation in promoting the objects of the [PAS]." Trego and Gibbons requested that the PAS send a delegation to present the petitions to the legislatures. The PAS assigned two of its lawyers with this task: William Elder and Thomas Earle.[45]

Elder and Earle traveled to Harrisburg in March 1846 to present the PAS petitions to the state legislature. They reported that a bill drafted "in partial conformity" to the PAS memorial had been presented to the House in February but rejected by Democrat James Burnside of Centre County. The house referred this bill to a "special committee known to be favorable to the prayers of the petitioners." This special committee granted Elder and Earle a private interview during which they freely discussed the petition, which although a "respectful" gesture, did not amount to much in terms of supporting the petitioners' goals. Real progress occurred on March 19, when Gibbons himself read a draft of the bill that included most of the PAS requests. However, Elder and Earle found this bill to be "defective," as it did not repeal sections of the 1826 liberty law that authorized Pennsylvania residents to arrest and recover fugitives from slavery. Nonetheless, the PAS delegation found a "friendly and favorable state of opinion and feeling" toward the petition and hoped that Gibbons's version of the bill, while not perfect, would pass before the legislature ended its session.[46]

Unfortunately, Earle and Elder reported that a deluge of "local and private bills" flooded the legislators at the eleventh hour, preventing the bill from coming up for a vote, let alone debate. As if to end on a good note, Earle and Elder concluded their report by stating that they expected the "friends of freedom" in the legislature to discuss the bill during the next session. Until that point, they advised Pennsylvania abolitionists to flood every state representative and senator with petitions. While a vital political strategy, petitioning alone could not force state legislators to pass the PAS bill; the national politics of slavery would once again resurface in Pennsylvania.[47]

Pennsylvania's "Native Sons" and the Tariff of 1846

From the perspective of legislators in Harrisburg, abolitionist appeals could not have come at a more pressing time. Beginning in January 1846 both houses of the state legislature examined the proposed Walker Tariff, which the national Congress debated throughout 1846. Named for President James K. Polk's secretary of the treasury, Robert J. Walker, a "Pennsylvania-reared" Mississippi Democrat who also drafted a highly influential pamphlet supporting annexation and the resettlement of African Americans in Latin America, this economic plan sought to reduce protective tariff rates in the Northern states, thus placating Southern slave states dependent on Northern and foreign manufacturers. Both houses of the Pennsylvania state legislature disapproved of this measure, with Whigs calling Democrats "rogues or fools" for supporting Polk, who had positioned himself as more amenable to protection during the 1844 election. This inconsistency, namely, electing Polk on the basis of his refusal to tamper with tariff rates (in this case, the Tariff of 1842, a boon to Northern industry), badgered national Democrats and Pennsylvania Democrats throughout 1846.[48]

Making matters worse, when the tariff came up for a vote in the national House of Representatives, Pennsylvania Whigs and Democrats as a group lined up to oppose the bill. Despite this show of solidarity toward Pennsylvania's rights, the bill passed the House. When it reached the Senate, the resulting vote produced a tie, which of course according to the Constitution required a tie-breaker vote from the vice president. In this case, Pennsylvanian and longtime Democratic party leader George Mifflin Dallas held what he saw as his obligation to "the Country, to the whole of the American People," in other words, the Union, and voted in support of Walker's Tariff in July 1846.[49]

Dallas's decision to vote for the tariff represented what two prominent historians of Pennsylvania called "one of the most courageous acts of his life." In the weeks leading up to the vote, Philadelphia newspapers noted the "magnitude of the interests involved, as relates to the whole Union, but more directly to our State," a state whose "business vitality is dependent upon [the] preservation" of the 1842 tariff rates. To vote or not to vote for the tariff placed Dallas in the unenviable position of having to decide between his state, his party, and his country. The Philadelphia *North American*, the city's Whig newspaper, warned Dallas that voting for the tariff would be "ruinous" to the state, and that he should be cautioned to "Save the Tariff, or lose the State." In other words, victories at the national level would jeopardize not only Dallas's political future in Pennsylvania but also the chances of Democrats to maintain their control over the state legislature, in what was after all an election year in Pennsylvania.[50]

Pennsylvania Democrats felt betrayed by the possibility of the tariff passing through the work of Dallas and Polk, both of whom James Buchanan assured state party leaders would protect tariff rates in the interests of Pennsylvania. "Surely a fatal blow is not about to be struck at Pennsylvania, and by one of her own sons," bemoaned the *Philadelphia Inquirer* in mid-July, "especially as he is well aware that the vast majority of the people of Pennsylvania, of all parties, are adverse to a change in the Tariff." Dallas even had to contend with familial concerns while deciding how to cast his vote: his niece was married to the bill's author, Robert J. Walker, the man who persuaded Dallas to support unrestrained expansion west and crafted the tariff bill in question. With the political bound to the personal, the fate of Pennsylvania's place within the Union seemed to hang in the balance.[51]

Knowing that his vote could cost him dearly in the Keystone State, Dallas acted for the Union and the Democracy when he proceeded as planned and voted for the tariff. As Dallas explained to the Senate, "if by thus acting, it be my misfortune to offend any portion of those who honored me with their suffrages, I have only to say to them, and to my whole country, that I prefer the deepest obscurity of private life, with an unwounded conscience, to the glare of official eminence, spotted by a sense of moral delinquency." Dreading the immediate fallout, Dallas wrote to his wife that "if there be the slightest indication of a disposition to riot in the city of Philadelphia, owing to the passage of the Tariff Bill, pack up and bring the whole brood to Washington." While riots failed to materialize in Philadelphia, Dallas was indeed burned in effigy in the city, and his Whig opponents paid "the charges" of those who posted insulting placards on his front door. Philadelphia newspapers excoriated Dallas, calling him a traitor for "deserting his own state" and his vote "the betrayal of Pennsylvania." "That our own people should be excited and indignant, is indeed natural," read an editorial in the *Philadelphia Inquirer*, for Dallas "disregarded the appeals of the people of Pennsylvania." Instead, Dallas placed party and sectional interests—more importantly, Southern slave state interests—above his native state. If one sought "an excuse for Mr. Dallas' vote, put it down to the fact that the South demanded it as the price of their party allegiance to Mr. Polk's administration," the *North American* editorialized. A Northern man with Southern principles, Dallas desired to toe the party line and revealed how Pennsylvania politicians who acted in the interests of the Union shared a common denominator. Whether they voted for a controversial tariff as Dallas did or curried a comity palatable to slaveholders who hunted human beings, they placed the Union, now synonymous with slaveholders' comity, above Pennsylvanians, Black and white.[52]

The outbreak of the war with Mexico occurred in the middle of the Walker Tariff debates, with Pennsylvania Whigs decrying the war and Pennsylvania Democrats embracing imperial aggrandizement. At the annual PASS meeting in 1846, Pennsylvania abolitionists excoriated the war as one of aggression "for the increase of the 'slave power' and the extension of the slave system."

PASS president Robert Purvis read a number of resolutions derived from a central thesis: opposing the Mexican War combined "all our efforts for the abolition of slavery." The PASS drafted petitions to the state legislature that asked to "free this Commonwealth from all connection with slavery." It also sent a petition to the national Congress claiming that continual attempts by state and national politicians "to unite freedom and slavery in one body politic" produced a Union that sacrificed freedom to slavery. The proper political solution for the American body politic was nothing short of "the immediate peaceful dissolution of the American Union."[53]

Pennsylvania abolitionists' lobbying efforts revealed two simple truths. First, abolitionists could not divorce themselves from the political sphere, even when asking for "peaceful dissolution." To wit, the personal was the political, especially when it came to street diplomats preventing violent dissolutions that enslaved Black Americans. Second, Pennsylvania abolitionists relied on Pennsylvania lawmakers to apply Pennsylvania's rights as a state in the Union to dictate their own slave policy within the state, and when necessary, interpose and nullify federal slave policy. In both cases, Pennsylvania abolitionists recognized that they and their state could and did represent a beacon of hope in a nation where African American freedom was insecure at best.[54]

The "hand-writing on the wall": Wilmot's Proviso

While Pennsylvania abolitionists met to debate and draft petitions, in early August 1846 Pennsylvania congressman David Wilmot proposed in the House of Representatives that Congress exclude slavery from the territories gained from Mexico. Wilmot's "Proviso" as it became known, threw the Second Party system into a panic and highlighted Wilmot's "independence and fearlessness" as a politician. Already Wilmot had bucked loyalty to his state in favor of party with his vote in support of the Tariff of 1846: he was the only Pennsylvania House member to vote for the tariff. Wilmot represented a lumbering district in north-central Pennsylvania, a region where, according to Democratic governor David Porter, "the only things the people manufactured were shingles, and they stole the lumber to make them, and the only protection they wanted was protection from the officers of the law." On the tariff question, Wilmot chose party principles; on the slavery question, Wilmot, like many other Northern Democrats, began to scorn the incommensurate power of Southerners within the party. This shift from voting with the slave power, as some Whigs and many abolitionists contended, to voting against party interests underscored how loyalties to state and party fluctuated. Wilmot thus represented the antislavery potential of Free Soil Democrats in places like Pennsylvania, and justified his position in this group of renegade Congressmen: "I will cheerfully stand by any organization established for the advancement of these principles, but if that is not enough, if it be further required that I shall submit in humble and slavish acquiescence to any organization based upon, and intended to promote the one object of slavery extension, then set me aside at once. I will never sustain any such organization, but will do all in my power to break it down." In sum, Wilmot and other Northern politicians, be they Whig or Democrat, were fed up with being used as tools of the South to promote national slavery. The vote for Wilmot's Proviso created a break within the Democratic Party: for the first time, Northern politicians presented a united front against Southern slavery; "a dire omen," wrote the historian James McPherson. And although Wilmot's Proviso failed to pass in the Senate, it certainly rocked the political landscape because it reconceptualized the borders between slavery and freedom in new territories, which as a consequence fanned the flames of slavery's insidious presence in the North, particularly Pennsylvania.[55]

Notably, both houses of the Pennsylvania state legislature approved of the proviso. An editorialist for the *Pennsylvania Freeman* warned Northerners not to remain idle while the slave power bound slavery to the conquest of Mexico: all Americans, especially proslavery politicians and indifferent Northerners, needed to "see in the Wilmot Proviso the 'hand-writing on the wall' . . . There is a point beyond which even Northern subserviency dare not go." It was fitting that it was a Pennsylvania politician who exposed and exploited this rift within an American political culture premised upon enslaving African Americans regardless of borders.[56]

Pennsylvania and the Election of 1846

The election of 1846 in Pennsylvania brought to the fore competing state, sectional, and party loyalties, and the Whigs capitalized on divisive national issues like the tariff and the war for slavery's expansion as a means to define both Pennsylvania states' rights and future expectations. The state's Whig Party linked Democratic ambivalence regarding the tariff of 1846 to the threats posed by the "southern slavery performances" of Dallas, Polk, and Walker. On the first issue, state Democrats were plagued by dissension in the national Congress. That some Democrats voted for the tariff and others against it, prompted the Whig-friendly *Pottsville Miner* to query voters, "Which is the Democratic Party, both cannot be." These "changings and twistings" of the

Democrats, claimed Philadelphia Whig Josiah Randall at a massive Whig rally on election day eve in October, distracted voters from the real issues at stake in the election. Polk and the Democrats "violated every pledge" regarding the protective tariff and "seized for subjugation what it had never dared to claim," in other words, territory once controlled by Mexico.[57]

Philadelphia Whigs viewed "subjugation" as a watchword for slavery and deemed such language essential to securing not only the votes of Pennsylvania Whigs but Pennsylvania abolitionists who still believed in the efficacy of the political process. Randall hoped that, unlike the 15,000 Whig abolitionists in New York who voted for the Liberty Party and gave Polk the presidency in 1844, Whig abolitionists in Pennsylvania would not abandon their principles and leave the state legislature in the hands of the Democrats. Philadelphia Whigs applied the logic of sectionalism to the Democracy's betrayal of Pennsylvania principles, i.e., the Democracy's embrace of the tariff and the slave power. If Democrats on the national stage willingly betrayed these principles, pondered Philadelphia Whig Joseph R. Ingersoll, what would prevent Pennsylvania Democrats from "cringing to the footstool of the South"?[58]

The Whigs handily defeated the Democrats on Election Day in Pennsylvania. Not only did the Whigs elect seventeen out of twenty-four seats in the national Congress, they also took control of both houses of the Pennsylvania state legislature. The Democrats had enjoyed a four-member majority in the state Senate and a more than two-to-one majority in the state House of Representatives before the election. After the election, Whigs carried a four-member majority in the Senate and a twelve-member majority in the House. One commentator for the Whig *North American* explained these major power shifts in the legislatures as the logical extension of how Pennsylvanians regarded slavery: "The state of public sentiment at the North upon the subject of slavery need not and cannot be concealed. Every man, women and child abhors it. And it has been ever so. The State of Pennsylvania, year after year, by the unanimous vote of its democratic legislature passed resolutions against it." While claims of Pennsylvania's legislative unanimity on the subject of slavery defied historical reality, the point remained that the Whigs utilized antislavery tropes as a means to "protect [Pennsylvania] from the efforts made [by the South] to overwhelm her." Here the writer for the *North American* espoused Pennsylvania states' rights and the perception of Pennsylvania's antislavery legacy and projected these rights and this legacy onto Pennsylvania residents. Indeed, a writer for the *Pennsylvania Freeman* linked Southern domination to slaveholders' inhumanity, noting that while many Pennsylvanians

voted for Whig promises of "financial prosperity and political economy"—
i.e., the Tariff of 1846—"so far as the question of slavery was involved [in the
election], humanity was triumphant." The Whigs (and their Free Soil Democrat allies) appeared as a protosectional party willing to limit the spread of
slavery. Thus, Pennsylvania abolitionists, white and Black, viewed the overwhelming Whig victory in their state as a prime opportunity to abolish slavery in Pennsylvania.[59]

Pennsylvania abolitionists greeted the Whig-dominated state legislature
in January 1847 with a petition designed "to prevent kidnapping, preserve the
public peace, prohibit the exercise of certain powers heretofore exercised by
Judges, Justices of the Peace, Aldermen and Jailors in this Commonwealth,
and to repeal certain slave laws." While the substance of the petition remained
unchanged from the previous year, the shift in political and public opinion
made it extremely likely that some version of the bill would pass; a writer for
the *North American* commented that "it behooves [Pennsylvania Whigs] . . . to
prove themselves worthy of the task." Were Pennsylvanians "worthy" enough
to overcome comity and bending their knees to the South, and did this "task"
include protecting Blacks? Both answers meant rehabilitating Pennsylvania's
place in the Union.[60]

The Whigs wasted little time, and upon their return to Harrisburg they
drafted and adopted a number of resolutions that supported Wilmot's Proviso, clear affronts to slaveholders' designs to spread slavery west. More importantly, the Whigs elected two speakers who bore antislavery credentials:
Speaker of the House James Cooper of Adams County and Speaker of the
Senate Charles Gibbons. Cooper recently defended fugitives from slavery in
his home county and, according to the historian David G. Smith, espoused
Pennsylvania's nascent "free soil" doctrines and declared during said trial that
the "moment [the enslaved] placed foot upon our soil, the shackles fell." Gibbons, who needed no introduction (see above), served as a counselor for the
PAS. What the historian Thomas D. Morris has called the "minimum of debate" on the way to the passage of the 1847 liberty law obscured this confluence of propitious events—the tariff, the war with Mexico, Wilmot's Proviso,
and the Whig ascendency in the state legislature—all of which were brought
to the fore by the experiences and efforts of white and Black street diplomats
in Philadelphia.[61]

The Pennsylvania state legislature passed the bill "to prevent kidnapping,
&c. &c.," by the end of February, and on March 3, 1847, Democratic governor
Francis Shunk signed it into law. The bill upheld slaveholders' constitutional

right to reclaim their property, but slaveholders could only retrieve said "property" without what the bill termed "illegal violence." However, as previous chapters have shown, rarely did retrieval efforts fail to include some form of violence, from the moment of seizure to the terminus of a godforsaken plantation. Determining how to avoid the violence of a patently violent series of interactions known as enslavement pushed the burden of retrieval firmly back onto slaveholders and their agents. As a states' rights document, the bill made the sale of the enslaved within the state illegal, permitted judges to issue writs of habeas corpus "to inquire into the causes and legality of the arrest or imprisonment of any human being within this commonwealth," and repealed a major component of Pennsylvania's 1780 gradual abolition act: slaveholders were no longer permitted to bring the enslaved with them to Pennsylvania for six months. Most importantly, the 1847 act rescinded Pennsylvania state assistance for federal slave rendition under the 1793 Fugitive Slave Act.[62]

As I have argued throughout this work, no law, whether local, state, or federal could ever completely prevent enslaved people from freeing themselves or slaveholders—*kidnappers all*—from attempting to retrieve fugitives from slavery; time and again these groups turned the streets of Philadelphia and the state of Pennsylvania into a battleground of freedom. The crises over fugitives from slavery continued to bind Pennsylvanians, like all Americans, to the scourge of national slavery even after the 1847 law, though Pennsylvania's liberty laws did upset federal retrieval efforts and thus forced slaveholders to pressure Congress to pass a revamped federal fugitive slave law in 1850. Those Black and white street diplomats who influenced and informed white politicians' legislating on liberty laws from 1820 onward adroitly outmaneuvered the local, state, and national slave powers arrayed against them and in 1847 forced Pennsylvania lawmakers to pass an aggressive nonpartisan states' rights bill that liberated Pennsylvania from the slavery-dominated federal government.[63]

Conclusion

The passage of the 1847 act elicited a variety of responses that depended largely upon where the writer stood regarding slavery. Pennsylvania abolitionists were, of course, thrilled by the act. The PAS wrote a letter thanking Charles Gibbons, who had informed them that the bill passed the Senate "without opposition." PASS members James and Lucretia Mott, who with Charles Burleigh acted as the main lobbyists for the bill in Harrisburg, cancelled their trip to the state capital, no doubt elated that the act had "received the signature of the Governor, and is now a law of the State." The Whig *North American* proclaimed that "slavery in Pennsylvania has received its death blow." A writer for the *Pennsylvania Freeman* even went so far as to encourage Southerners to bring the enslaved to Pennsylvania in order to place their recovery "out of the question"; "the more they bring, under the new law, the better." Unlike the previous decade in which Pennsylvanians debated allowing Black emigrants, the 1847 law, at least according to the interpretation of Pennsylvania abolitionists, encouraged Black emigration into the state. These abolitionists, Black and white, could rest assured, temporarily at least, that "the instant a slave treads on the soil of Pennsylvania, his freedom is in his own hands." The allies of freedom in Philadelphia—street diplomats all— redefined Pennsylvania as a free state.[64]

Slaveholders felt otherwise, calling the act a violation of comity. A writer for the *Macon Weekly Telegraph* explained: "Here then is an act of Congress [the 1793 Fugitive Slave Act] decided to be within the Constitution by the supreme judicature of the Union, and which the Legislature of Pennsylvania abrogates within her limits, on grounds that put at defiance those rights of Southern property which are solemnly guaranteed by that instrument."[65] More than nullifying a Supreme Court decision, Pennsylvania and her "rabid abolitionists" violated the sacred compact of Union, that original compromise over, with, and for slavery. Maryland and Virginia slaveholders alike complained that the human beings they owned, those enslaved African Americans who no doubt paid attention to such political developments, began fleeing the South in "gangs of tens and twenties." These fugitives from slavery came to and through the streets of Philadelphia, Pennsylvania, where they found willing assistance from those Black and white street diplomats like Robert Purvis, James McKim, and William Still, who labored for decades to perfect a system by which they could protect African Americans. Against slaveholders' hopes and dreams, the *Pennsylvania Freeman* declared Pennsylvania a free state, one where Black and white abolitionists would continue to spread the contagion of liberty "till the whole country shall become enlightened, and the public heart so changed that every vestige of slavery shall be swept from the land and from the face of the statute book." Only a revised federal fugitive slave act could stand in their way.[66]

The Famous Grasshopper War

"THE UNION MUST AND SHALL BE PRESERVED" declared the first page of a lengthy pamphlet published in November 1850 to commemorate the "Great Union Meeting" held in Philadelphia in the wake of the Compromise of 1850. Over 5,000 attendees of all political stripes affixed their names to this document and shared the common goal of remaining committed to the Union of a half-free, half-slave society called the United States of America. The illustrious speakers who held the rostrum represented the best political expedients that Pennsylvania could offer the nation. US senator John Sergeant, the proud defender of Pennsylvania states' rights in Congress over the Missouri Question, the PAS stalwart, and the key Whig leader who presided over the Pennsylvania state constitutional convention, reminded the audience that, because the Union was created by "the whole of the united people of the United States," all Americans must recognize the duties implicit in maintaining and enforcing the greatest product of the Union: the Federal Constitution. To Sergeant, Americans had "no choice about it."[1]

George Mifflin Dallas, the former vice president who sacrificed his state on the altar of slavery during the tariff debates, echoed Sergeant on the "binding" effect of the Constitution, especially with the recent passage of the Fugitive Slave Bill. "For better [or] for worse," the forefathers who consecrated the Union in Philadelphia demanded "a frank and fearless loyalty" to this bill. In keeping with Northern Democrat doughfacism, Dallas's loyalty depended on showing "our Southern brethren . . . a determination to enforce their rights." These rights, the slaveholder's right as a citizen of the Union, that solemn national compact that produced a Constitution and federal Fugitive Slave Act, demolished the border between freedom and slavery, a brutal fact understood and experienced by African Americans and their allies in Philadelphia.[2]

Throughout this book I have grappled with the question of when slavery ended in Pennsylvania. Struggles over the kidnapping and hunting of African Americans in Philadelphia created "grasshopper wars" that linked conflicts and compromises within the city to the state and nation. As the minister Noah Worcester wrote to longtime PAS member Roberts Vaux in 1822, "Two [Native American] children quarreled about a grasshopper, the women became enlisted for the children, and finally the men engaged in the quarrel, and commenced a war which occasioned the extermination of a great part of two tribes."[3]

What began as an individual's desire to live as a free human being regardless of their position in society soon transformed over time into a volatile concoction of overlapping boundaries and metastasizing political stakes. Faced with the choice of echoing the traditional periodization of 1865 or the more transgressive periodizations that link antebellum slavery to postwar debt peonage and in our own time, mass incarceration, my interpretation falls into the latter camp, as I view the history of slavery in Pennsylvania as a process of transposition. That is, similar to how a conductor might transpose a piece of music by adjusting the key while at the same time maintaining the instant familiarity of the song's melody, the work of transposing slavery in Pennsylvania became a series of intertwined victories and defeats for both antislavery and proslavery forces from 1820 to 1847.

The crises over removing fugitives from slavery and the kidnappings that transpired in Philadelphia during the 1850s merely exemplified the final battles at the tail end of a decades-long war. The 1850 Fugitive Slave Act was a "direct response" to the variety of means Black and white street diplomats implemented in places like Philadelphia to defend themselves as Americans. The act assigned all Americans the task of being slave catchers and kidnappers and brought to the fore those features of comity endured by street diplomats who fought in the midst of Philadelphia's own politics of slavery.[4]

As I have argued over the course of this book, African Americans bore the burden of freedom and slavery, and thus the burden of the Union through "street diplomacy," those up close and personal struggles over freedom and slavery that connected and produced local, state, and national ramifications. It seems ironic, then, that Philadelphia witnessed only a handful of removals through the revised 1850 Fugitive Slave Act. In keeping with the twists and turns of the cases I examined prior to 1850 and comporting to the perpetual dialectics between freedom and slavery, I analyze below one final example of street diplomacy and speak to the paucity of Philadelphia cases in the 1850s.

But first, the aggressive tone of the 1847 Pennsylvania liberty law and the "sudden unanimity" of the Pennsylvania politicians who passed it flew in the face of the 1793 Fugitive Slave Act as well as the *Prigg* decision. Here Pennsylvanians defined their rights as a state as superior to federal power by removing state assistance for cases of fugitives from slavery and empowering state judges to scrutinize or deny jurisdiction for any cases brought to them. Not only did Pennsylvania become a free state in this way, it did so primarily due to the efforts of a motley crew of abolitionists, politicians, and of course, ordinary African Americans, whose freedom was always subject to questioning regardless of their location in the Union. Southerners well understood that strengthening the 1793 Fugitive Slave Act at the federal level would be the only way to eclipse Pennsylvania's attempt to "destroy" their right to claim fugitives from slavery.[5]

While the intricate debates that led to the passage of the infamous 1850 Fugitive Slave Act lie beyond the scope of this work, the bill deserves a brief mention, as it applies directly to Pennsylvania's efforts to absolve itself of slavery. First, new federal commissioners would be appointed by federal courts to exercise the act. Second, federal marshals would work with commissioners to apprehend accused fugitives from slavery anywhere in the Union. Third, if in the course of the pursuit ordinary Americans failed to assist or obstructed the federal marshals, these bystanders could be fined or imprisoned. Finally, once the fugitive from slavery, whose testimony was disallowed under the act, appeared before the federal commissioner, the latter could decide the case in a summary manner and use "such reasonable force as is necessary to carry [the accused] back to slavery." This nightmarish process revoked the strides made by street diplomats from start to finish: local law enforcement would now collude with federal marshals, any effort to disrupt arrest or gather evidence would be punished, and supposed fugitives from slavery would be silenced in front of a federal judge, whose decision could destroy their lives and at the very least, flout the borders between freedom and slavery.[6]

And yet the Black and white Philadelphia abolitionists mustered their experience and the forces of freedom in response to the passage of the Fugitive Slave Act of 1850. A large group of African Americans gathered in Brick Wesley Church in South Philadelphia that October both to oppose the law but also, in the words of Andrew K. Diemer, to "make a larger case to the white public." This group resolved to pledge their lives, fortunes, and sacred honor to resist the new law, especially as the supposed and certainly manufactured popularity of the law—i.e., the Great Union Meeting—begged for African Americans and their allies to actualize the lessons of street diplomacy yet again.[7]

It was no coincidence that when the first case of a fugitive from slavery under the new law involving an African American man named Henry Garnett occurred in the city in October 1850, this community of street diplomats rose up with militant vigilance. One thousand African Americans along with their white allies accompanied Garnett to Independence Hall and brought him before the Associate Justice of the Supreme Court Robert Grier. Neither an admirer of abolitionists nor of African Americans, Grier patronized the Black audience at the hearing by telling them to avoid being "incited to violence by bad advisers," as rumors already spread across Philadelphia that a number of African Americans were arming themselves and preparing to riot if Garnett was not released. Grier promised to preserve law and order in Philadelphia, even if that meant he had to "walk through the blood of every colored person in the city." The potential for violence abated only due to the claimant's lawyer failing to produce the proper paperwork. Grier released Garnett to the hundreds of Black and white allies, street diplomats all.[8]

George Alberti, "A man of modest discretion"

"Who has not heard of Alberti?" opined *Frederick Douglass' Paper*. Among the many sobriquets devoted to George Alberti, including "the hangman," "the manstealer," "the resurrectionist," and "the constable," "the notorious kidnapper" outshone them all in the grimmest of ways. A figure who epitomized the struggle against African American freedom for forty years, Alberti seemed readymade to actualize the 1850 Fugitive Slave Act. Despite all of the laws passed to protect Black freedom in Pennsylvania, this man and other human beings like him relished the chance to use all of the tools at their disposal, from Black informants to local law enforcement to corrupt politicians and slave traders, relationships designed to perpetuate violence, artifice, and terror in the lives of African Americans. Unsurprisingly, the second case of a fugitive from slavery in light of the 1850 law involved Alberti. In late December 1850 Alberti arrested an African American man named Adam Gibson in Southwark, one of the hubs of Black Philadelphia. Gibson's crime? Allegedly stealing chickens, a stratagem devised to remand Gibson to his supposed "master" in Maryland. Alberti and his accomplices "the notorious kidnapper and desperado" James Frisby Price, a light-skinned African American man,

The 'Ruse' of the Sick Horse.

In 1825 a slaveholder hired George Alberti to retrieve a man who absconded to Haddonfield, New Jersey. Alberti contacted his informants in Haddonfield and discovered the man, a self-proclaimed "expert of horseology." However, the African American residents of Haddonfield well knew of Alberti's modus operandi. Alberti convinced the man to leave Haddonfield to tend to Alberti's "lame" horse. The man's wife ambushed Alberti just as she saw him strike her husband and shot the slave catcher with two horse pistols. Newspapers believed that Alberti suffered fatal wounds; he survived and continued to hunt human beings for the next forty years. "The Ruse of the Sick Horse," in *Life of the Notorious Kidnapper, George F. Alberti* [E441.A58 v. 118 No. 2], Historical Society of Pennsylvania

and his brother George brought Gibson to none other than Federal Slave Commissioner Edward J. Ingraham, who consistently defended slaveholders in Philadelphia. Ingraham sided with Alberti in order to "preserve the Union," and remanded Gibson to his supposed "owner" in Maryland, W. S. Knight. How did Knight react to the return of his "escaped property"? Knight stated plainly: "That is not my slave; I know this man, Adam . . . how he obtained his liberty, I do not know; he is not mine." This case of mistaken identity, i.e., a kidnapping, brought to light the immediate dangers of the revised Fugitive

Slave Act: kidnappers would still kidnap, and street diplomats would still consider any arrest of an African American a kidnapping, regardless of law or geography. Gibson arrived back in Philadelphia to a large throng of Black and white supporters, who greeted him with cheers and brought him to his wife and children, away from Alberti and the legal system that nearly stole Gibson away forever. Given their work in the previous decades, Philadelphia street diplomats knew how remanding an ordinary person like Adam Gibson in the name of Union clearly undermined the 1850 Fugitive Slave Act.[9]

Alberti's most publicized trial occurred less than six months later and inspired three fascinating print sources that represented the spectrum of freedom and slavery in Philadelphia. *Life of the Notorious Kidnapper, George F. Alberti*, written by the Philadelphia lawyer A. D. Byron, served as part biography, part excoriation of Alberti's life. *A Review of the Trial, Conviction, And Sentence, of George F. Alberti, for kidnapping*, written by another Philadelphia lawyer, named Peter Arrell Browne (see chapter 4), castigated Pennsylvania law and sympathized with Southern slavery. The final source was written by the presiding judge for the case, Anvil Virgil Parsons, who synthesized and conceptualized the entire litany of events. What follows is an attempt to thread these narratives together.[10]

The case began when an enslaved African American woman named Betsey Galloway, alias Catherine Thompson, escaped from Maryland slaveholder James Mitchell in 1845. Aided by Peregrine Berry, alias William Thompson, a freeman who lived on the plantation next to Mitchell, the pair left Maryland, married in Wilmington, Delaware, and settled in Burlington County, New Jersey, where in 1847 Catherine gave birth to a boy named Joel. In August 1850, Catherine and William were visited by James Frisby Price, who, unbeknownst to the Thompsons, was the aforementioned "notorious kidnapper and desperado" involved in Gibson's arrest. With cruel irony, Price claimed he was a lost hunter and made fast friends with the Thompsons. Price beckoned for Catherine to bring her new baby to meet Price's wife on Vernon Street in Philadelphia. Catherine obliged and visited the Prices numerous times in early August 1850.[11]

Catherine Thompson was a human being who fled slavery. Her potential capture and reenslavement always lurked in the back of her mind, and if she forgot that central fact of her existence, other human beings inside and outside of Philadelphia were keen to remind her. Byron claimed that Mitchell went to Philadelphia to enlist the help of Alberti in December 1847, again illustrating the ease with which slaveholders accessed networks of slave catchers who ignored borders. To wit, James Frisby Price must have obliterated borders regularly: he knew of the Thompsons "for some time before" because he resided not far from Mitchell in Cecil County during the 1840s. Ignorant of Mitchell's whereabouts and his alliance with Alberti, Catherine and Joel visited the Price household one final time on August 14, 1850. At some point over breakfast Price convinced Catherine to accompany him to the house of his friend, George Alberti. Of course, we will never know what Price said to her in that fateful moment, a moment of enslavement, a kidnapped moment—did he utter the name "Alberti"? Price's subterfuge worked: he appeared trustworthy as an ally, a friend even—all part of a plan to kidnap and enslave her. Catherine accompanied Price to Alberti's dwelling at Clare above Carpenter Street, located mere blocks away from the heart of Black Philadelphia.[12]

Alberti arrested Catherine as soon as she entered his house. Philadelphia County alderman William Allen, conveniently present at Alberti's, oversaw the arrest and, according to Byron "gave the affair the appearance of legal proceedings," before placing her in Alberti's custody. Mitchell's lawyer, Hugh Tener, was also in attendance, demonstrating again the premeditated nature of the arrest. Catherine implemented street diplomacy by requesting that her captors contact an abolitionist who lived nearby on Bank Street, someone who would clear her name and quite possibly initiate legal proceedings against Alberti and Price. Unfortunately for Catherine, the man she requested was none other than James Price's brother George, a man who when asked what his business was with Alberti in the Gibson case simply replied, "that is my business," i.e., we hunt and kidnap human beings. When George Price arrived, he maintained his abolitionist ruse and told her to cooperate in order to "extricate herself from the difficulties." The parties thus assembled—an accused woman, her baby, a slave catcher, an informant, a conman, an attorney, and a local political official—Catherine became a street diplomat.[13]

The main point of contention between Catherine and her captors was the position of Joel, a boy born to an enslaved mother in a free state. Price and Alberti insisted that Catherine leave the child with Alberti, perhaps suggesting that they, too, felt uneasy about potentially being arrested for kidnapping a free person—ironic, given Price's previous insistence that Catherine bring the baby with her to Philadelphia. Catherine was indeed caught in the slave catcher's trap: the trap of living as an African American north of slavery, the trap of creating a family and having futures dashed on the cornerstone of the Union. She refused to let Joel stay with Alberti and told him that her child was sickly. Viewed as an instance of street diplomacy, Catherine rested her hopes of freedom on Joel: if the boy went with her to Maryland, then there was a much better chance of Pennsylvania state kidnapping laws convicting Alberti and Price. Catherine wailed, pleaded, and clung tightly to Joel in the midst of her captors. She knew Alberti's strategy, one employed by countless slaveholders: Alberti would keep Joel until he was "grown up" and then sell him. Alberti "quieted" Catherine with his billy club, hitting her repeatedly as she shielded her son; Catherine would never let go of Joel. Soon thereafter a hack driver by the name of Thomas Richardson arrived at the Alberti household, picked up Alberti, Catherine, and Joel, and drove south to Elkton, Maryland, to meet with Mitchell. Upon seeing Catherine, Mitchell exclaimed, "We have got you, you Black bitch, at last!" Mitchell sold the pair to the Baltimore slave trader John Donovan, who offered to sell Catherine and Joel back to Philadelphia abolitionists "at a slight advance." The money for their freedom never materialized, so Donovan sold Catherine and Joel to the Deep South, where they disappeared from the historical record.[14]

With Joel and Catherine lost to slavery, Pennsylvanians pursued Alberti, Price, and Mitchell. In January 1851 a Philadelphia grand jury indicted Alberti and Price on the charge of kidnapping Joel "with the intention of selling him into slavery." In February Pennsylvania's Whig governor William F. Johnston sent multiple requests to Maryland governor Enoch Lowe demanding that he remand Mitchell to Philadelphia to stand trial for kidnapping. Lowe refused Johnston's requests for comity because Mitchell was never "personally present" in Pennsylvania and Joel was still enslaved by Mitchell. A month later in March 1851, Pennsylvania Whigs performed an about-face: they held a major gathering in Philadelphia where they praised the "compromise measures of the last Congress" and promised to repeal the "obnoxious" features of the 1847 Pennsylvania liberty law, namely, the section that prevented state prisons from housing accused fugitives from slavery. While not an abolitionist per se, Johnston imbibed the "free soil" doctrine permeating the Whig party, and thus pocket-vetoed a bill passed by the Pennsylvania legislature designed to open state prisons and repeal the 1847 law in general. For "spurning" this demand by Pennsylvanians who warily realigned themselves with slaveholders in the interest of preserving the Union, Johnston sacrificed his reelection prospects in 1852.[15]

Fittingly, Alberti and Price remained incarcerated in Philadelphia's Eastern State Penitentiary between their indictment and trial. This penitentiary was a well-known terminus for both men, as they had arrested and transported many supposed fugitives from slavery there over the course of their careers. The pair arrived in Judge A. V. Parsons's Court of Common Pleas on February 28, 1851. Parsons instructed the jury to take the law from him alone because of the dueling intricacies of the 1847 Pennsylvania liberty law and the 1850 Fugitive Slave Act. The prosecutors, including David Paul Brown, admitted that, while Catherine was an enslaved woman, her son Joel was free, having been born in New Jersey. Catherine's husband, William, testified as to the location of Joel's birth but said nothing to support or deny his wife's free status, merely stating that they were married in 1845 in Wilmington, Delaware. The prosecution also called Thomas Richardson, the hack driver who brought Catherine and Joel to Elkton. Richardson, a recently pardoned ex-convict, explained that Alberti told him that Catherine had stolen jewelry from Mitchell and that they were taking her to Elkton for that reason. Alberti and Price's defense team balked at Richardson's testimony, citing his status as an ex-convict, though one gets the sense that Richardson tried to save himself and place the burden of kidnapping on two well-known kidnappers.[16]

The defense team employed all of the schemes familiar to Philadelphia street diplomats. Mitchell's lawyer, Hugh Tener, testified that he told Alberti to leave Joel because Catherine "voluntarily and fully acknowledged that she was the slave of Mitchell," which again, spoke to the extemporaneous self-sacrifice a mother would perform to save her child: if Catherine was to be reenslaved, maybe she could let her son enjoy freedom. Next, the defense introduced Mitchell's letter of attorney he wrote to Alberti, but Parsons refused to accept the document even "if it had all the seals in Maryland to it" because Mitchell was not present in court to offer testimony—again, suggesting that Mitchell knew that he had kidnapped a free person and therefore did not want to cross the border into Pennsylvania. Parsons also dismissed the testimony of Alderman Allen because no Pennsylvania alderman was allowed to issue a certificate to remove accused fugitives from slavery and threatened to "bind him over to answer for it criminally." After hearing from a number of respectable witnesses who derided Richardson's character, the defense lawyer, General Horatio Hubbell, spoke. Hubbell argued that "the act of 1847 being but a re-enactment of the act of 1826, which the Supreme Court, in Priggs' case, held to be unconstitutional; that Priggs' case was applicable in deciding this case on the same grounds, and that under its ruling the act of 1847 was also unconstitutional."[17]

Hubbell's brief overview helps encapsulate the scope of this book and my argument for Pennsylvania's central place in the Union. Affronts to the 1780 Gradual Emancipation of the state's Black population inspired Pennsylvania's

1820 liberty law by increasing kidnapping fines and limiting state assistance when retrieving fugitives from slavery. The 1826 liberty law responded to slaveholders' pleas for their "property" and street diplomats' resistance and, in doing so, modified the retrieval process under the 1793 Fugitive Slave Act, a process that could and did result in the kidnapping of free people. The *Prigg* decision struck down the 1826 law because it modified the 1793 act but also left space for Pennsylvania to refuse to help slaveholders. Street diplomats exploited the confluence of events propelled by slaveholders, in particular, the invasion of Mexico and the tariff, thereby forcing Pennsylvanians to craft and pass the 1847 liberty law. This law ended slavery in the state by preventing state officials from participating in the rendition process, a maneuver that presaged the 1850 Fugitive Slave Act, which criminalized any American who refused to assist slaveholders in hunting human beings. Street diplomats in Philadelphia, Pennsylvania helped bring about the Civil War.[18]

Parsons brought the trial to an appropriate conclusion by discoursing on what he called a "national question." Indeed, slaveholders possessed the right to own and hunt human beings as laid out by the Constitution. At the same time, Pennsylvania possessed the right to protect its residents and punish those who would kidnap them. The consistent muddling within this case came from individuals making individual choices: Catherine chose to escape, chose to admit of her enslavement, chose to hold on to her son for dear life, and chose to resist as much as any human being could resist, street diplomat or otherwise. Alberti and his associates made choices, too, choices buttressed by a Federal Constitution that afforded limitless opportunities to kidnap, enslave, and inflict a "most brutal violence" upon two human beings, an African American mother and child. Alberti and Price's choice to participate in such deeds for money obscured how they conceived of themselves as staunch Unionists: without this *"fundamental"* ability to catch fugitives from slavery, Alberti and his ally Peter Arrell Browne argued, "the Union could not have been formed." A Union without slavery meant no Union at all; a Union with slavery and the ability to hunt human property meant comity. Parsons would not admit to this logic; he conceptualized the Union as one that "tolerated" slavery by law as much as one that "abhorred" the kidnapping of free people. The jury thus instructed, they quickly returned with their verdict: Alberti and Price were guilty. On March 24, 1851, Parsons sentenced Price to eight years in prison and fined him $700, while Alberti was to serve ten years hard labor and fined $1,000.[19]

Like many of the cases examined in this book, the conviction of Alberti and Price remained a half-victory. Catherine and Joel lost their futures indefinitely, while the kidnappers might serve their entire sentences unscathed. Thus, instead of a rapturous reaction to the sentencing of two infamous kidnappers, African Americans and their white allies present in the packed courtroom greeted the verdict with "murmurs of applause." The *Pennsylvania Freeman* castigated those who sympathized with Alberti due to his advanced age and long sentence; that people spoke in his defense inside and outside the courthouse illuminated the simple explanation that many Americans believed that the Fugitive Slave Act was necessary and proper for matters of Union. "Fools!" exclaimed the "Octogenarian" writing for the *Pennsylvania Freeman,* "do they not know that kidnapping is a necessary adjunct to slavery, and lies at the very foundation of it, and that neither of them can exist in this country, without the other?" This dark and prescient understanding of the Union as a union with slavery acted as the foundation of street diplomacy and collided with slaveholders' notions of justice. Proslavery writers from Baltimore and Washington, DC, applauded the Maryland State Legislature for refusing to extradite Mitchell and for sending money to Alberti while in prison; both actions effectively ignored comity. Alberti later claimed that he "never got a dollar" from the "corrupt set" that was the Maryland State Legislature, chalking up this failure to his lawyers William Lehman and Peter Arrell Browne contacting Maryland governor Enoch Lowe directly. At long last it seemed as though Philadelphia street diplomats had bested George Alberti.[20]

Newly elected Pennsylvania Democratic governor William F. Bigler chose comity with slavery over street diplomacy when he pardoned Alberti and Price in February 1852, not even a year into their sentences. This pardon came at the end of a bitter year: in September 1851 a major resistance effort erupted in Christiana, Pennsylvania, when a group of Maryland slave catchers ventured there to retrieve their human property; one of these slave catchers–cum–kidnappers lost their lives at the hands of African Americans led by local Black activist William Parker. That fall the Pennsylvania gubernatorial election season was underway, and Pennsylvania Democrats pilloried Governor Johnston for being "responsible" for what Democrats termed a "riot" because of his recent pocket veto of the state Senate bill to open state prisons to fugitives from slavery. Democratic candidate Bigler seized on this issue and took fellow Pennsylvanian James Buchanan's advice, who insisted that the Fugitive Slave Act must "sustain the Union." Buchanan hinted that the 1847 law would continue to create "riots" such as those Americans witnessed at Christiana. Democratic newspapers and politicians fanned these flames to such an extent that Governor Johnston himself experienced the wrath of rioters in late September, when an "infuriated mob" attempted to assault him as he made his way to Philadelphia.[21]

In light of this recent assault, Johnston waffled at a public meeting at Independence Hall a week before the election in October, claiming that the speed with which the amendments to the 1847 law passed prevented him from giving the new bill "due consideration." At a large Whig rally held in Philadelphia during the week of the election, pundits writing for the *North American* argued that despite what his Philadelphia Democratic critics might assert, Johnston was "no agitator" on the slavery question: Whigs in Pennsylvania, not unlike their Democratic counterparts, sought compromise on the slavery issue, a consensus which obviously jeopardized Johnston's campaign. This consensus maintained the Union and comity but led to Johnston's defeat. The newly sworn Governor Bigler made it clear that he would support slavery, that comity sustained the Union. Not only did he pardon Alberti and Price in February, "a most righteous act" according to the Democratic *Harrisburg Union:* two months later he signed into law the bill created by Pennsylvania Democrats and Union-minded Whigs in the state legislature that closed Pennsylvania state jails to fugitives from slavery.[22]

"Liberty at the cost of life"

I return now to Philadelphia in 1852, where the new Fugitive Slave Act inspired the crucial context for the reorganization of the Philadelphia Vigilance Committee in December of that year. This group of passionate Black and white abolitionists were "synonymous" with the Underground Railroad, according to the organization's secretary, William Still. Their efficient methods derived from the decades of knowledge accrued by Black and white street diplomats in Philadelphia, who rendered the fugitive from slavery and potential free kidnapping victim as one and the same person and placed them at the center of political change. In a time when the law and the lawmakers themselves could neither precipitate nor guarantee Black freedom, Still's work alongside other Black and white abolitionist stalwarts, like Robert Purvis and James Miller McKim, gave hope to African Americans living in and passing through Philadelphia.[23]

In the words of William Still, Vigilance Committee members well understood that African American fugitives from slavery were "determined to have liberty at the cost of life," a notion familiar to free African Americans in Pennsylvania who may never have experienced enslavement. Thus, while it is well established how fugitives from slavery pushed white politicians to make desperate compromises "in the coming of the Civil War," free African Americans like Purvis and Still faced violence, racism, riots, and kidnapping threats that made their lives akin to living under slavery. Formal legislative efforts made by those same white politicians to maintain comity foisted the burden of the Union onto African Americans, fugitives from slavery or otherwise. The inability of Americans to clearly delineate the freedom or enslavement of African Americans in Pennsylvania meant that their very beings and futures sustained the Union. Unsure as African Americans were of their futures, Black and white street diplomats charged their future, our present, with bringing to light those who participated in "officially, professionally, or as volunteers, in hunting down the fugitive slave, and delivering him over to his master"— people like Alberti, Price, and Bigler. Obscure as these Americans sound to us, they disrupted the lives, worlds, and futures of African Americans living in Philadelphia, Pennsylvania, and no doubt the lives, worlds, and futures of those who resided in other Northern locales.[24]

Philadelphia served as a hotbed for slave catching, wayward slaveholders, fugitives from slavery, and abolitionists. It is curious then, that only eleven federal cases under the 1850 law transpired in the city. I attribute this dearth to the successes of the Underground Railroad, which in many ways institutionalized both the idea of street diplomacy, as well as actual human beings who acted as street diplomats. A lack of cases in a formal legal setting like a courtroom betrays the hundreds of individual successes of Philadelphia's Underground Railroad, many of which were "sad and thrilling" stories communicated orally that left deep impressions upon Blacks and whites alike. Thankfully, we do possess William Still's magisterial work on the Underground Railroad, which recounted hundreds of rescues in the city. In addition, historians have consulted Still's "Journal C of Station No. 2" of the Underground Railroad and created an index of over 900 fugitives from slavery who ventured to and through Philadelphia from 1852 to 1857. Given that "Journal 'C' " may presuppose a journal A and a journal B, that "Station No. 2" certainly presupposes other "stations," that William Still was not the only "conductor" in Philadelphia, and that the Philadelphia network was one of at least ten Underground Railroad routes that we know of in Pennsylvania, African Americans who fled slavery seemed to have more Black and white street diplomats at their disposal who were willing to assist them and do so with great success because of decades of experience. When all else failed, the 1850s gave African Americans plenty of examples of rescues through which they could free themselves and defend their freedom, putting into practice lessons gleaned from the streets of Philadelphia.[25]

The struggles experienced by African Americans in Pennsylvania in general and Philadelphia in particular revealed that hard-fought compromises over slavery produced short-lived victories for freedom. These victories emerged through the process of street diplomacy, in which local, state, and national concerns were shaped by the contested battleground and porous borders of slavery and freedom in Pennsylvania. Pennsylvania politicians who attempted to prevent the spread of slavery could do so only by compromising with Southern slaveholders—hardly a compromise, especially when the latter group threatened to secede from the Union, which protected their rights to own and hunt human beings. The 1850 Fugitive Slave Act represented the desperate attempt by politicians to pledge their love and loyalty to the Union, and as such, these same politicians failed to learn the lesson of African American life in Pennsylvania from 1820 to 1850: compromising with slavery inexorably led to violent conflict. These conflicts through compromise destroyed the Second Party system, reified the social, political, and racial inequality of African Americans through the Dred Scott decision, and elected a president who refused to accept the expansion of slavery as the basis of the Union. The Civil War became street diplomacy writ large; yet slavery in all its intricacies could never completely fade away in America—or the world. We are living in the shadow of the charge made by Robert Purvis in 1865 to remain at our posts "until slavery goes down so effectually that about it we can have no question or doubt." Questioning slavery's origins, politics, and realities today remains paramount if historians hope to realize the brute fact of slavery long, long ago.[26]

Introduction

1. A note on language: throughout this work I employ language that defers to the guide "Writing about Slavery?" by Professor Gabrielle Foreman et al. "Writing about Slavery? Teaching about Slavery?: This Might Help" community-sourced document, accessed August 17, 2021, https://naacpculpeper.org/resources/writing-about-slavery-this-might-help; "Interview with George Alberti," *National Anti-Slavery Standard [NASS]*, February 19, 1859. Unless stated otherwise, all italics are in the original.

2. "Interview with George Alberti," February 19, 1859; William Still, *The Underground Rail Road: A Record of Facts, Authentic Narratives, Letters, &c., narrating the Hardships, Hairbreadth Escapes and Death Struggles of the Slaves in their Efforts for Freedom, as related by themselves and others, or witnessed by the author,* [. . .] (Medford, NJ: Plexus Publishing, 2005), 654–659; Ira V. Brown, "Miller McKim and Pennsylvania Abolitionism." *Pennsylvania History* 30 (January 1963): 56–73.

3. Pennsylvania Abolition Society General Meeting Minutes, 1825–1847, December 31, 1835; Robert Purvis, *A Tribute to the Memory of Thomas Shipley, The Philanthropist* (Philadelphia: Merrihew and Gunn, 1836), 6–7. See also Isaac Parrish, *Brief Memoirs of Thomas Shipley and Edwin P. Atlee, Read Before the Pennsylvania Society for Promoting the Abolition of Slavery* (Philadelphia: Merrihew and Gunn, 1838).

4. While texts on the history of Philadelphia are legion, I relied mainly but not exclusively, upon on the following works: Gary Nash, *First City: Philadelphia and the Forging of Historical Memory* (Philadelphia: University of Pennsylvania Press, 2006), 147; Gary Nash and Jean Soderlund, *Freedom by Degrees: Emancipation in Pennsylvania and Its Aftermath* (New York: Oxford University Press, 1991), 179–192; Gary Nash, *Forging Freedom: The Formation of Philadelphia's Black Community, 1720–1840* (Cambridge, MA: Harvard University Press, 1988); Erica Armstrong Dunbar, *A Fragile Freedom: African American Women and Emancipation in the Antebellum City* (New Haven, CT: Yale University Press, 2008); Russell F. Weigley, ed., *Philadelphia: A 300 Year History* (New York: Norton, 1982); Richard Newman and James Mueller, eds., *Antislavery and Abolition in Philadelphia: Emancipation and the Long Struggle for Racial Justice in the City of Brotherly Love* (Baton Rouge: Louisiana State University Press, 2011); Andrew Keith Diemer, "Black Nativism: African American Politics, Nationalism and Citizenship in Baltimore and Philadelphia, 1817 to 1863" (PhD diss., Temple University, 2011); Andrew K. Diemer, *The Politics of Black Citizenship: Free African Americans in the Mid-Atlantic Borderland, 1817–1863* (Athens: University of Georgia Press, 2016); Richard S. Newman, *The Transformation of American Abolitionism: Fighting Slavery in the Early Republic* (Chapel Hill: University of North Carolina Press, 2002); Allen F. Davis and Mark H. Haller, eds., *The Peoples*

of Philadelphia: A History of Ethnic Groups and Lower-Class Life, 1790–1940 (Philadelphia: University of Pennsylvania Press, 1998); Bruce Laurie, Working People of Philadelphia, 1800–1850 (Philadelphia: Temple University Press, 1980); Michael Feldberg, The Philadelphia Riots of 1844: A Study of Ethnic Conflict (Westport, CT: Greenwood Press, 1975); Noel Ignatiev, How the Irish Became White (New York: Routledge, 1995); Jean Soderlund, Quakers and Slavery: A Divided Spirit (Princeton, NJ: Princeton University Press, 1985); Sam Bass Warner, The Private City: Philadelphia in Three Periods of Growth (Philadelphia: University of Pennsylvania Press, 1987); Beverly C. Tomek, Pennsylvania Hall: A "Legal Lynching" in the Shadow of the Liberty Bell (New York: Oxford University Press, 2014); David Grimsted, American Mobbing, 1828–1861: Toward Civil War (Oxford: Oxford University Press, 1998). See also W. E. B. Du Bois, The Philadelphia Negro: A Social Study (Philadelphia: University of Pennsylvania Press, 1899); J. Thomas Scharff and Thompson Westcott, History of Philadelphia, 1609–1884 (Philadelphia: L. H. Everts & Co., 1884); Henry Simpson, Lives of Eminent Philadelphians, Now Deceased (Philadelphia: William Brotherhead, 1859).

On Pennsylvania history in general, see Randall M. Miller and William Pencak, eds., Pennsylvania: A History of the Commonwealth (University Park: Pennsylvania State University Press, 2002); Philip S. Klein and Ari Hoogenboom. A History of Pennsylvania (University Park: Pennsylvania State University Press, 1980); Philip S. Klein, Pennsylvania Politics, 1817–1832: A Game without Rules (Philadelphia: Historical Society of Pennsylvania, 1940); Charles M. Snyder, The Jacksonian Heritage: Pennsylvania Politics, 1833–1848 (Harrisburg: Pennsylvania Historical and Museum Commission, 1958); John F. Coleman, The Disruption of the Pennsylvania Democracy (Harrisburg: Pennsylvania Historical and Museum Commission, 1958); David G. Smith, On the Edge of Freedom: The Fugitive Slave Issue in South Central Pennsylvania, 1820–1870 (New York: Fordham University Press, 2013). Edward Raymond Turner's work on African Americans in Pennsylvania reigns supreme in the historiography; see Edward Raymond Turner, The Negro in Pennsylvania: Slavery-Servitude-Freedom, 1639–1861 (New York: Negro Universities Press, 1969).

On the shocks of which I speak, see Charles Sellers, The Market Revolution: Jacksonian America, 1815–1846 (New York: Oxford University Press, 1991); Jacqueline Jones, American Work: Four Centuries of Black and White Labor (New York: Norton, 1999); James Brewer Stewart, "The Emergence of Racial Modernity and the Rise of the White North, 1790–1840," Journal of the Early Republic 18, no. 2 (Summer 1998): 181–217, and responses, pp. 218–236; Alexander Saxton, The Rise and Fall of the White Republic: Class Politics and Mass Culture in Nineteenth Century America (New York: Verso, 1990); Lawrence Kohl, The Politics of Individualism: Parties and the American Character during the Jacksonian Era (New York: Oxford University Press, 1989); Elizabeth Varon, Disunion! The Coming of the American Civil War, 1789–1859 (Chapel Hill: University of North Carolina Press, 2008); Stanley Harrold, Border War: Fighting over Slavery before the Civil War (Chapel Hill: University of North Carolina Press, 2010); Frederick J. Blue, No Taint of Compromise: Crusaders in Antislavery Politics (Baton Rouge: Louisiana State University Press, 2005); Jean Baker, Affairs of Party: The Political Culture of Northern Democrats during the Nineteenth Century (Ithaca, NY: Cornell University Press, 1983); Leon Richards, The Slave Power: The Free North and Southern Domination, 1780–1860 (Baton Rouge: Louisiana University Press, 2000); Larry Tise, Proslavery: A History of the Defense of Slavery in America, 1701–1840 (Athens: University of Georgia Press, 1987); William Freehling, The Road to Disunion, vol. 1: Secessionists at Bay, 1776–1854 (New York: Oxford University Press, 1991); William Freehling, The Road to Disunion, vol. 2: Secessionists Triumphant, 1854–1861 (New York: Oxford University Press, 2008); John Ashworth, Slavery, Capitalism, and Politics in the Antebellum Republic, vol. 1: Commerce and Compromise, 1820–1850 (New York: Cambridge University Press, 1995); Walter Johnson, River of Dark Dreams: Slavery and Empire in the Cotton Kingdom (Cambridge, MA: Belknap Press of Harvard University Press, 2013); Robert H. Gudmestad, *A Troublesome Commerce: The Transfor-mation of the Interstate Slave Trade* (Baton Rouge: Louisiana State University Press, 2003).

5. On northern complicity in slavery, see Anne Farrow, Joel Lang, and Jenifer Frank, *Complicity: How the North Promoted, Prolonged, and Profited from Slavery* (New York: Bal-lantine Books, 2006); Sven Beckert and Seth Rockman, eds., *Slavery's Capitalism: A New History of American Economic Development* (Philadelphia: University of Pennsylvania Press, 2016); Edward E. Baptist, *The Half Has Never Been Told: Slavery and the Making of American Capitalism* (New York: Basic Books, 2014). Earlier works on Pennsylvania political history emphasize the connections between Pennsylvania and the slave states, in particular, South Carolina; cf. Daniel Kilbride, *An American Aristocracy: Southern Planters in Antebellum Philadelphia* (Columbia: University of South Carolina Press, 2006). In making these connec-tions between states, I am grateful for Jonathan D. Wells's scholarship (and friendship!); see Jonathan Daniel Wells, *The Origins of the Southern Middle Class, 1800–1861* (Chapel Hill: University of North Carolina Press, 2004).

6. Dunbar, *A Fragile Freedom*, xvi; Nash, *Forging Freedom*, 134–171, quotation on 143. On the fugitives from slavery and kidnapping crises in the United States, Philadelphia and Penn-sylvania, in particular, I consulted Harrold, *Border War*; Julie Winch, "Philadelphia and the Other Underground Railroad," *Pennsylvania Magazine of History and Biography* 111, no. 1 (Jan. 1987): 3–25; Carol Wilson, *Freedom at Risk: The Kidnapping of Free Blacks in America, 1780–1865* (Lexington: University Press of Kentucky, 1994); Stanley W. Campbell, *The Slave Catchers: Enforcement of the Fugitive Slave Act, 1850–1860* (Chapel Hill: University of North Carolina Press, 1968); John Runcie, "'Hunting the Nigs' in Philadelphia: The Race Riot of August 1834," *Pennsylvania History* 39, no. 2 (Apr. 1972): 187–218; Joseph A. Boromé, Jacob C. White, Robert B. Ayres, and J. M. McKim, "The Vigilant Committee of Philadelphia," *Pennsyl-vania Magazine of History and Biography* 92, no. 3 (Jul. 1968): 320–351; Nat and Yanna Kroyt Brandt, *In the Shadow of the Civil War: Passmore Williamson and the Rescue of Jane Johnson* (Columbia: University of South Carolina Press, 2007); William J. Switala, *Underground Rail-road in Pennsylvania* (Mechanicsburg, PA: Stackpole Books, 2001); Smith, *On the Edge of Freedom*; Erica Armstrong Dunbar, *Never Caught: The Washingtons' Relentless Pursuit of Their Runaway Slave, Ona Judge* (New York: Simon & Schuster, 2017); Richard Bell, *Stolen: Five Free Boys Kidnapped into Slavery and Their Astonishing Odyssey Home* (New York: Simon & Schuster, 2019); Milt Diggins, *Stealing Freedom along the Mason-Dixon Line: Thomas Mc-Creary, the Notorious Slave Catcher from Maryland* (Baltimore: Maryland Historical Society, 2015); David Fiske, *Solomon Northup's Kindred: The Kidnapping of Free Citizens before the Civil War* (Santa Barbara, CA: Praeger, 2016); R. J. M. Blackett, *The Captive's Quest for Freedom: Fugitive Slaves, the 1850 Fugitive Slave Act, and the Politics of Slavery* (New York: Cambridge University Press, 2018); Kellie Carter Jackson, *Force and Freedom: Black Abolitionists and the Politics of Violence* (Philadelphia: University of Pennsylvania Press, 2019); Manisha Sinha, *The Slave's Cause: A History of Abolitionism* (New Haven, CT: Yale University Press, 2016).

7. On New York City, I am referring particularly to Eric Foner, *Gateway to Freedom: The Hidden History of the Underground Railroad* (New York: Norton, 2016); Jonathan Daniel Wells, *The Kidnapping Club: Wall Street, Slavery, and Resistance on the Eve of the Civil War* (New York: Bold Type Books, 2020). On Boston I am referring particularly to Stephen Kantro-witz, *More than Freedom: Fighting for Black Citizenship in a White Republic, 1829–1889* (New York: Penguin, 2012); Edmund Morgan, *American Slavery, American Freedom: The Ordeal of Colonial Virginia* (New York: Norton, 2003). On Independence Hall, see Charlene Mires, *Independence Hall in American Memory* (Philadelphia: University of Pennsylvania Press, 2002). Other studies of the urban north not included in previous endnotes but featuring similar struggles over freedom and slavery, especially rescues, include Gordon S. Barker, *The Imperfect Revolution: Anthony Burns and the Landscape of Race in Antebellum America* (Kent,

OH: Kent State University Press, 2010); Gary Lee Collison, *Shadrach Minkins: From Fugitive Slave to Citizen* (Cambridge, MA: Harvard University Press, 1997); Albert Von Frank, *The Trials of Anthony Burns: Freedom and Slavery in Emerson's Boston* (Cambridge, MA: Harvard University Press, 1998); H. Robert Baker, *The Rescue of Joshua Glover: A Fugitive Slave, the Constitution, and the Coming of the Civil War* (Athens: Ohio University Press, 2006); Scott Christianson, *Freeing Charles: The Struggle to Free a Slave on the Eve of the Civil War* (Chicago: University of Illinois Press, 2010); Graham Russell Gao Hodges, *David Ruggles: A Radical Black Abolitionist and the Underground Railroad in New York City* (Chapel Hill: University of North Carolina Press, 2010); Jayme A. Sokolow, "The Jerry McHenry Rescue and the Growth of Northern Antislavery Sentiment during the 1850s," *Journal of American Studies* 16, no. 3 (Dec. 1982): 427–445; Seth Rockman, *Scraping By: Wage Labor, Slavery, and Survival in Early Baltimore* (Baltimore, MD: Johns Hopkins University Press, 2009); Steven Lubet, *Fugitive Justice: Runaways, Rescuers, and Slavery on Trial* (Cambridge, MA: Harvard University Press, 2010). See also Stanley Harrold, *Subversives: Antislavery Community in Washington, D.C., 1828–1865* (Baton Rouge: Louisiana State University Press, 2003); Corey M. Brooks, "Reconsidering Politics in the Study of American Abolitionists," *Journal of the Civil War Era* 8, no. 2 (June 2018): 291–317.

8. David Waldstreicher, *Slavery's Constitution: From Revolution to Ratification* (New York: Hill and Wang, 2009), 8–14, 115; Don E. Fehrenbacher, *The Slaveholding Republic: An Account of the United States Government's Relations to Slavery* (Oxford: Oxford University Press, 2001), 209–212. See also Paul Finkelman, "The Kidnapping of John Davis and the Adoption of the Fugitive Slave Act of 1793," *Journal of Southern History* 56, no. 3 (Aug. 1990): 397–422.

9. Fehrenbacher, *Slaveholding Republic*, 211–212; Thomas D. Morris, *Free Men All: The Personal Liberty Laws of the North, 1780–1861* (Baltimore, MD: Johns Hopkins University Press, 1974), 25–26; Dunbar, *Never Caught*, 105–106.

10. Wilson, *Freedom at Risk*, 8; Ira Berlin, *Generations of Captivity: A History of African-American Slaves* (Cambridge, MA: Belknap Press of Harvard University Press, 2003), 159–244; Steven Deyle, *Carry Me Back: The Domestic Slave Trade in American Life* (New York: Oxford University Press, 2005), 56–60, 146; Walter Johnson, *Soul by Soul: Life inside the Antebellum Slave Market* (Cambridge, MA: Harvard University Press, 1999); Johnson, *River of Dark Dreams*; Adam Rothman, *Slave Country: American Expansion and the Origins of the Deep South* (Cambridge, MA: Harvard University Press, 2005), 191–210. See also Michael Tadman, *Speculators and Slaves: Masters, Traders, and Slaves in the Old South* (Madison: University of Wisconsin Press, 1989), and Gudmestad, *A Troublesome Commerce*.

11. On the politics of slavery, I am referring to William Cooper, *The South and the Politics of Slavery, 1828–1856* (Baton Rouge: Louisiana State University Press, 1978). Morris, *Free Men All*; H. Robert Baker, *Prigg v. Pennsylvania: Slavery, the Supreme Court, and the Ambivalent Constitution* (Lawrence: University Press of Kansas, 2012); William R. Leslie, "The Pennsylvania Fugitive Slave Act of 1826," *Journal of Southern History* 18, no. 4 (Nov. 1952): 429–445; Paul Finkelman, *An Imperfect Union: Slavery, Federalism, and Comity* (Chapel Hill: University of North Carolina Press, 1980); Fehrenbacher, *The Slaveholding Republic*. Steven Hahn's work on Black political consciousness in the South spoke to northern Blacks' political consciousness; see Steven Hahn, *A Nation under Their Feet: Black Political Struggles in the Rural South from Slavery to the Great Migration* (Cambridge, MA: Harvard University Press, 2005). I concur with Paul Polgar's rationale for the importance of the mid-Atlantic region, though I view Philadelphia's role in the politics of slavery and freedom as more integral than New York City for the reasons explained above. See Paul J. Polgar, *Standard-Bearers of Equality: America's First Abolition Movement* (Chapel Hill: University of North Carolina Press, 2019), 18–19.

12. Many thanks to Richard Bell for encouraging me to reframe my definition of "street diplomacy" by brushing up on "practical abolition"! Hodges, *David Ruggles*, 4–6, 63–101; Eric

Foner, *Gateway to Freedom: The Hidden History of the Underground Railroad* (New York: Norton, 2016), 20; Richard Bell, "Counterfeit Kin: Kidnappers of Color, the Reverse Underground Railroad, and the Origins of Practical Abolition," *Journal of the Early Republic* 38 (Summer 2018): 199–230; Diemer, *The Politics of Black Citizenship*, 196 ft. 15; Van Gosse, *The First Reconstruction: Black Politics in America from the Revolution to the Civil War* (Chapel Hill: University of North Carolina Press, 2021). On the spectacle of enslavement, see Saidiya V. Hartman, *Scenes of Subjection: Terror, Slavery, and Self-Making in Nineteenth-Century America* (New York: Oxford University Press, 1997).

13. Harrold, *Border War*, 72–93. Thank you to Stanley Harrold for his incisive critique of these terms. Kate Masur links these activists to a broader Antebellum civil rights movement, see her *Until Justice Be Done: America's First Civil Rights Movement, From the Revolution to Reconstruction* (New York: Norton, 2021).

14. From Herodotus of Halicarnassus to Noam Chomsky, the state's imagining, imposing, and enforcing of arbitrary borders is nothing new to world history, and examples are legion. See Joanne P. Sharp, *Geographies of Postcolonialism: Spaces of Power and Representation* (London: SAGE Publications, Ltd., 2009); Anthony Arnove, ed., *The Essential Chomsky* (New York: The New Press, 2008); Mark Simpson, *Trafficking Subjects: The Politics of Mobility in Nineteenth-Century America* (Minneapolis: University of Minnesota Press, 2005); Mae Ngai, *Impossible Subjects: Illegal Aliens and the Making of Modern America* (Princeton, NJ: Princeton University Press, 2004); Benedict Anderson, *Imagined Communities: Reflections on the Origin and Spread of Nationalism* (London: Verso, 2006); Edward W. Said, *Orientalism* (New York: Vintage Books, 1979), 49–72, esp. 54–55.

15. Sinha, *The Slave's Cause*, 391; Richard S. Newman, " 'Lucky to be born in Pennsylvania': Free Soil, Fugitive Slaves and the Making of Pennsylvania's Anti-Slavery Borderland," *Slavery & Abolition* 32, no. 3 (Sept. 2011): 413–430. The perpetual terror of daily life for African Americans in Philadelphia evinced on a micro-scale the dynamics of a hemispheric perspective of enslavement, a perspective on events both mundane and "momentous." See Robin Blackburn, *The American Crucible: Slavery, Emancipation, and Human Rights* (London: Verso, 2013), chapters 12 and 14, esp. "Crucibles and Stews," 475–477.

16. On interracial cooperation, see Still, *The Underground Rail Road*; Wilbur Henry Seibert, *The Underground Railroad from Slavery to Freedom* (New York: The MacMillan Company, 1898); Larry Gara, *The Liberty Line: The Legend of the Underground Railroad* (Lexington: University of Kentucky Press, 1961); John Stauffer, *The Black Hearts of Men: Radical Abolitionists and the Transformation of Race* (Cambridge, MA: Harvard University Press, 2002); David W. Blight, *Passages to Freedom: The Underground Railroad in History and Memory* (Washington, DC: Smithsonian Books, 2004); Fergus M. Bordewich, *Bound For Canaan: The Underground Railroad and the War for the Soul of America* (New York: HarperCollins, 2005); Christopher James Bonner, *Remaking the Republic: Black Politics and the Creation of American Citizenship* (Philadelphia: University of Pennsylvania Press, 2020), 95; Foner, *Gateway to Freedom*, 14–15; Sinha, *The Slave's Cause*.

17. Bell, "Counterfeit Kin." See also Winch, "Philadelphia and the Other Underground Railroad"; Stewart, "The Emergence of Racial Modernity"; Jean R. Soderlund, "[The Emergence of Racial Modernity and the Rise of the White North, 1790–1840]: Comment," *Journal of the Early Republic* 18, no. 2 (Summer 1998): 218–221; James Oliver Horton, "[The Emergence of Racial Modernity and the Rise of the White North, 1790–1840]: Comment," *Journal of the Early Republic* 18, no. 2 (Summer 1998): 222–225; Ronald G. Walters, "[The Emergence of Racial Modernity and the Rise of the White North, 1790–1840]: Comment," *Journal of the Early Republic* 18, no. 2 (Summer 1998): 226–232; James Brewer Stewart, "[The Emergence of Racial Modernity and the Rise of the White North, 1790–1840]: Comment," *Journal of the Early Republic* 18, no. 2 (Summer 1998): 233–236; Johnson, *Soul by Soul*; Walter Johnson, ed., *The*

Chattel Principle: Internal Slave Trade in the Americas (New Haven, CT: Yale University Press, 2004); Walter Johnson, "On Agency," *Journal of Social History* 37, no. 1 (Oct. 2003): 113–124; Martha Hodes, "The Mercurial Nature and Abiding Power of Race: A Transnational Family Story," *American Historical Review* 108, no. 1 (Feb. 2003): 84–118. On the fragmentary nature of source material relating to slavery, past and present (and historical evidence in general), I am influenced by Niall McKeown, *The Invention of Ancient Slavery* (London: Duckworth, 2007). On using race as a strategy to enslave, I call upon Joseph Miller's work on the process of slaving derived from marginalized groups in Joseph C. Miller, *The Problem of Slavery as History: A Global Approach* (New Haven, CT: Yale University Press, 2012).

18. Hartman, *Scenes of Subjection*; Daina Ramey Berry, *The Price for Their Pound of Flesh* (Boston: Beacon Press, 2017). See also Sven Beckert and Seth Rockman, *Slavery's Capitalism: A New History of American Economic Development* (Philadelphia: University of Pennsylvania Press, 2016); James W. C. Pennington, *The Fugitive Blacksmith; or, Events in the History of James W. C. Pennington, Pastor of a Presbyterian Church, New York, Formerly a Slave in the State of Maryland, United States* (London: Charles Gilpin, 1849); Walter Johnson, "On Agency" and *Soul by Soul*. On the unity of opposites, see "Heraclitus," in *Early Greek Philosophy*, Jonathan Barnes, ed. (London: Penguin Books, 1987), 100–126; Edward Hussey, "Heraclitus," in *The Cambridge Companion to Early Greek Philosophy*, Arthur Long, ed. (Cambridge: Cambridge University Press, 1999), 88–112; W. E. B. Du Bois's notion of "double-consciousness" might be helpful in dissecting the unity-of-opposites, in that Du Bois grappled with being Black and being American much in the same way that African Americans struggled with being Black and being free. See W. E. B. Du Bois, *The Souls of Black Folk* (New York: Penguin Books, 2018), chapter 1. On maintaining the ability to project a future, I draw upon the terminology of Martin Heidegger, who asserted the inseparable nature of human existence (or in his words, *Dasein* [trans. "being-there"]) from human beings' active engagement in the world. In other words, our "being-in-the-world" reflects the fact that *Dasein* is inseparable from its world and other human beings. In my study, the relationships between these human beings (slaveholders, slave catchers, kidnappers, fugitives from slavery, free(d) African Americans, and abolitionists) as such evinced the "project" of slavers slave catching and kidnapping African Americans to sell into slavery as well as free and fugitive African Americans and their abolitionist allies preserving or (re)asserting African American freedom. This "project" and thus the project's participants demonstrated a "ready-to-hand" relationship in which individuals (the aforementioned slaveholders et al.) utilized each other as instruments within the context of their own personal projects of freeing or (re)enslaving African Americans, and thus failed to acknowledge the latter's existence as fundamentally engaged in a world with others. In short, I suggest that while slaveholders viewed African Americans as ready-to-hand instruments in their overall project of enslaving, African Americans and their allies viewed fugitives or would-be kidnapping victims as sites of a human potential toward becoming free. Martin Heidegger, *Being and Time*, trans. Joan Stambaugh (Albany: State University of New York Press, 1996), 62–83, esp. 67. On the role of time under slavery, see Mark M. Smith, *Mastered by the Clock: Time, Slavery, and Freedom in the American South* (Chapel Hill: University of North Carolina Press, 1997), 12–16 and 215 ft. 44.

19. Reinhart Koselleck, *Sediments of Time: On Possible Histories,* trans. Sean Franzel and Stefan-Ludwig Hoffman (Stanford, CA: Stanford University Press, 2018), 41–59. While not adopting the language of "mentalité," throughout my research I found ample evidence of historical personages actualizing a worldview that understood African Americans as potentially free and potentially subject to enslavement. See Aldo Schiavone, *The End of the Past: Ancient Rome and the Modern West,* trans. Margery J. Schneider (Cambridge, MA: Harvard University Press, 2000), 108–164.

20. Christopher J. Bonner, "Runaways, Rescuers, and the Politics of Breaking the Law," in

New Perspectives on the Black Intellectual Tradition, Keisha N. Blain, Christopher Cameron, and Ashley D. Farmer, eds. (Evanston, IL: Northwestern University Press, 2018), 201–217, quotation on 212. I admire how Sarah L. H. Gronningsater problematizes teleology in Sarah L. H. Gronningsater, "'On Behalf of His Race and the Lemmon Slaves': Louis Napoleon, Northern Black Legal Culture, and the Politics of Sectional Crisis," *Journal of the Civil War Era* 7, no. 2 (June 2017): 210–229. Kate Masur's recent magisterial work shows how freedom was far from a "foreordained" success for Antebellum civil rights activists; see Masur, *Until Justice Be Done*.

21. See Varon, *Disunion!*

22. On transposing enslavement, I am inspired by Arthur Schopenhauer's view of history, especially his "Eadem, sed aliter [the same, but different]," from Arthur Schopenhauer, *The World as Will and Representation*, vol. 2, trans. E. F. J. Payne (New York: Dover Publications, Inc., 1966), 439–446.

Chapter 1 · A Precarious Freedom

1. *Franklin's Gazette*, Jan. 21, 1820; *Poulson's American Daily Advertiser* (hereafter "*Poulson's*"), Jan. 25, 1820; *Journal of the Thirtieth House of Representatives of the Commonwealth of Pennsylvania* [microform] *commenced at Harrisburg, Tuesday the Seventh of December . . . 1819* (Harrisburg: Peacock, 1819–1820), 323 (hereafter "*House Journal, 1819–1820*"); Mayor's Court of Philadelphia, Record Group 130.1 Docket. 12–31–1819; *McElroy's Philadelphia City Directory*, 1819 (hereafter "*Philadelphia Directory*"); PAS Series 1.5 Acting Committee Minute Book, 1810–1822, Jul., 17, 1820 and Sept. 5, 1820 (hereafter "PAS 1.5").

2. Sarah L. H. Gronningsater, "'On Behalf of His Race and the Lemmon Slaves': Louis Napoleon, Northern Black Legal Culture, and the Politics of Sectional Crisis," *Journal of the Civil War Era* 7, no. 2 (June 2017): 210–229.

3. This chapter calls upon the following studies on antebellum borders: Stanley Harrold, *Border War: Fighting over Slavery before the Civil War* (Chapel Hill: University of North Carolina Press, 2010); William Freehling, *The Road to Disunion*, vol. 1: *Secessionists at Bay, 1776–1854* (New York: Oxford University Press, 1991); Walter Johnson, *Soul by Soul: Life inside the Antebellum Slave Market* (Cambridge, MA: Harvard University Press, 1999); William Cooper, *The South and the Politics of Slavery, 1828–1856* (Baton Rouge: Louisiana State Press, 1978); Larry Tise, *Proslavery: A History of the Defense of Slavery in America, 1701–1840* (Athens: University of Georgia Press, 1987); Steven Hahn, *Political Worlds of Slavery and Freedom* (Cambridge, MA: Harvard University Press, 2009); Seth Rockman, *Scraping By: Wage Labor, Slavery, and Survival in Early Baltimore* (Baltimore, MD: Johns Hopkins University Press, 2009); R. J. M. Blackett, *The Captive's Quest for Freedom: Fugitive Slaves, the 1850 Fugitive Slave Act, and the Politics of Slavery* (New York: Cambridge University Press, 2018); James W. C. Pennington, *The Fugitive Blacksmith; or, Events in the History of James W. C. Pennington, Pastor of a Presbyterian Church, New York, Formerly a Slave in the State of Maryland, United States* (London: Charles Gilpin, 1849).

4. No historians have analyzed the 1820 debates and passage through the lens of the case studies under consideration in this chapter. See Thomas D. Morris, *Free Men All: The Personal Liberty Laws of the North, 1780–1861* (Baltimore, MD: Johns Hopkins University Press, 1974); William R. Leslie, "The Pennsylvania Fugitive Slave Act of 1826," *Journal of Southern History* 18, no. 4 (Nov. 1952): 429–445; Stanley W. Campbell, *The Slave Catchers: Enforcement of the Fugitive Slave Act, 1850–1860* (Chapel Hill: University of North Carolina Press, 1968); Edward Raymond Turner, *The Negro in Pennsylvania: Slavery-Servitude-Freedom, 1639–1861* (New York: Negro Universities Press, 1969); Michel-Rolph Trouillot, *Silencing the Past: Power and the Production of History* (Boston: Beacon Press, 2015), esp. chapter 1. See also the debate over Northern states' rights in Gronningsater, "'On Behalf of His Race and the Lemmon Slaves.'"

5. *House Journal, 1819–1820*, 26.

6. *House Journal, 1819–1820*, 20–28; Philip Shriver Klein, *Pennsylvania Politics, 1817–1832: A Game without Rules* (Philadelphia: Historical Society of Pennsylvania, 1940), 75–112; Pennsylvania House of Representatives, *The Parole and Documentary Evidence, Delivered before a Committee of the House of Representatives, Appointed to Inquire into the Conduct of the Governor of the Commonwealth of Pennsylvania* (J. Wyeth: Philadelphia, 1820), 5; *The Kaleidoscope: Or, Literary and Scientific Mirror* 13, no. 102 (Sept. 26, 1820); William C. Armor, *Lives of the Governors of Pennsylvania* (Norwich: T. H. Davis & Co., 1874), 331; Pennsylvania, *Laws, Statutes, etc., 1819 Resolutions Relative to Preventing the Introduction of Slavery into New States* (Harrisburg, 1819).

7. *House Journal, 1819–1820*, 20–28; *The Kaleidoscope*; Armor, *Lives of the Governors of Pennsylvania*; Pennsylvania, *Laws, Statutes, etc., 1819 Resolutions Relative to Preventing the Introduction of Slavery into New States* (Harrisburg, 1819). On the "lapse," see Richard S. Newman and James Mueller, eds., *Antislavery and Abolition in Philadelphia: Emancipation and the Long Struggle for Racial Justice in the City of Brotherly Love* (Baton Rouge: Louisiana State University Press, 2011).

8. Gary Nash and Jean Soderlund, *Freedom by Degrees: Emancipation in Pennsylvania and Its Aftermath* (New York: Oxford University Press, 1991), 2–18; "African American Migration," *The Encyclopedia of Greater Philadelphia*, accessed January 28, 2017, http://philadelphia encyclopedia.org/archive/African American-migration/; "Free Black Communities," *The Encyclopedia of Greater Philadelphia*, accessed June 23, 2020, https://philadelphiaencyclopedia .org/archive/free-Black-communities; John Purdon, *A Digest of the Laws of Pennsylvania, from the year One Thousand Seven Hundred, to the Thirteenth Day of October, One Thousand Eight Hundred and Forty* (Philadelphia: McCarty and Davis, 1841), 788–793; *Proceedings and Debates of the House of Representatives of the United States at the Second Session of the Second Congress, Begun at the City of Philadelphia, November 5, 1792*, "Annals of Congress, 2nd Congress, 2nd Session (November 5, 1792 to March 2, 1793)," 1414–1415; Paul J. Polgar, *Standard-Bearers of Equality: America's First Abolition Movement* (Chapel Hill: University of North Carolina Press, 2019), 69–76.

9. *National Anti-Slavery Standard*, Dec. 12, 1840, Daniel Meaders, *Kidnappers in Philadelphia: Isaac Hopper's Tales of Oppression, 1780–1843* (New York: Garland, 1974), 65–68.

10. Matthew Mason, *Slavery and Politics in the Early American Republic* (Chapel Hill: University of North Carolina Press, 2006), 107–110; Steven Deyle, *Carry Me Back: The Domestic Slave Trade in American Life* (New York: Oxford University Press, 2005), 15–39, 94–141.

11. Campbell, *The Slave Catchers*, 8–9; Paul Finkelman, *An Imperfect Union: Slavery, Federalism, and Comity* (Chapel Hill: University of North Carolina Press, 1980), 64–65.

12. John Cole Lowber, *Ordinances of the Corporation of the City of Philadelphia: To which are Prefixed, the Original Charter, the Act of Incorporation, and Other Acts of Assembly Relating to the City* [. . .]" (Philadelphia: J. Maxwell, 1812), 37–38; Howard O. Sprogel, *The Philadelphia Police, Past and Present* (Philadelphia, 1887), 70–72.

13. Sam Bass Warner, *The Private City: Philadelphia in Three Periods of Growth* (Philadelphia: University of Pennsylvania Press, 1987), 141–144; Gary Nash, *Forging Freedom: The Formation of Philadelphia's Black Community, 1720–1840* (Cambridge, MA: Harvard University Press, 1988), 166–168; Gary Nash, *First City: Philadelphia and the Forging of Historical Memory* (Philadelphia: University of Pennsylvania Press, 2013), 144–152.

14. Richard S. Newman, *Freedom's Prophet: Bishop Richard Allen, the AME Church, and the Black Founding Fathers* (New York: New York University Press, 2008), 89, 101.

15. Van Gosse, *The First Reconstruction: Black Politics in America from the Revolution to the Civil War* (Chapel Hill: University of North Carolina Press, 2021), 64–67; Julie Winch, *A Gentleman of Color: The Life of James Forten* (New York: Oxford University Press, 2002), 152–154; Scott J. Hammond, Kevin R. Hardwick, and Howard Lubert, eds., *The American*

Debate over Slavery, 1760–1865: An Anthology of Sources (Indianapolis: Hackett Publishing Company, Inc., 2016), 50–52.

16. Turner, *The Negro in Pennsylvania*, 126–127, 151; *House Journal, 1812–1813*, 216, 432, 567, 588, 589; Daniel Bowen, *A history of Philadelphia: with a notice of villages in the vicinity, designed as a guide to citizens and strangers* [. . .] (Philadelphia: D. Bowen, 1839), 19; Wilkes University, "The Wilkes University Election Statistics Project," accessed Jun. 25, 2020, http://staffweb.wilkes.edu/harold.cox/legis/37H.pdf; PAS Series 1.2 General Meeting Minute Book, Mar. 13, 1813.

17. Winch, *A Gentleman of Color*, 152–153, 169–174; Julie Winch, "The Making and Meaning of James Forten's 'Letters from a Man of Colour,'" *William and Mary Quarterly* 64, no. 1 (Jan. 2007): 136; Julie Winch, "Web Supplement for 'The Making and Meaning of James Forten's 'Letters from a Man of Colour,'" *William and Mary Quarterly* 64, no. 1 (Jan. 2007): 1–6; *House Journal, 1813–1814*, 216, 388–389, 417, 481; *Philadelphia City Directory*, 1816; PAS 1.5, Dec. 26, 1815, Jan. 4, 1817, Oct. 3, 1817, Nov. 6, 1817, May 19, 1818 (decided) District Court, PCA Group Philadelphia County District Court Records, 22.20 Minute Book, December 1814, March 2, 1815, October 11, 1817, and May 15, 1818; Willard Sterne Randall and Nancy Nahra, *Forgotten Americans: Footnote Figures Who Changed American History* (Cambridge: Da Capo Press, 1999), 156.

18. PAS 5.6, Benjamin C. Bacon and Charles Gardner, *Committee to Visit the Colored People: Census Facts Collected by Benjamin C. Bacon and Charles Gardner, 1838*; Richard Bell, *Stolen: Five Free Boys Kidnapped into Slavery and Their Astonishing Odyssey Home* (New York: Simon & Schuster, 2019), 239 ft. 26.

19. Nash and Soderlund, *Freedom by Degrees*, 137–139; Nash, *Forging Freedom*, 165–169, 192–193, 227; Polgar, *Standard-Bearers of Equality*, 63–67, 72–73. See also Erica L. Ball, *To Live an Antislavery Life: Personal Politics and the Antebellum Black Middle Class* (Athens: University of Georgia Press, 2012), esp. chapter 1; Newman, *Freedom's Prophet*, 55.

20. Erica Armstrong Dunbar, *A Fragile Freedom: African American Women and Emancipation in the Antebellum City* (New Haven, CT: Yale University Press, 2008), 48–51; Eric Ledell-Smith et al., "Notes and Documents: Rescuing African American Kidnapping Victims in Philadelphia as Documented in the Joseph Watson Papers at the Historical Society of Pennsylvania," *Pennsylvania Magazine of History and Biography* 129, no. 3 (Jul. 2005): 320–321; Winch, "Web Supplement," 5; *National Anti-Slavery Standard*, Dec. 12, 1840.

21. Nash and Soderlund, *Freedom by Degrees*, 169–173; *National Gazette*, Nov. 22, 1825; *Berks and Schuylkill Journal*, Nov. 26, 1825.

22. Ledell-Smith et al. "Notes and Documents." On the American Convention, see Richard Newman, *The Transformation of American Abolitionism: Fighting Slavery in the Early Republic* (Chapel Hill: University of North Carolina Press, 2002), 1–38. Peters Jr. served as judge of the District Court of the United States, located in Philadelphia. Richard Peters, Jr., "To the Abolition and Manumission Societies of the United States," 1817; PAS, American Convention Acting Committee Minute Book, Series 5.16, Sept. 1, 1817 (hereafter "PAS 5.16"); American Convention for Promoting the Abolition of Slavery, "Minutes of the Proceedings of the Fifteenth American Convention" (Philadelphia: Merritt, 1817), 9–10; Wayne J. Eberly, *The Pennsylvania Abolition Society, 1775–1830* (University Park: Pennsylvania State University, 1973), 62–66.

23. Polgar, *Standard-Bearers of Equality*, 4–5, 9–10 ft. 6–7. I agree with Polgar and Manisha Sinha's views that "isolating" abolitionists based upon race tends to overracialize, that is, assumes that "conservative" or "traditional" or "abolitionism" equates to white Americans, and that somehow African Americans did not work within an inter- or "cross-racial" paradigm. See Manisha Sinha, *The Slave's Cause: A History of Abolitionism* (New Haven, CT: Yale University Press, 2016). See also Nicholas P. Wood, "'A Class of Citizens': The Earliest Black

Petitioners to Congress and Their Quaker Allies," *William and Mary Quarterly,* 3d Ser., LXXIV [2017], 109–144.

24. John Stauffer, *The Black Hearts of Men: Radical Abolitionists and the Transformation of Race* (Cambridge, MA: Harvard University Press, 2002); PAS, Series 5.16, Sept. 1, 1817; American Convention for Promoting the Abolition of Slavery, "Minutes"; Eberly, *The Pennsylvania Abolition Society.* For other examples of interracial political activism, see Stanley Harrold, *Subversives: Antislavery Community in Washington, D.C., 1828–1865* (Baton Rouge: Louisiana State University Press, 2003); Gronningsater, " 'On Behalf of His Race and the Lemmon Slaves' "; Andrew K. Diemer, *The Politics of Black Citizenship: Free African Americans in the Mid-Atlantic Borderland, 1817–1863* (Athens: University of Georgia Press, 2016); Polgar, *Standard-Bearers of Equality.*

25. Sinha, *The Slave's Cause,* 160–191; Gronningsater, " 'On Behalf of His Race and the Lemmon Slaves,' " 228–229. See also Donald J. Ratcliffe, "The Decline of Antislavery Politics, 1815–1840," in John Craig Hammond and Matthew Mason, eds., *Contesting Slavery: The Politics of Bondage and Freedom in the New American Nation,* Jeffersonian America (Charlottesville: University of Virginia Press, 2011), 267–290.

26. Crystal Lynn Webster, *Beyond the Boundaries of Childhood: African American Children in the Antebellum North* (Chapel Hill: University of North Carolina Press, 2021), 22–23. See also Bell, *Stolen.* PAS 1.5, Jun. 24, 1817, Nov. 6, 1817; Philadelphia City Archives, Mayor's Court 130.1 Docket, Nov. 1 and 12, 1817; PAS Series 1.1 General Meeting Minute Book (hereafter "PAS 1.1"), Jan. 25, 1817.

27. For unknown reasons Milnor did not appear at trial, PAS 1.5, Nov. 6, 1817; Lydia Maria Child, *Isaac T. Hopper: A True Life* (Boston: John P. Jewett and Company, 1860), 140–141; PAS 1.1, Jan. 25, 1817.

28. PAS 1.1, Jan. 25, 1817, Mar. 27, 1817, Jan. 5, 1818, Jan. 16, 1818; John F. Reed, "Jonathan Roberts," *Bulletin of the Historical Society of Montgomery County, Pennsylvania* 15 (Fall 1967–Spring 1968): 5–15; Jonathan Roberts and Philip Shriver Klein, "Notes and Documents: Memoirs of a Senator from Pennsylvania: John Roberts, 1771–1854," *Pennsylvania Magazine of History and Biography* 61, no. 4 (Oct. 1937): 449–450; Robert Pierce Forbes, *The Missouri Compromise and Its Aftermath: Slavery and the Meaning of America* (Chapel Hill: University of North Carolina Press, 2007), 75–81; Glover Moore, *The Missouri Controversy, 1819–1821* (Lexington: University of Kentucky Press, 1953), 69–75. Unfortunately, Hopkinson's "masterly" speech does not survive; see *Alexandria Gazette,* Nov. 5, 1819; *Daily National Intelligencer,* Nov. 9, 1819.

29. PAS 1.1, Jan. 25, 1817; Newman, *Transformation of American Abolitionism,* 29–30, 58; Morris, *Free Men All,* 35–40, Sergeant quote on 39; H. Robert Baker, "The Fugitive Slave Clause and the Antebellum Constitution," *Law and History Review* 30, no. 4 (Nov. 2012): 1146–1148; Finkelman, *An Imperfect Union,* 46–69.

30. Richard Bell, "Counterfeit Kin: Kidnappers of Color, the Reverse Underground Railroad, and the Origins of Practical Abolition," *Journal of the Early Republic* 38 (Summer 2018): 199–230. See also Winch, "Philadelphia and the Other Underground Railroad"; Martha Hodes, "The Mercurial Nature and Abiding Power of Race: A Transnational Family Story," *American Historical Review* 108, no. 1 (Feb. 2003): 85, 112, 118.

31. PAS 1.5, Dec. 11, 1817; *Poulson's,* Oct. 1, 1818; *Hallowell Gazette,* Oct. 14, 1818. For more examples of Badger's tendency to call for "further examination," see PAS 1.5, Apr. 22, 1817, May 2, 1817, Mar. 9, 1819, Sept. 18, 1820, Apr. 3, 1835, Sept. 1, 1835.

32. *Poulson's,* Oct. 1, 1818; *Hallowell Gazette,* Oct. 14, 1818; Simon P. Newman, *Embodied History: The Lives of the Poor in Early Philadelphia* (Philadelphia: University of Pennsylvania Press, 2003), 45.

33. On the "second" middle passage, see Ira Berlin, *Many Thousands Gone: The First Two*

Centuries of Slavery in North America (Cambridge: Harvard University Press, 1998); *Poulson's*, Oct. 1, 1818.

34. Solomon Northup's brutal travails represent the most famous example of the distances kidnappers would compel their victims to travel; Solomon Northup, *Twelve Years a Slave: Narrative of Solomon Northup, a Citizen of New-York, Kidnapped in Washington City in 1841, and Rescued In 1853* (Auburn: Derby and Miller, 1853) [electronic edition: https://docsouth .unc.edu/fpn/northup/northup.html], accessed June 24, 2021. On the internal slave trade, see Deyle, *Carry Me Back*; Bell, *Stolen*; Walter Johnson, *River of Dark Dreams: Slavery and Empire in the Cotton Kingdom* (Cambridge, MA: Belknap Press of Harvard University Press, 2013); Michael Tadman, *Speculators and Slaves: Masters, Traders, and Slaves in the Old South* (Madison: University of Wisconsin Press, 1989); John H. Powell, *Richard Rush: Republican Diplomat, 1780–1859* (Philadelphia: University of Pennsylvania Press, 1942), 202–203; *Poulson's*, Oct. 1, 1818; PAS 1.5, Jul. 19, Sept. 5, 1820.

35. *Poulson's*, Oct. 1, 1818; *Hallowell Gazette*, Oct. 14, 1818.

36. *Poulson's*, Oct. 1, 1818; *Hallowell Gazette*, Oct. 14, 1818.

37. "Replevin," Cornell University Law School, accessed January 28, 2017, https://www.law .cornell.edu/wex/replevin; Baker, "The Fugitive Slave Clause and the Antebellum Constitution," 1146; Morris, *Free Men All*, 42; Leslie, "The Pennsylvania Fugitive Slave Act," 432–433; Newman, *Transformation of American Abolitionism*, 81–83, Finkelman, *An Imperfect Union*, 47–65; "Wright v. Deacon," University of Chicago, accessed January 28, 2017, http://press-pubs .uchicago.edu/founders/documents/a4_2_3s11.html; H. Robert Baker, "A Better Story in *Prigg v. Pennsylvania?*," *Journal of Supreme Court History* 39, no. 2 (Jul. 2014): 169–189.

38. Leslie, "The Pennsylvania Fugitive Slave Act," 433; *Poulson's*, Oct. 1, 1818; *Hallowell Gazette*, Oct. 14, 1818.

39. Elizabeth Varon, *Disunion! The Coming of the American Civil War, 1789–1859* (Chapel Hill: University of North Carolina Press, 2008), 41–46; Forbes, *The Missouri Compromise and Its Aftermath*, 33–86. See also Richard Kreitner, *Break It Up: Secession, Division, and the Secret History of America's Imperfect Union* (Boston: Little, Brown and Company, 2020).

40. Forbes, *The Missouri Compromise and Its Aftermath*, 33–86.

41. Mason, *Slavery and Politics in the Early American Republic*, 120–129; John Sergeant, "Speech on the Missouri Question, delivered in the House of Representatives of the United States, on the Eighth and Ninth of February 1820," in *Selected Speeches of John Sergeant* (Philadelphia: E. L. Carey and A. Hart, 1832), 220–221, 246–247.

42. Sergeant, "Speech on the Missouri Question," 238–239.

43. On Hudson's manumission, see Document 9, "Testimony from Nathan Luff"; Document 3, "Henry Hudson's Certificate of Freedom," Series III: Miscellany re: Henry Hudson (a runaway slave), Box 119, Folder 417, Wyck Association Collection, American Philosophical Society (hereafter Series/Box/Folder/Wyck Papers, APS).

44. Sandra F. Mackenzie, "'What a Beauty there is in Harmony': The Reuben Haines Family of Wyck" (MA thesis, University of Delaware, 1979), 3–19, quote on 19, 51–57; see also John M. Groff, "'All that Makes a Man's Mind more Active': Jane and Reuben Haines at Wyck, 1812–1831," in *Quaker Aesthetics: Reflections on a Quaker Ethic in American Design and Consumption*, Emma Jones Lapsansky and Anne A. Verplanck, eds. (Philadelphia: University of Pennsylvania Press, 2002), 90–121.

45. Garrigues's interviews appeared in Abraham W. Garrigues to Reuben Haines, ?/1819, II/17/216, Wyck Papers, APS; PAS, *Centennial anniversary of the Pennsylvania Society for Promoting the Abolition of Slavery* (Philadelphia: Grants, Faires & Rodgers, Printers, 1875) 58; Abraham M. Garrigues to Reuben Haines, Apr. 30, 1819, Series II/17/213, Wyck Papers, APS.

46. *Poulson's*, May 18, 1819; *Baltimore Patriot*, May 7, 1819. Newspapers that advertised the reward included the *Commercial Advertiser of New York*, May 8, 1819; *The Times Connecticut*,

244 Notes to Pages 39–44

May 18, 1819; *Illinois Emigrant,* June 5, 1819; *Alexandria Gazette,* Jun. 1 through Sep. 25, 1819; Reuben Haines to Jane Haines, May 30, 1819, II/22/324, Wyck Papers, APS.

47. Ephraim Carsons to Reuben Haines, May 19, 1819, II/17/324, Wyck Papers, APS; Document 8, "Statement of the mysterious disappearance of Henry Hudson from 'Ketter Fields' Near Germ. 4th Mo 30th and of his return 10m 30th" (hereafter "Statement") III/119/417, Wyck Papers, APS.

48. James Canby of Wilmington to Arthur Davis and Richard Lockwood of Middletown DE, May 24, 1819, II/17/213, Wyck Papers, APS. According to the 1820 United States Federal Census, Lockwood owned four slaves in 1820; see US Census Bureau, *1820 United States Federal Census, Ancestry.com,* accessed December 28, 2020 (hereafter "[*Census Year*] *United States Federal Census*"). In 1822 a Black man named Joseph Wilson stabbed Lockwood in the head when the latter arrested him as a supposed fugitive from slavery. See, PAS 1.5, Jan. 10, 1822, and Jun. 22, 1822; PAS American Convention Assorted Materials (Undated), Series 5.36, Letter from Isaac Barton [?] regarding Joseph Wilson.

49. "Statement," Wyck Papers, APS; Reuben Haines to Jane B. Haines, May 27, 1819, II/22/324, Wyck Papers, APS. Letters from Haines and his mother Hannah revealed how they sought to assure Jane Haines of her husband's safety. See Hannah Haines to Jane B. Haines, May 23, 1819, II/22/324, Wyck Papers, APS. Reuben Haines to Jane B. Haines, May 27, 1819, II/22/324, Wyck Papers, APS; Hannah Haines to Jane B. Haines, May 28, 1819, II/22/ 324, Wyck Papers, APS.

50. "Statement," Wyck Papers, APS; R. Campbell to Reuben Haines, Jun. 16, 1819, II/17/214.

51. "Statement," Wyck Papers, APS; Henry Hudson to Reuben Haines, Oct. 4, 1819, II/17/215, Wyck Papers, APS; *McElroy's Philadelphia City Directory,* 1820. According to the 1820 United States Federal Census, Habersham owned eight enslaved people and Campbell owned three enslaved people; *1820 United States Federal Census.*

52. "Statement," Wyck Papers, APS. See also Abraham W. Garrigues to Reuben Haines, undated, II/17/213 and II/17/216.

53. *Poulson's,* May 18, 1819, Nov. 6, 1819.

54. Webster, *Beyond the Boundaries of Childhood,* 65–72; *Poulson's,* May 18, 1819, Nov. 6, 1819; *New York Commercial Advertiser,* Jul. 9, 1819; PAS 1.5, May 11, Jun. 15, 1819. While Betsey's living circumstances prior to her kidnapping remain unknown, census information and the 1821 *Philadelphia Directory* offered clues. A successful African American oysterman named Elijah Everson lived on Pine Street with an adult woman of color and three children in 1820. The family resided in Cedar Ward, which placed them mere blocks away from the treacherous kidnapping territory: the Philadelphia wharves. Such circumstantial evidence linked Betsey to Elijah. Elijah placed notices in the *Democratic Press* warning readers not to trust his wife Roxanna Everson "for anything at all," adding that he would not hold himself accountable for "any debt she may contract." We will never know if Betsey was Roxanna, as Elijah submitted these notices in 1811. See *Democratic Press,* Jan. 29–30, 1811; *Philadelphia Directory,* 1821; *1820 United States Federal Census.*

55. *Poulson's,* May 18, 1819, Nov. 6, 1819; *New York Commercial Advertiser,* Jul. 9, 1819; PAS 1.5, May 11, Jun. 15, 1819; Bell, *Stolen,* 47.

56. *Poulson's,* May 18, 1819; PAS Loose Correspondence, Incoming 1796–1819, R. Lane to Thomas Shipley, May 28, 1819; PAS 1.5, Jun. 15, 1819.

57. Gertrude MacKinney, ed., *Pennsylvania Archives: Ninth Series,* vol. 7: *1818–1821* (Philadelphia: 1931), 4875, 5130; *Franklin's Gazette,* Jan. 3, 1820; *McElroy's Philadelphia City Directory,* 1819–1820; PAS 1.5, 1.5 Jul. 6, 1819, Sept. 5, 1820, Oct. 23, 1820; PAS Correspondence, Incoming 1796–1819, James Trimble to PAS, Sep. 1, 1819.

58. PAS 1.5, Jun. 15, 23, 1819; Henry Simpson, *Lives of Eminent Philadelphians, Now Deceased* (Philadelphia: William Brotherhead, 1859), 26–28; Robert Allan Gates, ed., *Eighteenth*

and *Nineteenth Century American Drama* (New York: Irvington Publishers, 1983), 121–122; *Farmer's Repository*, Feb. 2, 1820; James Nelson Barker, *An Oration Delivered at Philadelphia On the Forty-First Anniversary of American Independence* (Philadelphia: Binns, 1817), 1–18; *Franklin's Gazette*, Jul. 7, 1818.

59. *New York Commercial Advertiser*, Jul. 9, 1819; PAS 1.5, Jun. 15, 23, Aug. 20, Nov. 24, Nov. 30, 1819; *Poulson's*, Nov. 16, 1819; *The National Advocate*, Oct. 21, 1819; *Poulson's*, Nov. 25, 1819.

60. PAS Loose Correspondence, Incoming 1796–1819, John Jones of Wilmington to Samuel Hagerman, Jun. 28, 1819. Interestingly, a "Reverend Ware" suggested to Reuben Haines and Joseph Paxson that James Welsh may have kidnapped Henry Hudson. See Reverend Professor Ware to Reuben Haines or Mr. Joseph R. Paxson, ?/1819, II/15/157, Wyck Papers, APS; PAS 1.5, Nov. 24 and Nov. 30, 1819.

61. PAS 1.5, Nov. 30, 1819.

62. PAS 1.5, Nov. 30, 1819. On the Cannon-Johnson gang, see George Alfred Townsend, *The Entailed Hat, or, Patty Cannon's Times: A Romance* (New York: Harper and Brothers, 1884); Sammy Miller, "Patty Cannon: Murderer and Kidnapper of Free Blacks, A Review of the Evidence," *Maryland Historical Magazine* 72, no. 3 (Fall 1977): 419; Richard Bell, " 'Thence to Patty Cannon's': Gender, Family, and the Reverse Underground Railroad," *Slavery & Abolition* 37, no. 4, 661–679; Bell, *Stolen*.

63. PAS 1.5, Nov. 30, 1819.

64. PAS 1.5, Nov. 30, 1819. Carol Wilson erred in her reading of this case. Willits explained, "Not being myself permitted to accompany them, I have no personal knowledge of the events which transpired during the search, nor of the victims incarcerated within the walls of this detestable prison. From Miller however I afterwards learned the following particulars." Carol Wilson, *Freedom at Risk: The Kidnapping of Free Blacks in America, 1780–1865* (Lexington: University Press of Kentucky, 1994), 19–20. See also Stauffer, *The Black Hearts of Men*.

65. PAS 1.5, Nov. 30, 1819.

66. PAS 1.5, Nov. 30, 1819.

67. Sewell E. Slick, "William Wilkins: Pittsburgh Extraordinary," *Western Pennsylvania Historical Magazine* 22, no. 4 (Dec. 1939): 217–236; *Franklin's Gazette*, Jan. 8, 1820; *House Journal, 1819–1820*, 175.

68. *Franklin's Gazette*, Jan. 13, 1820; *House Journal, 1819–1820*, 987–990.

69. *House Journal, 1819–1820*, 337–341; *Weekly Aurora*, Jan. 31 and Jul. 24, 1820; *Poulson's*, Apr. 8, 1820; John Codman Hurd, *The Law of Freedom and Bondage in the United States* (Boston: Little, Brown, and Company, 1862), 70–71.

70. *House Journal, 1819–1820*, 987–990.

71. *House Journal, 1819–1820*, 341. On this lack of debate, see *House Journal, 1819–1820*, 983, 987, 1069, 1081, 1088; *Franklin's Gazette*, Jan. 24, 1820. In addition, some members used the opportunity to dredge up the issue of limiting Black emigration, but the House left these attempts on the table. *Franklin's Gazette*, Jan. 21, 1820; *House Journal, 1819–1820*, 341; *Poulson's*, Apr. 8, 1820.

72. *Poulson's*, Apr. 8, 1820; Morris, *Free Men All*, 45–46; Leslie, "The Pennsylvania Fugitive Slave Act," 433.

Chapter 2 · *Street Diplomacy*

1. PAS Series 1.5 Acting Committee Minute Book, 1810–1822 (hereafter "PAS 1.5"), Sept. 24, 1822.

2. PAS 1.5, Sept. 24, 1822.

3. According to the 1820 US Federal census, Gale owned seven enslaved people in 1820. US Census Bureau, *1820 United States Federal Census, Ancestry.com,* accessed December 28,

2020 (hereafter "[*Census Year*] *United States Federal Census*"). Details of the Ann Chambers case also appeared in PAS 1.5, Jan. 11, 1823. Interestingly enough, Clarke cited the illegal dealings of the Cannon-Johnson gang in his letter to PAS. See PAS Papers Series II, Correspondence, Loose Correspondence, incoming 1820–1863 (hereafter "PAS 2.4"), James Clarke to William Masters, Sept. 17, 1822; PAS member Isaac Barton contacted John Cummings of Smyrna, Delaware, to see if he could find additional details about Chambers. The latter had nothing to report. See PAS 2.4, John Cummings to Isaac Barton, Sept. 19, 1822; PAS 2.4, James Clarke to Isaac Barton, Jan. 20, 1823. On constable Weisener, see PAS 1.5, Sept. 3, 1834.

4. Thomas D. Morris, *Free Men All: The Personal Liberty Laws of the North, 1780–1861* (Baltimore, MD: Johns Hopkins University Press, 1974), 45–46.

5. Historians typically cite how the failed removal of John Reed in 1820 epitomized the continuing struggle for black freedom after the passage of the 1820 anti-kidnapping law. After explaining the Read incident, scholars then shift their focus primarily to what Stanley Harrold calls "interstate diplomacy," or the debates over freedom, slavery, and comity between white politicians. The key element to Harrold's approach is that he shows how these diplomatic efforts failed to stave off border wars and eventually the Civil War. The merits of emphasizing the key role of Lower North states like Pennsylvania notwithstanding, the idea of interstate diplomacy lacks a clear analysis of how African American "diplomats" dealt with the threat of removal and (re)enslavement, a perspective essential to understanding the 1826 liberty law debates. See [Unknown Author], "What Right Had a Fugitive Slave of Self-Defence against His Master?" *Pennsylvania Magazine of History and Biography* 13, no. 1 (Apr. 1889): 106–109; William R. Leslie, "The Pennsylvania Fugitive Slave Act of 1826," *Journal of Southern History* 18, no. 4 (Nov. 1952): 429–445; Stanley W. Campbell, *The Slave Catchers: Enforcement of the Fugitive Slave Act, 1850–1860* (Chapel Hill: University of North Carolina Press, 1968), 1–25; Morris, *Free Men All*, 43–58; Paul Finkelman, *An Imperfect Union: Slavery, Federalism, and Comity* (Chapel Hill: University of North Carolina Press, 1980), 46–69; Carol Wilson, *Freedom at Risk: The Kidnapping of Free Blacks in America, 1780–1865* (Lexington: University Press of Kentucky, 1994), 83–116; Don E. Fehrenbacher, *The Slaveholding Republic: An Account of the United States Government's Relations to Slavery* (Oxford: Oxford University Press, 2001), 205–230; Stanley Harrold, *Border War: Fighting over Slavery before the Civil War* (Chapel Hill: University of North Carolina Press, 2010), 72–93; Richard S. Newman, "'Lucky to be born in Pennsylvania': Free Soil, Fugitive Slaves and the Making of Pennsylvania's Anti-Slavery Borderland," *Slavery & Abolition* 32, no. 3 (Sept. 2011): 413–430; H. Robert Baker, *Prigg v. Pennsylvania: Slavery, the Supreme Court, and the Ambivalent Constitution* (Lawrence: University Press of Kansas, 2012), 65–81; H. Robert Baker, "The Fugitive Slave Clause and the Antebellum Constitution," *Law and History Review* 30, no. 4 (Nov. 2012): 1133–1174; David G. Smith, *On the Edge of Freedom: The Fugitive Slave Issue in South Central Pennsylvania, 1820–1870* (New York: Fordham University Press, 2013), 87–114.

6. Kim T. Phillips, "Democrats of the Old School in the Era of Good Feelings," *Pennsylvania Magazine of History and Biography* 95, no. 3 (Jul. 1971): 363–382; Philip S. Klein and Ari Hoogenboom, *A History of Pennsylvania* (University Park: Pennsylvania State University Press, 1980), 132–133; Philip S. Klein, *Pennsylvania Politics, 1817–1832: A Game without Rules* (Philadelphia: Historical Society of Pennsylvania, 1940), 75–112; *Weekly Aurora*, Mar. 20, 1820.

7. *Franklin's Gazette*, Mar. 17, 1820. To save face on switching to the convention system, the *Franklin's Gazette* noted that "Mr. Findlay is the properly nominated and acknowledged candidate of the democratic party for Governor of Pennsylvania; and we should presume that no real democrat would engage in a cabal for the purpose of subtracting even a single vote from the republican party on that occasion"; see *Franklin's Gazette*, Mar. 18, 1820.

8. *Franklin's Gazette*, Jul. 19–20, 1820.

9. *Franklin's Gazette*, Jul. 19–20, Aug. 2, 15, 1820; *Lancaster Free Press*, Jul. 6, 1820; *Weekly*

Aurora, Sep. 25, 1820; John Codman Hurd, *The Law of Freedom and Bondage in the United States* (Boston: Little, Brown, and Company, 1862), 69–70; Cathy Matson, "Mathew Carey's Learning Experience: Commerce, Manufacturing, and the Panic of 1819," *Early American Studies* 11, no. 3 (2013): 477–478. It should be noted that Duane's *Weekly Aurora* focused mostly on Findlay's misconduct as state treasurer and governor. See, for example, the *Aurora* of August 21, 1820, in which Duane lists twenty reasons not to elect Findlay, seventeen of which dealt with corruption. Andrew K. Diemer, *The Politics of Black Citizenship: Free African Americans in the Mid-Atlantic Borderland, 1817–1863* (Athens: University of Georgia Press, 2016), 49–52.

10. PAS Series 1.1 General Meeting Minute Book (hereafter "PAS 1.1"), Mar. 30, Apr. 13, and Jun. 29, 1820.

11. Bruce Irwin Ambacher, "George M. Dallas: Leader of the 'Family' Party" (PhD diss., Temple University, 1970), 29–30; Klein, *Pennsylvania Politics*, 105–112, 408; Phillips, "Democrats of the Old School in the Era of Good Feelings," 363–382; Klein and Hoogenboom, *A History of Pennsylvania*, 133.

12. Gary Nash, *Forging Freedom: The Formation of Philadelphia's Black Community, 1720–1840* (Cambridge, MA: Harvard University Press, 1988), 165–169; Erica Armstrong Dunbar, *A Fragile Freedom: African American Women and Emancipation in the Antebellum City* (New Haven, CT: Yale University Press, 2008), 48–69.

13. "What Right had a Fugitive Slave of Self-Defence against his master?,'" 106–109; *Poulson's*, Dec. 25, 1820; Diemer, *The Politics of Black Citizenship*, 52–53, 56.

14. "What Right had a Fugitive Slave of Self-Defence against his master?,'" 106–109; *Poulson's*, Dec. 25, 1820.

15. Linda Myrsiades, "Legal Practice and Pragmatics in the Law: The 1821 Trials of John Reed, 'Fugitive Slave,'" *Pennsylvania Magazine of History and Biography* 138, no. 3 (July 2014): 305–338.

16. Leslie, "The Pennsylvania Fugitive Slave Act of 1826," 434; Myrsiades, "Legal Practice and Pragmatics in the Law," 333.

17. *The Berks and Schuylkill Journal*, Dec. 1, 1821; *Poulson's*, Dec. 25, 1820; Myrsiades, "Legal Practice and Pragmatics in the Law," 330; *Niles Weekly Register*, Dec. 1, 1821, 214. On the trappings of Black masculinity and the resistance of the enslaved, see François Furstenberg, "Beyond Slavery and Freedom: Autonomy, Agency, and Resistance in Early American Political Discourse," *Journal of American History* 89, no. 4 (Mar. 2003): 1295–1330.

18. Diemer, *The Politics of Black Citizenship*, 52–53.

19. *Niles' Weekly Register*, Oct. 2, 1824, 79.

20. *Niles' Weekly Register*, Oct. 2, 1824, 79; John Bioren, *Laws of the Commonwealth of Pennsylvania*, vol. 2 (Philadelphia: John Bioren, 1810), 443–446.

21. *Niles' Weekly Register*, Oct. 2, 1824, 79; John Bioren, *Laws of the Commonwealth of Pennsylvania*, vol. 2 (Philadelphia: John Bioren, 1810), 443–446.

22. See also *Wright alias Hall v. Deacon*, 5 Sergeant and Rawle 62 in John Codman Hurd, *The Law of Freedom and Bondage in the United States* (Boston: Little, Brown, and Company, 1862), 634–638.

23. The 1820 census listed Lowe as owning ten enslaved people; the 1830 census listed him as owning nine; *1820* and *1830 United States Federal Census*; Irwin F. Greenberg, "Charles Ingersoll: The Aristocrat as Copperhead," *Pennsylvania Magazine of History and Biography* 93, no. 2 (Apr. 1969): 190–217. See also Larry Tise, *Proslavery: A History of the Defense of Slavery in America, 1701–1840* (Athens: University of Georgia Press, 1987), 250–254; Lydia Maria Child, *Isaac T. Hopper: A True Life* (Boston: Jewett and Company, 1860), 185–186; Daniel E. Meaders, ed., *Kidnappers in Philadelphia: Isaac Hopper's Tales of Oppression, 1780–1843* (New York: Garland, 1994), 203–206.

24. Child, *Isaac T. Hopper*, 185–186; Meaders, *Kidnappers in Philadelphia*, 203–206.

25. Child, *Isaac T. Hopper,* 185–186; Meaders, *Kidnappers in Philadelphia,* 203–206; *National Gazette,* Jan. 1, 1824.

26. Child, *Isaac T. Hopper,* 33–35, 185–186, 201; Meaders, *Kidnappers in Philadelphia,* 203–206; *National Gazette,* Jan. 1, 1824. Although Hopper took the witness stand, the *Gazette* does not mention him. Samuel Mason also served as one of the secretaries for the PAS from 1823 to 1827. The *National Anti-Slavery Standard* also published seventy-nine of Hopper's "Tales of Oppression" between 1840 and 1842.

27. Child, *Isaac T. Hopper,* 185–186; Meaders, *Kidnappers in Philadelphia,* 203–206; *National Gazette,* Jan. 1, 1824.

28. *Easton Gazette,* Jul. 27, 1822.

29. *Easton Gazette,* Jul. 27, 1822.

30. *Easton Gazette,* Jul. 27, 1822.

31. Herbert A. Johnson, "Bushrod Washington," paper presented at 2008 Symposium on Neglected Justices at Vanderbilt University, *Vanderbilt Law Review* 62, no. 2 (Mar. 2009): 447–490; Lynn Price, "Bushrod Washington: Slavery and Colonization in the Shadow of George Washington," Washington Papers, accessed Jun. 30, 2020, https://washingtonpapers .org/bushrod-washington-slavery-and-colonization-in-the-shadow-of-george-washington/; Horace Binney, *Bushrod Washington* (Philadelphia: C. Sherman & Son, 1858), 1–29; Diemer, *The Politics of Black Citizenship,* 14.

32. Hill v. Lowe, case no. 6,494, Circuit Court, E.D. Pennsylvania, 12 F. Cas. 172; 1822 U.S. App. Lexis 406; 4 Wash. C.C. 327, October 1822, Term.; *National Gazette,* Jan. 1, 1824; Salmon P. Chase, *Reclamation of Fugitives from Service: An argument for the defendant, submitted to the Supreme Court of the United States, at the December term, 1846 in the Case of Wharton Jones vs. John Vanzandt* (Cincinnati: R. P. Donogh and co., 1847), 18–20.

33. *National Gazette,* Jan. 1, 1824; Child, *Isaac T. Hopper,* 185–186; Tise, *Proslavery,* 251; Greenberg, "Charles Ingersoll," 192.

34. *National Gazette,* Jan. 1, 1824; Child, *Isaac T. Hopper,* 185–186.

35. *National Gazette,* Jan. 1, 1824; Child, *Isaac T. Hopper,* 185–186.

36. Manisha Sinha, *The Slave's Cause: A History of Abolition* (New Haven, CT: Yale University Press, 2016), 391; Daina Ramey Berry, *The Price for Their Pound of Flesh* (Boston, MA: Beacon Press, 2017), xiii.

37. Leslie, "The Pennsylvania Fugitive Slave Act of 1826," 435–436; *American State Papers,* 17th Congress, First Session, No. 506 "Recovery of Fugitive slaves," Dec. 17, 1821; Morris, *Free Men All,* 45 ft. 15.

38. Interestingly enough, several Maryland state legislators had been rebuffed while trying to retrieve their slaves in Pennsylvania; see Jeffrey R. Brackett, *The Negro in Maryland: A Study of the Institution of Slavery* (Baltimore: N. Murray, 1889), 87; *Easton Gazette,* Jul. 20, 1822. The *Baltimore Patriot* said that "the laws relating to runaway negroes appear to be defective" and demanded the interposition of the state legislature; *Baltimore Patriot,* Jan. 25, 1822; George Edward Reed, ed., *Pennsylvania Archives, Fourth Series,* vol. 5: *Papers of the Governors* (Harrisburg: Wm. Stanley Ray, 1900), 371–373; PAS 1.5, Apr. 4, 1821; PAS Series 1.1, May 14 and Dec. 27, 1821.

39. *1830 United States Federal Census;* Pierre Islam, *Perplexing Patriarchies: Fatherhood among Black Opponents and White Defenders of Slavery* (Wilmington, DE: Vernon Press, 2019), 124; Reed, *Pennsylvania Archives,* 371–373; PAS 1.1, May 14 and Dec. 27, 1821. The PAS also contacted Hiester because it lacked the funds to track down kidnapping victims; see PAS 1.1, Mar. 29, 1821, and Feb. 28, 1823; PAS Series 5.1, Miscellaneous 1784–1866, PAS to his Excellency, Joseph Hiester, Governor of the State of Pennsylvania, 1821.

40. Chambers owned at least one enslaved person, according to the 1820 US Census; Goldsborough owned approximately sixty-two enslaved people in 1830; *1820 and 1830 United*

States Federal Census; Whitman H. Ridgway, *Community Leadership in Maryland: A Comparative Analysis of Power in Society* (Chapel Hill: University of North Carolina Press, 2018), 107 n. 87; William M. Wiecek, *The Sources of Anti-Slavery Constitutionalism in America, 1760–1848* (Ithaca, NY: Cornell University Press, 2018), 158; Conway W. Sams and Elihu S. Riley, eds., *The Bench and Bar of Maryland, A History: 1634–1901*, vol. 2 (Chicago: Lewis Publishing Company, 1901), 378–383; Paul Finkelman, ed., *Fugitive Slaves and American Courts: The Pamphlet Literature* (New York: Garland Publishing, 1988), 41; *Pennsylvania Archives Ninth Series*, vol. 8, 6403; Baker, *Prigg v. Pennsylvania*, 76; *Pennsylvania Archives Fourth Series*, 627–629; *Genius of Universal Emancipation*, Feb. 18, 1826; Harrold, *Border War*, 72–93.

41. *Easton Gazette*, Feb. 25, 1826; *Poulson's*, Feb. 13, 1826; Harrold, *Border War*, 72–93; Pennsylvania Abolition Society, *Centennial anniversary of the Pennsylvania Society for Promoting the Abolition of Slavery* (Philadelphia: Grants, Faires & Rodgers, Printers, 1875), 53; "Belmont Mansion," American Women's Heritage Society, accessed Jul. 2, 2020, https://www.belmontmansion.org/history_belmont_mansion.html; "Cornelia Wells," American Women's Heritage Society, accessed Jul. 2, 2020, https://www.belmontmansion.org/CorneliaWellsWeb.pdf.

42. *National Gazette*, Feb. 14 and 16, 1826. The bill also revived the idea of a pass system, which had floated around the legislature for a number of years; African Americans traveling without a pass or clear account of their freedom were to be put in prison.

43. *National Gazette*, Feb. 14 and 16, 1826.

44. *Baltimore Patriot*, Feb. 4 and 8, 1826; *Easton Gazette*, Feb. 25, 1826.

45. *National Gazette*, Feb. 11 and 14, 1826; *Poulson's*, Feb. 14, 15, and 16, 1826.

46. *National Gazette*, Feb. 23, 1826; Diemer, *The Politics of Black Citizenship*, 56–57, quotation on 57.

47. Richard Newman, *Freedom's Prophet: Bishop Richard Allen, the AME Church, and the Black Founding Fathers* (New York: New York University Press, 2008), 159; Jonathan Roberts to Eliza Roberts, Feb. 27, 1820, Letters 1815–1832, Jonathan Roberts Papers, Historical Society of Pennsylvania; *National Gazette*, Feb. 14, 18, 20, 1826.

48. *Poulson's*, Feb. 13, 1826; *American Sentinel*, Feb. 15, 1826; John Henderson to Joseph Watson, Jan. 2, 1826, Joseph Watson Papers, Historical Society of Pennsylvania; PAS 2.4, Joseph Watson to William Rawle, Jul. 4, 1826; Jesse Green to Joseph Watson, Mar. 12, 1827, Joseph Watson Papers, Historical Society of Pennsylvania; Thomas Shipley to Joseph Parrish, Feb. 16, 1826, Cox-Parrish-Wharton Papers, Historical Society of Pennsylvania. See also Richard Bell, *Stolen: Five Free Boys Kidnapped into Slavery and Their Astonishing Odyssey Home* (New York: Simon & Schuster, Co., 2019).

49. PAS 2.4, William Rawle to PAS, Feb. 10, 1826; PAS Series 1.2, General Meeting Minute Book, Feb. 11, 1826; *National Gazette*, Feb. 14, 1826.

50. Meredith defeated Josiah Randall by seventy-eight votes in a special election for Philadelphia City representative held on January 17, 1826. *National Gazette*, Jan. 19, 1826; Robert Vaux to Stephen Duncan and William M. Meredith, Feb. 9, 1826, Meredith Family Papers (Historical Society of Pennsylvania; Richard Newman, *The Transformation of American Abolitionism: Fighting Slavery in the Early Republic* (Chapel Hill: University of North Carolina Press, 2002), 39–44. On extraterritoriality, see Ralph Keller, "Extraterritoriality and the Fugitive Slave Debate," *Illinois Historical Journal* 78, no. 2 (1985): 113–128; Paul Finkelman, "Prigg v. Pennsylvania: Understanding Justice Story's Proslavery Nationalism," *Journal of Supreme Court History* 22, no. 2 (Dec. 1997): 51–64. See also Diemer, *The Politics of Black Citizenship*, 57–59.

51. William Meredith to William M. Meredith, Feb. 13, 1826, Meredith Family Papers (HSP).

52. Richard Allen to William M. Meredith, Feb. 14, 1826, Meredith Family Papers (HSP).

53. Richard Allen to William M. Meredith, Feb. 14, 1826.

54. Richard Allen to William M. Meredith, Feb. 14, 1826; PAS 2.4, Adam Brown to Richard Allen, Jan. 15, 1826; Robert Layton to James Forten, May 5, 1825. See Walter Johnson, *River of Dark Dreams: Slavery and Empire in the Cotton Kingdom* (Cambridge, MA: Belknap Press of Harvard University Press, 2013), and the career of the abolitionist Jacob Barker, whose letters to the PAS spoke to liberating African Americans from New Orleans jails; see PAS 1.5, Sept. 23, 1839, Jan. 28, Feb. 10, 1840; Jan. 8, Apr. 20, Jun. 24, Dec. 7, 1840, Jun. 16, Jul. 26, Sept. 28, 1841, Jun. 9, 1842, and R. D. Turner, *The Conspiracy Trials of 1826 and 1827: A Chapter in the Life of Jacob Barker* (Philadelphia: George W. Childs, 1864); Edie L. Wong, *Neither Fugitive nor Free: Atlantic slavery, Freedom Suits, and the Legal Culture of Travel* (New York: New York University Press, 2009), 188–189; Michael Alan Schoeppner, "Navigating the Dangerous Atlantic: Racial Quarantines, Black Sailors, and United States Constitutionalism" (PhD diss., University of Florida, 2010), 222–223.

55. Gary Nash, *First City: Philadelphia and the Forging of Historical Memory* (Philadelphia: University of Pennsylvania Press, 2006), 147–151; Nash, *Forging Freedom*, 221–227.

56. Richard Allen to William M. Meredith, Feb. 14, 1826, Meredith Family Papers (HSP).

57. Leslie, "The Pennsylvania Fugitive Slave Act of 1826," 438; Baker, *Prigg v. Pennsylvania*, 78; *National Gazette*, Feb. 23, 1826; Morris, *Free Men All*, 50–51.

58. Leslie, "The Pennsylvania Fugitive Slave Act of 1826," 438; *National Gazette*, Feb. 23, 1826; Morris, *Free Men All*, 50–51.

59. Leslie, "The Pennsylvania Fugitive Slave Act of 1826," 440–443; Thomas Shipley to Joseph Parrish, Feb. 16, 1826, Cox-Parrish-Wharton Papers (HSP).

60. Leslie, "The Pennsylvania Fugitive Slave Act of 1826," 440–443. While a record of the vote does not survive, seventy-seven Democrats and twenty-three Federalists presided over the Pennsylvania House of Representatives during the 1825–1826 session, which indicated that legislators crossed party lines to vote for the bill; similarly, the composition of the state Senate (twenty-seven Democrats to six Federalists) required legislators to cross party lines and vote 16–12 in favor of the kidnapping bill. See Morris, *Free Men All*, 46 ft. 19, 51, and Wilkes University, "The Wilkes University Election Statistics Project," accessed Feb. 4, 2017, http://staff web.wilkes.edu/harold.cox/legis/; *National Gazette*, Feb. 18 and 23, 1826; Thomas Shipley to Joseph Parrish, Feb. 16, 1826, Cox-Parrish-Wharton Papers (HSP); Diemer, *The Politics of Black Citizenship*, 59.

61. Francis J. Troubat and William W. Haly, *A digest of the acts of Assembly of Pennsylvania: passed in the sessions of 1824–5, 1825–6, 1826–7, 1827–8, and 1828–9, with an appendix containing the acts passed in 1829–30. With notes of judicial decisions* (Philadelphia: Robert H. Small, 1830), 105–111.

62. Troubat and Haly, *A digest of the acts of Assembly of Pennsylvania*, 105–111; Morris, *Free Men All*, 52.

63. Troubat and Haly, *A digest of the acts of Assembly of Pennsylvania*, 105–111.

Chapter 3 · Fugitive Freedom in Philadelphia

1. Anonymous to PAS Acting Committee, July 25, 1826, PAS Series 2.4 (hereafter PAS 2.4), Loose Correspondence, Incoming 1820–1863, Historical Society of Pennsylvania.

2. On the revolutionary nature of the era, see Charles Sellers, *The Market Revolution: Jacksonian America, 1815–1846* (New York: Oxford University Press, 1991); Daniel Walker Howe, *What Hath God Wrought: The Transformation of America, 1815–1848* (Oxford: Oxford University Press, 2007); Sean Wilentz, *The Rise of American Democracy: Jefferson to Lincoln* (New York: Norton, 2005); Jacqueline Jones, *American Work: Four Centuries of Black and White Labor* (New York: Norton, 1999); Alexander Saxton, *The Rise and Fall of the White Republic: Class Politics and Mass Culture in Nineteenth Century America* (New York: Verso, 1990);

Lawrence Kohl, *The Politics of Individualism: Parties and the American Character during the Jacksonian Era* (New York: Oxford University Press, 1989); John Ashworth, *Slavery, Capitalism, and Politics in the Antebellum Republic*, vol. 2: *The Coming of the Civil War, 1850–1861* (New York: Cambridge University Press, 2007).

3. J. Thomas Scharff and Thompson Westcott, *History of Philadelphia, 1609–1884* (Philadelphia: L. H. Everts & Co., 1884), 617.

4. William R. Leslie, "The Pennsylvania Fugitive Slave Act of 1826," *Journal of Southern History* 18, no. 4 (Nov. 1952): 429–455; John Henderson to Joseph Watson, Jan. 2, 1826, Joseph Watson Papers, HSP (hereafter "WP"); PAS 2.4, Jul. 4, 1826; Jesse Green to Joseph Watson, Mar. 12, 1827. See also Eric Ledell-Smith et al., "Notes and Documents: Rescuing African American Kidnapping Victims in Philadelphia as Documented in the Joseph Watson Papers at the Historical Society of Pennsylvania," *Pennsylvania Magazine of History and Biography* 129, no. 3 (Jul. 2005): 317–345, esp., 323; "Narrative of Samuel Scomp," *African Observer* (May 1827): 39–41. Much of my account of the 1826 kidnapping crisis comports with the aforementioned work by Richard Bell, *Stolen: Five Free Boys Kidnapped into Slavery and Their Astonishing Odyssey Home* (New York: Simon & Schuster, Co., 2019). The presence of African Americans amongst the kidnappers is best discussed in Richard Bell, "Counterfeit Kin; Kidnappers of Color, the Reverse Underground Railroad, and the Origins of Practical Abolition," *Journal of the Early Republic* 38 (Summer 2018): 199–230.

5. Henderson to Watson, Jan. 2, 1826, Watson Papers; *Poulson's American Daily Advertiser* (hereafter "*Poulson's*"), Feb.13, 1826.

6. Ledell-Smith et al., "Notes and Documents," 317–318. Daniel Neal served as vice president of the PAS in 1820, his son Daniel Jr. served as the PAS secretary in 1838; Isaac Parrish joined the PAS in 1784; his son Dr. Isaac Parrish served as vice president of the PAS in 1832; Dr. Joseph Parrish served as the PAS president in 1816 and attended the American convention as a Philadelphia delegate; Dillwyn Parrish also served as PAS president in 1832 and his brother William Parrish served as PAS secretary in 1842. See Pennsylvania Abolition Society, *Centennial Anniversary of the Pennsylvania Society* (Philadelphia: Grant, Faires & Rodgers, 1875), 51–66.

7. Watson to Hamilton, Feb. 24, 1826; Watson to Hamilton and Henderson, Mar. 10, 1826; Henderson to Watson, Mar. 20, Apr. 17, May 5 and 8, 1826; "Abstract: A list of documents forwarded to John Henderson and J. W. Hamilton," all in Watson papers. "Narrative of Samuel Scomp," 39–41; Ledell-Smith et al., "Notes and Documents," 327; Gertrude MacKinney, ed., *Pennsylvania Archives: Ninth Series, Volume IX* (Harrisburg: Wm. Stanley Ray, State Printer, 1934), 6619.

8. Trimble to Watson, Mar. 29, 1826, WP; *African Observer* (May 1827), 42; Job Brown to Watson, July 5, 1826, WP; MacKinney, *Pennsylvania Archives: Ninth Series, Volume IX*, 6418. Rumors spread that the Johnsons returned to New Jersey at some point in early 1826. There Gloucester County justice of the peace Job Brown heard from a farmer who had recently hired Purnell to work for him in recent weeks. The farmer cited the article in *Poulson's* detailing the travails of the victims, and even mentioned how Purnell bragged "that he could sometimes make from fifty to an hundred dollars in a Week" kidnapping African Americans. See Job Brown to Watson, July 5, 1826, WP.

9. Samuel J. Garrigues to Watson, Mar. 23 and 27, 1826, WP; Ledell-Smith et al. "Notes and Documents," 323, 327; *Philadelphia Democratic Press*, Jan. 25, 1827.

10. Jesse Green to Watson, Mar. 12, 1827, WP; Ledell-Smith et al., "Notes and Documents," 327; Carol Wilson, *Freedom at Risk: The Kidnapping of Free Blacks in America, 1780–1865* (Lexington: University Press of Kentucky, 1994), 32–33; Bell, *Stolen*, 199–207.

11. *Poulson's*, June 15 and 19, 1827; Ledell-Smith et al., "Notes and Documents," 327–328.

12. *Poulson's,* June 15 and 19, 1827; *Freedom's Journal,* June 22, 1827; *African Observer* (Aug. 1827, 139). Carr left Philadelphia and died in either Alabama or Arch Street Prison in 1828; see Ledell-Smith et al., "Notes and Documents," 327, ft. 46, and Bell, *Stolen,* 280–281 ft. 45, for the conflicting accounts. In a fascinating turn of events, Samuel Scomp changed his name to Samuel Hill and went to live with and work for the renowned abolitionist Thomas Shipley— we know that he did so because of a hard-to-find-record of an assault and battery case in Philadelphia's Mayor's Court in 1835. Apparently Scomp assaulted Shipley "with intent to murder" and was sentenced to a year in prison. Scomp fades from the historical record shortly thereafter. Mayor's Court of Philadelphia, Record Group 130.1 Docket. Oct. 6, 1835. See also Bell, *Stolen,* 291 ft. 4.

13. *Poulson's,* June 19, 1827. Parker may have been "Simeon Parker," a Black cordwainer listed in the 1825 *Philadelphia Directory.*

14. *Poulson's,* June 19, 1827; "Narrative of Samuel Scomp."

15. On the economic vulnerability of Black children, see Bell, *Stolen*; Crystal Lynn Webster, *Beyond the Boundaries of Childhood: African American Children in the Antebellum North* (Chapel Hill: University of North Carolina Press, 2021), 65–89.

16. Pennsylvania Abolition Society Series 1.2 (hereafter "PAS 1.2"), General Meeting Minute Book, Volume 3, 1825–1847, Sept. 27, 1827; *Freedom's Journal,* Dec. 19, 1828; *African Observer* (May 1827): 37; Henderson to Watson, July 16, 1827, WP. The PAS created a committee to compensate Garrigues for his work, though it was unclear how much or if they paid him anything. See PAS 1.2 Sept. 5, 1828.

17. *Freedom's Journal,* Feb. 15, 1828, May 23, 1828, July 25, 1828.

18. *Freedom's Journal,* Feb. 15, 1828, Apr. 25, 1828, May 23, 1828, July 25, 1828. For 1842 as the year that the PAS became integrated, see Richard S. Newman, "The PAS and American Abolitionism: A Century of Activism from the American Revolutionary Era to the Civil War," *Historical Society of Pennsylvania* via http://hsp.org/sites/default/files/legacy_files/migrated /newmanpasessay.pdf, 9.

19. William J. Switala, *Underground Railroad in Pennsylvania* (Mechanicsburg, PA: Stackpole Books, 2001), 143–144. William Kashatus argued that informal anti-kidnapping groups may have existed in Pennsylvania as early as 1786; see William C. Kashatus, *William Still: The Underground Railroad and the Angel at Philadelphia* (Notre Dame: Notre Dame Press, 2021), 49–57. *Freedom's Journal,* Dec. 5, 1828, suggested that New York abolitionists adopt the Philadelphia model of forming a "protecting society."

20. I rely on two main sources for the account of Emory Sadler: Isaac Hopper's article in the *National Anti-Slavery Standard* from April 15, 1841, and the PAS 1.5 records. Where there is a discrepancy over dates and details, I defer to the PAS records both because they were written closer to and during the entire ordeal and because they square with government records from the Pennsylvania archives. Daniel E. Meaders, *Kidnappers in Philadelphia: Isaac Hopper's Tales of oppression, 1780–1843* (New York: Garland, 1994), 105–106; PAS 1.5, Jan. 18, 1826. On "interstate diplomacy," see Stanley Harrold, *Border War: Fighting over Slavery before the Civil War* (Chapel Hill: University of North Carolina Press, 2010), 72–93. On John Shulze, see William Crawford Armor, *Lives of the Governors of Pennsylvania, with the Incidental History of the State, from 1609–1873* (Philadelphia: James K. Simon, 1873), 342–349.

21. Meaders, *Kidnappers in Philadelphia,* 105–106; PAS 1.5, Jan. 18, 1826. Information on William Pritchett comes from the *Philadelphia Directory, 1825.* Perhaps inspired by Sadler, Pritchett joined the PAS in 1829; see *Centennial Anniversary of the Pennsylvania Society,* 64. On the role played by hiring out in the collapse of the Union, see William A. Link, *Roots of Secession: Slavery and Politics in Antebellum Virginia* (Chapel Hill: University of North Carolina Press, 2003), and Seth Rockman, *Scraping By: Wage Labor, Slavery, and Survival in Early Baltimore* (Baltimore, MD: Johns Hopkins University Press, 2009).

22. PAS 1.2, Dec. 29, 1825; MacKinney, *Pennsylvania Archives: Ninth Series, Volume IX,* 6333, 6391.

23. PAS 1.2, Dec. 29, 1825; MacKinney, *Pennsylvania Archives: Ninth Series, Volume IX,* 6333, 6391.

24. PAS 1.5, Dec. 25, 1826; Meaders, *Kidnappers in Philadelphia,* 109.

25. PAS 1.5, Jun. 23, 1826. The secondary literature does not mention William Welch in the list of Maryland commissioners who ventured to Harrisburg in 1826. Welch owned two enslaved people in 1820. See Kevin Hemstock, "Then & Now: A Former Slave Helped Pioneer a Black Community," My Eastern Shore, accessed July 9, 2020, https://www.myeasternshoremd .com/opinion/kent_county/then-now-a-former-slave-helped-pioneer-a-black-community -feb-16/article_2fc37d5c-bbc0-599f-b6d2-b9c365bf44f5.html; US Census Bureau, *1820 United States Federal Census, Ancestry.com,* accessed December 28, 2020.

26. PAS 1.5, Jun. 23, 1826; MacKinney, *Pennsylvania Archives: Ninth Series, Volume IX,* 6634–35, 6638–39, 6576; *Baltimore Gazette and Daily Advertiser,* May 14, 1827; *Republican Star and General Advertiser,* May 15, 1827. Reward posted in *Easton Gazette,* June 16, 1827; *Genius of Universal Emancipation,* Jun. 1827, volume 2, issue 30, p. 239; *Genius of Universal Emancipation,* Jun. 1827, volume 2, issue 31, p. 248.

27. On the expansion of the cotton economy, see Adam Rothman, *Slave Country: American Expansion and the Origins of the Deep South* (Cambridge, MA: Harvard University Press, 2005), and Walter Johnson, *River of Dark Dreams: Slavery and Empire in the Cotton Kingdom* (Cambridge, MA: Belknap Press of Harvard University Press, 2013). The sources are mute as to who contacted Rawle. PAS 1.5, Sept. 25, 1827; PAS 1.2, Feb. 5, Jun. 25, Dec. 31, 1829, Mar. 31, 1831.

28. *Republican Star and General Advertiser,* Jan. 10, 1826.

29. *National Gazette,* Apr. 29; *Richmond Inquirer,* May 30, 1826; Joseph Hemphill, *Speech of Mr. Hemphill on the Missouri Question in the House of Representatives of the U. States* (Washington, DC: Unknown Publisher, 1819), 1–27.

30. PAS 1.5, Dec. 26, 1815, Jan. 4, Oct. 4, Nov. 6, 1817, May 19, 1818; Alberti's accomplice was a man named James Robinson. The 1815 *Philadelphia Directory* lists three people with that name: a white rigger, a white ship captain, and a Black mariner. *Democratic Press,* Jan. 25, 1827; Don E. Fehrenbacher, *The Slaveholding Republic: An Account of the United States Government's Relations to Slavery* (Oxford: Oxford University Press, 2001), 215–216.

31. *National Gazette,* May 27, 1826; *Genius of Universal Emancipation,* Nov. 10, 1827, volume 1, issue 19, p. 148; Charles Miner, *Speech of Mr. Miner, of Pennsylvania, Delivered in the House of Representatives* (Washington, DC: Unknown Publisher, 1829). See also "Minutes of the twentieth session of the American Convention for Promoting the Abolition of Slavery, and Improving the Condition of the African Race: convened at Philadelphia, on the second of October, 1827," last modified 2021, http://www.loc.gov, and "Minutes of the twenty-first biennial American Convention for Promoting the Abolition of Slavery, and Improving the Condition of the African Race: convened at the city of Washington, December 8, A.D. 1829: and an appendix, containing the addresses from various societies, together with the constitution and by-laws of the convention," last modified 2021, http://www.loc.gov. Green was also frazzled by the recent meeting of the American Convention in Philadelphia and especially that group's plan to relocate to Washington DC for its next meeting; see *Genius of Universal Emancipation,* Nov. 17, 1827, volume 1, issue 20, p. 159.

32. Philip Shriver Klein, *Pennsylvania Politics, 1817–1832: A Game without Rules* (Philadelphia: Porcupine Press, 1974), 248–249; *Genius of Universal Emancipation,* Sept. 6, 1828, volume 3, issue 1, p. 6; *Genius of Universal Emancipation,* Oct. 4, 1828, volume 3, issue 4, p. 25.

33. Klein, *Pennsylvania Politics, 1817–1832,* 251, 409; *Freedom's Journal,* July 20, 1827. For *Freedom's Journal's* reportage on Jackson in Pennsylvania and other states, see Sept. 14 and

254 Notes to Pages 100–106

Dec. 14, 1827, Feb. 8, Apr. 25, June 13, July 4, Sept. 12, 1828; Andrew K. Diemer, *The Politics of Black Citizenship: Free African Americans in the Mid-Atlantic Borderland, 1817–1863* (Athens: University of Georgia Press, 2016), 60–62.

34. Emma Jones Lapsansky, "'Since They Got Those Separate Churches': Afro-Americans and Racism in Jacksonian Philadelphia," *American Quarterly* 32, no. 1 (Spring 1980): 64–68.

35. Webster, *Beyond the Boundaries of Childhood*, 90–103; *Baltimore Gazette*, Nov. 25, 1829; *New York Evangelist*, Aug. 11, 1842; Jeremiah Gloucester, *An Oration, Delivered on January 1, 1823 in Bethel Church: On the Abolition of the Slave Trade* (Philadelphia: John Young, 1823), 12, 15; Julie Winch, *Philadelphia's Black Elite: Activism, Accommodation, and the Struggle for Autonomy, 1787–1848* (Philadelphia: Temple University Press, 1988), 125; Matthew Hopper, *From Refuge to Strength: The Rise of the African American Church in Philadelphia* (Philadelphia: Preservation Alliance for Greater Philadelphia, 2015), 7–10, 13. See also "Preservation Alliance for Greater Philadelphia," last Modified 2015, www.preservationalliance.com/files/aa churches.pdf. On Gloucester's license to preach the Gospel, see *Christian Repository*, Nov. 7, 1823; *Freedom's Journal*, May 11, 1827. *Freedom's Journal* Jan. 11 and 25, 1828, reported on Gloucester's death; Saxton, *Rise and Fall of the White Republic*, 148–149.

36. John M. Werner, *Reaping the Bloody Harvest: Race Riots in the United States during the Age of Jackson, 1824–1849* (New York: Garland, 1986), 169 ft. 11; Scharff and Westcott, *History of Philadelphia*, 624; *Baltimore Gazette*, Nov. 25, 1829; PAS 1.5, June 8, 1827; *New York Spectator*, Nov. 27, 1829; *Newport Mercury*, Nov. 28, 1829; *National Gazette*, June 6,1829; *Philadelphia Directory*, 1829.

37. Werner, *Reaping the Bloody Harvest*, 169–170.

38. PAS 1.2, Nov. 12, 1829; *Genius of Universal Emancipation*, Nov. 20, 1829, volume 4, issue 11, 41–42, 53; "Minutes of the twenty-first biennial American Convention [. . .] 1829."

39. "This absoluteness of the act of choice does not alter the relativity of each epoch." See Jean-Paul Sartre, *Existentialism and Human Emotions* (New York: Citadel Press, 1985), 39–40. See also Kellie Carter Jackson, *Force and Freedom: Black Abolitionists and the Politics of Violence* (Philadelphia: University of Pennsylvania Press, 2019).

40. *Philadelphia Inquirer*, Apr. 19, 1830; *Saturday Evening Post*, Apr. 24, 1830.

41. *Philadelphia Inquirer*, Apr. 19, 1830; *Saturday Evening Post*, Apr. 24, 1830. A constable named "Dunhart" does not appear in the 1830 *Philadelphia Directory*, so perhaps these papers mistook him for another constable.

42. National Convention, *Minutes and Proceedings of the First Annual Convention of the People of Colour* (Philadelphia: Committee of Arrangements, 1831).

43. National Colored Convention, *The Proceedings of the Convention with Their Address to Free Persons of Colour in the United States* (Philadelphia: J. W. Allen, 1831); National Convention, *Minutes and Proceedings of the First Annual Convention of the People of Colour* (Philadelphia: Committee of Arrangements, 1831); Winch, *Philadelphia's Black Elite*, 94; Diemer, *The Politics of Black Citizenship*, 84–86.

44. National Colored Convention, *Minutes and Proceedings of the First Annual Convention of the People of Colour* (Philadelphia: Committee of Arrangements, 1831); Michel Foucault, *The Order of Things: An Archaeology of the Human Sciences* (New York: Vintage Books, 1994), 3–16.

45. On Turner, see Kenneth S. Greenberg, ed., *The Confessions of Nat Turner and Related Documents* (New York: Bedford / St. Martin's, 1996).

46. *Philadelphia Inquirer*, Sept. 19, 1831; *National Gazette*, Aug. 30, 1831.

47. *Liberator*, Oct. 8, 1831; Saxton, *Rise and Fall of the White Republic*, 148–150. On the *Liberator* in the *Philadelphia Inquirer*, see *Philadelphia Inquirer*, Jan. 8, Jan. 22, Sept. 26, 1831. On the relationship between print culture and nationalism, see Benedict Anderson, *Imagined Communities: Reflections on the Origin and Spread of Nationalism* (London: Verso, 2006),

47–65; David Waldstreicher, *In the Midst of Perpetual Fetes: The Making of American National-ism, 1776–1820* (Chapel Hill: University of North Carolina Press, 1997); "MVB to Thomas Ritchie, 13 January 1827," The Papers of Martin Van Buren, 1782–1862, accessed July 16, 2020, http://vanburenpapers.org/document-mvb00528. On the spectacle of violence inherent in a slave society, see Saidiya V. Hartman, *Scenes of Subjection: Terror, Slavery, and Self-Making in Nineteenth-Century America* (New York: Oxford University Press, 1997), 32–44, quotation on p. 33.

48. *Liberator,* Dec. 10, 1831.

49. *Liberator,* Dec. 10, 1831; Beverly C. Tomek, *Colonization and Its Discontents: Emanci-pation, Emigration, and Antislavery in Antebellum Pennsylvania* (New York: New York Uni-versity Press, 2011), 153–154; *Philadelphia Inquirer,* Aug. 30, Sept. 13, Dec. 1, 22–23, 1831; see also Paul J. Polgar, *Standard-Bearers of Equality: America's First Abolition Movement* (Chapel Hill: University of North Carolina Press, 2019), 318–325, where he explains the relationship between the rise of colonization and the decline of antislavery activism. See also Diemer, *The Politics of Black Citizenship,* 68–69, quotation on 68.

50. *Liberator,* Dec. 10, 1831.

51. *Liberator,* Dec. 10, 1831.

52. Leon Litwack, *North of Slavery: The Negro in the Free States* (Chicago: University of Chicago Press, 1961), 69–70; Winch, *Philadelphia's Black Elite,* 131–133; Tomek, *Colonization and Its Discontents,* 154; House of Representatives of the Commonwealth of Pennsylvania, *Journal of the Forty-Second House of Representatives of the Commonwealth of Pennsylvania: Volume 1* (Harrisburg: Henry Welsh, 1831), 48, 117–118, 143, 153, 338; *Philadelphia Inquirer,* Dec. 31, 1831; Diemer, *The Politics of Black Citizenship,* 70–72.

53. *Liberator,* Apr. 14, 1832; *Hazard's Register of Pennsylvania Volume IX,* June 9, 1832, 361.

54. *Liberator,* Apr. 14, 1832.

55. *Easton Gazette,* Jan. 28, 1832.

56. *Liberator,* Feb. 11, 1832; *National Gazette,* Jan. 28, 1832.

57. John Bowers, *To the Honourable Senate and House of Representatives of the Common-wealth of Pennsylvania* (Philadelphia: Unknown publisher, 1833), 11–12; Winch, *Philadelphia's Black Elite,* 132–133.

58. Christopher James Bonner, *Remaking the Republic: Black Politics and the Creation of American Citizenship* (Philadelphia: University of Pennsylvania Press, 2020), 11–37, quotation on 16; National Colored Convention, *Minutes and Proceedings of the Second Annual Conven-tion of the Free People of Color* (Philadelphia: Benj. Paschal, Thos. Butler, and Jas. C. Matthews, 1832), 17, 19, 32–36.

59. Bowers, *To the Honourable Senate and House of Representatives,* 3, 7, 9, 11.

60. Bowers, 10–11.

61. Julie Winch, *A Gentleman of Color: The Life of James Forten* (New York: Oxford Uni-versity Press, 2002), 292–293; Samuel Breck, *Report of the Committee Appointed in the Senate of Pennsylvania to Investigate the Cause of an Increased Number of Slaves being returned for that Commonwealth, by the Census of 1830, over that of 1820* (Harrisburg: Henry Welsh, 1833), 1–7.

62. Breck, *Report of the Committee,* 1–7; Bowers, *To the Honourable Senate and House of Representatives,* 1–12; Charles M. Snyder, *The Jacksonian Heritage: Pennsylvania Politics, 1833–1848* (Harrisburg: Pennsylvania Historical and Museum Commission, 1958), 26–27; Russell F. Weigley, ed., *Philadelphia: A 300 Year History* (New York: Norton, 1982), 303.

Chapter 4 · *Domestic Sanctuary*

1. *Baltimore Gazette and Daily Advertiser,* July 6, 1835; *United States Gazette,* June 18, 1835; *Liberator,* July 18, 1835.

2. *Philadelphia Inquirer*, July 10, 1835; *Liberator*, Sept. 19, 1835; *National Gazette*, June 23, 1835.

3. The historiography on this series of riots includes, John Runcie, "'Hunting the Nigs' in Philadelphia: The Race Riot of August 1834," *Pennsylvania History* 39, no. 2 (Apr. 1972): 187–218; Carl E. Prince, "The Great 'Riot Year': Jacksonian Democracy and Patterns of Violence in 1834," *Journal of the Early Republic* 5, no. 1 (Spring 1985): 1–19; Alexander Saxton, *The Rise and Fall of the White Republic: Class Politics and Mass Culture in Nineteenth Century America* (New York: Verso, 1990); Emma Jones Lapsansky, "'Since They Got Those Separate Churches': Afro-Americans and Racism in Jacksonian Philadelphia," *American Quarterly* 32, no. 1 (Spring 1980): 64–68; Paul Gilje, *Rioting in America* (Bloomington: Indiana University Press, 1996); Leonard Richards, *Gentlemen of Property and Standing: Anti-Abolition Mobs in Jacksonian America* (New York: Oxford University Press, 1970); David Grimsted, *American Mobbing, 1828–1861: Toward Civil War* (Oxford: Oxford University Press, 1998); Elizabeth M. Geffen, "Industrial Development and Social Crisis, 1841–1854," in *Philadelphia: A 300 Year History* (New York: Norton, 1982), 307–363; Noel Ignatiev, *How the Irish Became White* (New York: Routledge, 1995).

4. *Hazard's Register of Pennsylvania Volume IX*, 6/1832.

5. William Lloyd Garrison, *Selections from the Writings of W. L. Garrison* (Boston: R. F. Wallcut, 1852), 66–71.

6. Margaret Hope Bacon, *But One Race: The Life of Robert Purvis* (Albany: State University of New York, 2007); Ira Brown, "Miller McKim and Pennsylvania Abolitionism," *Pennsylvania History* 30, no. 1 (Jan. 1963): 55–72.

7. *Pennsylvanian*, Dec. 14, 1833; *Liberator*, Feb. 1, 1834; *New York Spectator*, Feb. 15, 1834; *Richmond Enquirer*, Dec. 19, 24, 1833; *Boston Courier*, Dec. 12, 1833; *Christian Watchman*, Dec. 20, 1833; *Philadelphia Inquirer*, Dec. 7, 1833.

8. Edwin Atlee and Dillwyn Parrish also served on this board. "Joseph Cassey. No. 36 South Fourth Street," advertisement in *United States Directory for the Use of Travellers and Merchants* (Philadelphia: James Maxwell, 1823); Library Company of Philadelphia, "Black Founders: The Free Black Community in the Early Republic," last modified 2011, http://www .librarycompany.org/Blackfounders/section9.htm. See also Janine Black and T. L. Hill, "The Rise and Fall Of Joseph Cassey: How Environmental Munificence and Social Networks Enhance and Constrain Minority Entrepreneurship (Interactive Paper)," *Frontiers of Entrepreneurship Research* 29, no. 9 (2009): article 4; Julie Winch, *Philadelphia's Black Elite: Activism, Accommodation, and the Struggle for Autonomy, 1787–1848* (Philadelphia: Temple University Press, 1988), 81–83; Philadelphia Anti-Slavery Society, *Constitution of the Philadelphia Anti-Slavery Society* (Philadelphia: Thomas Town, 1834), v–vi.

9. The College of Pharmacy was located at Seventh and Zane Streets: P. J. Gary, *Philadelphia as it is: And Citizens' Advertising Directory Containing a General Description of the City and Environs*, [. . .] (Philadelphia: P. J. Gary, 1834). For other cases involving Randall, see PAS 1.5, Dec. 26, 1833, Mar. 1 and 17, 1834, Apr. 3, 1835, Jun. 25, 1835, Sept. 1, 1835, Oct. 1, 22, 26, 1835, Jan. 14, 1836, Mar. 3, 1836, Jul. 21, 1836, as well as the Mary Gilmore case, as detailed below; *Philadelphia Inquirer*, May 1, 1834.

10. *Philadelphia Inquirer*, May 1, 1834; *Philadelphia Directory*, 1835–1836; Donnehower (also spelled Donohower and Donnahower) figured largely as another Alberti-type character who plied his trade as a petty law enforcement officer and slave catcher in Philadelphia and New Jersey; his career appears just as prolific as Alberti's, though unlike Alberti little is known of Donnehower's life after 1839. For other cases involving Donnehower, see, for example, PAS 1.5, Mar. 17, 1834, Apr. 3, Oct. 20, 1835, Jan. 16, June 14, 21, July 21, Sept. 6, Oct. 31, Nov. 21, 1836, June 30, 1837, and Sept. 23, 1839.

11. Kellie Carter Jackson, *Force and Freedom: Black Abolitionists and the Politics of Violence*

(Philadelphia: University of Pennsylvania Press, 2019), 28–30; Edwin G. Burrows and Mike Wallace, *Gotham: A History of New York City to 1898* (New York: Oxford University Press, 1999), 558; Prince, "The Great 'Riot Year,'" 1; *Journal of Commerce*, July 10, 11, 1834.

12. Prince, "The Great 'Riot Year,'" 18–19. Steven Hahn presented a compelling argument for equating free Black life in the North with maroon communities in Steven Hahn, *The Political Worlds of Slavery and Freedom* (Cambridge, MA: Harvard University Press, 2009), 1–55. I concur with Andrew K. Diemer's rationale in his *The Politics of Black Citizenship*, 92–93, 207 ft. 48, 216 ft. 42, though the process by which African Americans "decamped" during these riots suffers from a paucity of sources, i.e., we simply do not know if African Americans found solace or sanctuary from other Blacks, whites, or both after the riots. Ignatiev, *How the Irish Became White*; David Roediger, *The Wages of Whiteness: Race and the Making of the American Working Class* (New York: Verso, 2007).

13. Gary Nash, *Forging Freedom: The Formation of Philadelphia's Black Community, 1720–1840* (Cambridge, MA: Harvard University Press, 1988), 47–53. On the "hardening" of racial categories and the celebration of "whiteness" as a political strategy, see James Brewer Stewart, "The Emergence of Racial Modernity and the Rise of the White North, 1790–1840," *Journal of the Early Republic* 18, no. 2 (Summer 1998): 181–217; Saxton, *The Rise and Fall of the White Republic*. See also Eric Lott, *Love and Theft: Blackface Minstrelsy and the American Working Class* (New York: Oxford University Press, 1993); Mark E. Neely, *The Boundaries of American Political Culture in the Civil War Era* (Chapel Hill: University of North Carolina Press, 2005); *Freedom's Journal*, Mar. 14, 1828; *Philadelphia Monthly Magazine*, July 11, 1828.

14. Edward Strutt Abdy, *Journal of a Residence and Tour in the United States of North America, From April 1833 to October 1834, Volume III* (London: John Murray, 1835), 316–317; *Pennsylvania Enquirer*, Jul. 14, 1834. On residential segregation in Philadelphia during the nineteenth century, see Theodore Hershberg, "Free Blacks in Antebellum Philadelphia: A Study of Ex-Slaves, Freeborn, and Socioeconomic Decline," *Journal of Southern History* 5, no. 2 (Winter 1971–1972): 183–209; Emma Jones Lapsansky-Werner, *Neighborhoods in Transition: William Penn's Dream and Urban Reality* (New York: Garland, 1994), 71–97.

15. Abdy, *Journal of a Residence and Tour*, 319–321, 324; Julie Winch, *A Gentleman of Color: The Life of James Forten* (New York: Oxford University Press, 2002), 288–290; Lapsansky, "'Since They Got Those Separate Churches,'" 59; *Pennsylvanian*, Aug. 14, 1834; *United States Gazette*, Aug. 15, 1834; *Weekly Aurora*, Aug. 16, 1834; Ric N. Caric, "From Ordered Buckets to Honored Felons: Fire Companies and Cultural Transformation in Philadelphia, 1785–1850," *Pennsylvania History* 72, no. 2 (Spring 2005): 117–158; Hibernia Fire Company, *The Hibernia Fire Engine Company* (Philadelphia: J. B. Chandler, 1859), 98.

16. *Pennsylvanian*, Aug. 14, 1834; *Philadelphia Gazette*, Aug. 18, 1834; *United States Gazette*, Aug. 14, 1834; *Hazard's Register of Pennsylvania Volume XIV*, Aug. 23, 1834.

17. *Pennsylvanian*, Aug. 14, 1834; Runcie, "'Hunting the Nigs' in Philadelphia," 194, 197–198, 209; *Philadelphia Directory, 1835–1836*, lists John Cox as a tavern owner on the northeast corner of 6th and Small Streets. On early policing in Philadelphia, see Howard O. Sprogle, *The Philadelphia Police: Past and Present* (Philadelphia, 1887); US Bureau of the Census, "Table 6. Population of the 90 Urban Places: 1830," accessed July 17, 2020, https://www.census .gov/population/www/documentation/twps0027/tab06.txt.

18. *Pennsylvanian*, Aug. 15, 1834; *Workingman's Advocate*, Aug. 16, 1834.

19. *Pennsylvanian*, Aug. 15, 1834; *Workingman's Advocate*, Aug. 16, 1834; Matthew Hopper, *From Refuge to Strength: The Rise of the African American Church in Philadelphia* (Philadelphia: Preservation Alliance for Greater Philadelphia, 2015), 13; William T. Catto, *A semicentenary discourse, delivered in the First African Presbyterian church, Philadelphia, on the fourth Sabbath of May, 1857: with a history of the church from its first organization: including a brief notice of Rev. John Gloucester, its first pastor* (Philadelphia: Joseph M. Wilson, 1857), 110.

20. *Pennsylvanian*, Aug. 15, 1834; *Hazard's Register of Pennsylvania Volume XIV*, Aug. 23, 1834. Information for Fitzgerald and Nicholson came from the 1830 US Federal Census and *Philadelphia Directory*, 1833, 1835–1836. US Census Bureau, *1830 United States Federal Census, Ancestry.com*, accessed December 28, 2020 (hereafter "[*Census Year*] *United States Federal Census*").

21. *Pennsylvanian*, Aug. 15, 1834; Abdy, *Journal of a Residence and Tour*, 321, 325–328.

22. *Pennsylvanian*, Aug. 16, 1834; *Hazard's Register of Pennsylvania Volume XIV*, 9/1834, 202; Abdy estimated 5,000 served in the posse, while the *Pennsylvanian* noted that "several hundred men" comprised the anti-mob force. See Abdy, *Journal of a Residence and Tour*, 321, and *Philadelphia Gazette*, Aug. 15, 1834; Pennsylvania Abolition Society Series 1.14 (hereafter "PAS 1.14") General Meeting Reports, 1788–1847, & undated materials, 379–380 [undated materials], HSP.

23. *Pennsylvanian*, Aug. 16, 1834; *Philadelphia Gazette*, Aug. 15, 1834; *Hazard's Register of Pennsylvania Volume XIV*, 9/1834, 202.

24. *Pennsylvanian*, Aug. 16, 1834; Abdy, *Journal of a Residence and Tour*, 321; PAS 1.14, 379–380 [undated materials].

25. Abdy, *Journal of a Residence and Tour*, 324–325; PAS 1.14, 379–380 [undated materials]; *Hazard's Register of Pennsylvania Volume XIV*, 9/1834, 202; J. Thomas Scharff and Thompson Westcott, *History of Philadelphia, 1609–1884* (Philadelphia: L. H. Everts & Co., 1884), 638.

26. *Hazard's Register of Pennsylvania Volume XIV*, 9/1834, 200–203. Thomas Shipley attended the initial meeting, which called for a committee on September 3, 1834. According to the *Liberator*, his voice and concerns were shouted down by the other attendees. See *Liberator*, Sept. 13, 1834; Ignatiev, *How the Irish Became White*, 144–161; Runcie, "'Hunting the Nigs' in Philadelphia," 197.

27. *Hazard's Register of Pennsylvania Volume XIV*, 9/1834, 201; Abdy, *Journal of a Residence and Tour*, 323, 329.

28. PAS 1.5, Nov. 15, 1834.

29. National Colored Convention, *Fifth Annual Convention for the Improvement of the Free People of Colour* (Philadelphia: William P. Gibbons, 1835), 17–19, 22–27. See also Diemer, *The Politics of Black Citizenship*, 94.

30. *Philadelphia Inquirer*, Jul. 10, 1835; *Liberator*, Sept. 19, 1835; *National Gazette*, June 23, 1835. Robert Aitken did not own any enslaved people in 1830, according to the 1830 census. *1830 United States Federal Census*.

31. *Philadelphia Inquirer*, July 10, 1835.

32. *Philadelphia Inquirer*, July 10, 1835.

33. *Philadelphia Inquirer*, July 10, 1835; Duke University Libraries, "'Ten Dollar Reward': advertisement written by Robert Aitken for the return of an 8 or 9 year old girl named Emily," John W. Williams papers, 1822–1835 and undated, accessed July 18, 2020, https://archives.lib .duke.edu/catalog/williamsjohnw_aspace_ref20_f74.

34. *National Gazette*, June 23, 1835; *Philadelphia Inquirer*, July 10, 1835; PAS 1.5, Jan. 14, 1836. Five people lived in the Gilmore household at the time of the 1830 census: two free African American males between the ages of 10 and 23, one free African American male (Jacob Gilmore), one free African American female (Gilmore's wife), and one free African American female between the ages of 10 and 23; this last person was in all likelihood Mary Gilmore; why the census taker recorded her as African American remains unclear, though again, it would not be beyond the scope of possibility that he assumed her to be African American, seeing as she lived in a house with other African Americans. *1830 United States Federal Census*.

35. *Baltimore Gazette and Daily Advertiser*, July 6, 1835; *United States Gazette*, June 18, 1835; *Liberator*, July 18, 1835. Numerous John Hills appeared in the 1835 *Philadelphia Directory*; all were white. It is possible that this John Hill worked as a distiller at 12th and Lombard. An

African American John Hill was listed as living in New Market ward in the 1840 United States Federal Census. *1840 United States Federal Census.*

36. *Philadelphia Inquirer,* June 24, 1835.

37. *Philadelphia Inquirer,* June 24, 1835; Mayor's Court Docket, 1835 (Record Group 130.1), Philadelphia City Archives; Index of Prisoners, 1835 (Record Group 38.37), Philadelphia City Archives.

38. *Philadelphia Inquirer,* July 11, 1835; *Liberator,* July 18, 1835.

39. *Philadelphia Inquirer,* July 10 and 11, 1835.

40. *Philadelphia Inquirer,* July 11, 1835.

41. *Philadelphia Inquirer,* July 11, 1835.

42. *Philadelphia Inquirer,* July 11, 1835.

43. *Liberator,* Apr. 14, 1832, and July 18, 1835.

44. *Liberator,* July 18, Aug. 22, and Sept. 10, 1835.

45. Philadelphia Anti-Slavery Society, *First Annual Report of the Board of Managers of the Philadelphia Anti-Slavery Society* (Philadelphia: Philadelphia Anti-Slavery Society, 1835), 9–11; Elizabeth Varon, *Disunion! The Coming of the American Civil War, 1789–1859* (Chapel Hill: University of North Carolina Press, 2008), 87–124.

46. Philadelphia Anti-Slavery Society, *Address of the Members of the Philadelphia Anti-Slavery Society to their Fellow Citizens* (Philadelphia: Board of Managers, 1835), 6, 12–14, 16–17.

47. Emma Jones Lapsansky-Werner agreed with the newspaper accounts of Juan's motives; see Lapsansky, " 'Since They Got Those Separate Churches,' " 76. See also Werner, *Reaping the Bloody Harvest,* 182–184; *Philadelphia Inquirer,* Jul. 14, 1835; *Hazard's Register of Pennsylvania Volume XVI,* 7/1835, 35. Stewart's grave memorialized the attack; see "Robert Ralston Stewart," last modified Apr. 26, 2007, http://www.findagrave.com/cgi-bin/fg.cgi?page=gr&GRid =19103598, and "Waterhouse Symbolism Newsletter, Issue 14, August 1, 2007," last modified 2007, http://freepages.history.rootsweb.ancestry.com/~waterhousesymbolism/newsletter /14.pdf.

48. *Hazard's Register of Pennsylvania Volume XVI,* 7/1835, 35; *Philadelphia Inquirer,* July 14, 1835; Stewart, "The Emergence of Racial Modernity"; Saxton, *The Rise and Fall of the White Republic.*

49. *Liberator,* July 25, 1835; Mayor's Court Minute Books, 1835 (Record Group 130.2), Philadelphia City Archives; Pennsylvania Abolition Society Series 4.2, Manumission Book G, 1792–1853, HSP; "A Guide to the Papers of the Pennsylvania Abolition Society," last modified 2015, http://www.slavery.amdigital.co.uk.libproxy.temple.edu/Essays/content/PASguide.aspx.

50. *Liberator,* July 25, 1835; *Philadelphia Gazette,* July 13, 1835; *Philadelphia Inquirer,* July 14 and 15, 1835; *Hazard's Register of Pennsylvania Volume XVI,* 7/1835, 36.

51. *Hazard's Register of Pennsylvania Volume XVI,* 7/1835, 36; *Philadelphia Inquirer,* July 16, 1835; Grimsted, *American Mobbing;* Saidiya V. Hartman, *Scenes of Subjection: Terror, Slavery, and Self-Making in Nineteenth-Century America* (New York: Oxford University Press, 1997), 82–86.

52. *Hazard's Register of Pennsylvania Volume XVI,* 7/1835, 36; *Atkinson's Saturday Evening Post,* July 18, 1835; *Philadelphia Inquirer,* July 16, 1835.

53. *Hazard's Register of Pennsylvania Volume XVI,* 7/1835, 37; *National Gazette,* July 18, 1835; *Philadelphia Inquirer,* July 16 and 28, 1835; *Liberator,* July 25, 1835.

54. Martin Heidegger, *Being and Time,* trans. Joan Stambaugh (Albany: State University of New York Press, 1996), 62–67.

55. George Edward Reed, ed., *Pennsylvania Archives: Fourth Series, Volume VI* (Harrisburg: Wm. Stanley Ray, State Printer, 1901), 241–242; Charles M. Snyder, *The Jacksonian Heritage: Pennsylvania Politics, 1833–1848* (Harrisburg: Pennsylvania Historical and Museum Commission, 1958), 61.

56. On the Great Postal Campaign, see Bertram Wyatt-Brown, "The Abolitionists' Postal Campaign of 1835," *Journal of Negro History* 50 (Oct. 1965): 227–238; James Stewart, *The Holy Warriors: The Abolitionists and American Slavery* (New York: Hill and Wang, 1976), and Susan Wyly-Jones, "The 1835 Anti-Abolition Meetings in the South: A New Look at the Controversy over the Abolition Postal Campaign," *Civil War History* 47, no. 4 (2001): 289–309; *Philadelphia Inquirer*, Jul. 21, 29, Aug. 4, 7, and 15, 1835; *Philadelphia Gazette*, Aug. 8, 1835, via *Connecticut Courant*, Aug. 17, 1835; *Richmond Enquirer*, July 24, 1835; *Southern Patriot*, July 29 and Aug. 1, 1835.

57. *Philadelphia Inquirer*, Aug. 14 and 15, 1835; *New Bedford Mercury*, Aug. 28, 1835.

58. *Philadelphia Inquirer*, Aug. 19, 1835.

59. "(1836) James Forten, Jr. 'Put on the Armour of Righteousness,'" last modified 2015, http://www.Blackpast.org/1836-james-forten-jr-put-armour-righteousness; Pennsylvania Abolition Society Series 5.40, Miscellaneous, Young Men's Anti-Slavery Society; Winch, *Philadelphia's Black Elite*, 174–177; Pennsylvania Abolition Society, *Centennial Anniversary of the Pennsylvania Society*; *Philadelphia Directory*, 1835–1836; *Emancipator*, May 26, 1835; *Philadelphia Inquirer*, Aug. 19, 1835; Erica Armstrong Dunbar, *A Fragile Freedom: African American Women and Emancipation in the Antebellum City* (New Haven, CT: Yale University Press, 2008), 82–85.

60. *Philadelphia Inquirer*, Aug. 21, 24, 25, and Sept. 11, 1835.

61. On the Orr family, see Paul R. Begley, "James Lawrence Orr," *South Carolina Encyclopedia*, accessed July 19, 2020, http://www.scencyclopedia.org/sce/entries/orr-james-lawrence/; *1830 United States Federal Census*. Interestingly enough, Morton McMichael worked at the law office of David Paul Brown; see Robert L. Bloom, Morton McMichael's "North American," *Pennsylvania Magazine of History and Biography* 77, no. 2 (Apr. 1953): 164–180. Robert Conrad wore many hats besides that of a newspaper editor and politician; see Henry Simpson, *Lives of Eminent Philadelphians, Now Deceased* (Philadelphia: William Brotherhead, 1859), 246–247, and Philadelphia Repeal Association, *Oration delivered by the Hon. Robert T. Conrad, at the celebration of the anniversary of American independence by the Philadelphia Repeal Association, at the Arch Street Theatre, July 5, 1841* (Philadelphia: Charles Alexander, 1841); Snyder, *The Jacksonian Heritage*, 58, 86; *Philadelphia Inquirer*, Aug. 25, 1835; *Philadelphia Directory*, 1835–1936; Saxton, *The Rise and Fall of the White Republic*. Steven Deyle outlined the question of being "soft" on the slavery question in the South, which I suggest permeated Northerners' impressions of how best to display their loyalty to Southern slaveholders. See Steven Deyle, "An 'Abominable' New Trade: The Closing of the African Slave Trade and the Changing Patterns of U.S. Political Power, 1808–60," *William and Mary Quarterly* 66, no. 4 (Oct. 2009): 833–850.

62. *Philadelphia Inquirer*, Aug. 25, 1835.

63. *Hazard's Register of Pennsylvania Volume XVI*, 163–165; *Philadelphia Inquirer*, Aug. 25, 1835; David Paul Brown, *Eulogium on Joseph Reed Ingersoll* (Philadelphia: Collins, 1869), 10. On the portents of disunion, see Varon, *Disunion!*

64. *Hazard's Register of Pennsylvania Volume XVI*, 163–165. On this "friend-enemy" distinction, I am alluding to Carl Schmitt's notion of the friend-enemy antithesis. See Carl Schmitt, *The Concept of the Political* (Chicago: University of Chicago Press, 2007), 25–27.

65. *Philadelphia Inquirer*, Aug. 25, 1835.

66. *Boston Courier*, Aug. 31, 1835; *Philadelphia Inquirer*, Aug. 26, 1835; Louis Filler, *The Crusade against Slavery, 1830–1860* (Harper's: New York, 1960), 98.

67. *Emancipator*, May 26, 1835; Richard S. Newman, *The Transformation of American Abolitionism: Fighting Slavery in the Early Republic* (Chapel Hill: University of North Carolina Press, 2002), 84–85, 106; *National Enquirer*, Nov. 12, 1836. Scott also served as a delegate to the

American convention; see Pennsylvania Abolition Society, *Centennial Anniversary of the Pennsylvania Society*, 65.

68. *Philadelphia Inquirer*, Aug. 26, 1835.

Chapter 5 · A Theatre of Scenes

1. Samuel Webb, *History of Pennsylvania Hall, which was Destroyed by a Mob, on the 17th of May, 1838* (Philadelphia: Merrihew and Gunn, 1838), 27–29; *Concord Gazette*, Mar. 15, 1808; *Poulson's American Daily Advertiser*, Feb. 22, 1808. On Pennsylvania Hall generally, see Beverly C. Tomek, *Pennsylvania Hall: A "Legal Lynching" in the Shadow of the Liberty Bell* (New York: Oxford University Press, 2014); Ira V. Brown, "Racism and Sexism: The Case of Pennsylvania Hall," *Phylon, the Atlanta University Review of Race and Culture* 37, no. 2 (Jun. 1976): 126–136.

2. Carl E. Prince, "The Great 'Riot Year': Jacksonian Democracy and Patterns of Violence in 1834," *Journal of the Early Republic* 5, no. 1 (Spring 1985): 1–19; Elizabeth M. Geffen, "Industrial Development and Social Crisis, 1841–1854," in Russell F. Weigley, ed., *Philadelphia: A 300 Year History* (New York: Norton, 1982), 307–363; Alexander Saxton, *The Rise and Fall of the White Republic: Class Politics and Mass Culture in Nineteenth Century America* (New York: Verso, 1990); Eric Lott, *Love and Theft: Blackface Minstrelsy and the American Working Class* (New York: Oxford University Press, 1993); James Brewer Stewart, "The Emergence of Racial Modernity and the Rise of the White North, 1790–1840," *Journal of the Early Republic* 18, no. 2 (Summer 1998): 181–217.

3. Noel Ignatiev, *How the Irish Became White* (New York: Routledge, 1995), 88–91; Russell F. Weigley, ed., *Philadelphia: A 300 Year History* (New York: Norton, 1982), 275–281; Lawrence Kohl, *The Politics of Individualism: Parties and the American Character during the Jacksonian Era* (New York: Oxford University Press, 1989), esp. chapters 1–3. See also, Charles G. Sellers, *The Market Revolution: Jacksonian America, 1815–1846* (New York: Oxford University Press, 1991).

4. Charles M. Snyder, *The Jacksonian Heritage: Pennsylvania Politics, 1833–1848* (Harrisburg: Pennsylvania Historical and Museum Commission, 1958), 68–95.

5. On whiteness and racism, see Ignatiev, *How the Irish Became White*, and Saxton, *The Rise and Fall of the White Republic*; Pennsylvania Abolition Society [PAS], *The present state and condition of the free people of color, of the city of Philadelphia and adjoining districts, as exhibited by the report of a committee of the Pennsylvania society for promoting the abolition of slavery, &c. Read first month (Jan.) 5th, 1838* (Philadelphia: Merrihew and Gunn, 1838), 10–12, 21; PAS, *A Statistical Inquiry into the Condition of the People of Colour of the City and Districts of Philadelphia* (Philadelphia: Kite and Walton, 1849), 34–36.

6. PAS, *Centennial Anniversary of the Pennsylvania Society for Promoting the Abolition of Slavery* (Philadelphia: Grants, Faires & Rodgers, Printers, 1875), 11, 61; Wayne J. Eberly, *The Pennsylvania Abolition Society, 1775–1830* (University Park: Pennsylvania State University, 1973), 227–228. A cursory look at the Acting Committee records yields plenty of examples of Shipley's successes (and failures) as a member of that body. See, for example, PAS 1.5, Jan. 10, 1816, Sept. 8, 1818, Sept. 5, 1820, June 23, 1822, Jan. 18, 1826, Jun. 23, 1826, Nov. 15, 1834, Mar. 29, 1839; Richard S. Newman, *The Transformation of American Abolitionism: Fighting Slavery in the Early Republic* (Chapel Hill: University of North Carolina Press, 2002), 84, 116, 119. On Shipley's relationship with Samuel Scomp, see chapter 3 of this book.

7. Isaac Parrish, *Brief Memoirs of Thomas Shipley and Edwin P. Atlee, Read Before the Pennsylvania Society for Promoting the Abolition of Slavery* (Philadelphia: Merrihew and Gunn, 1838), 26–27; *National Enquirer*, Oct. 15, 1836; Robert Purvis, *A Tribute to the Memory of Thomas Shipley, The Philanthropist* (Philadelphia: Merrihew and Gunn, 1836), 8, 16–17.

8. Purvis, *Tribute to the Memory of Thomas Shipley*, 8, 16–17. See also *Liberator*, Sept. 24, Oct. 10, 15, 24, 1836.

9. Purvis, *Tribute to the Memory of Thomas Shipley*, 6; Margaret Hope Bacon, *But One Race: The Life of Robert Purvis* (Albany: State University of New York, 2007), 75; Christopher James Bonner, *Remaking the Republic: Black Politics and the Creation of American Citizenship* (Philadelphia: University of Pennsylvania Press, 2020), 108.

10. On the case of Thomas Dorsey, see PAS 1.5, Aug. 24, 1838; Robert C. Smedley, *History of the Underground Railroad in Chester and the Neighboring Counties of Pennsylvania* (Lancaster: John A. Hiestand, 1883), 352–358; Bacon, *But One Race*, 76; Richard Bell, "Counterfeit Kin; Kidnappers of Color, the Reverse Underground Railroad, and the Origins of Practical Abolition," *Journal of the Early Republic* 38 (Summer 2018): 199–230.

11. Smedley, *History of the Underground Railroad*, 352–358.

12. Smedley, 352–358.

13. Smedley, 358–359.

14. Smedley, 359–361; Bell, "Counterfeit Kin."

15. Smedley, 359–361; *National Enquirer*, Jul. 27, Aug. 3, 8, 10, 17, 1837; *Colored American*, Sept. 2, 1837.

16. *Pennsylvania Freeman*, Nov. 12, Dec. 3, 17, 24, 31, 1836; Pennsylvania Abolition Society Series 1.2 (hereafter "PAS 1.2"), General Meeting Minute Book, Volume 3, 1825–1847, Jan. 5, 1837. See also Pennsylvania Abolition Society Series 5.40, Miscellaneous, Young Men's Anti-Slavery Society.

17. Kathleen Smith Kutolowski, "Antimasonry Reexamined: Social Bases of the Grass-Roots Party," *Journal of American History* 71 (Sept. 1984): 269–293; William Preston Vaughn, *The Antimasonic Party in the United States, 1826–1843* (Lexington: University Press of Kentucky, 1983); Snyder, *The Jacksonian Heritage*, 66–81; Michael Holt, *The Rise and Fall of the American Whig Party* (New York: Oxford University Press, 1999), 54, 97–98; "Governor Joseph Ritner," accessed Jul 1, 2016, http://www.phmc.state.pa.us/portal/communities/governors/1790 -1876/joseph-ritner.html.

18. *Pennsylvania Inquirer*, Dec. 10, 1836. As I wrote in chapter 4, Philadelphians witnessed a preemptive gag rule during the late riots of 1835, when a crowd dumped thousands of abolitionist tracts into the Delaware River.

19. *Pennsylvania Freeman*, Jan. 14, 1837; PAS 1.2, Dec. 16, 1836; "John Greenleaf Whittier (1807–1892). The Poetical Works in Four Volumes. 1892," accessed Jul. 1, 2016, http://www .bartleby.com/372/242.html.

20. *Niles Weekly Register*, Mar. 18, 1837; below are the Philadelphia state senators who voted to reject jury trials for fugitives. (District, name, party, term expiration, vote)

— 1 Philadelphia City, Miller, Abraham Dem 1839—Reject
— 1 Philadelphia City, Toland, George W. Dem 1838—Reject
— 2 Philadelphia, Baker, George N. Dem 1837—Reject
— 2 Philadelphia, Burden, Jesse R. Dem 1838—Reject
— 2 Philadelphia, Peltz, Alexander M. Dem 1840—Absent
— "Tri-Partisan" support to grant a jury trial to fugitives from slavery:
— 21 Allegheny, Darragh, Cornelius AM 1839
— 25 Beaver, Butler Dickey, John Dem 1837
— 8 Dauphin, Lebanon Harper, John AM 1838
— 4 Chester, Delaware James, Francis Dem 1838
— 14 York, Adams McConkey, James AM 1839
— 14 York, Adams Middlecoff, David Whig 1837
— 3 Montgomery, Paul, James Dem 1839

— 16 Cumberland, Perry Penrose, Charles B. Whig 1837
— 7 Lancaster, Strohm, John AM 1838
— 23 Crawford, Erie, Mercer, Cunningham, Thomas S. Dem 1837

See Wilkes University, "The Wilkes University Election Statistics Project," accessed Jul. 1, 2016, http://staffweb.wilkes.edu/harold.cox/legis/61S.pdf; James C. Scott, *Domination and the Arts of Resistance: Hidden Transcripts* (New Haven, CT: Yale University Press, 1990), 37.

21. Snyder, *The Jacksonian Heritage*, 96–111.

22. Julie Winch, *A Gentleman of Color: The Life of James Forten* (New York: Oxford University Press, 2002), 293; Sarah L. H. Gronningsater, "'Expressly Recognized by Our Election Laws': Certificates of Freedom and the Multiple Fates of Black Citizenship in the Early Republic," *William and Mary Quarterly* 75, no. 3 (July 2018): 468–471, 497; Ira Berlin, "Slavery, Freedom, and Philadelphia's Struggle for Brotherly Love," in *Antislavery and Abolition in Philadelphia: Emancipation and the Long Struggle for Racial Justice in the City of Brotherly Love*, Richard Newman and James Mueller, eds. (Baton Rouge: Louisiana State University Press, 2011), 19–44, quotation on 31.

23. Van Gosse, *The First Reconstruction: Black Politics in America from the Revolution to the Civil War* (Chapel Hill: University of North Carolina Press, 2021), 101–106. See also Nicholas Wood, "A Sacrifice on the Altar of Slavery: Doughface Politics and Black Disenfranchisement in Pennsylvania, 1837–1838," *Journal of the Early Republic* 31, no. 1 (Spring 2011): 75–106; Sarah N. Roth, "The Politics of the Page: Black Disfranchisement and the Image of the Savage Slave," *Pennsylvania Magazine of History and Biography* 134, no. 3 (Jul. 2010): 209–233; Christopher Malone, "Rethinking the End of Black Voting Rights in Antebellum Pennsylvania: Racial Ascriptivism, Partisanship and Political Development in the Keystone State," *Pennsylvania History* 72, no. 4 (Autumn 2005): 466–504; Eric Ledell-Smith, "The End of Black Voting Rights in Pennsylvania: African Americans and the Pennsylvania Constitutional Convention of 1837–1838," *Pennsylvania History* 65, no. 3 (Summer 1998): 279–299; Julie Winch, "Free Men and 'Freemen': Black Voting Rights in Pennsylvania, 1790–1870," *Suffrage in Pennsylvania, Pennsylvania Legacies* 8, no. 2 (2008): 14–19; Winch, *A Gentleman of Color*, 292–295; Andrew Diemer, *The Politics of Black Citizenship: Free African Americans in the Mid-Atlantic Borderland, 1817–1863* (Athens: University of Georgia Press, 2016), 49. See also Erica L. Ball, *To Live an Antislavery Life: Personal Politics and the Antebellum Black Middle Class* (Athens: University of Georgia Press, 2012).

24. *Colored American*, Jun. 10, 1837; Stephen Kantrowitz, *More than Freedom: Fighting for Black Citizenship in a White Republic, 1829–1889* (New York: Penguin, 2012), 13–40, esp. 24.

25. John Agg, ed., *Proceedings and Debates of the Convention of the Commonwealth of Pennsylvania to Propose Amendments to the Constitution, Commenced at Harrisburg, May 2, 1837* (14 vols., Harrisburg, PA, 1837–39), vol. 2, 199–202; James Bergquist, "Immigration (1790–1860)," *The Encyclopedia of Greater Philadelphia*, http://philadelphiaencyclopedia.org/archive/immigration-1790–1860/, accessed July 11, 2016; Ignatiev, *How the Irish Became White*, 45–46.

26. Agg, *Proceedings and Debates*, vol. 2, 199–202; John W. Jordan, *A History of the Juniata Valley and its People* (New York: Lewis Historical Publishing Company, 1913), 146; Biographical Dictionary of the United States Congress, "DARLINGTON, William, (1782–1863)," http://bioguide.congress.gov/scripts/biodisplay.pl?index=D000059, accessed July 11, 2016.

27. Agg, *Proceedings and Debates*, vol. 2, 472–479; 540–541; Wood, "A Sacrifice on the Altar of Slavery," 80, ft. 5, 83–84; J. H. Battle, *History of Bucks County, Pennsylvania: Including an Account of Its Original Exploration, Its Relation to the Settlements of New Jersey and Delaware, Its Erection Into a Separate County, Also Its Subsequent Growth and Development, with Sketches of Its Historic and Interesting Localities, and Biographies of Many of Its Representative*

Citizens (Philadelphia: A. Warner & Co., 1887), 261; Saxton, *Rise and Fall of the White Republic*, 148–149; Winch, *A Gentleman of Color*, 296; Ledell-Smith, "The End of Black Voting Rights in Pennsylvania," 288.

28. Agg, *Proceedings and Debates*, vol. 3, 82–84.

29. Wood, "A Sacrifice on the Altar of Slavery," 101–102, 103 ft. 35; *Emancipator*, Mar. 29, 1838. The Pennsylvania Supreme Court ruled on the case after the convention for political reasons, namely, so that the state legislature could rule on the issue of Black voting prior to the ruling, which disenfranchised Black Pennsylvanians prior to the vote to approve the state Constitution in October 1838.

30. Wood, "A Sacrifice on the Altar of Slavery," 89; Agg, *Proceedings and Debates*, vol. 5, 414–423.

31. Ledell-Smith, "The End of Black Voting Rights in Pennsylvania," 291–292; John Fox, *Opinion of the Hon. John Fox, against the exercise of Negro suffrage in Pennsylvania: also, the vote of the members of the Pennsylvania convention on the motion of Mr. Martin to insert the word "white" as one of the proposed amendments to the constitution* (Harrisburg: Packer, Barrett and Parke, 1838), 10–13.

32. Agg, *Proceedings and Debates*, vol. 9, 321–322.

33. Agg, *Proceedings and Debates*, vol. 9, 346–353, 365. Here I am alluding to the use of the word "disunion" as a threat, best argued in Elizabeth Varon, *Disunion! The Coming of the American Civil War, 1789–1859* (Chapel Hill: University of North Carolina Press, 2008), 1–17, and esp. chapters 3 and 4.

34. Malone, "Rethinking the End of Black Voting Rights in Antebellum Pennsylvania," 496; Agg, *Proceedings and Debates*, vol. 9, 346–353, 365.

35. Agg, *Proceedings and Debates*, vol. 10, 16–22, 79–81.

36. Agg, *Proceedings and Debates*, vol. 10, 40–44; W. W. Thomson, *Chester County and its People* (Chicago: The Union History Company, 1898), 550–553.

37. Gosse, *The First Reconstruction*, 139; Ledell-Smith, "The End of Black Voting Rights in Pennsylvania," 293–294; Agg, *Proceedings and Debates*, vol. 10, 106; *Pennsylvania Freeman*, Jan. 25, 1838; Julie Winch, ed., *The Elite of Our People: Joseph Willson's Sketches of Black Upper-Class Life in Antebellum Philadelphia* (University Park: Pennsylvania State University Press, 2000); 1837 *Philadelphia Directory*. All but three Democrats voted to disenfranchise; see Wood, "A Sacrifice on the Altar of Slavery," 101.

38. Robert Purvis, *Appeal of Forty Thousand Citizens, Threatened with Disenfranchisement, to the People of Pennsylvania* (Philadelphia: Merrihew and Gunn, 1838), 5–6, 16–17; Ledell-Smith, "The End of Black Voting Rights in Pennsylvania," 293.

39. On abolitionist rhetoric relating to empathy and winning the "hearts" of African Americans, see Ronald G. Walters, *The Antislavery Appeal: American Abolitionism after 1830* (New York: Norton, 1978); Stanley Harrold, *The Rise of Aggressive Abolitionism: Addresses to the Slaves* (Lexington: University of Kentucky Press, 2005), esp. chapter 2; Timothy Patrick McCarthy and John Stauffer, eds., *Prophets of Protest: Reconsidering the History of American Abolitionism* (New York: New Press, 2006), 220–234; John Stauffer, *The Black Hearts of Men: Radical Abolitionists and the Transformation of Race* (Cambridge, MA: Harvard University Press, 2002); Purvis, *Appeal of Forty Thousand Citizens*, 17–18; Thomas D. Morris, *Free Men All: The Personal Liberty Laws of the North, 1780–1861* (Baltimore, MD: Johns Hopkins University Press, 1974), 84–88; Agg, *Proceedings and Debates*, vol. 11, 252, 296–297; Julie Winch, *Philadelphia's Black Elite: Activism, Accommodation, and the Struggle for Autonomy, 1787–1848* (Philadelphia; Temple University Press, 1988), 137–138. Black Philadelphians lamented the death of James C. Biddle in 1838, even going so far as to call Biddle "a great and good man, the ornament of his profession" who supported the rights of an "oppressed and suffering class of the community." See *Pennsylvania Freeman*, Sept. 6, 1838.

40. Tomek, *Pennsylvania Hall*, ix–xiv, 69–70; Beverly Tomek, "Pennsylvania Hall," *The Encyclopedia of Greater Philadelphia*, https://philadelphiaencyclopedia.org/archive/pennsyl vania-hall/, accessed July 22, 2020. Webb, *History of Pennsylvania Hall*, 6; *Pennsylvania Anti-Slavery Society Minute Book, 1838–1846*; Erica Armstrong Dunbar, *A Fragile Freedom: African American Women and Emancipation in the Antebellum City* (New Haven, CT: Yale University Press, 2008), 70–95.

41. Diemer, *The Politics of Black Citizenship*, 102; Larry Tise, *Proslavery: A History of the Defense of Slavery in America, 1701–1840* (Athens: University of Georgia Press, 1987), 248–254 (quotation on 251); William Montgomery Meigs, *Life of Charles Jared Ingersoll* (Philadelphia: J. B. Lippincott Company, 1897), 252; Agg, *Proceedings and Debates*, vol. 11, 297; Webb, *History of Pennsylvania Hall*, 8; US Census Bureau, *1830* and *1840 United States Federal Census, Ancestry.com*, accessed December 28, 2020; Pennsylvania Historical & Museum Commission, "An Act for the Gradual Abolition of Slavery," accessed July 22, 2020, http://www.phmc.state.pa.us /portal/communities/documents/1776–1865/abolition-slavery.html; United States House of Representatives, *Abstract of the Returns of the Fifth Census* (Washington: Duff Green, 1832), 12–13.

42. Webb, *History of Pennsylvania Hall*, 13, 22–23, 33–34, 123–127.

43. Webb, 71–72, 75, 117–120.

44. Webb, 134–138; Brown, "Racism and Sexism," 130–131.

45. Webb, 137–140; "Pennsylvania Hall, Retrospective Newspaper Articles," Triptych Tri-College Digital Library, http://triptych.brynmawr.edu/cdm/ref/collection/HC_QuakSlav/id /4592; Tomek, "Pennsylvania Hall."

46. Webb, *History of Pennsylvania Hall*, 134–140; *Public Ledger*, May 18, 1838; "Pennsyl-vania Hall Association, Board of Managers Minutes," Triptych Tri-College Digital Library, http://triptych.brynmawr.edu/cdm/ref/collection/HC_QuakSlav/id/4223; Daniel R. Biddle and Murray Dubin, *Tasting Freedom: Octavius Catto and the Battle for Equality in Civil War America* (Philadelphia: Temple University Press, 2010), 53–56; Crystal Lynn Webster, *Beyond the Boundaries of Childhood: African American Children in the Antebellum North* (Chapel Hill: University of North Carolina Press, 2021), 58–61.

47. Webb, *History of Pennsylvania Hall*, 156; *Daily Picayune*, May 26, 1838; Biddle and Dubin, *Tasting Freedom*, 56; Bacon, *But One Race*, 71–72; *Macon Weekly Telegraph*, May 28, 1838.

48. "Daniel Neall Papers, 5–21–1838 Letter," Triptych Tri-College Digital Library, http:// triptych.brynmawr.edu/cdm/ref/collection/HC_QuakSlav/id/8814; Junior Anti-Slavery Society of Philadelphia Constitution and Preamble, 1836 and Minute Book, 1836–1846, Jun. 1 and 24, 1838; Deborah C. De Rosa, *Domestic Abolitionism and Juvenile Literature, 1830–1865* (Albany: SUNY Press, 2003), 112.

49. Joseph A. Boromé, Jacob C. White, Robert B. Ayres, and J. M. McKim, "The Vigilant Committee of Philadelphia," *Pennsylvania Magazine of History and Biography* 92, no. 3 (Jul. 1968): 323–326. Contemporaries used the terms "Vigilant Committee of Philadelphia" and "Philadelphia Vigilant Association" interchangeably; see Boromé et al., "The Vigilant Com-mittee of Philadelphia"; *Pennsylvania Freeman*, Jul. 5, 1838, Jul. 26, 1838, Dec. 27, 1838. For two examples of African Americans faking their "fugitive" status, see *Philadelphia Inquirer*, Nov. 18, 1831, and Jan. 15, 1848; Bacon, *But One Race*, 79–80; Vigilant Committee of Philadelphia Records, 1839–1844, 1–29.

50. Snyder, *The Jacksonian Heritage*, 128–131; *Richmond Enquirer*, Oct. 2, 1838; Diemer, *The Politics of Black Citizenship*, 103–104.

51. Snyder, *The Jacksonian Heritage*; Andrew Diemer, "Black Nativism: African American Politics, Nationalism, and Citizenship in Baltimore and Philadelphia, 1817–1863" (PhD diss., Temple University, 2011), 178–181; *Emancipator*, Oct. 4, 1838; Diemer, *The Politics of Black Citizenship*, 104.

52. Sarah L. H. Gronningsater, "'Expressly Recognized by Our Election Laws': Certificates of Freedom and the Multiple Fates of Black Citizenship in the Early Republic." *William and Mary Quarterly* 75, no. 3 (July 2018): 465–471, quotation on 467.

53. 1839 *Philadelphia Directory*; PAS 1.5, Mar. 29, 1838. On Hope Hull Slatter, see Bryan Prince, *One More River to Cross* (Toronto: Dundurn Natural Heritage, 2012); Ann Arbor District Library, "Slatter's Slave Prison—Baltimore—*Signal of Liberty*, January 5, 1842" accessed July 22, 2020, https://aadl.org/signalofliberty/SL_18420105-p1–09. See also Calvin Schermerhorn, *The Business of Slavery and the Rise of American Capitalism, 1815–1860* (New Haven, CT: Yale University Press, 2005), 124–168.

54. PAS 1.5, Mar. 29, 1838.

55. Case of Williams, Case No. 17,709 District Court, E.D. Pennsylvania 1839 U.S. Dist. LEXIS 3; 29 F. Cas. 1334; 1 Crabbe 243; 2 Law Rep. 104, LexisNexis Academic; Henry Simpson, *The Lives of Eminent Philadelphians, Now Deceased* (Philadelphia: William Brotherhead, 1859), 596–600; PAS 1.5, Mar. 29, 1838.

56. Case of Williams; PAS 1.5, Mar. 29, 1838.

57. Case of Williams; PAS 1.5, Mar. 29, 1838; "Ignatius Beck," accessed Jul. 1, 2016, https://southwarkhistory.org/2013/01/29/ignatius-beck/; "Ignatius Beck," accessed Jul. 1, 2016, https://bethelburyinggroundproject.com/2015/01/18/ignatius-beck-was-a-common-man-and-lies-buried-at-bethel-burying-ground/; Daniel E. Meaders, *Kidnappers in Philadelphia: Isaac Hopper's Tales of Oppression, 1780–1843* (Cherry Hill: Africana Homestead Legacy Publishers, 2009), 255–256.

58. Case of Williams; PAS 1.5, Mar. 29, 1838; *National Gazette*, Aug. 13, 1839; *Liberator*, Mar. 22, 1839.

59. Case of Williams; PAS 1.5, Mar. 29, 1838.

60. H. Robert Baker, *Prigg v. Pennsylvania: Slavery, the Supreme Court, and the Ambivalent Constitution* (Lawrence: University Press of Kansas, 2012), 108–109; Diemer, *The Politics of Black Citizenship*, 119–120; Morris, *Free Men All*, 94–106; *Niles Register*, Mar. 5, 1842.

61. *Niles Register*, May 25, 1839; Baker, *Prigg v. Pennsylvania*, 151; Paul Finkelman, "*Prigg v. Pennsylvania*: Understanding Justice Story's Proslavery Nationalism," *Journal of Supreme Court History* 22, no. 2 (Dec. 1997): 51–64; *Prigg v. Commonwealth of Pennsylvania* no. 32 (1842).

62. *Prigg v. Commonwealth of Pennsylvania* no. 32 (1842).

63. *Liberator*, Mar. 11, 18, 1842; Luther Rawson Marsh, *Writings and Speeches of Alvan Stewart on Slavery* (New York: A. B. Burdick, 1860), 387–389.

64. Philadelphia Female Anti-Slavery Society Minute Book, 1839–1844, Sept. 2, Oct. 11, 1841, Jun. 9, Sept. 8, 1842; Jean R. Soderlund, "Priorities and Power: The Philadelphia Anti-Slavery Society," in Jean Fagan Yellin and John C. Van Horne, eds., *The Abolitionist Sisterhood: Women's Political Culture in Antebellum America* (Ithaca, NY: Cornell University Press, 1994), 80–84; Erica Armstrong Dunbar, *A Fragile Freedom: African American Women and Emancipation in the Antebellum City* (New Haven, CT: Yale University Press, 2008), 70–91; Boromé et al., "The Vigilant Committee of Philadelphia," 325 ft. 17, 331–351; Vigilant Committee of Philadelphia Records, 1839–1844, 1–29.

65. Winch, *A Gentleman of Color*, 86–87, 122–124, 327, 331; *National Anti-Slavery Standard*, Apr. 21, 1842.

66. Stephen H. Gloucester, *A Discourse Delivered on the Occasion of the Death of Mr. James Forten, Sr. in the Second Presbyterian Church of Colour of the City of Philadelphia, April 17, 1842, before the Young Men of the Bible Association of said Church* (Philadelphia: I. Ashmead and Co., 1843), 10–13, 15, 17, 23, 27.

67. PAS 1.5, Jun. 9, 1842, whoever took the minutes for this meeting added other cases that

extended well into 1842; *Philadelphia Inquirer*, Jun. 3, 1842; *North American*, Jun. 2, 1842; *Public Ledger*, Jun. 2, 3, 1842; 1842 *Philadelphia Directory*.

68. Baker, *Prigg v. Pennsylvania*, 144–151.

69. PAS 1.5, Jun. 9, 28, Sept. 23, 1842.

70. PAS 1.5, Jun. 9, 28, Sept. 23, 1842.

71. PAS 1.5, Jun. 28, Sept. 23, 1842; *Emancipator and Free American*, Jun. 16, 1842.

72. PAS 1.5, Jun. 9, 1842; 1842 *Philadelphia Directory*.

73. *Emancipator and Free American*, Sept. 1, 1842; Jack Brubaker, "Stephen Smith, Early Black Leader, Subject of 'Rare' Portrait," *Intelligencer Journal*, Feb. 23, 2010.

74. Kellie Carter Jackson, *Force and Freedom: Black Abolitionists and the Politics of Violence* (Philadelphia: University of Pennsylvania Press, 2019), 15–47; *Philadelphia Inquirer*, Aug. 4, 1842; *North American*, Aug. 3, 1842; *Public Ledger*, Aug. 2, 4, 5, 1842; *Liberator*, Aug. 12, 1842; United States Constitution, Amendment I.

75. *Public Ledger*, Aug. 5, 1842.

76. *Liberator*, Aug. 12, 1842; *Philadelphia Inquirer*, Aug. 4, 5, 1842; 1842 *Philadelphia Directory*; Bacon, *But One Race*, 98–99; John M. Werner, *Reaping the Bloody Harvest: Race Riots in the United States during the Age of Jackson, 1824–1849* (New York: Garland, 1986), 204–209.

77. *Public Ledger*, Aug. 4, 8, 1842; *North American*, Aug. 11, 1842.

78. *Public Ledger*, Aug. 4, 8, 1842; *Pennsylvanian*, Aug. 6, 1842. The managers of Smith's Beneficial Hall and the Second Presbyterian Church were later awarded damages by the Pennsylvania Supreme Court; see Samuel Otter, *Philadelphia Stories: America's Literature of Race and Freedom* (New York: Oxford University Press, 2010), 135–136; Werner, *Reaping the Bloody Harvest*, 204–209.

79. Robert Purvis to Henry Clarke Wright, Aug. 22, 1842, C. Peter Ripley, ed., *Black Abolitionist Papers* (Chapel Hill: University of North Carolina Press, 1985), 3:389–390.

80. *Liberator*, Sept. 9, 1842.

Chapter 6 · Interlocking Opportunities

1. Pennsylvania Abolition Society 5.48 Pennsylvania Anti-Slavery Society Executive Committee minute book [hereafter "PAS 5.48"], Aug. 18, 1846.

2. *Public Ledger*, Oct. 20, 1842.

3. Senate of the Commonwealth of Pennsylvania, *Appendix to Volume II of the Journal of the Senate, Session 1836–1837* (Harrisburg: Emanuel Guyer, 1837), 194; US Census Bureau, *1840 United States Federal Census*, Ancestry.com, accessed December 28, 2020; *Public Ledger*, Oct. 20, 1842.

4. *Public Ledger*, Oct. 20, 21, 1842.

5. *Public Ledger*, Oct. 20, 1842.

6. *Public Ledger*, Oct. 20, 1842.

7. *Public Ledger*, Oct. 20, 1842; H. Robert Baker, *Prigg v. Pennsylvania: Slavery, the Supreme Court, and the Ambivalent Constitution* (Lawrence: University Press of Kansas, 2012), 135, 138–139; Richard Peters and Frederick C. Brightly, *Reports of Cases Argued and Adjudged in the Supreme Court of the United States, January Term 1842* (New York: The Banks Law Publishing Company, 1903), 599.

8. *Public Ledger*, Oct. 24, 1842; Baker, *Prigg v. Pennsylvania*, 77–79.

9. *Public Ledger*, Oct. 24, 1842.

10. *Public Ledger*, Oct. 25, 1842.

11. *Public Ledger*, Oct. 25, 1842.

12. *Public Ledger*, Oct. 25, 1842; *Emancipator*, Dec. 1 and 22, 1842.

13. *Public Ledger*, Oct. 25, 1842; *Emancipator*, Dec. 1 and 22, 1842. On slaveholders and

purchasers projecting their identities through slaves, see Walter Johnson, *Soul by Soul: Life Inside the Antebellum Slave Market* (Cambridge, MA: Harvard University Press, 1999), 135–161; Robert H. Gudmestad, *A Troublesome Commerce: The Transformation of the Interstate Slave Trade* (Baton Rouge: Louisiana State University Press, 2003), 169–202, esp. 190.

14. *Public Ledger*, Oct. 25, 1842; *Emancipator*, Dec. 1 and 22, 1842; "Trespass," 2016, in *Dictionary of Legal Terms: Definitions and Explanations for Non-Lawyers*, Steven H. Gifis, Hauppauge: Barron's Educational Series, http://search.credoreference.com/content/entry /barronsgkwm/trespass/0.

15. Richard Newman, *The Transformation of American Abolitionism: Fighting Slavery in the Early Republic* (Chapel Hill: University of North Carolina Press, 2002), 39–59; *National Anti-Slavery Standard*, Feb. 2, 1843; PAS Series 1.2 Minutes and Reports, General Meeting, Minutes 1825–1916 (hereafter "PAS 1.2"), Jan. 13 and 27, 1843; Thomas D. Morris, *Free Men All: The Personal Liberty Laws of the North, 1780–1861* (Baltimore, MD: Johns Hopkins University Press, 1974), 117, esp. ft. 50.

16. W. E. B. Du Bois, *The Philadelphia Negro: A Social Study* (Philadelphia: University of Pennsylvania Press, 1899), 36, 47; PAS 5.6, Benjamin C. Bacon and Charles Gardner, *Committee to Visit the Colored People: Census Facts Collected by Benjamin C. Bacon and Charles Gardner, 1838*; Ira V. Brown, "Miller McKim and Pennsylvania Abolitionism," *Pennsylvania History* 30, no. 1 (Jan. 1963): 55–72; Minute Book of the Vigilant Committee of Philadelphia 1839–1844, Dec. 28, 1843, Feb. 19, Mar. 11, 1844. The number of people assisted by the Vigilant Committee comes from Joseph A. Boromé, Jacob C. White, Robert B. Ayres, and J. M. McKim, "The Vigilant Committee of Philadelphia," *Pennsylvania Magazine of History and Biography* 92, no. 3 (Jul. 1968). The committee handled two cases per week in the spring of 1841; that number rose to about three cases per week that fall; over 160 cases transpired between January and September 1842. Robert Purvis recollected that the committee assisted about one fugitive from slavery each day between 1837 and 1852, though as Boromé pointed out, Purvis's age (85) at the time of these recollections and the lack of a paper trail may have distorted these numbers. See Boromé, "The Vigilant Committee," 325 ft. 17.

17. Recently Van Gosse wrote of the long-term failure of the Vigilant Committee but did not consider how that group inspired the success of the Underground Railroad; see Van Gosse, *The First Reconstruction: Black Politics in America from the Revolution to the Civil War* (Chapel Hill: University of North Carolina Press, 2021), 142–144; William J. Switala, *Underground Railroad in Pennsylvania* (Mechanicsburg, PA: Stackpole Books, 2001), 11–28, 141–152; *National Anti-Slavery Standard*, Feb. 2, 1843; *Liberator*, May 19, 1843; William C. Kashatus, *William Still: The Underground Railroad and the Angel at Philadelphia* (Notre Dame: University of Notre Dame Press, 2021), 56–61.

18. PAS 5.48, Aug. 14, 1843.

19. PAS 5.48, Aug. 14, 1843; Boromé et al., "The Vigilant Committee," 327–328. Boromé noted that the revamped Philadelphia Vigilant Committee paled in comparison to the original committee as well as the 1852 reorganization due to the 1842 riot, the removal of Purvis to Byberry, and feuds within Philadelphia's elite Black community that "crippled" the chances of statewide cooperation. While these three stumbling blocks played a role in the relative inefficacy of the Philadelphia Vigilant Committee from 1843 to 1848, perhaps the group's apparent ineffectiveness derived from the paucity of historical records concerning the Acting Committee of the PAS (no minutes survive from after 1842), the PASS (rarely mentioned the vigilant committee in its records from 1836 to 1848), and the records of the Philadelphia Vigilant Committee itself, of which none exist after 1844. It is significant to note that the PASS heaped praise on the Philadelphia Vigilant Committee at its annual meetings in 1841, 1843, and 1844. See PAS 5.48, May 6, 1841, and Aug. 12, 1844; Julie Winch, ed., *The Elite of Our*

People: *Joseph Willson's Sketches of Black Upper-Class Life in Antebellum Philadelphia* (University Park: Pennsylvania State University Press, 2000), 90–97, 102–110.

20. Andrew Heath "Philadelphia County, Pennsylvania," *The Encyclopedia of Greater Philadelphia*, accessed July 26, 2020, https://philadelphiaencyclopedia.org/archive/philadelphia-county-pennsylvania/.

21. Elizabeth M. Geffen, "Industrial Development and Social Crisis, 1841–1854," in Russell F. Weigley, ed., *Philadelphia: A 300 Year History* (New York: Norton, 1982), 307–363, esp. 307–309; Noel Ignatiev, *How the Irish Became White* (New York: Routledge, 1995), 45–46, 173; Alexander Saxton, *The Rise and Fall of the White Republic: Class Politics and Mass Culture in Nineteenth Century America* (New York: Verso, 1990), 148–149.

22. Michael Feldberg, "The Crowd in Philadelphia History," *Labor History* 15, no. 3 (Summer 1974): 334; David Montgomery, "The Shuttle and the Cross: Weavers and Artisans in the Kensington Riots of 1844," *Journal of Social History* 5, no. 4 (Jul. 1972): 411–446; Sam Bass Warner, *The Private City: Philadelphia in Three Periods of Growth* (Philadelphia: University of Pennsylvania Press, 1987), 141–144. See also Michael Feldberg, *The Philadelphia Riots of 1844: A Study of Ethnic Conflict* (Westport, CT: Greenwood Press, 1975). It is worthy to note that one of the most cited books on Philadelphia history was written by two well-known Nativists, J. Thomas Scharff and Thompson Westcott. See their *History of Philadelphia, 1609–1884* (Philadelphia: L. H. Everts and Company, 1884), 663–668; Ignatiev, *How the Irish Became White*, 48, 144–168; *North American*, Jun. 4 and 8, 1844.

23. *Liberator*, May 17, Jul. 12 and 19, 1844; *Public Ledger*, Jul. 6–9, 1844; Ignatiev, *How the Irish Became White*, 174–176.

24. Ignatiev, *How the Irish Became White*, 99, 176–177; Andrew K. Diemer, "Black Nativism: African American Politics, Nationalism and Citizenship in Baltimore and Philadelphia, 1817 to 1863" (PhD diss., Temple University, 2011); ProQuest [AAT 91516], 229–232; Norm Cohen, *American Folk Songs: A Regional Encyclopedia, Volume 1* (Westport, CT: Greenwood Press, 2008), 144–148; Edward Needles, *A Statistical Inquiry into the Condition of the People of Colour, of the City and Districts of Philadelphia* (Philadelphia: Kite and Walton, 1849), 10–11; Theodore Hershberg, "Free Blacks in Antebellum Philadelphia: A Study of Ex-Slaves, Freeborn, and Socioeconomic Decline," *Journal of Social History* 5, no. 2 (Dec. 1971): 192–193.

25. Sidney George Fisher, *Philadelphia Perspective: The Civil War Diary of Sidney George Fisher* (Bronx: Fordham University Press, 2007), 4.

26. PASS 5.48, Aug. 12, 1844; Joel H. Silbey, *Storm over Texas: The Annexation Controversy and the Road to Civil War* (New York: Oxford University Press, 2005), 25–26.

27. "Martin Van Buren to William Henry Hammet, 20 April 1844," The Papers of Martin Van Buren, 1782–1862, accessed July 27, 2020, http://vanburenpapers.org/document-mvb03868; The Wilkes University Election Statistics Project, "Pennsylvania Election Statistics: 1682–2004," http://staffweb.wilkes.edu/harold.cox/legis/68S.pdf and http://staffweb.wilkes.edu/harold.cox/legis/68H.pdf; Silbey, *Storm over Texas*, 52–79; Charles McCool Snyder, *The Jacksonian Heritage: Pennsylvania Politics, 1833–1848* (Harrisburg: Pennsylvania Historical and Museum Commission, 1958), 183; Philip S. Klein and Ari Hoogenboom, *A History of Pennsylvania* (University Park: Pennsylvania State University Press, 1980), 154–156, 176; *North American*, May 31, 1844; *Liberator*, Jun. 14 and 28, Aug. 31, 1844; PASS 5.48, Aug. 12, 1844.

28. *North American*, May 31, 1844; *Liberator*, Jun. 14 and 28, Aug. 31, 1844; PASS 5.48, Aug. 12, 1844.

29. *Liberator*, Jun. 14 and 28, Aug. 31, 1844; PASS 5.48, Aug. 12, 1844; Snyder, *The Jacksonian Heritage*, 182–186.

30. *Liberator*, Nov. 8, 15, and 29, 1844; *Palladium of Liberty*, Jun. 12, 1844; *North American*, Jan. 11, 1845.

31. *Palladium of Liberty*, Jun. 12, 1844; Elizabeth Varon, *Disunion! The Coming of the American Civil War, 1789–1859* (Chapel Hill: University of North Carolina Press, 2008), 152–154; *Liberator*, May 20 and Jul. 26, 1844. On Garrison's political education, see Henry Mayer, *All on Fire: William Lloyd Garrison and the Abolition of Slavery* (New York: St. Martin's Press, 1998), esp. chapters 15 and 16.

32. PASS 5.48, Aug. 12, 1844.

33. *Public Ledger*, Jan. 28, 1845. The case of Hawkins was also reported on by the *North American*, Jan. 27, 1845, and *Liberator*, Feb. 14, 1845. The *Boston Courier* entitled its brief article on Hawkins "Negro Hunting"; see *Boston Courier*, Jan. 30, 1845. For more on Thomas Finnegan, see Meghan Linsley Bishop, "Slave to Freewoman and Back Again: Kitty Payne and Antebellum Kidnapping" (MA thesis, Indiana University, 2007). For more on Nathaniel B. Eldred, see *Harrisburg Telegraph*, Aug. 16, 1884.

34. *Philadelphia Inquirer*, Feb. 10, 1845; William Henry Egle, *History of the Counties of Dauphin and Lebanon, in the Commonwealth of Pennsylvania: Biographical and Geographical* (Philadelphia: Everts and Peck, 1883), 514.

35. Thomas Cushing, *A Genealogical and Biographical History of Allegheny County, Pennsylvania* (Baltimore: Clearfield Company, 2007), 553; *New Hampshire Sentinel*, Feb. 5, 1845; *Public Ledger*, Feb. 10, 12, and 2, 1845. Morris and Turner enumerate the attempts to modify *Prigg* in Morris, *Free Men All*, 117 ft. 51, and Edward Raymond Turner, *The Negro in Pennsylvania: Slavery, Servitude, Freedom, 1639–1861* (New York: Negro University Press, 1969), 238 ft. 49.

36. *Philadelphia Inquirer*, Feb. 10, 1845.

37. PAS 5.48, Aug. 11, 1845.

38. PAS 5.48, Aug. 11–13, 1845. On the rise of the slave power, see Leonard Richards, *The Slave Power: The Free North and Southern Domination, 1780–1860* (Baton Rouge: Louisiana State University Press, 2000).

39. PAS 5.48, Aug. 11–13, 1845; Edwin Bronner, *Thomas Earle as a Reformer* (Philadelphia: International Printing Company, 1948), 26–29, 40–41.

40. PAS 5.48, Aug. 13, 1845.

41. PAS 5.48, Aug. 13, 18, 1845; Paul Finkelman, "Story Telling on the Supreme Court: Prigg v Pennsylvania and Justice Joseph Story's Judicial Nationalism," *Supreme Court Review* 1994 (1994): 247–294.

42. The Pennsylvania state legislature passed a minor bill in 1827 to "prevent certain abuses of the laws" that encouraged the kidnapping of free African Americans. See Gettysburg College, "Pennsylvania Legislation Relating to Slavery," accessed August 4, 2021, https://cupola.gettysburg.edu/ach/vo19/iss1/8. On street diplomacy elsewhere in the United States, see, for example, the trial of George Latimer in Boston, which influenced the Massachusetts Liberty Law of 1843 that withdrew the state "entirely from the process of reclaiming" fugitives from slavery. See Newman, *The Transformation of American Abolitionism*, 131–151; *Boston Atlas*, Nov. 11, 1842; Scott Gac, "Slave or Free? White or Black? The Representation of George Latimer," *New England Quarterly* 88, no. 1 (March 2015): 73–103; *Liberator*, Oct. 28, Nov. 4 and 11, 1842; Queens Borough Public Library, "The George Latimer Case: A Benchmark in the Struggle for Freedom," accessed July 8, 2020, http://edison.rutgers.edu/latimer/glatcase.htm; Morris, *Free Men All*, 114–115; Marion Gleason McDougall, *Fugitive Slaves, 1619–1865* (New York: Berman Publishers, 1969), 67–68.

43. Morris, *Free Men All*, 118 ft. 56. Petitioning efforts by abolitionists in south central Pennsylvania no doubt contributed to the 1847 law; see David G. Smith, *On the Edge of Freedom: The Fugitive Slave Issue in South Central Pennsylvania, 1820–1870* (New York: Fordham University Press, 2013), 86–87, 105; Snyder, *The Jacksonian Heritage*, 195.

44. PAS, 1.2, Jan. 22 and Jun. 25, 1846; *Pennsylvania Freeman*, Jan. 29, 1846.

45. PAS 1.2, Jun. 25, 1846; Solomon W. Roberts, "Obituary Notice of Charles B. Trego," *Proceedings of the American Philosophical Society* 14, no. 94 (Jan.–Jun. 1875): 356–358; Bryan Prince, *One More River to Cross* (Toronto: Dundurn Natural Heritage, 2012), 47; *Public Ledger*, Aug. 15, 1884; John Russell Young, *Men and Memories: Personal Reminiscences* (New York: F. T. Neely, 1901), 44.

46. PAS 1.2, Jun. 25, 1846.

47. PAS 1.2, Jun. 25, 1846.

48. Snyder, *The Jacksonian Heritage*, 195; Klein and Hoogenboom, *A History of Pennsylvania*, 156–157; Charles G. Sellers, *The Market Revolution: Jacksonian America, 1815–1846* (New York: Oxford University Press, 1991), 415, 425–426.

49. Snyder, *The Jacksonian Heritage*, 195.

50. Klein and Hoogenboom, *A History of Pennsylvania*, 157; *North American*, Jun. 29 and Jul. 10, 1846.

51. *Philadelphia Inquirer*, Jul. 11, 1846.

52. James P. Shenton, *Robert John Walker: A Politician from Jackson to Lincoln* (New York: Columbia University Press, 1961), 85; John K. Kane et al., *Life of George Mifflin Dallas: Vice President of the United States* (Philadelphia: Times and Keystone, 1847), 15–16; *Philadelphia Inquirer*, Jul. 30, 1846; *North American*, Aug. 8, 1846.

53. See Michel Holt, *The Rise and Fall of the American Whig Party: Jacksonian Politics and the Onset of the Civil War* (New York: Oxford University Press, 1999), 248–257, and Henry R. Mueller, *The Whig Party in Pennsylvania* (New York: Columbia University, 1922); PAS 5.48, Aug. 5–7, 1846, Sept. 1, 1846. The PAS sent a similar set of petitions to the state legislature and national Congress. See PAS 1.2, Jul. 9, 1846.

54. Varon, *Disunion!*, 1–16.

55. James H. Duff, "David Wilmot, the Statesman and Political leader," *Pennsylvania History: A Journal of Mid-Atlantic Studies* 13, no. 4 (Oct. 1946): 283–289; Klein and Hoogenboom, *A History of Pennsylvania*, 157; James McPherson, *Battle Cry of Freedom: The Civil War Era* (New York: Oxford University Press, 1988), 52–60, esp. 52–53; Varon, *Disunion!* 182–184.

56. *Pennsylvania Freeman*, Nov. 19, 1846; *North American*, Nov. 18, 1846.

57. *North American*, Oct. 12, 1846; *Pottsville Miners' Journal*, Oct. 3, 1846, quoted in Snyder, *The Jacksonian Heritage*, 197 ft. 39.

58. *North American*, Oct. 12, 1846. It is interesting to point out that erstwhile PAS acting committee stalwart, now Alderman George Griscom, represented the 2nd voting district at the Whig meeting; *Pennsylvania Freeman*, Oct. 8, 1846.

59. The Wilkes University Election Statistics Project, "Pennsylvania Election Statistics: 1682–2004," http://staffweb.wilkes.edu/harold.cox/legis/indexlegis.html; Snyder, *The Jacksonian Heritage*, 197; *North American*, Oct. 26–27, 1846; *Pennsylvania Freeman*, Oct. 22, 1846.

60. PAS 5.48, Jan. 26 and Mar. 15, 1847; *Baltimore Sun*, Jan. 1, 1847; Morris, *Free Men All*, 118; *North American*, Oct. 26, 1846. Gosse, *The First Reconstruction*, 146–147.

61. Smith, *On the Edge of Freedom*, 100–102; Mueller, *The Whig Party in Pennsylvania*, 133–135.

62. *North American*, Feb. 8, 1847; Morris, *Free Men All*, 118–119.

63. *North American*, Feb. 8, 1847; Morris, *Free Men All*, 118–119; Andrew K. Diemer, *The Politics of Black Citizenship: Free African Americans in the Mid-Atlantic Borderland, 1817–1863* (Athens: University of Georgia Press, 2016), 138–139. The either/or model of "slave societies" or "societies with slaves" stemming from Moses Finley's original definition of slave societies and continuing through the magisterial works of Ira Berlin—both scholars whose scholarship continues to inspire countless thinkers, including myself—snares historians with a subtle (though alluring) tendency to bifurcate immensely complicated historical processes, whether micro, macro, or anywhere in between. Moses I. Finley, *Ancient Slavery and Modern Ideology*

(Princeton: Markus Weiner Publishers, 2017); Ira Berlin, *Generations of Captivity: A History of African-American Slaves* (Cambridge, MA: Belknap Press of Harvard University Press, 2003). For new conceptual undertakings that problematize "canonical" views of slave societies, see Noel Lenski and Catherine M. Cameron, eds., *What Is a Slave Society: The Practice of Slavery in Global Perspective* (Cambridge: Cambridge University Press, 2018), 1–60, esp. 46. Thank you to Cory James Young's conclusion in Cory James Young, "For Life of Otherwise: Abolition and Slavery in South Central Pennsylvania, 1780–1847" (PhD diss., Georgetown University, 2021).

64. PAS 1.2, Mar. 25, 1847; PAS 5.48, Mar. 15, 1847.

65. *Macon Weekly Telegraph*, Mar. 23, 1847.

66. Morris, *Free Men All*, 119. See also *Niles Register*, Mar. 20, 1847; *Liberator*, Mar. 19, 1847; Don E. Fehrenbacher, *The Slaveholding Republic: An Account of the United States Government's Relations to Slavery* (Oxford: Oxford University Press, 2001), 222 ft. 259. On enslaved African Americans' political consciousness throughout the Antebellum Era, I am referring to Steven Hahn's discussion of the "grapevine telegraph," which he of course borrowed from Booker T. Washington. See Steven Hahn, *A Nation under Our Feet: Black Political Struggles in the Rural South from Slavery to the Great Migration* (Cambridge, MA: Harvard University Press, 2003), 66, 131; Booker T. Washington, *Up from Slavery: An Autobiography* (New York: Doubleday, Page & Co., 1901), 8, 19.

Epilogue

1. John M. Scott, *Proceedings of the Great Union Meeting* (Philadelphia: B. Mifflin, 1850), 5.

2. Scott, *Proceedings of the Great Union Meeting*, 9–11; *Daily National Intelligencer*, Nov. 21, 1850.

3. Noah Worcester to Roberts Vaux, Dec. 12, 1822, Vaux Family Papers (Collection 684), The Historical Society of Pennsylvania. See also Noah Worcester [Philo Pacificus], *The Friend of Peace*, vol. 4 (Cambridge: Hilliard, Metcalf, and Co., 1827), 361–364; John Witthoft, "The 'Grasshopper War' Folktale," *Journal of American Folklore* 66, no. 262 (Oct.–Dec. 1953): 295–301.

4. Christopher James Bonner, *Remaking the Republic: Black Politics and the Creation of American Citizenship* (Philadelphia: University of Pennsylvania Press, 2020), 96.

5. Thomas D. Morris, *Free Men All: The Personal Liberty Laws of the North, 1780–1861* (Baltimore, MD: Johns Hopkins University Press, 1974), 118–119.

6. Morris, *Free Men All*, 144–145; *The North Star*, Oct. 24, 1850; "Fugitive Slave Act of 1850," Yale Law School, accessed August 9, 2020, https://avalon.law.yale.edu/19th_century/fugitive.asp.

7. Andrew K. Diemer, *The Politics of Black Citizenship: Free African Americans in the Mid-Atlantic Borderland, 1817–1863* (Athens: University of Georgia Press, 2016), 137–147, 161.

8. *Weekly Herald*, Oct. 19, 1850; *Farmer's Cabinet*, Oct. 24, 1840; *Public Ledger*, Oct. 25, 1850; *Daily Picayune*, Oct. 26, 1850; "Fugitive Slave Case, #4 Garnett," National Archives Catalog, accessed August 9, 2020, https://catalog.archives.gov/id/279015. See also Kellie Carter Jackson, *Force and Freedom: Black Abolitionists and the Politics of Violence* (Philadelphia: University of Pennsylvania Press, 2019), 50–53.

9. *Frederick Douglass' Paper*, Aug. 12, 1853; *National Era*, Jan. 2, 1851; *Pennsylvania Freeman*, Mar. 6, 1851; *Public Ledger*, Dec. 24, 1850; A. D. Byron, *Life of the Notorious Kidnapper, George F. Alberti* (Philadelphia: Published by the author, 1851), 24–25. On Alberti's career as a "resurrectionist," see Byron's biography; that Alberti enmeshed himself in kidnapping the living and the dead squares with the underground market of "ghost values" and body-snatching pervasive throughout the Antebellum Era. See Daina Ramey Berry, *The Price for Their Pound*

of Flesh (Boston: Beacon Press, 2017), chapter 6, and Michael Sappol, *A Traffic of Dead Bodies: Anatomy and Embodied Social Identity in Nineteenth-Century America* (Princeton: Princeton University Press, 2002). James Frisby Price's race is a subject of debate. As the historian David Fiske points out, judicial proceedings did not state his race, but Alberti's 1869 obituary identified Price as a "colored man." However, Price identified himself as white in the 1850 and 1860 censuses and his death certificate stated his race as "white." The question then becomes why Alberti's obituary would include "colored man" in describing Price when throughout his life Price did not identify himself that way. I agree with David Fiske's assigning of Price as African American, though I would go a step further and state that Price was light-skinned and thus could pass over racial borders, which in turn facilitated his work as a decoy for Alberti. See David Fiske, *Solomon Northup's Kindred: The Kidnapping of Free Citizens before the Civil War* (Santa Barbara, CA: Praeger, 2016), 160 ft. 388; *New York Times*, July 27, 1869; Milt Diggins, *Stealing Freedom along the Mason-Dixon Line: Thomas McCreary, the Notorious Slave Catcher from Maryland* (Baltimore: Maryland Historical Society, 2015), 56–59; Richard M. Blackett, *The Captive's Quest for Freedom: Fugitive Slaves, the 1850 Fugitive Slave Act, and the Politics of Slavery* (New York: Cambridge University Press, 2018), 340; *Ancestry.com*, "James F. Price" in *Philadelphia, Pennsylvania, Death Certificates Index, 1803–1915*, accessed August 11, 2020; US Census Bureau, *1850* and *1860 United States Federal Census, Ancestry.com*, accessed December 28, 2020.

10. Peter A. Browne, *A Review of the Trial, Conviction, And Sentence, of George F. Alberti, for kidnapping* (Philadelphia: s.n., 1851); A. V. Parsons, *Cases in Equity and at Law, Argued and Determined in the Court of Common Pleas*, vol. 2 (Philadelphia: T. and J. W. Johnson, 1851), 495–502.

11. *National Era*, Jan. 2, 1851; Byron, *Life of the Notorious Kidnapper*, 24–26; Browne, *Review of the Trial*, 1–3; Parsons, *Cases in Equity and at Law*, 496.

12. *Philadelphia Directory*, 1850; Browne, *Review of the Trial*, 4; Byron, *Life of the Notorious Kidnapper*, 24–26; *Public Ledger*, Dec. 23, 1850; Parsons, *Cases in Equity and at Law*, 497; *National Era*, Jan. 2, 1851.

13. Byron, *Life of the Notorious Kidnapper*, 25; Browne, *Review of the Trial*, 2–3; Parsons, *Cases in Equity and at Law*, 496; *National Era*, Jan. 2, 1851.

14. Byron, *Life of the Notorious Kidnapper*, 25; Browne, *Review of the Trial*, 2–3; Parsons, *Cases in Equity and at Law*, 497–498; *Times-Picayune*, Mar. 27, 1851.

15. Diggins, *Stealing Freedom along the Mason-Dixon Line*, 56–59; *Philadelphia Legal Intelligencer*, May 9, 1851; *Baltimore Sun*, Jan. 13, 1852; *Pennsylvania Freeman*, Mar. 6, 1851; Pennsylvania Anti-Slavery Society, *Fourteenth Annual report presented to the Pennsylvania Anti-Slavery Society by its Executive committee, October 7 1851: with the proceedings of the annual meeting* (Philadelphia: Merrihew & Thompson, 1851), 40–43.

16. Browne, *Review of the Trial*, 5; Parsons, *Cases in Equity and at Law*, 497; Fiske, *Solomon Northup's Kindred*, 105–107; Byron, *Life of the Notorious Kidnapper*, 25–26.

17. Browne, *Review of the Trial*, 5–6; Byron, *Life of the Notorious Kidnapper*, 25–26; Parsons, *Cases in Equity and at Law*, 497.

18. Morris, *Free Men All*, 118–119; H. Robert Baker, "A Better Story in *Prigg v. Pennsylvania?" Journal of Supreme Court History* 39, no. 2 (2014): 169–189.

19. Byron, *Life of the Notorious Kidnapper*, 501–502; Browne, *Review of the Trial*, 13, 16.

20. *Pennsylvania Freeman*, Mar. 27, Apr. 3, Oct. 2, 1851; *National Era*, Mar. 27, 1851; State of Maryland, *Debates and Proceedings of the Maryland Reform Convention to Revise the State Constitution*, 2 vols. (Annapolis: William McNeir, 1851), 614.

21. On the Christiana Riot, see Thomas P. Slaughter, *Bloody Dawn: The Christiana Riot and Racial Violence in the Antebellum North* (New York: Oxford University Press, 1991);

Castner Hanway, and a Member of the Philadelphia bar, *A History of the Trial of Castner Hanway and Others for Treason: At Philadelphia in November, 1851: With an Introduction Upon the History of the Slave Question* (Philadelphia: U. Hunt & Sons, 1852); Morris, *Free Men All*, 155–156; *North American*, Sept. 27, Oct. 3, 13, 1851.

22. *North American*, Oct. 13, 1851; *Pennsylvania Freeman*, Oct. 2, 1851, Feb. 26, 1852; Morris, *Free Men All*, 155–156; *National Anti-Slavery Standard*, Oct. 16, 1851; John F. Coleman, *The Disruption of the Pennsylvania Democracy, 1848–1860* (Harrisburg: The Pennsylvania Historical and Museum Commission, 1975), 42–48, 168; *Richmond Enquirer*, Feb. 10, 1852.

23. Joseph A. Boromé, Jacob C. White, Robert B. Ayres, and J. M. McKim, "The Vigilant Committee of Philadelphia," *Pennsylvania Magazine of History and Biography* 92, no. 3 (Jul. 1968): 329. On Still's efficiency and the overall scope of the Vigilance Committee, see chapters 4 and 5 of Andrew K. Diemer, "Still Draft" (unpublished manuscript, June 9, 2021), electronic. See also Eric Foner, *Gateway to Freedom: The Hidden History of the Underground Railroad* (New York: Norton, 2016), 145–150.

24. Boromé et al., "The Vigilant Committee"; William Still, *The Underground Rail Road: A Record of Facts, Authentic Narratives, Letters, &c., narrating the Hardships, Hair-breadth Escapes and Death Struggles of the Slaves in their Efforts for Freedom, as related by themselves and others, or witnessed by the author,* [. . .] (Philadelphia: Porter & Coates, 1872), 2–6. See also Samuel May, *The Fugitive Slave Act and Its Victims* (Freeport: Books for Libraries Press, 1970); Wilbur Henry Seibert, *The Underground Railroad from Slavery to Freedom* (New York: The MacMillan Company, 1898); Larry Gara, *The Liberty Line: The Legend of the Underground Railroad* (Lexington: University of Kentucky Press, 1961); David W. Blight, *Passages to Freedom: The Underground Railroad in History and Memory* (Washington, DC: Smithsonian Books, 2004); Fergus M. Bordewich, *Bound for Canaan: The Underground Railroad and the War for the Soul of America* (New York: HarperCollins Publishers, Inc., 2005); Pennsylvania Anti-Slavery Society, *Fourteenth Annual Report*, 11. On fugitives from slavery and the coming of the Civil War, see John Ashworth, *Slavery, Capitalism, and Politics in the Antebellum Republic*, vol. 1: *Commerce and Compromise, 1820–1850* (New York: Cambridge University Press, 1995); John Ashworth, *Slavery, Capitalism, and Politics in the Antebellum Republic*, vol. 2: *The Coming of the Civil War, 1850–1861* (New York: Cambridge University Press, 2007); Manisha Sinha, *The Slave's Cause: A History of Abolitionism* (New Haven, CT: Yale University Press, 2016); R. J. M. Blackett, *The Captive's Quest for Freedom: Fugitive Slaves, the 1850 Fugitive Slave Act, and the Politics of Slavery* (New York: Cambridge University Press, 2018); Kellie Carter Jackson, *Force and Freedom: Black Abolitionists and the Politics of Violence* (Philadelphia: University of Pennsylvania Press, 2019); Jonathan Daniel Wells, *The Kidnapping Club: Wall Street, Slavery, and Resistance on the Eve of the Civil War* (New York: Bold Type Books, 2020). For examples of other such Northern locales, see Christopher Cameron, *To Plead Our Own Cause: African Americans in Massachusetts and the Making of the Antislavery Movement* (Kent, OH: Kent State University Press, 2014); Graham Russell Hodges, *David Ruggles: A Radical Black Abolitionist and the Underground Railroad in New York City* (Chapel Hill: University of North Carolina Press, 2010); Jonathan Daniel Wells, *The Kidnapping Club: Wall Street, Slavery, and Resistance on the Eve of the Civil War* (New York: Bold Type Books, 2020).

25. Stanley W. Campbell, *The Slave Catchers: Enforcement of the Fugitive Slave Act, 1850–1860* (Chapel Hill: University of North Carolina Press, 1968), 199–205; Still, *The Underground Rail Road*, 2–6; "Underground Railroad—The McGowan Index," Temple University, accessed December 28, 2020, https://libguides.tcnj.edu/aahistory1/underground; William C. Kashatus, *William Still: The Underground Railroad and the Angel at Philadelphia* (Notre Dame: University of Notre Dame Press, 2021). "Journal C of Station No. 2 of the Underground Railroad, Agent William Still," Historical Society of Pennsylvania, accessed August 12, 2020, https://hsp.org/sites/default/files/still_journal_c_0.pdf; William J. Switala, *Underground Railroad in*

Pennsylvania (Mechanicsburg, PA: Stackpole Books, 2001). For works on rescuing fugitives from slavery and kidnapping victims, see citations in the introduction to this book; Jackson, *Force and Freedom*, 48–79.

26. *National Anti-Slavery Standard*, May 20, 1865.

PRIMARY SOURCES

Archival Material

American Antiquarian Society, Worcester, Massachusetts.
Anti-Slavery Collection, Boston Public Library, Boston, Massachusetts.
Bigler Papers, Historical Society of Pennsylvania, Philadelphia.
Cox-Parrish-Wharton Papers, Historical Society of Pennsylvania, Philadelphia.
Mayor's Court of Philadelphia, Record Group 130.1 Docket, Philadelphia City Archives.
Meredith Family Papers, Historical Society of Pennsylvania, Philadelphia.
Pennsylvania Abolition Society Papers, Historical Society of Pennsylvania, Philadelphia.
Pennsylvania Anti-Slavery Society Records, Historical Society of Pennsylvania, Philadelphia.
Rawle Family Papers, Historical Society of Pennsylvania, Philadelphia.
Roberts Papers, Historical Society of Pennsylvania, Philadelphia.
David M. Rubenstein Rare Book & Manuscript Library, Duke University.
Schomburg Center, Manuscripts and Archives, New York Public Library.
Vigilant Committee of Philadelphia Records, 1839–1844, Historical Society of Pennsylvania, Philadelphia.
Joseph Watson Papers, Historical Society of Pennsylvania, Philadelphia.
Wyck Association Collection, American Philosophical Society, Philadelphia.

Periodicals

African Observer (New York)
Alexandria Gazette (Virginia)
American Sentinel (Philadelphia)
Atkinson's Saturday Evening Post (Philadelphia)
Baltimore Gazette and Daily Advertiser
Baltimore Patriot
Baltimore Sun
The Berks and Schuylkill Journal (Pennsylvania)
Boston Courier
Christian Repository (Vermont and Pennsylvania)
Christian Watchman (Massachusetts)
Colored American (New York)
Concord Gazette (New Hampshire)
Connecticut Courant
Daily Picayune (New Orleans)
Democratic Press (Philadelphia)

Easton Gazette (Maryland)
Emancipator (New York)
Emancipator and Free American (New York)
Emigrant (Illinois)
Franklin's Gazette (Philadelphia)
Freedom's Journal (New York)
Genius of Universal Emancipation (Baltimore)
Hallowell Gazette (Maine)
Harrisburg Telegraph
Journal of Commerce (New York)
The Kaleidoscope: Or, Literary and Scientific Mirror (Liverpool, UK)
Lancaster Free Press (Pennsylvania)
Liberator
Macon Weekly Telegraph (Georgia)
National Anti-Slavery Standard (New York)
National Enquirer (Philadelphia)
National Gazette (Philadelphia)
New Bedford Mercury (Massachusetts)
New Hampshire Sentinel
New York Commercial Advertiser
New York Evangelist
New York Spectator
Newport Mercury (Rhode Island)
Niles' Weekly Register (Baltimore)
North American (Philadelphia)
Palladium of Liberty (Ohio)
Pennsylvania Enquirer
Pennsylvania Freeman
Pennsylvanian
Philadelphia Democratic Press
Philadelphia Gazette
Philadelphia Inquirer
Philadelphia Monthly Magazine
Pottsville Miners' Journal (Pennsylvania)
Poulson's Daily American Advertiser (Philadelphia)
Public Ledger (Philadelphia)
Republican Star and General Advertiser (Easton)
Richmond Inquirer
Saturday Evening Post (Philadelphia)
Southern Patriot (SC and NC)
The Times Connecticut
United States Gazette (Philadelphia)
Weekly Aurora (Philadelphia)
Workingman's Advocate (Massachusetts)

Abdy, Edward Strutt, 124
abolitionism: during 1840s, 200–206; gradual vs immediate, 145–46, 148, 154; immediate, 12, 116, 117–20, 135, 142, 147, 148, 167, 194; practical, 6, 148, 167; presidential election (1828) and, 99–100; as threat to interstate comity, 167–68, 169, 170–71, 192; white opposition, 120, 140, 142–46
abolitionists (Black), 100–101; convention movement and, 103–4; violence of, 183
abolitionists (interracial), 1–2, 3, 12, 15, 24, 46, 72, 117–20, 143, 164, 175; "first movement," 28–29, 241n23; Great Postal Campaign, 12, 140–47, 144, 260n56; networks, 8; personal liberty law (1847) and, 215; white opposition to, 12, 121, 140–46, 166. See also Pennsylvania Abolition Society (PAS); Philadelphia Anti-Slavery Society (PASS); Young Men's Anti-Slavery Society
abolitionists (white): convention movement and, 104; interstate comity position, 77–78; Southern, 97
abolition societies (Black): white members, 118; William Young case and, 33–34
Adams, John, 30
African Observer, 91
Aitken, Robert, 115–16, 128–29, 130, 131, 132–34, 258n30n33
Alberti, George F., Jr., 1–2, 17, 18, 26, 88, 98, 151, 221–28, 230, 272n9; Catherine Thompson case, 1, 15–16, 223–28; trial, sentencing, and pardon, 1, 225–28; William Stansbury case, 171–73
aldermen, 21, 143; certificates of removal/warrants issued by, 17, 22, 47, 66, 179, 226; kidnapping cases' involvement, 33–34, 67, 103, 244; limitation

of powers, 48, 49, 215, 226; response to riots, 122; as slaveholders' agents, 22; white mob attacks on, 122
Alexander, Archibald, 123
Allen, John, 94
Allen, Richard, 24, 27, 76, 94, 103–4, 173–74; personal liberty law (1826) position, 76, 78–80, 81–82
Allen, William, 224, 226
Alter family, 156
amalgamation, 121–22, 162
American Anti-Slavery Society, 118–19, 142, 177; Great Postal Campaign, 140–46
American Colonization Society, 69, 106
American Convention of Abolition Societies, 29, 101–2
American Republican Association, 199
"An Act for the Gradual Abolition of Slavery" (1788), 5, 21, 59, 64, 136–37
"An Act to Prevent Kidnapping." See personal liberty law (1820)
Anti-Masonic Party, 156–57, 158, 165, 170
assumed identities, of fugitive slaves, 148

Bache, Richard, 58
Bacon, Benjamin, 26
Badger, Samuel, 33–34
Baker, H. Robert, 176
Baltimore Chronicle, 105
Baltimore Commercial Chronicle, 129
Baltimore Patriot, 39
Bank of the United States, 149
Barker, James Nelson, 43–44
Beck, Ignatius, 173–74

Bell, Richard, 33

Beneficial Hall, 182, 184

Benezet Hall, 54, 110, 125–26

Bennet, Benjamin, 34, 51

Berlin, Ira, 5, 158

Berry, Daina Ramey, 9

Berry, Peter, 63–65

Biddle, James C., 165

Bigler, William F., 1, 15, 228, 229, 230

Bill of Rights, 159

Binns, John, 99, 179, 180

Birdseye, Ezekiel, 97

Black, Charles, 186

Black, Richard, 189, 193

Black activists: response to threatened disenfranchisement, 13–14, 164–65. *See also* abolitionists
(Black)

Black Americans: collusion with slave catchers, 1,
15, 33–36, 90–93, 221–22; migration into Philadelphia, 21, 23–24, 25

Black children: education, 117; free, born of enslaved parents, 175–76, 224–26; kidnapping of,
11–12, 76–77, 78–79, 85, 87–93; rescued from
slaveholders, 119–20

Black cultural institutions, 24, 26, 60, 137, 138. *See
also* churches (Black)

Black Founding Fathers, 79. *See also* Allen,
Richard; Forten, James

Black identity, Mary Gilmore case and, 127–34

Black Pennsylvanians, disenfranchisement, 13, 171,
185, 264n29

Black Philadelphians, 2, 3; 1828 presidential election
and, 100; comparison with Irish immigrants,
102; criminal activity by, 150; emigration debate,
107–13; leadership, 26; memorials/petitions to
legislative bodies, 24–25, 76, 110–12, 117, 159,
208–9, 212; opposition to Fugitive Slave Act
(1850), 220–21; population, 13, 20, 26, 195, 198;
precarious position, 5–6, 17–18; settlement
pattern, 198; social mobility, 100–101, 103, 123,
160, 185; vulnerable position, 8, 9–10, 60, 85–86;
white resentment of achievements of, 101–2, 103,
116, 121, 122, 123

Blayney, William, 139

Bonner, Christopher J., 8, 10, 110, 152

borders, of slavery, 4, 7, 237n14

Bosserman, Mr., 190, 193–94

Boston Courier, 118

Boston Post, 202

Breck, Samuel, 13, 112–13, 158

Brick Wesley Church, 220–21

Brown, Adam, 79

Brown, David Paul, 118–19, 128, 132, 133, 134, 148,
154–55, 226; Great Postal Campaign and, 140,
142; Pennsylvania Hall speech, 166–67; William
Stansbury case and, 171, 172, 173

Browne, Peter Arrell, 124, 223, 227, 228

Buchanan, James, 201, 210, 228

Burden, Jesse, 143

Burleigh, Charles C., 167, 205, 216–17

Burnside, James, 209

Burr, Aaron, Jr., 164

Burr, John P., 164

Bush, Orange, 43

Butler, Thomas, 164

Campbell, George W., 43

Campbell, Robert, 40

Canby, James, 39

Cannon, Jesse, 44–45, 46

Cannon, Patty, 45, 76, 90

Cannon-Johnson gang, 45, 76–77, 89–90, 93,
98–99

Caric, Ric N., 121–22

Carmalt, Caleb, 80–81

Carr, Henry, 90–93

Carsons, Ephraim, 39, 40

Case, Peter, 63–65

Cassey, Joseph, 118–19

Cedar Ward, Philadelphia, PA, 23–24, 43, 60, 101,
138, 139, 150, 168, 184, 198, 244n54

certificates: of freedom, 38, 39–40; of ownership,
32; of removal, 22, 47, 49, 66–67, 73–74, 172

Chambers, Ann, 53, 55, 56–57, 73–74

Chambers, Ezekiel F., 73, 96, 248n40

chattel principle, 5, 9, 18

churches (Black), 137; convention movement and,
103, 104; moral leadership role, 24; white mob
attacks on, 24–28, 100–101, 116, 120, 123, 124–25,
168, 183–84

churches (Irish Catholic), Nativist mob attacks on,
199

citizenship rights, of Black Pennsylvanians, 109,
111, 158, 163–64

Civil War, 5, 9, 15, 120, 231

Clay, Cassius, 204

Clay, Henry, 201, 203, 208

Collins, Thomas, 88

Colored Temperance Hall, 182, 184–85

Commonwealth v. Case, 72

Compromise of 1850, 218. *See also* Fugitive Slave Act (1850)

Congo, Maria, 115–16, 128–29, 130–32, 134

congressional elections: 1838, 170–71; 1846, 213–16

Conrad, Robert T., 143

constables: abuse of power, 47; anti-Black violence, 13, 27, 50, 67, 168; Black Philadelphians attacks on, 102–3; cooperation with slaveholders / slave catchers, 22, 27, 50, 55, 78, 88, 147, 153, 179; fugitive slaves' resistance to, 101; rights of arrest, 111–12; riot responses, 122; sympathetic to slavery, 74

Constitution (PA), Black suffrage under, 158–60, 165

Constitution (US), 25, 48, 117; Article IV, 176; Black "free ingress and regress" rights under, 111; emancipation under, 208; extradition clause, 89, 95; "fugitive slave" clause, 4; interstate comity under, 73, 145, 204; slaveholders' rights under, 188, 191–93, 215–16, 218–19, 227; Three-Fifth Clause, 4

Constitutional Convention (PA), 157–65, 170, 218

Constitutional Convention (US), 3, 23

convention movement, 103–4

Cook, Alexander A., 202–3

Cooper, Hezekiah, 63–65, 83

Cooper, James, 215

Cope, Thomas P., 5

Corbin, Mr., 63–64, 65

Cox, John, 122

Crawford, James, 179–80, 181–82, 184

Cross, Sarah, 148

Cummins, John, 159–60

Dallas, George Mifflin, 58, 124, 187, 201, 210–11, 213, 218–19

Darlington, Isaac, 62–63

Darlington, William, 159–60, 164

deceased persons, free identity of, 63–65

Declaration of Independence, 3, 23, 25, 31, 110, 117, 159

"Declaration of Sentiments," 117–18

decoys, 48, 90

Deep South, slavery's expansion in, 5, 58–59, 79

Delaware, 2; anti-Black violence, 105; fugitive slave act, 73; kidnappers operating out of, 30–31, 34, 40–41, 42, 43, 45, 88, 89–90, 179; street diplomacy in, 131–32

Democratic Party, 59, 97, 106, 107, 126, 139, 143, 198; annexation of Texas and, 200–201; anti-abolitionist position, 167; elections (1820), 57–60; elections (1846), 213–14; Free Soil, 212–13, 215; Irish immigrants' allegiance to, 13, 23, 121, 149–50, 199, 201; Jacksonian, 143, 205; newspapers sympathetic to, 106, 123; "Old School" and "New School," 57–58; PA legislature members, 81, 107; Southern influence on, 212, 213–15; Walker Tariff and, 210–11

Diemer, Andrew K., 59, 63, 69, 81, 100, 106, 170, 220

Dolbert, John, 43

Donnehower, Michael, 119, 122, 147, 256n10

Donovan, John, 225

Dorden, John, 34, 51

Dorsey brothers, 153–55, 185–86

"Doughface-ism," 74, 98, 218

Downingtown Standard, 134

Duane, William, 48, 57–58

Dunbar, Eric Armstrong, 3

Duncan, Benjamin, 126

Duval, Dennis, 173

Earle, Thomas, 149–50, 205–6, 209

Eastern State Penitentiary, Philadelphia, 1, 225–26

Easton Gazette, 75

education: of Black children, 117; religious discrimination in, 199

Elder, William, 209

Eldred, Nathaniel B., 203

Elton, Anthony, 31

emancipation, 3, 219; as "freedom by degrees," 20–21; gradual, 98, 99; Tallmadge amendment and, 36–37; West Indian Emancipation celebration, 13, 177, 182–85, 197; white fears of, 105, 118, 135, 143, 144. *See also* abolitionism; Gradual Abolition Act (1780)

emancipation, in Pennsylvania, 15, 21–22, 28, 156, 188, 202, 207–8; William Findlay's address on, 20. *See also* Gradual Abolition Act (1780). *See also* personal liberty law (1847)

Emancipator, 155

emigration, Black, 21, 23–24, 25, 106–7, 117, 161, 195; debates, 19, 107–13, 217; personal liberty law (1847) and, 217; proposed legislative restrictions, 109–13, 127, 159

Emmons, Mary, 164

enslaved persons: registration of, 26, 58, 136–37; right to freedom, 193. *See also* fugitives from slavery

Everson, Betsey, 42–44

"Family Party," 58

Federalists, 57, 250n60

federal law, protective of slavery: conflict with state law, 99. *See also* Fugitive Slave Act (1793); Fugitive Slave Act (1850)

federal property rights, of slaveholders, 30, 35–36, 48; Black "support" for, 109; constitutionality, 188, 191–93, 215–16; under Fugitive Slave Act (1793), 71; under Maryland's proposed slave-holders' right bill, 74–75; under personal liberty law (1820), 55; under personal liberty law (1847), 215–16; as threat to interstate comity, 192

Federal Slave Commissioner, 221–22

Female Vigilant Association, 13, 170, 177

Fifth Annual Colored Convention, 127

Findlay, William, 19–20, 35, 36, 43, 47, 49, 57–60

Finnegan, Thomas, 202–3

fire companies, 121–22, 138, 149, 198

First African Presbyterian Church, 100, 123

Fisher, Sidney George, 200

Flannery, Margaret, 42, 43, 44

Flint, William, 66–67

Fogg, William, 161

Foner, Eric, 6

Forsett, Smith, 38

Forten, Harriet, 118

Forten, James, 23–24, 25–26, 27, 67, 79, 112, 151, 158; anti-Black riots and, 122, 124; convention movement and, 103–4; death, 177–78, 185; emigration proposals and, 108; PASS and, 134; Underground Railroad and, 14, 195, 197

Forten, James, Jr., 142, 164

Forten, Margaretta, 142, 177

Forten, Sarah, 142, 177

Forten, Thomas, 122, 124

Foss v. Hobbs, 161

Founding Fathers, 4; Black, 79

Fox, John, 162

Franklin Gazette, 58, 59

Franklin Institute Hall, 102, 116

Franklin's Gazette, 20

Frederick Douglass' Paper, 221

Free African Society, 24

Freedom's Journal, 100

Freeman, Ezekiel, 65–71, 83

Free Soil doctrine, 212–13, 215, 225

free state status, of Pennsylvania, 1–4, 5, 10, 14–15, 16, 20–21, 29–30; gubernatorial election (1820) debates, 57–60; nominal nature, 50–51, 57, 204. *See also* personal liberty law (1847); interstate comity

Frisby, Flora, 17

Frisby, Perry, 17–18, 27, 51, 53

fugitives from slavery: conflation with free Black kidnapping victims, 7, 11, 13, 14, 82–83; murders, 189–93

fugitives from slavery, retrievals. *See* kidnappings

Fugitive Slave Act (1793), 4–5, 11, 18, 22, 24–25, 28, 30, 40, 74, 113, 153; constitutionality, 35–36, 188, 217, 218–19; enforcement, 4–5, 6, 83, 108, 188, 206–7; fugitive slave removal protocol, 172–73, 179; House bill 446 and, 110; interstate comity and, 67–68; personal liberty law (1820) and, 11, 48–50; personal liberty law (1847) and, 15, 216, 217; proof of enslavement, 172–73; proposed revision, 32; Section 4, 69

Fugitive Slave Act (1850), 15, 22, 219–21, 227, 229; cases tried under, 221–23, 226, 230; George Alberti and, 221–23, 226, 230

gag rule, 156, 170, 204

Gale, Lewis, 53, 55

Galloway, Betsey, 223

Gardner, Charles, 26, 151, 159, 184, 195

Garnett, Henry, 221

Garrett, Thomas, 76, 179

Garrigues, Abraham, 38–39

Garrigues, Samuel P., 89–90, 93, 125–26

Garrison, William Lloyd, 104, 105–6, 117, 142, 146, 167, 169, 176, 205

Genius of Universal Emancipation, 73, 97, 99

Germantown protest (1688), 3

Gholson, James Herbert, 180

Gibbons, Charles, 208–9, 215, 216

Gibbons, Hettey, 79

Gibson, Adam, 221–23

Gibson, John, 161

Gilmore, Jacob, 54, 115, 128, 129–30, 131, 132, 133, 134, 258n34

Gilmore, Mary, 115–16, 127–34, 142, 258n34

Gilpin, Charles, 128, 171, 172

Gloucester, Jeremiah, 100–101

Gloucester, John, 100, 123

Gloucester, John, Jr., 5, 101

Gloucester, Stephen, 54, 76, 81–82, 123, 177, 178, 183–84

Goldsborough, Robert H., 73, 248n40

Gosse, Van, 158

Gradual Abolition Act (1780), 5, 7–8, 20–21, 64, 162, 203, 208, 216, 226–27; "Quaker" amendments, 80–81

"grasshopper war," 219

Great Postal Campaign, 12, 140–47, 260n56

Great Union Meeting, 218, 220–21

Green, Duff, 99

Green, Jesse, 89–90

Grice, Hezekiah, 103

Grier, Robert, 221

Griffith, Samuel, 61–62, 63

Grimstead, David, 120, 138

Griscom, George, 128

Gronningsater, Sarah L. H., 18

gubernatorial elections: 1820, 57–60; 1838, 170–71; 1844, 201; 1851, 225, 228–29

habeas corpus, 32, 216

Habersham, Richard W., 40

Hagerman, Sarah, daughter's kidnapping, 42–47, 51, 76

Haines, Reuben III, 38–41, 51

Hall, George, 188–89, 193

Hall, John, 188–90, 193–94

Hall, William W., 172

Hallowell Gazette, 35

Hamilton, John, 76, 88, 89, 93

Harman, Eli, 85, 93

Harrisburg Republican, 58

Harrisburg Union, 229

Harrold, Stanley, 6, 246n5

Hawkins, Peter, 202–3, 204

Hemphill, Joseph, 26, 98–99

Henderson, John, 76, 88, 93

Hiester, Joseph, 57–60, 72–73

Hill, John, 130, 258n35

Hinton, Frederick, 159

Hobbs, Hiram, 161

Hodges, Graham Russell Gao, 6

Hopkinson, Joseph, 31, 171, 172–73, 174–75

Hopper, Edward, 142

Hopper, Isaac T., 21, 31, 67, 68, 148, 174

Horn, Henry, 99

Hubbell, Horatio, 226

Hudson, Henry, 38–41, 42, 47–48, 51

Huston, Charles, 64–65

Igbo-African ancestry, 135, 136

immediatism, 12, 94, 119, 135, 140, 142, 143, 204

Incorporated Colored Benezet Society, 125–26

Independence Hall, Philadelphia, PA, 4, 23, 27, 31, 54, 119, 124, 229

informants, 29, 45, 61, 94, 98, 171–72, 189, 222; Black, 45, 61, 90, 113–14, 115–16, 128–29, 130–31, 172, 221

Ingersoll, Charles Jared, 54, 66, 70, 149–50, 166–67, 170, 171, 201

Ingersoll, Joseph R., 70, 144–45, 147, 214

Ingraham, Edward D., 132, 171, 172, 173, 221–22

interracial activism, 6, 12, 13, 38, 114, 116, 117, 119–20, 144–45. *See also* abolitionism (interracial); Underground Railroad

interstate comity, 3, 130–31, 229; abolitionists as threat to, 166–67, 169; abolitionists' opposition to, 117–18; Alberti trial and, 227, 228, 229; in apprehension of kidnappers, 89; Black Americans' role, 15, 126; Black Philadelphians' definition of, 111; Black suffrage and, 163–64, 165; compromise in, 231; constitutionality, 145; governors' role, 94–98, 225; Great Postal Campaign and, 140–46; impact of street diplomacy on, 6–7; intermediaries in, 94–98; liberty law (1820) and, 50; racial comity and, 135; Ritner on, 156; street diplomacy as threat to, 116; William Stansbury case and, 174–75

interstate diplomacy, 6, 246n5

Irish Catholicism, 199, 201

Irish identity, of Mary Gilmore, 115–16, 127–34, 142, 258n34

Irish immigrants, 60; in anti-Black riots, 13, 101, 120, 121, 122, 125–26, 198; comparison with Black Philadelphians, 102, 159–60; competition with Black Philadelphians, 101, 149, 159, 182; Democratic Party and, 13, 23, 121, 149, 150, 198, 199, 201;

Irish immigrants (*cont.*)
Nativist antagonism toward, 199–200; "white"
identity, 121, 149

Jackson, Andrew, 43, 98, 99–100, 140, 143, 149, 157
Jackson, Kellie Carter, 120
Jacksonian Era, race riots of, 115
Jacobs, Arnold, 95–97
Jefferson, Thomas, 43, 57
Jenkins, David, 202
Johnson, Ebenezer, 76, 78, 88
Johnson, John, 43, 45, 148
Johnson, Joseph, 45–46, 76, 88, 92
Johnson, Ovid, 190–91
Johnston, William F., 225, 228–29
John Upton's Hotel, 106–7
Jones, Absalom, 24
Journal of Commerce, 120
Joyce, John, 148
Juan riot, 116, 135–40
Junior Anti-Slavery Society of Philadelphia,
169–70

Kantrowitz, Stephen, 159
Keen, Richard, 26, 98
Kendall, Amos, 145
Kennedy, Isaac, 101
Kenrick, Joseph, 199
Kent, Joseph, 73, 89, 113
kidnappers, 17, 18; Black Americans' collusion with,
1, 15, 33–36, 90–93, 221–22; Black resistance to,
61–63, 102, 222, 228; distance escapes from,
88–91, 230–31; extradition, 89, 94–98, 175, 225,
228; prosecution, 1, 11, 21, 43–44, 47–48, 49, 71,
98, 188, 202–3, 206, 225–28
kidnapping court cases, 1, 10, 11, 60–72, 90–91,
108–9, 155–57, 203, 221–23; 1816–1820s, 30–36,
49–52; 1840s, 14–15; Black Americans' presence
in courtrooms, 119–20, 124; Black witnesses, 17,
119, 131, 132, 133–34, 173–75, 190; cited in personal
liberty law (1820) debates, 29–36, 38–47, 50–52;
jury trials, 62–63, 71, 108–9, 155–57, 165, 170, 203,
262n20; kidnappers' trials, 15, 23, 64–65, 90,
95–96, 98, 179–80, 190–93, 202–3, 225–28;
Missouri Compromise debates and, 36–38; for
murders of kidnappers, 62–63; for obstruction
of fugitive slave arrests, 188–93; proof of enslavement requirement, 172–73; slaveholders' ex parte

testimony, 172, 173, 206; trial by jury, 155–57, 165,
203, 262n20
kidnapping gangs, 30, 42–47, 51, 76–77
kidnappings, 2, 7, 17–19, 82–83; after personal
liberty law (1820) passage, 53, 55–56; attempted
rescues from, 38–41, 42–47, 51, 102, 116, 178–81;
escapes from, 65–71, 88–91, 195, 197; Fugitive
Slave Act (1850) and, 219–20; obstruction, 61–63,
66–71, 74, 101, 126–27, 188–94, 189–94, 220;
plausible deniability and, 21, 47, 56, 63, 65, 74,
79–80, 88, 101, 172; unknown fate of victims,
42–47, 51, 86, 225, 227. *See also* kidnappings;
personal liberty law(s)
King, Edward, 124
Kittera, Thomas, 99
Knight, W. S., 222–23
Kunkel, John C., 203

law enforcement officials: certificates of removal
issued by, 22, 47, 49, 66–67, 74; cooperation
with slave catchers and slaveholders, 17, 18, 22,
26, 28, 47–48; Irish immigrants as, 198. *See also*
constables; police
Lea, David, 21
Leavitt, Joshua, 155
Lee, Archibald, 73
Lehman, William, 228
Leslie, William R., 49, 72
Lewis, Evan, 40
Liberator, 105, 106, 107, 109, 118–19, 134, 136, 201
Liberty Party, 201, 202, 205, 214
Life of the Notorious Kidnapper, George F. Alberti
(Byron), 223–24
Lockwood, Richard, 40
Louden, Jabez, 178–79
Louden, Mary, 178–81, 185–86
Loughead, Robert L., 122
Lowe, Enoch, 225, 228
Lowe, Solomon, 65–66, 67, 69–71, 247n23
Luff, Alice, 38
Luff, Nathaniel, 38
Lundy, Benjamin, 99–100, 104

Macon Weekly Telegraph, 217
Madison, James, 31, 43
Manlove, Alexander, 88, 90
manumission papers, 26, 58, 95, 98, 136, 148
marriage, interracial, 120

Martin, Benjamin, 161, 162–63
Martin, John, 85
Maryland, 154–55; Black children kidnapping cases
    and, 76–77; George Alberti trial and, 228; inter-
    state comity with Pennsylvania, 95–98; personal
    liberty law (1826) compromise, 11, 72–75, 76,
    80–82, 83
Mason, Matthew, 21, 37
Mason, Samuel, Jr., 67–71, 77
Massey, Ebenezer, 95
Mathias, Peter, 148, 185–86
McCrummell, James, 177, 195, 197
McCrummell, Sarah, 170
McDowell, E. T., 160
McKee, John, 42–44
McKim, James Miller, 1–2, 8, 118, 195, 197, 217, 229
McMichael, Morton, 143
McVay, Jonathan, 189–91, 193
Meredith, William, 77–80, 83, 163, 191–93, 249n50
Meredith, William, Sr., 78
Mexican War, 15, 102, 187–88, 207–8, 211–12, 213,
    214, 227
Miller, William, 30, 31
Milnor, John, 30, 31
Miner, Charles, 99
Missouri Compromise debates (1819–1822), 20,
    31–32, 36–38, 43–44, 49, 51
Missouri Question, 59–60, 98
mistaken identity, 101, 172, 222–23. *See also* plau-
    sible deniability
Mitchell, Jacob, 25
Mitchell, James, 223–24, 225, 226
Monroe, Abraham, 188–94
Monroe, James, 57–58
Morgan, Margaret, 175–76, 185–86
Morris, Henry, 184
Morris, Thomas D., 55, 207, 215
Mother Bethel AME Church (Philadelphia, PA),
    24, 27–28, 54, 101, 103, 159, 168–69, 184; as
    Underground Railroad station, 195, 197
Mott, James, 88, 126, 216–17
Mott, Lucretia, 88, 216–17
Moyamensing, Philadelphia, 54, 60, 122, 179, 184,
    198
Murphy, Robert, 43

Nash, Gary, 3–4, 20–21
National Gazette, 74, 109, 175

National Republican Party, 112
Native Americans, 21, 219
Nativist/Native American Party, 199–200, 201
Neales, Samuel, 30–31
Neall, Daniel, Jr., 169
Needles, Edward, 208–9
Newport, PA, Abraham Monroe and, 188–94
North American, 210, 211, 214, 215, 217
Northerners, complicity with slavery, 3

Olmstead, Edward, 139
Orr family, 143, 260n61
oyster shops, 90–93

Palladium of Freedom, 202
Panic of 1819, 57–58, 60
Parker, Simon Wesley, 91–93
Parker, William, 228
Parsons, Anvil Virgil, 223, 226, 227
PAS. *See* Pennsylvania Abolition Society
PASS. *See* Philadelphia Anti-Slavery Society
Patterson, William C., 143
Payne, Daniel, 184
Payne, Hiram, 163–64
Pennington, James W. C., 9, 18–19
Pennsylvania, as Black refuge, 72, 161, 192
Pennsylvania Abolition Society (PAS), 1–2, 24, 25,
    26, 73, 74, 101–2, 118–19; anti-abolitionists' view
    of, 144–45; *Centennial Anniversary*, 150; eman-
    cipation petitions, 208; Emory Sadler case and,
    95–97; General Committee, 31; gradualist
    approach, 8, 144–46, 155; informants, 61; jury
    trial resolution, 156; Lombard Street riots and,
    181–82; Mary Gilmore case and, 128–29; Mary
    Louden case and, 180; Pennsylvania Hall and,
    165–69; personal liberty law (1826) and, 80–81,
    83; personal liberty law (1847) and, 216; petition
    to Congress, 194; Protecting Society, 93–94;
    registration of enslaved persons with, 136–37;
    Thomas Shipley and, 1–2, 118–19, 150; William
    Rawle as president, 96–97
Pennsylvania Abolition Society (PAS) Acting
    Committee, 17, 28–29, 67; distribution of anti-
    slavery publications, 59–60; kidnapping cases
    recorded by, 10–11, 29–47, 50–52, 53, 55, 85,
    144–45; Thomas Shipley and, 17, 72
Pennsylvania Anti-Slavery Society, 165–66, 195,
    197, 200–201, 202, 205; anti-political

Pennsylvania Anti-Slavery Society (*cont.*)
participation resolutions, 205–6; emancipation
petitions, 208; meeting (1844), 200–201, 202,
205; opposition to Mexican War, 211–12; personal liberty law (1847) and, 216–17; Vigilance
Committee, 164
Pennsylvania Freeman, 213, 214–15
Pennsylvania Fugitive Slave Act (1826). *See* personal liberty law (1826)
Pennsylvania Gazette, 58, 121
Pennsylvania Hall, 13, 54, 148, 165–71, 182, 185
Pennsylvanian, 106, 122, 123–24
Pennsylvanian Freeman, 195, 228
Pennsylvania state legislature: Black memorials/
petitions presented to, 24–25, 76, 110–12, 117, 159;
election of 1846, 213–16; emancipation and anti-
kidnapping legislation, 20–22, 29, 203, 270n42;
fugitive slave retrieval position, 202–4; House
Bill 446, 110; PAS kidnapping cases and, 31–32,
35, 38; personal liberty law debates, 47–50,
76–80, 207–9, 225, 250n60; proposed anti-
kidnapping legislation, 194–95; proposed Black
emigration ban, 25
Pennsylvania state officials, fugitive slave laws and,
47–48, 74, 180; limited or prohibited enforcement, 19, 49, 50, 80, 82, 176, 188–93, 206, 208;
required enforcement, 19, 22, 28, 45, 49, 50, 82,
83–84, 176, 191, 206
Pennsylvania Supreme Court decisions, 35–36, 72,
161, 175, 203, 217, 227, 264n29, 267n78; *Commonwealth v. Case*, 72; *Fogg v. Hobbs*, 161; *Wright v.
Deacon*, 36–37, 72
Perry, Oliver Hazard, 19
personal liberty law(s), 7–8, 10, 50, 48–50, 98, 176
personal liberty law (1820), 10, 18, 19, 29, 30, 56–84,
62–63, 108–9, 206; debates, 47–50, 239n4; Fugitive Slave Act (1793) and, 48–50, 64–65, 67–68,
108; legal penalties under, 64; proposed repeal
or revision, 108; proslavery provisions, 110; street
diplomacy and, 63; violations, 63–65
personal liberty law (1826), 11, 13–14, 72–84,
108–9, 216, 250n69; debates, 11, 71–84, 87–88,
96, 250n60; Fugitive Slave Act (1793) and, 55–56,
108, 133, 227; House bill 446 and, 111–12; as
legislative compromise, 11, 72–75, 76, 80–82, 83,
206; proposed repeal, 108; unconstitutionality
under *Prigg v. Pennsylvania*, 13–14, 175–78,
191–92, 206–7, 226–27

personal liberty law (1847), 3, 11, 14, 111, 176, 188,
225, 226, 229; debates, 206–16; Fugitive Slave Act
(1793) and, 220; proposed repeal, 225; unconstitutionality, 226
personal liberty law (1850), 82, 84
Peters, Richard, Jr., 28, 53, 54, 67–69, 70, 73–74, 75
Philadelphia, 54; as Black refuge, 2, 3; political
culture, 198–200. *See also* Black Philadelphians;
white Philadelphians
Philadelphia Anti-Slavery Society (PASS), 169;
founding, 118–19, 134–40
Philadelphia Chronicle, 101
Philadelphia Female Anti-Slavery Society, 142,
165–66, 177
Philadelphia Gazette, 136, 143
Philadelphia Inquirer, 105, 109, 128, 130–31, 134, 138,
140, 142, 145, 203, 210–11
Philadelphia Sun, 199
Philadelphia Vigilant Association, 170
Philadelphia Vigilant Committee, 13, 170, 177, 178,
183, 195–98, 229–31, 268n19
Pindall, James, 32
plausible deniability, 21, 47, 56, 63, 65, 74, 79–80,
88, 101, 172
Polgar, Paul J., 28
police: defense of Black Philadelphians, 124;
"Flying Horses" riot and, 122, 124
politics, of slavery, 14; economics of, 149–50; at
local level, 98–100. *See also* interstate comity
Polk, James K., 201–2, 209, 213, 214
Porter, David R., 170–71, 175, 212
posse comitatus, 124–25
Pottsville Miner, 213
Poulson's Daily American Advertiser, 39, 42, 43, 44,
75, 88
presidential elections: 1828, 98, 99–100; 1844,
201–2, 210
Price, George, 221–22, 224–26, 230
Price, James Frisby, 1, 54, 221–22, 221–24, 223–24,
272n9
Prigg v. Pennsylvania, 82, 84, 175–78, 185, 188,
203; Abraham Monroe case and, 190–91; PASS
resistance to, 197–98, 206; personal liberty law
(1826) and, 13, 191–92, 206–7
Pritchett, William, 95, 97
Protecting Society, 93–94
Public Ledger, 168–69, 184
Purnell, John, 88, 89, 90–93

Purvis, Harriet Forten, 170

Purvis, Robert, 2, 13, 118, 151–55, 169, 212, 217, 229, 231; Black disenfranchisement and, 164–65; emigration proposals and, 108; eulogy for James Forten, 177–78; riots (1842) and, 184, 185, 195; Underground Railroad and, 14, 151–54, 195–97; Vigilance Committee and, 13, 170, 177, 195

Quakers, 21, 24, 31, 88

Quomoney, Abraham, 30–33, 38

race mixing: Mary Gilmore case and, 127–34; whites' fear of, 12, 118, 121–22, 127

racial traits: essentialization of, 136; skin color, 115–16, 127–34, 258n34

racism, 9, 26, 112, 163, 169, 185, 192, 193, 229–30, 261n5; "hard" and "soft," 116, 160; of Irish immigrants, 198–99

Randall, Archibald, 119, 120, 129, 130, 133, 249n50

Randall, Josiah, 47–48, 149, 213–14

Randolph, John, 100

Rawle, William, 38, 77

Reed, John, 61–63, 65, 83, 246n5

Reed, Joseph, 66

religious discrimination, toward Irish immigrants, 199

religious institutions, supportive of slavery, 204

Republican Party, 105–6

Review of the Trial, Conviction, and Sentence, of George F. Alberti, for kidnapping (Browne), 223

Richards, Benjamin Wood, 101

Richardson, Thomas, 225, 226

Richmond Inquirer, 118

Richmond Whig, 109

riots, 3, 5, 8–9, 106, 143–44; 1829–1830, 100–103; 1834–1835, 12, 115–27, 146–47, 148; after Turner rebellion, 106; anti-abolitionist, 118, 140; as assault on Governor Joseph Johnston, 228–29; Black property damage focus, 8–9, 122–26, 138, 139, 183–84; as Black resistance, 61, 103, 115–16, 119–20, 139; causes, 126–27; Christiana, 228–29, 273n21; "Flying Horses" (1834), 116, 120–27, 168; as fugitive slave retrieval obstruction, 101–3; Juan riot (1835), 116, 135–40; Lombard Street (1842), 13–14, 181–85, 197; Nativist anti-Irish (1844), 199–200, 201; Pennsylvania Hall destruction, 168–69

Ritner, Joseph, 148, 155–57, 170–71

"Ritner" (Whittier), 157

Roberts, Jonathan, 31–32, 76

Robinson, Joseph, 26

Ross, John, 62

Ruggles, David, 198

Runcie, John, 122

Rush, Lewis, 25

Rush, Ricard, 34–36

Sadler, Emory, 11–12, 54, 94–98, 113, 252n20

Scomp, Samuel, 88, 89, 90–91, 92

Scott, Dred, 231

Scott, John, 180, 184

Scott, William H., 145–46

Second African Presbyterian Church, 100–101, 116

Second Annual Convention of the People of Color, 110–11

Second Bank of the United States, 112, 143

Second Colored Presbyterian Church, 183–84

second middle passage, 5, 58–59, 79

Second Party system, 149–50, 212, 231

self-emancipation, 177, 192–93, 194, 195, 197

Sergeant, John, 32, 36, 37–38, 59–60, 70–71, 99, 149, 158, 218

Sergeant, Thomas, 25, 58

Shellito, George, 162

Shelter for Colored Orphans, 168–69

Shipley, Peter, 61–62, 63

Shipley, Thomas, 1–2, 8, 17, 72, 76–77, 88, 102, 104, 118, 125, 133; death, 13, 150–51, 185; "Flying Horses" riot and, 125, 126; Mary Gilmore case and, 133, 134; PAS and, 118–19; PASS and, 134; personal liberty law (1826) and, 80–81

Shoemaker, Abraham, 67

Shulze, John, 73, 81, 89, 94–96, 97–98

Shunk, Francis R., 201, 215

Sinclair, Cornelius, 90

Slatter, Hope, 171–72

slave catchers: Black Americans' collusion with, 1, 15, 33–36, 90–93, 221–22; methods, 171–72. *See also* kidnappers

slaveholders: constitutional concessions to, 4; legal punishments, 15; liberty laws and, 50; response to personal liberty law (1847), 217. *See also* federal property rights, of slaveholders

slavery: as 1828 presidential election issue, 99–100; Constitutional concessions to, 4; domestic

slavery (*cont.*)
    expansion, 5, 11, 14, 15, 102, 187–88, 201–2, 204–5,
    207–8, 211–12, 213, 214, 227. *See also* Missouri
    Compromise
Smith, David G., 215
Smith, Stephen, 83–184, 182
Soderlund, Jean, 20–21
Sollers, Sabrett, 153–54, 155
Southern states: enslaved population, 93. *See also*
    interstate comity
Southwark, Philadelphia, 60, 122, 198, 221
Sprigg, Samuel, 72–73
Stansbury, William, 171–75, 185–86
state officials: non-cooperation with slave catchers,
    188–93
Sterigere, John B., 160, 163
Stevens, Samuel, 113
Stevens, Samuel, Jr., 95–96, 97–98
Stevens, Thaddeus, 156, 159, 160
Stewart, Alvan, 176–77
Stewart, Robert, 135–37, 139
Still, William, 54, 196, 217, 229–30; Underground
    Railroad and, 1, 14, 195–97, 229, 230
Stockson, Richard, 89
Story, Joseph, 176, 188, 206
street diplomacy, 6–7, 53–84, 60–71; 1820 personal
    liberty law and, 11; definition, 6–7, 11, 56–57;
    interracial nature of, 6; as interstate comity
    threat, 116, 145; Robert Purvis and, 151–55; of
    white Philadelphians, 66–71
suffrage, for Black Pennsylvanians: disenfranchise-
    ment, 13, 171, 185; Pennsylvania Constitutional
    Convention debates, 158–65
Sullivan, Charles, 203, 204
"Supplementary Act," 21
Swift, John, 33, 54, 122, 123, 124, 125–26, 131, 137, 139,
    168
Swift, William, 128–29

Talbot, Samuel, 30–31
Tallmadge, James, 36–37
Taney, Roger, 163–64
Tappan, Arthur, 104, 120, 122
Tappan, Lewis, 120, 122
Tariff of 1846 (Walker Tariff), 15, 187, 205–6, 212,
    213–15, 227
Tener, Hugh, 224, 226
Texas, 14, 200–202, 204–5, 205–6

Thackara, James, 47–48
Thatcher, George, 25
Thompson, Catherine, 15–16, 223–28
Thompson, Joel, 15, 223–25
Thompson, Joseph, 96, 97–98
Thompson, William, 223–24, 226
Three-Fifth Clause, 4
Tilghman, Enos, 88, 89, 90–91
Tilghman, William, 35–36, 64, 72
Todd, Alexander, 78
Trego, Charles B., 208–9
trials: of Black rioters, 119–20. *See also* kidnapping
    court cases
Turner, Edward Raymond, 25
Turner, Nat, 12, 104–7, 108, 109–10, 146, 158–59
Tyson, Isaac, 39

Underground Railroad, 14, 79, 94, 177, 195–97, 229;
    Black churches as stations on, 24; Robert Purvis
    and, 14, 151–54, 195–97; William Still and, 1, 14,
    195–97, 229, 230
United States Gazette, 109
Upton, John, 106–7
US Supreme Court decisions, 193; *Prigg v. Pennsyl-*
    vania, 13, 82, 84, 175–78, 185, 188, 190–92, 191–92,
    193, 194, 197–98, 203, 206–7, 226

Van Buren, Martin, 43, 105–6, 201
Vansant, Franklin, 107–8
Varon, Elizabeth R., 36
Vaux, Richard, 179–80
Vaux, Roberts, 38, 77–78, 219
Veazey, Thomas, 175
vigilance committees, 13, 182, 198. *See also* Phila-
    delphia Vigilant Committee
violence: anti-abolitionist, 199–200; toward slave-
    holders, 135–40. *See also* riots
violence, anti-Black, 8–9, 26–28, 27–28, 109, 121,
    137–40, 193, 229–30; by fire companies, 121–22;
    following Turner's rebellion, 105, 106; "inso-
    lence" justification for, 101–2; by Irish immi-
    grants, 149–50; Pennsylvania Hall destruction,
    13, 148, 165–71, 182, 185; by white employers, 137

Waldstreicher, David, 4
Walker, Robert J., 209–10, 211, 213
Walker Tariff (1846), 15, 187, 205–6, 207–8, 209–12,
    213–15

War of 1812, 21, 31, 186

Washington, Bushrod, 68–69

Washington, George, 4, 69, 123

Washington, Henry, 102–3

Watson, Joseph, 76, 88–90, 93, 94

Wedgwood, Josiah, 99

Weekly American, 57–58

Weekly Aurora, 74–75

Weisener, John, 88

Welch, William, 96

Wells, Cornelia, 74

Welsh, James, 42–44

Wesleyan Church, 104

Wharton, Robert, 30–31

Wheatley, Anthony, 44–45

Whig Party, 14, 23, 126, 149, 150, 163, 198, 199, 203,
  206, 212, 225; congressional elections of 1846,
  213–16; emancipation petitions and, 208–9; Free
  Soil doctrine, 225; gubernatorial election (1851)
  and, 229; political alliances, 156, 157, 158, 165,
  201; position on US territorial expansion, 200;
  Walker Tariff and, 210

Whipper, William, 108

White, Elizabeth, 170, 177

White, Jacob C., 195, 197

white Philadelphians: anti-abolitionist/pro-slavery
  sentiments, 116, 140, 142–47; anti-Black sentiments, 106–8, 109–10, 113–14; Black attacks on,
  135–40; hatred of Black achievements, 101–2, 103,
  116, 121, 122, 123, 182; response to Black street
  diplomacy, 87; street diplomacy of, 66–71, 147.
  See also violence, anti-Black

white slavery, 165

white women, as fugitives from slavery. *See*
  Gilmore, Mary

white women, racial mingling, 168

Whittier, John Greenleaf, 157

Wiesner, John, 53, 55

Wilkins, William, 47, 48, 58

Williams, Edward, 63–64

Williams, John W., 128, 133

Williams, Ruth, 171–72, 173, 174

Williamson, Daniel, 123

Willits, John H., 44–46

Wilmot, David, 212–13

Wilmot's Proviso, 15, 187–88, 207–8, 212–13, 215

Wimberly, Lewis, 85

Winch, Julie, 158

Winder, Emily, 128, 133

Winder, Milly (Amelia), 128, 129, 132–33

Witman, George, 132

Wolf, George, 139–40, 147

Wood, John, 34, 51

Woodward, George, 163

Worcester, Noah, 219

Wright, Hatfield, 45

Wright v. Deacon, 35–36, 64

Young, William, 33–36, 38, 51

Young Men's Anti-Slavery Society, 140, 142, 145–46,
  155–57

Young Men's Vigilant Association, 182–83

Zollificker, Henry, 103

Printed in the USA
CPSIA information can be obtained
at www.ICGtesting.com
LVHW092043131023
761032LV00035B/912/J